Variegated Economies

Variegated Economies

Jamie Peck

OXFORD
UNIVERSITY PRESS

Oxford University Press is a department of the University of Oxford. It furthers
the University's objective of excellence in research, scholarship, and education
by publishing worldwide. Oxford is a registered trade mark of Oxford University
Press in the UK and certain other countries.

Published in the United States of America by Oxford University Press
198 Madison Avenue, New York, NY 10016, United States of America.

© Oxford University Press 2023

All rights reserved. No part of this publication may be reproduced, stored in
a retrieval system, or transmitted, in any form or by any means, without the
prior permission in writing of Oxford University Press, or as expressly permitted
by law, by license, or under terms agreed with the appropriate reproduction
rights organization. Inquiries concerning reproduction outside the scope of the
above should be sent to the Rights Department, Oxford University Press, at the
address above.

You must not circulate this work in any other form
and you must impose this same condition on any acquirer.

Library of Congress Cataloging-in-Publication Data
Names: Peck, Jamie, author.
Title: Variegated economies / Jamie Peck.
Description: New York, NY : Oxford University Press, [2023] |
Includes bibliographical references.
Identifiers: LCCN 2023004664 (print) | LCCN 2023004665 (ebook) |
ISBN 9780190076931 (hardback) | ISBN 9780190076948 (paperback) |
ISBN 9780190076962 (epub)
Subjects: LCSH: Economic geography.
Classification: LCC HF1025 .P378 2021 (print) | LCC HF1025 (ebook) |
DDC 330.9—dc23/eng/20230324
LC record available at https://lccn.loc.gov/2023004664
LC ebook record available at https://lccn.loc.gov/2023004665

DOI: 10.1093/oso/9780190076931.001.0001

Paperback printed by Marquis Book Printing, Canada
Hardback printed by Bridgeport National Bindery, Inc., United States of America

Contents

List of Tables and Figure vii
Acknowledgments ix
Abbreviations xi

1. Different Again: Encounters with Economic Geography 1
2. Remaking Heterodoxy: Navigating Economic Geographies 18
3. Socioeconomic Geographies: Networks, Embeddedness, and More 50
4. Rascal Concepts: Tangling with Neoliberalism 72
5. Relocating Variety: Toward Variegated Capitalism 102
   with Nik Theodore
6. Confounding Variety? Neither Mao nor Market 131
   with Jun Zhang
7. Mapping Economies: Substantivism in Space 160
8. Arid Comparisons? Economies of Difference 187
9. After Variety: Unevenly Developing Capitalism(s) 222
10. Situating Method: Exploring Conjunctural Capitalism(s) 270

Notes 305
Bibliography 353
Index 367

List of Tables and Figure

Tables

4.1	Between Neoliberalism as Exception and Neoliberalism Inside/Out	96
5.1	Varieties of Capitalism versus Variegated Capitalism	127
6.1	Varieties of Capitalism versus the Chinese Model	135
7.1	Mapping Economic Methodologies	173
7.2	Contrasting Modes of Economic Integration	176
9.1	Capitalist Variegation and Reflexive Methodologies	267
10.1	Contrasting Methodological Orientations	283
10.2	Some Rules of Thumb for Relational Comparison	285
10.3	Some Rules of Thumb for Conjunctural Analysis	299

Figure

8.1	A Pilbara welcome	212

Acknowledgments

There are far too many people to thank here, and too many debts to repay, so what must suffice is to recognize the (actually unmeasurable) contributions of my long-term collaborators over the years, whose influence and ideas are present in all kinds of ways and all over the place in the pages that follow, even as the caveat about the particular responsibility remaining mine must hold: Trevor Barnes, Neil Brenner, Helga Leitner, Eric Sheppard, Nik Theodore, Adam Tickell, and Jun Zhang. I am especially grateful to Nik and Jun for allowing me to reproduce some of our shared work in Chapters 5 and 6. More formally, I acknowledge the support provided by the Social Sciences and Humanities Research Council of Canada, from the Canada Research Chairs program and through the research grants #430-2018-00468 and #435-2021-0634.

I dedicate the book to the three Peters (Lloyd, Dicken, and Bibby), who each in their own way played significant parts in getting this project on the rails.

Gibsons, BC
July 2022

Abbreviations

ACFTU	All China Federation of Trade Unions
AEC	Australian Employment Covenant
CCP	Chinese Communist Party
CDEP	Community Development Employment Program
CME	coordinated market economy
FIFO	fly-in/fly-out (work system)
LME	liberal market economy
NES	new economic sociology
NWIRU	North West Industry Research Unit
R4R	Royalties for the Regions
RDA	regionally decentralized authoritarianism
SOE	state owned enterprise
TVE	township and village enterprise
UCD	uneven and combined development
VoC	varieties of capitalism

1
Different Again

Encounters with Economic Geography

This book is about approaching and analyzing economies as geographically differentiated and unevenly developed phenomena. It is staged from the loosely bounded field known as economic geography, although not as an introspective project but as one that seeks to make connections, and build bridges, especially to the complementary fields of critical political economy and heterodox economic studies. The book, in line with economic geography's remit, seeks to advance a series of arguments concerning the inherent—and highly consequential—spatiality of economic forms, worlds, and lives, and to do so in ways that engage themes and currents that have been bubbling to the surface in a number of interdisciplinary (and postdisciplinary) conversations—particularly around the diversity of capitalism(s), around late-stage neoliberalization, around uneven geographical development, and around relational-conjunctural modes of analysis. The book's mode of engagement is dialogical and cumulative. It is not about the revelation (or recitation) of a ready-made framework or fixed approach; neither does it make the case for the adoption of some singular theory or methodology. Rather, it describes—and takes the form of—something more like a journey, and a continuing one at that. As with all journeys, it began somewhere, and so there is a need to account for that, and along the way there have been encounters and conversations which have sometimes been course-changing and sometimes course-affirming. Some of the particularities (and perhaps peculiarities) do need to be acknowledged, not least to underscore the point that there really is no inherent claim here to typicality or universality. Inescapably, it is tangled up with my own biography and research sites, mainly in the United Kingdom, North America, Australia, and parts of Asia, but also with a somewhat cumulative series of engagements in political-economic theory, the most significant and enduring of which have been Polanyian socioeconomics, the restructuring approach in economic geography, theories of regulation and labor segmentation, and some currents in institutionalist economics and economic sociology. This reflects an approach to the ongoing work of "theorizing" in economic geography that is not exclusively abstract and effectively disembodied, but which in important ways is grounded, contextual, and particular.

My own approach to these things was certainly not mapped out from the start, or constructed from known coordinates; instead, the journey has been somewhat improvised and to a certain degree shaped by happenstance, but not least by conjunctural circumstances—beginning in the early years of Thatcherism, as experienced in the north of England, following the mainstreaming of neoliberal modes of governance and unequal patterns of growth during the "globalization decade" of the 1990s, and stretching into the extended interregnum that followed the global financial crisis of 2008, marked by the rise of China and the hegemonic humbling of the American model of capitalism. If this journey had indeed started out with a map of some kind, it would have had to be radically redrawn several times, so the process has been more like one of exploration, learning and relearning, and a fair amount of stumbling around. Certainly, it bears little to no resemblance to a one-way trip to "discovery." This book is not a travelogue, though; its concern is with the always moving terrains of the economic, and with the development, revision, and reconstruction of explanatory frameworks that might be equal to the challenge of making sense of this situation, where the ground is always moving under foot.

Variegated Economies tries to get at the question of the reproduction of economic difference—economic geographies, in other words—with the aid of a variety of resources, theories, and methodological guides, all of which are engaged from the staging ground that is the field and research community of economic geography. Characteristically eclectic and pluralistic, economic geography does not pretend to lay claim to its own entirely separate and homegrown theoretical canon, but it does have a point of view, and it is a point of view continually shaped by a series of encounters with various branches of critical social theory and heterodox economics. Speaking for myself, but also from a position perhaps similar to that of many economic geographers, I think it is fair to say that few in this field aspire to be the architects of grand theoretical designs, or even experts in a particular methodological craft; the economic geographer's somewhat more modest position within the academic division of labor is more like that of a general contractor, the particular skill sets of which tend to be more concerned with the interpretation, operationalization, and reconstruction of theoretical designs, adapted to the circumstances of this or that site, coupled with more or less successful attempts to pick up and combine the tricks of various trades. And general contractors are, of course, in the business of "construction," and sometimes deconstruction; what they learn, they learn by doing, and by making and rectifying mistakes, understood as an ongoing and largely experiential process. They know that no two projects are ever really the same and that there are no universal fixes; they tend to be skeptical of prefabricated and one-size-fits-all solutions.

Rather than stretch this metaphor any further, it can be said that the commitments and dispositions of economic geographers are nevertheless quite distinct from those that prevail in the various other branches of (generally heterodox) economic studies, like economic sociology or economic anthropology, even as they overlap here and there. Geographers recognize, perhaps most notably, that place, perspective, and positionality all matter. Economic worlds, institutions, and cultures have never been singular, and neither is there any evidence of a historical trend toward convergence or the erasure of local differences. But here, *place* is more than a signifier of elemental spatial difference, say the difference between Detroit and Dubai. Economic geographers will often encounter and engage "the economy" not by means of abstract representations but through the medium of (such) proper-noun places. With this comes a commitment to grounded forms of analysis, sufficiently "close" to see and interact with agents, institutions, and social action, and on the other hand, also a concern to situate and contextualize theory claims. Place is consequently more than a signifier of the intrinsic specificity, particular history, or "internal" characteristics of this or that location. Places are also uniquely *positioned* in the world, each possessing a unique array of relations with other places (including positions in spatial divisions of labor, regimes of unequal exchange, the interstate system, and all manner of interdependencies). Along with these uniquely situated places, furthermore, come different and distinctive vantage points and lines of sight; they facilitate particular *perspectives* on the world (such that the meaning, form, and implications of "globalization," for example, are quite different when viewed from Wall Street, the Russian gas fields, or the barrios of Buenos Aires).

To this three Ps reading of some of the basic commitments in the field of economic geography, the approach of this book can be captured by the addition of three Rs: concerns with the real, with processes of restructuring, and with the principles of relationality. To begin with the concern with the *real*, this echoes an emphasis on (and commitment to) actually existing places and situated understandings of economies inescapably shaped by uneven geographical development. Economic geographers have long practiced their own version of what Polanyi called "substantivism," and styles of reflexive theorizing always in dialogue with the movements of empirical economies, typically confronted in the here and now. My own approach, all along, has also been informed by a critical-realist approach, as pioneered in the field by Andrew Sayer and Doreen Massey, with its depth ontology and commitments to the interrogation of mediations between persistently enduring social structures (or tendencies) and contingently realized concrete outcomes. The second R, *restructuring*, also owes a debt to this mode of inquiry, with its license to explore the persistently patterned but never mechanistically predetermined configurations and ongoing reconfigurations of labor practices, technological affordances, state policies, institutional forms, and so on. "Restructuring" here implies more than mere change, signaling instead the continuing and unevenly developed transformation of socioeconomic forms, dynamic and politically shaped processes of institutionalization, and not least, shifts in the relations through which economies (expansively read) are constituted. These conceptions of structures in change and their uneven geographical development are, it follows, necessarily *relational*. They imply a rejection of reductionism and economism, together with the limiting assumptions of methodological individualism, in favor of a conjunctural emphasis on economic transformations as the multicausal and mediated outcome of intersecting, interacting, and deeply interdependent social processes, forces, and relations.

This bundle of concerns—with site and situation, with the interdependencies between sites and situations, and with contextually rich approaches to explanation and theorization—means that economic geographers tend to write from somewhere, rather than nowhere in particular, and also that their accounts are more likely to be quite cluttered and granular rather than spare and parsimonious. Characteristically, they will work *through* complexities and contingencies, rather than filtering them out or attempting to "control" for them. This certainly does not mean that the field is dispositionally atheoretical, although it does imply that "theories" are handled in a particular way (or ways), not in a deterministic or dogmatic manner, but in a relatively eclectic and "decentralized" fashion. Theories and proto theories, it might be said, are almost always in the mix, but rarely are they bases for iron-clad and unchanging commitments. (Stereotypically, both orthodox Marxism and neoclassical economics will often attract the accusation that they imply fixed and inflexible modes of analysis, and for sure each has its blind spots, but in truth the traces and manifestations of both in economic-geographical scholarship tend to be of the less doctrinaire variety.) None of this is to suggest, of course, that economic geography is a space of consensus. It is not. But there is in the heterodox theory-culture of the field not just a tolerance of different approaches, but an expectation of a fairly persistent state of flux and explanatory churn, more often than not in critical dialogue with the movements of actually existing economies, their representations, contestations, counterprojects, and so on. To the extent that an economic-geography "project" can be identified, it is one that operates with an exploratory ethos and relatively open horizons. It is not a formally framed and delimited project, on a mission to achieve some kind of closure.

This means that the (ongoing) journey that is described in the remainder of this book has itself to be accounted for—contextualized, one might say—since in no sense was it pregiven or predictable, let alone typical. What follows will certainly not take the form of the disembodied disclosure of theory claims, or the enunciation of an all-purpose methodology. Instead, the book will recount (and look forward from) a journey that has involved a particular series of encounters with approaches to heterodox economic studies, both inside and beyond the field of economic geography. In turn, this has involved a more or less continual reconstruction of theory and method, passing through numerous iterations and formulations of the former, while moving toward a recalibration of the latter. The fact that the book ends, at Chapter 10, with a discussion of methodology underlines the point that this is a not a matter of refining some prefabricated framework. Rather, it is about fashioning a mode of analysis in dialogue with various strands of (heterodox and critical) economic theory and methodological practice, many of them complementary but none of them complete.

Venturing into a first-person narrative in places, at least where this seems to be warranted and appropriate, I will tell this story (indeed *can* only tell this story) in a way that reflects my own positionality and situation. This said, this is not some kind of academic diary, but an account that is attentive to the need to account for itself, with a certain degree of "declared" reflexivity. It is written from a position in the field and research community of economic geography that is an established one, but also with the sense that there is little that has been certain or secure, over the past four decades, about what it means to "be" an economic geographer, or to "do" economic geography. My own research career began on the fringes of what was then generally known as industrial geography, but it was grounded in literatures that at the time lay mostly outside the field—labor studies, institutional political economy, the socioeconomics of Karl Polanyi, influences from French regulation theory. It took some years—most of the 1980s in fact—before it felt like there might be a place on the "inside" of economic geography, rather than on the margins, looking in. The de facto career paths for most "industrial" geographers in Britain during the 1980s were aimed toward local government, unions, and maybe some other parts of the public sector; with few, if any, openings, the academic route did not seem to be even available, and I do not remember the idea of it really coming up when I was a graduate student. To find myself, first, in a postdoctoral position in Australia, and then in an academic job back in Manchester, at the very end of that turbulent decade, came as something of a surprise, but the path from there was hardly a predictable one either.

My point in saying this is to recognize that journeys into and through what has been known since the early 1990s as economic geography are diverse, varied, always contingent, and not necessarily convergent. To enter the field in the early 1990s did not feel like arriving in a field that was predefined or institutionalized. It seemed to be in a state of flux then, and in some ways it has remained that way ever since. Economic geography's restless energy, its always emergent character, improvised eclecticism, and occasionally discordant pluralism mean that it has tended to be rather unbounded, unruly, and less "disciplinary" on the inside, if maybe less than fully postdisciplinary. Accounting for how and why this is so, or at least how and why I understand it to be so, seems like a necessary step to explaining how it is that questions of economic difference, diversity, and variegation have come to be seen, in particular ways, from this position and perspective. This is why this opening chapter begins on somewhat autobiographical terrain, rather than because this is conventional or even particularly comfortable. It is because some degree of transparency and reflexivity is called for at the start of what can only be a particular (and path-dependent) journey around the still-somewhat-elusive problematic of economic spatiality, which is perhaps more about a direction (and means) of travel, and the recognition of certain lines of sight, than it is about some surefooted path toward an ultimate destination. This chapter and the book as a whole therefore start off where I started off, before moving on in Chapter 2 to explore in a more concerted way what it is that is distinctive about the perspective—and the socially produced theory-culture—of economic geography.

I know that I am not alone when I say that it feels like the process of "becoming" an economic geographer was more by accident than design (although in many ways a fortunate one). I did not so much "choose" what has since become my career as tumbled into it, largely (and quite appropriately) as a result of conjunctural circumstances. Four decades ago, after completing an undergraduate geography degree at Manchester University, I was without a job (or anything much) to go to, and certainly nothing approaching a plan. Then, out of the blue really, a doctoral grant became available, having been declined by the original awardee. Frankly, I had not considered applying for graduate school, but in utilitarian terms I had no viable alternative. It paid more than the dole, plus the award came with an internship at a municipal council in East Manchester (so that might be a pathway to a job, I remember thinking). And so I began to learn about research, from my academic supervisor Peter Lloyd, who along with Peter Dicken had established the North

West Industry Research Unit (NWIRU), and Peter Bibby, who was my mentor at Tameside council. The matter of finding a research topic seemed to have little to do with "the literature," about which I knew only little, and less still about weighty matters of theory. Both at NWIRU ("the Unit") and at the council, the overriding and in some ways existential questions were those of a declining industrial economy and its associated communities. They were questions about jobs, job losses, and the historically new phenomenon of mass unemployment. Some of us at the Unit were doing PhDs, but that hardly seemed to be the most important thing, as we moved from one project to another. We were half a dozen or so contract researchers mostly working on employment surveys and industrial sector studies, commissioned by local and national government agencies and sometimes by academic funders. This was my start in economic geography; it was applied and problem-oriented, it was regionally focused, and it involved working collaboratively.

Much later on, after I had started to teach economic geography, to go to conferences, and to mix with other economic geographers, I started to think of the field as an island of sorts, an island of acculturated practices, the work and "output" of which has less to do with the refinement of a singular, definitive approach or model of the world, and more as an open-ended and exploratory mandate to tackle an array of real-world problems with tools fashioned for, or around, that purpose.[1] Allen Scott captures this well when he writes:

> The history of economic geography over the second half of the twentieth century is characterised by a complex series of twists and turns of substantive focus and sudden changes of theoretical mood. Over time, economic geography has behaved in a manner quite different to that which might be expected of a rationally ordered discipline pursuing some pre-ordained epistemological mission. Its historical course has been notably responsive to changes in external economic conditions, to the unfolding of political events, and to the play of professional ambitions and rivalries.[2]

Starting out on my own uncertain path, I must confess to barely thinking much at all about these disciplinary conditions (and conventions), even as some of them were no doubt passed on through customary practice. All that seemed to matter, in Manchester in the 1980s, were the problems at hand, and adequate responses to those problems.

The doctoral award that had unexpectedly come my way had been designed around the planning of local-authority industrial estates, which while perhaps worthy struck me as rather dull. Instead, I fixed upon an issue that was getting a lot of attention in the mid-1980s, the new generation of labor-market programs that the Thatcher government was introducing, many of which were targeted at young people, whose attitudes and expectations apparently needed to be adjusted along with their "reservation wages." Since geographers at the time did not really "do" labor markets, the relevant literature was mostly outside the discipline as such. A class that I took in orthodox labor economics promptly confirmed that, if anything, neoclassical approaches to unemployment and wage setting were part of the problem rather than the solution. Instead, much more productive and relevant were those heterodox approaches to labor-market studies that went under the label of segmentation theory.[3] This approach lent itself to empirical inquiries situated at the nexus of productive restructuring, socially structured (and segmented) labor supplies, and shifting modes of state regulation. While it paid attention to national institutions, most of this work was basically "spaceless," however. None of it took seriously the questions of uneven geographical development, spatial divisions of labor, or the "local" construction of labor markets, which would eventually gel as the framing for my own dissertation research.[4] Beyond production-centric accounts, which tended to read the changing geographies of labor from the vantage point of industrial restructuring and changes in workplace labor processes, my own approach took shape as an intersectional understanding of local labor markets as multifaceted socioeconomic formations, the continuous remaking of which was partly down to those drivers on the demand side, but just as importantly was also shaped by processes of social reproduction on the so-called supply side, and especially, by the vagaries of state policies and governance. The latter, "regulative" institutions, processes, and practices were positioned in between these demand-side and supply-side factors, mediating them and managing their contradictions, at least up to a point.

This approach was positioned alongside, while being somewhat distinct from, the influential program of work initiated by Doreen Massey, Andrew Sayer, and others under the rubric of "restructuring," with its signature conception of the spatial division of labor.[5] Some of the researchers in this restructuring tradition, concerned as it was with connections between workplace transformations, class and gender relations, and so-called locality effects, later toyed with the idea that local labor markets warranted recognition as a decisive explanatory terrain, but in the final analysis made little meaningful headway in this direction.[6] Another characteristic of restructuring studies, and another telling lacuna from the perspective of segmentation theory, was that the state, social regulation, and governance were for the most part secondary concerns, subject to inconsistent and largely pre-theoretical treatment. Perhaps this was too much to take on, or too messy and complicated. Whatever the reason, restructuring studies did not much go there, and so the question of how labor markets were actually regulated was left to the side. Meanwhile, orthodox treatments offered virtually nothing and, worse still, seemed to be synthesizing with "neoliberal" arguments about competition, marketization, and so-called deregulation.[7] Actually existing labor markets bear little resemblance to the orthodox model of a self-regulating commodity market; they exist almost entirely out of equilibrium and in fact are sites of intractable and enduring regulatory dilemmas, the responses to which are always politically mediated and functionally incomplete.

Empirically, these questions concerning how labor markets actually worked, what motivated the large-scale "interventions" of the Thatcher government, and how things worked out on the ground, in different places, were those that animated my doctoral research in the 1980s. What would subsequently be understood as almost classically neoliberal interventions, launched in the name of "helping markets work better," along with a strategic assault on the unions, premonitions of systemic welfare reform, and campaigns to socialize and normalize "flexible" working practices, was anything but a retreat of the state. Rather, it represented one of the earlier manifestations of neoliberalization as a state-led project geared to the imposition and enforcement of market rule, the scope and significance of which seemed, even then, to be undeniably programmatic if not, from some perspectives, paradigmatic.[8] Theoretically, this line of inquiry prompted what would prove to be long-term engagements with Karl Polanyi's unique brand of substantivist economics and with French regulation theory, read in both cases more for their open-ended potential than as fixed or final frameworks.[9] Axiomatic for both of these approaches is the recognition of the *diversity* of (socio)economic forms and patterns of institutionalization, matched in both cases with an appreciation of their decidedly lumpy and discontinuous histories. On the other hand, the handling of uneven development and spatial relations has been underdeveloped in both traditions, for all their telling compatibilities with "geographical" treatments. The regulation approach has been limited by an abiding methodological nationalism, coupled with a legacy of Eurocentrism, while the geographical implications of Polanyian analysis remain for the most part latent and uncodified.[10]

An important thread that runs through the writings collected and synthesized in this book is the attendant concern to "spatialize" these and other complementary approaches to heterodox political economy. Rather than encountering questions of spatiality, geographical diversity, and uneven development as confounding complications, all too often addressed, as David Harvey has reflected, only "at the end of the analysis," the challenge here is to confront them frontally and at the outset.[11] What has on my part been a continuously evolving approach to neoliberalization (and one with which

I remain episodically engaged, decades later) is a case in point: this began not with some structural theory or epochal form(ul)ation, imposed as if from on high, but with an extended series of grounded investigations of economic policymaking in the wild (and in the regions), and with the incremental reconstruction of local institutional systems in the netherworld of implementation. Only later did this engage with questions relating to the theorization of more-than-local regulatory relations, patterns of "diffusion" and interdependence, and variegated processes of reproduction.[12] The chapters that follow represent a series of attempts to grapple with variants of the "space question" in political economic theory, analysis, and methodological practice. Drawing on work conducted sometimes on my own and sometimes in collaboration, going back well over a decade, these interventions take inspiration from the distinctively restless and creative field of economic geography, just as they often overflow its especially porous boundaries. Economic geographers do not subscribe to a stable repertoire of theories and methods, and neither are they particularly constrained in their choice of empirical questions. On the contrary, there is a tendency to be drawn to (explanations of) the new and the novel, to prioritize the leading and bleeding edges of contemporary transformations, and to collect data at first hand and in real time. This tendency to work in what I have called the "restructuring present" is a source of dynamism and (productive) disruption, but it is also reflected in a presentist and sometimes fickle disposition.[13] Allen Scott characterized the field as a "palimpsest" of accumulated practices, one marked by certain continuities, habits, and recurrent points of reference, but also by a compulsion to move on to the next thing.[14] Borrowing a different metaphor, this one from Doreen Massey, it can be said that the field of economic geography is constantly remade by new rounds of intellectual "investment," often spurred by reactions (positive or negative) against what went before, and frequently in dialogue with other fields, as well as with developments in actually existing economies, their representations and crises.[15] The overall outcome is a sort of "layering" effect, rather than a linear pattern of cumulative development, as new foci of interest and new approaches come, often in tandem, to unevenly displace and succeed the old. In the process, some concerns, habits, and convictions are passed along, while others become discredited or simply fade into disuse, sometimes to be rediscovered or revisited.

When I made my own way into the field of economic geography, in England in the late 1980s, it was hardly unified but, in that part of the world at least, felt quite strongly centered—most notably around urgent questions of deindustrialization and job loss, around the problematic of industrial restructuring, and around approaches that were strongly influenced by (neo)Marxist theories and critical-realist methodologies.[16] By the 1990s, even in the United Kingdom but certainly elsewhere, this was giving way to a new cluster of concerns (and approaches) focused on the dynamics of growth, growth politics, and growth regions, while the previous preoccupation with class relations anchored at the point of production had been met by telling and consequential critiques, particularly from feminist geographers, out of which emerged new research programs concerned with servicing (and later caring) economies, gendered employment regimes, workplace cultures, the restructuring of public services, and more.[17] And all of this was overlaid, of course, with increasing engagements with questions of globalization—as corporate practice, as a cultural condition, as an object of statecraft, as an ideology, and so forth. As Trevor Barnes and Brett Christophers have observed, these shifting concerns and conditions would intermix with "economic geography's open-mindedness toward theory and method," married to a notable "willingness to remake itself in light of changing circumstances," such that, for the field as a whole, increasingly:

> anything goes. In particular, [economic geography] has been unflinching in its inclination to experiment.... Only rarely in the course of its history has it believed that there were any holy cows to violate. You choose the theoretical framework that seems most appropriate for the (shifting) geographical process at hand rather than choosing one because it was always used. As a result, economic geographers might take their theoretical framework from science and technology studies, or from cultural theory, or from feminism, or from Marxism, or from institutionalism, or from orthodox economics.... [Sometimes, these influences] might come a pure form, drawing on a single tradition. Or it might be a mix and match, an eclectic style of theorization, a bricolage, a DIY approach to theory construction. Likewise ... the methods used to assemble the data to be explained are also increasingly varied and assorted.[18]

One of the recurring themes at the Summer Institute in Economic Geography, a workshop for early-career researchers in economic geography and adjacent fields that has been meeting since the turn of the twenty-first century, is that almost no one in attendance feels that their own work occupies the "center," if indeed such a center can be identified.[19] And one of the cultural characteristics of such a decentered field, as a result, is a certain degree of circumspection, and an in-built check on overconfidence. When this is married, as it tends to be, to a relatively grounded, exploratory ethos, and a flexible approach to theory and method, it speaks to a disciplinary culture that for the most part is more pragmatic than it is dogmatic, more centrifugal than centered, more adaptive and contingent than programmatically committed, and more critical than it is conservative. Inquiries tend to be at least somewhat inductive, but rarely simply descriptive; theorizing tends to be an ongoing, widely distributed, and creative practice, more than it involves deference to formalized frameworks or fixed principles; and methodological practice tends to be eclectic and sometimes improvised rather than prescriptive.

This bundle of attributes means that in terms of its scholarly disposition and sociology, there is a certain "there there" in economic geography, or what might be thought of as a theory culture and community of practice. Yet even as certain behavioral patterns and traits are unevenly reproduced over time, there is hardly anything approaching a firmly anchored and intersubjectively accepted canon or "core." And even though the orientation toward regionally indexed *industrial* geographies was more strongly evident in the 1980s, when I made my start, than at any time since, as interests and approaches in the field have continued to proliferate, my own subjective experience at the time was hardly a "centered" one—notwithstanding the fact that I was employed in an *industrial* research unit with a *regional* remit. To be working with labor-market segmentation and regulation theories on questions of state intervention and policy implementation, as I was back then, was somewhat marginal to prevailing disciplinary norms. It was not until I did my postdoctoral work, with Michael Webber at the University of Melbourne in the late 1980s, that I had occasion to work on an "industry" proper (in that case, on the clothing industry), such that I might be able to lay a claim of sorts to the kind of "sectoral" knowledge around which much of the field was structured at the time.[20] (To be an industrial geographer, one had to have an industry!) By this time, however, the period in which (manufacturing) industries, in the conventional sense, served as the principal containers of economic-geographical knowledge (commonsensically, as containers of data, as ways to engage the world) was already coming to an end, and not only because "industries" themselves were disintegrating and unbundling in real time.[21] Never really as sustained and institutionalized as the word "paradigm" might suggest, this industry-oriented tradition in economic geography gave way in the early 1990s to a more diverse array of approaches and perspectives variously concerned with nodes and networks, institutions and culture, growth and globalization, allied to an equally diverse array of theoretical and methodological influences, including feminism, poststructuralism, the new economic sociology, evolutionary economics, and convention, state, and regulation theories, and often involving a turn toward more qualitative methods.[22]

In the process, it has become increasingly clear that there is no single, central tendency in the research programs of economic geography, let alone a recognizable "core." Instead, the field became more heterogeneous, diverse, and "cellular," its attention, energies, and creativity becoming more widely distributed, not least through a series of "boundary" conversations with critical development studies, political ecology, social studies of finance, science studies, and so on. The extent to which this increasingly heterodox theory culture represents a truly "engaged" and transformative pluralism has itself become an important debating point in the field.[23] Intersecting with these debates, but also extending beyond them, have been important critiques of, and responses to, economic geography's persistent and to some extent constitutive Anglo-centrism.[24] These various decenterings of the field remain ongoing, productive, contested, and incomplete. They have been shaping what have been broadly centrifugal processes and practices of reproduction over the period since the 1980s, which without doubt is today more diverse, more heterodox, less provincial, and less introspective than it once was, even if it has certainly not shaken off all of the old habits.

While economic geography as a field and as a research community seems destined to remain a restive, porous, eclectic, unsettled, and somewhat decentered enterprise, if there is a commitment that most in its general orbit tend to share, this arguably lies in some form or another with the *recognition of economic difference* across the various registers and optics of site, situation, subjectivity, scale, and spatiality.[25] Rather than some source of friction or complication, persistent—and persistently *changing*—spatial differences play an animating role in economic geography, disrupting the field and any would-be orthodoxies, and keeping researchers on their toes, not just in service of the mundane documentation of difference, contrasting this place with that, but rather, with the imperative to continually sift and reassess questions of position and perspective, context and conjuncture, causality and contingency. Even as they encounter such questions of economic difference in different ways, economic geographers tend, broadly speaking, to distance themselves from claims to universalism or convergence. Theirs is instead an unevenly developed world of deeply ingrained (and profoundly consequential) geographical differences, the restive state of which is one of lumpiness, an always moving terrain over which there is no perfect, god's-eye view, but instead a multiplicity of vantage points, all of them differently situated. This, in turn, is related to an epistemological preference for engaging "the economic" not as a discrete domain governed by its own self-acting principles, but as a socially structured, "instituted," polymorphic, and politically contested space, what in (neo)Polanyian terms can be seen as an always-and-everywhere embedded economy, or an unevenly globalizing ecology of differently embedded economies.[26] For the most part, economic geographers are comfortable with the proposition that economic forms, relations, processes, and practices are "localized," and by the same token that "globalization" signals not some ultimate state of market-assisted integration—the flat and featureless earth of the orthodox economic imagination—but a *relational* condition of uneven interdependencies. Something along these lines might be considered to be the field's epistemological premise, while the proposition that there are *always* alternatives to existing ways of seeing and modes of economic organization—if not here, then over there—is widely taken for granted, if not its (*sotto voce*) rallying cry.

Making these arguments within the community of economic geographers, broadly defined, is rather like preaching to the choir, albeit a choir that is far from committed to merrily singing from the same hymn sheet. Beyond the field itself, across the much more diverse domains of heterodox economics and critical political economy, "space talk" is much less commonplace; meaningful recognition of uneven geographical development is sporadic at best; varieties of methodological nationalism, tacit or explicit, remain pervasive; and tolerance of contingent and cluttered modes of exposition and explanation, grounded in place and attentive to positionality, is often in short supply. Of course, this is not a universal or uniform condition. In fact, it may be the exceptions that best illustrate the more general rule, since these can also be seen as openings where there has been some degree of interdisciplinary bridge-building (or engaged pluralism, perhaps) around spatial, scalar, and geographical problematics. The renewed interest, among economic sociologists, in trust, tacit knowledge, localized industrial "atmospheres," and "untraded" interdependencies, emerged in the 1990s as one such trading zone.[27] Soon after, highly productive lines of research around commodity chains, global value chains, and global production networks have also been somewhat postdisciplinary from the start, with geographical questions and geographical interlocutors playing prominent roles.[28] In the extended wake of the (hyper)globalization theories of the 1990s, and their one-best-way discourses, approaches committed to grounding, contextualizing, or otherwise "holding down" the global, along with intersectional treatments of place and globality, have gained widespread traction, notably among ethnographers.[29] And the renewal of interest in uneven and combined development in fields including international political economy, historical sociology, critical development studies, and Marxian anthropology has served to re-energize these questions in economic geography itself.[30]

It is in the spirit of these more-than-disciplinary conversations that I seek to make a contribution with this volume, reciprocating parallel developments in economic sociology, socioeconomics, institutionalism, and heterodox political economy in particular. Drawing on and drawing together, within the same frame, different aspects of my research program over the past decade or so, it seeks to pull together a series of hopefully cumulative arguments concerning the "difference that space makes" in heterodox economics and critical political economy, to recall the title of a well-known book chapter by Andrew Sayer.[31] This chapter is well known, I should add, in human geography, but much less well known beyond that, despite the expansive implications of the arguments that he developed there, and which I propose to pick up in a different but complementary fashion in the chapters that follow.

The result is a rather long book probably not suitable for a single sitting. *Variegated Economies* surely reflects some of the idiosyncrasies and path dependencies of my own travels into and occasionally beyond economic geography, but my hope is that it also presents a number of potential jumping-in points and opportunities for engagement across a fairly wide range of issues and approaches. Chapter 2 continues where this introductory discussion has left off, exploring the remit, outlook, and promise of economic geography as a *distinctively* heterodox project, both in its own terms and in relation to the archipelago of related fields that make up the world of heterodox economic studies. Some of these themes are carried further in Chapter 3, which traces various through-lines from the new economic sociology and neoPolanyian economics, as well as some of the limits of these approaches. Beyond the heuristic-cum-metaphor of embeddedness, it is argued that the remit for critical *and contextualized* economic theorizing is in fact considerably wider, and more challenging, themes that are picked up in much of the remainder of the book.

It is in Chapter 4, which ventures into the sometimes fraught and still controversial debates around the political economy of neoliberalism, that some of the book's key arguments concerning variation first come into focus, not least by virtue of the nature of neoliberalization as a rolling and roiling process of regulatory transformation. To say that neoliberalism has become globally hegemonic but that it also comes in varieties is insufficient. As a tendential process, neoliberalization is not trending toward a state of completion or uniformity, but produces, reproduces, and responds to uneven geographical development as it carves its zigzagging way. There is no original, pure, or template form against which "others" can be judged; there is only and can only be a world of conjuncturally situated and coevolving processes of neoliberalization, which over time have evidently become increasingly interdependent and mutually referential. As a reactive and reactionary political-economic project, neoliberalism will often fight its battles territorially (against "incumbent" institutions and interests like those associated with

European welfare states or varieties of state socialism, or against social and labor movements of different kinds), such that the conditions of its emergence are profoundly variegated even if similar use might sometimes be made of the "same" routines and strategies (such as privatization measures or culture of welfare critiques). Ontologically conjunctural, neoliberalization is the complex outcome *both* of these situated and always particular histories *and* of their interactions and mutual adaptions, the family resemblances resulting less from some singular lineage, more from admixture and interbreeding, the consequences and contradictions of which tend to ramify rather than simply "add up." Variegation is therefore a constitutive property of neoliberalization as a multiply-conjunctural process, and one that is not reducible to empirical variation.

The next pairing of chapters, 5 and 6, develops these arguments further in relation to the variegation of capitalism, first through a transformative critique of the varieties of capitalism (VoC) approach and then by way of an engagement with the ostensibly confounding case of China. The role of these chapters is to develop an analytical vocabulary of variegation, in part through critique and in part through an orthogonal application. Following this, the next pairing of chapters, 7 and 8, has the shared objective of refining this emergent approach, cutting it together with a reconsideration of Polanyian socioeconomics, the methodology of substantivism, and the open-ended project (initiated by Polanyi toward the end of his life) of "comparative economy." These chapters work with a constructive reading of Polanyi as arguably the original theorist of economic diversity and hybridity—certainly one of the most creative. The goal here is to specify and operationalize an approach to socioeconomic difference, within as well as between places, that is true to Polanyian principles but not detained by issues relating to the (understandably) incomplete nature of his own research program. Here, cues are also taken from Michael Burawoy's approach to theoretical "stress-testing" and case-study "extension," by exploring the resulting framework in a sharply bifurcated regional economy in outback Australia. This speaks to one of the ways in which "context," contextualized economic behavior, instituted or embedded economic practices, and so forth—in other words, traces of the spatial constitution of economic life—*stretch* social theories beyond their tacit "comfort zones," to interrogate them in sites and situations that present explanatory disjunctures, anomalies, and contradictions, and in sites and situations where the taken-for-granted and the hypothesized are readily disturbed. Rather than pre-emptively negating received social theories or moving to grant exceptions, this turns discrepancies and questions of "fit" into opportunities for the ongoing reconstruction of theory. This should not be read as cover for remaining stubbornly loyal to this or that theory, but as an invitation to work creatively with what might be thought of as the locational politics of research design and with the frictions generated by extending theories across contexts.

The closing chapters of the book, 9 and 10, seek to draw the preceding arguments together, plotting a course from relatively orthodox treatments of (advanced) capitalist variety through to a new generation of heterodox and critical approaches to the question of capitalist "diversity," before moving on to a reconsideration of relational theories of uneven geographical development and the neglected but vital principle of "combination." Despite its presence at the birth of the concept of uneven and combined development (UCD), both in commonplace usage and in analytical exegesis the C has since become largely silent. Attending to the problematic of combination, and the *recombination* of socioeconomic forms old and new, near and far, becomes one of the ways to animate and interrogate the principle of variegation. Furthermore, if UCD is understood not simply as an intractable fact of the social world, more as a constitutive facet of "spatialized" social theory-building, then there are generative implications for theory selection and research design. Ostensibly "capacious" theories like variegated capitalism and neoliberalization have utility here for the reason that they make space for UCD on the "inside," contrary to the misleading assertion that they are "loose," or proxies for universalizing claims. The book ends, in Chapter 10, by building a bridge from these issues of baked-in variegation and UCD to matters of methodology, focusing in particular on the potential of approaches to relational comparison and conjunctural analysis. One of the concerns here is with "locational politics" of case selection and research design (or where to start and which directions to pursue), which themselves become opportunities for theoretical reflexivity and reconstruction. Ultimately, of course, the value of methodological approaches like relational comparison and conjunctural analysis can only be truly realized through critical application and ongoing, iterative development, although this must be the work of other projects, other books.

2
Remaking Heterodoxy

Navigating Economic Geographies

This chapter began life as a presentation at the opening reception of the Fourth Global Conference on Economic Geography at Oxford University. The setting was a particularly striking if somewhat disconcerting one, at least for the speaker. The reception took place in the famous dinosaur gallery of the Museum of Natural History, which for the audience presented no shortage of distractions: a room overflowing with friends old and new, rows of display cases packed with intriguing exhibits, a menacing, life-size replica skeleton of a *Tyrannosaurus rex,* and an open bar. The circumstances demanded some sort of acknowledgment (assuming that, on its own, one of the more obvious dinosaur jokes would not suffice) of the elephant-sized presence in the room. And they also called for some recognition of the diversity in the room itself, and the audience of several hundred economic geographers, not all of whom necessarily defined themselves as such, but by being there were at least field-adjacent.

My gesture to the unusual surroundings began with a reference to the history of this storied Victorian pile, which in 1860 had hosted the meetings of the British Association for the Advancement of Science. That was the setting for the legendary debate between Thomas Huxley, a leading advocate of Darwin's theory of evolution, and the bishop of Oxford, Samuel Wilberforce. Plenty of weighty themes suggested themselves, from the principles of evolutionary development to the status of scientific truth claims, but there was also an intriguing footnote from the early days of what was known at the time as "geographical botany" that struck a chord: mention of a rough-and-ready distinction drawn between "lumpers" and "splitters." There were, it was said, two tribes of scientific taxonomists: the habit among splitters, who tended to have a sharp eye for difference and detail, was to disaggregate and proliferate categories of analysis, favoring generally smaller units and freely identifying new species and varieties, while the inclination among lumpers on the other hand was to focus on bigger-picture connections and resemblances, staying loyal to more generic and overarching categories, and emphasizing recurring traits over smaller differences. Darwin, for his part, valued the contributions of both, believing that scientific progress was well served by back-and-forth debates between these alternate positions and indeed perspectives. "It is good to have hair-splitters and lumpers," he once wrote, just as it was productive to attack a problem from different angles and vantage points.[1]

The institutional economist Geoffrey Hodgson has pointed out that one of Darwin's significant legacies is a distinctive way of thinking with difference, keyed into the (generative) diversity of populations and ecosystems, rather than resorting to so-called typologism and "averaging out" across those differences in the interest of sustaining a standard or universal model.[2] In the Darwinian style of evolutionary thinking, diversity and difference are themselves constitutive of a particular kind of dynamic (dis)order. From this perspective, diversity and difference are not to be (re)presented as sources of interference, disruption, or impediment to an otherwise natural order or equilibrium condition—be that in the form of the self-regulating market, or the presumption that American capitalism equates to a standard model, "purer" than its others. The implications of this kind of "population thinking" are far-reaching, not least for theories of capitalism, for which there has never been a pure form and where protean dynamics of difference continue to defy standard models and universal templates (for all their appeal in many quarters). Hodgson puts it this way:

> Multiple coexisting capitalisms, or multiple firms in an industry, have to be understood in population terms. Crucially, variation within a population (of capitalisms or firms) is part of its species essence rather than a disturbance from one natural state. *The essence itself embraces variation.* We cannot identify an essence by seeking an illusory natural state for the species.[3]

An axiomatic emphasis on economic diversity and difference—and the *coexistence* of multiple economic forms—is also a feature of the thinking of Karl Polanyi, for whom modes of economic organization were always plural and actually existing economies always heterogeneous, even as in different circumstances some modes of organization display "instituted" dominance.[4] And a parallel emphasis on economic diversity and difference lies at the heart of the project of contemporary economic geography, the business of which is concerned with not just documenting (and taxonomizing) but *explaining* the causes and consequences of economic differentiation across space, and doing so in ways that account for connections, relays, and interdependencies in a world comprising a plethora of "localized" economic forms. Economic geographers, it is fair to say, do not have a singular or settled way of accounting for these differences and interdependencies, even as this is the terrain on which they ply their trade.

Back in the dinosaur gallery, in the company of several hundred economic geographers, the distinction between lumpers and splitters provided a point of entry—albeit a somewhat whimsical and metaphorical one—into a discussion of the characteristically restive, eclectic, and diverse theory-culture of the field, understood as a heterodox and pluralistic enterprise in spirit as well as in practice. And it also provided the premise for what was envisaged as a methodological intervention, inspired by the late-Polanyian project of substantivist "comparative economy," which might set up a different kind of conversation between those who might be considered analytical lumpers, dedicated to the refinement and reconstruction of more generalized, capacious, and durable categories of analysis, and their interlocutors, the analytical splitters, whose inclination is to work outside (or against) such tacitly accepted categories, favoring their deconstruction and displacement. Even if lumpers and splitters continue to disagree, perhaps Darwin was right that there is something to be gained not only from their continuing cohabitation but also from their ongoing (if ultimately irresolvable) dialogue. This dialogue, I will suggest here, holds particular importance for those concerned with questions of economic difference, diversity, and variation, and more specifically for economic geography's heterodox theory-culture,[5] the ongoing concerns of which tend to revolve around the unruly problematic of economic spatiality, its constitution, causality, and consequences.

Splitting Differences

Contemporary economic geography can be considered to be heterodox in the weak (and somewhat negative) sense that the pull of orthodox neoclassical economics has not been a defining current in field (although this has been changing), which alone might stand as qualification as a branch of heterodox economics. But the discipline can also be said to be heterodox in the stronger (and indeed positive) sense that it displays a theory-culture that reserves an important role for (ongoing) critique, and which is robustly polycentric and pluralist. Across the always shifting diversity of the field, epistemological and ontological orientations frequently hew toward heterodox positions and perspectives too.[6] These include the widespread recognition of, and engagement with, inter alia, the emergent, instituted, and socially processual character of economic lives, worlds, and systems; the constitutive roles of uneven (and combined) development, spatiality, relationality, and localized embeddedness as non-transient features of the economic world; and the inseparability of the economic from the political, the natural, the cultural, and so forth. The discipline's methodological tolerances are also relatively wide, spanning ethnography, modeling, discourse analysis, and much in between, albeit with a concentration on qualitative case studies conducted in various registers but often linked to a concern with midlevel theorizing.

Contemporary economic geography shows no sign of becoming unified around a single program or dominant perspective, frequently bridling, in fact, at the very suggestion. This means that the field, at least since the late 1970s, has been not only diverse but boldly unbounded and intellectually eccentric (in a constructive sense of the word, tilting against any would-be center), while its shared worldview and purpose is difficult to marshal under anything resembling a succinct, parsimonious description. In the absence (notably) of a received definition, it can be said that this is a field that works with and from the recognition of economic-geographical difference (formally stated, the more-than-contingent or constitutive spatiality of the economic), mapping and explaining the differences that spatiality, site, and situation make across an array of economic processes, practices, and performances.[7] This means that depicting, parsing, and accounting for economic-geographical difference—the interpretative spectrum of which includes the lumper's mandate, of finding patterns, connections, and interdependencies *across* economic diversity, while accommodating (not erasing) that diversity on the inside of their categories, and the no-less-important splitter's charge, of mapping localizations, anomalies, exceptions, and alternatives, extending the field of the visible beyond extant categories of analysis and ways of seeing—are enduring features of economic geography's restlessly heterogeneous theory-culture. Echoing the field's contested interpretations to the economic world, this is an intellectual culture marked by persistent disequilibrium.

In this context, the title of this chapter, "Remaking Heterodoxy," is intended to signal two things. First, it picks up a theme from Chapter 1, recognizing that there is no single pathway into, or through, economic geography (even if some are more well-trodden than others). It follows that there is no privileged vantage point from which to survey or read this diverse field. Situated knowledge is therefore more than a poststructuralist caveat; it is a necessary recognition of diversity and positionality. Second, the title hints at the sense that commitments to, and within, economic geography are rarely once-and-for-all matters of certitude. The ground is always moving, as are the field's coordinates, communities, and constituencies, and it is in the nature of economic geography's heterogeneous theory-culture that there is no consensus on analytical frameworks or methodological strategies, and little that is fixed in either substantive research priorities or centers of influence. Characteristically restless, economic geography is not a discipline with a strong gravitational center, with canonical beliefs and long-lived sacred texts, or with determinate objects of analysis. Drawing the contrast with the monism of orthodox economics, with its "implacable centre," Barnes and Sheppard aptly observe that "[f]rom the beginning economic geography has been a discipline with a centre that did not hold."[8]

This does not mean, however, that there is no "there, there." At the very least (and this is probably not a small thing), there would seem to be something like a "structure of feeling," to borrow Raymond Williams's term, the patterned reproduction of a shared culture, spirit, or consciousness in economic geography. (Anecdotally, those located "outside" economic geography, and looking in, will routinely remark that there is.) But even if there are elements of a shared culture, this does not mean that economic geographers are all joined together, arm in arm, around the same campfire. Far from it. Presumptuous claims made on a core project or programmatic mission for economic geography are liable to generate ambivalence, unease, or even hostility. And maybe it is such *responses* that are the most telling indicators of a shared culture—an unsettled, decentered, pluralist heterodoxy. "Turns" may be declared from time to time in economic geography, but they are never complete and neither do they ever completely hold; rather, they symbolize a restive theory-culture that is actively resistant to consensus or consolidation, and generally more inclined to "turn again." The field has for some time been characterized by an "anti-canonical [and] open-ended" spirit of inquiry that endlessly breaks down and through any boundaries created for itself.[9] Over the past two decades, in particular, economic geography has taken to narrating and re-narrating its own story, which surely cannot be put down (at least not entirely) to disciplinary narcissism or intellectual insecurity. It has more to do with the fact that neither the provenance of, nor perspectives in, economic geography are self-evident or pre-given, and that no single (situated) account can ever do. These are circumstances that call for a certain degree of reflexivity, both epistemologically and sociologically; which render unstable, provisional, and contestable any pan-disciplinary claims to a singular identity or dominant direction; and which demand that questions of position and perspective are not just passively acknowledged but actively addressed. Positionality and context, in other words, really matter.

One aspect of the theory-culture of economic geography that I have highlighted here is the back and forth between positions that might be equated with those of lumpers and splitters, an alternating debate that will never be settled in any final way. There are well-established positions and perspectives on both sides; both have valid things to say as well as their own limitations; neither is inclined to give up or cede the argument. After all, these debates are intractable; they are not about whether the world is flat or round. They two sides are engaged in debates around the interpretation of an always emergent and always changing economy—or economies; they are both working on a moving terrain. In this respect, at least, maybe some things were not really all that different in Darwin's day. This is how a contributor to the prominent Victorian periodical *Cornhill* (self-describing not only as a "convinced and consistent" lumper, but as the bearer of "conscientious objections to splitting") characterized his differences with the gentleman botanist William Borrer, by all accounts an "abandoned splitter":

> [M]odern biologists are divided into the two camps of the splitters and the lumpers. The first are in favour of making a species out of every petty local race or variety; the second are all for lumping unimportant minor forms into a single species.[10]

The lumpers were said to favor inclusive, integrative categories; they chose to live with a relatively high degree of intra-category heterogeneity, opting to attach overriding significance to similarity, family resemblance, recurrence, and connectivity; on some accounts they were intellectually more conservative, at least in the sense that the default position was to work with and defend extant categories, incorporating new discoveries within established schema. The gaze of the splitters, on the other hand, was irresistibly drawn toward separation rather than similarity, and (the cultivation of) difference and deviation rather than connectivity and conformity; drawn to new species and varieties, they would call for the subdivision of existing categories or the creation of new ones, validating smaller variations in the specification of less promiscuous, more "local" units of analysis. (Mr. Borrer, for example, whose life goal had been to cultivate, and then classify, each and every British species, had scrupulously sought to distinguish some seventeen varieties of the dogwood plant, and no less than forty strains of the native blackberry.)

Similar bifurcations have been witnessed in scientific enterprises ever since, not only among geographical botanists. In the wake of the millennial protest movements ignited in Seattle, Porto Alegre, and elsewhere, the analyst of comparative political systems, Sidney Tarrow, restated the case for "splitting the biggest lumps" off some of the most amorphous categories in the contemporary social sciences, namely the one-lump conception of globalization as free-market homogenization, which had been hitched to a hastily assembled other, the hardly less promiscuous concept of "global resistance."[11] Around the same time, the renowned economic historian Charles Kindleberger stumbled across the distinction between lumpers and splitters, having been intrigued to see his habit of drawing cross-contextual analytical generalizations portrayed as the work of an arch-lumper. Following an impromptu investigation of the origins of the term, he was relieved to discover that the label was not intended to be pejorative, conceding that it was indeed "more or less true that I believe financial crises have broad similarities."[12] A thoroughly heterodox scholar himself, Kindleberger's mediation on lumping and splitting in economics did not lead him all the way back to Darwin, but his instinctive wariness of intellectual monocultures led him also to reach the conclusion that ongoing dialogue and debate between the two camps represented a healthy state of affairs.

With this in mind, the chapter proceeds in three steps. It begins by considering the nature of heterodox theory-cultures across the field of economic studies, which are often defined against the foil of neoclassical orthodoxy. Second, the chapter elaborates the claim that contemporary economic geography is—in both a formal and a temperamental sense—a heterodox discipline, prompted by the assertion that some of the central tendencies in the discipline can be enveloped by the signifier "geographical political economy," the patterns of devotion, deviation, and dissent from which reveal a field still somewhat haunted by Marx but also to varying degrees in the throes of a poststructuralist exorcism. And third, since healthy heterodoxies should really be dynamic, evolving, and contestable, rather than settled or static, a heterodox intervention is proposed in the form of a constructive methodological challenge. Here, the chapter draws upon a reinterpretation of Karl Polanyi's notion of substantivism, an anthropological formulation originally elaborated in opposition to the methodological norms of neoclassical formalism, as a prompt to a different kind of heterodox conversation. The debt here is not to the more familiar Polanyi (the originator of that now freighted term, "embeddedness"), but to the rather less well-known postwar Polanyi—Polanyi the comparative economist. His was a project of heterodox economics, programmatically concerned with the spatial and the social; it was never completed, although its guiding principles and methodological spirit remain suggestively provocative.

Economic Heterodoxies

What does it mean to characterize economic geography as not just generically heterodox, but as a branch of heterodox economics? On the face of it, as a signifier of weak-center multipolarity and restive critique-cum-reformulation, this captures something about the contrarian spirit of the field, and its limited tolerance of orthodoxies of just about any stripe. On the other hand, there is surely more at work here than dissent and negation, or the mere absence of orthodoxy. Strictly speaking, however, the label "heterodox" establishes no more than a state of exception (hence the *Oxford English Dictionary* definition: "Not in accordance with established doctrines or opinions, or those generally recognized as right or 'orthodox'"). In the language of economics, of course, heterodoxy carries very particular connotations. Across the broad and heterogeneous field of heterodox economics—which spans everything from economic history to feminist economics, and institutionalism to Marxism, and much else besides—the shadow of the Big Other that is neoclassical economics looms dauntingly large. As Sheila Dow puts it, "heterodox economists cannot *but* be aware" of this outsized orthodoxy, against which they are unevenly unified in dissent, even if their own disparate priorities and purposes are not so easily bracketed as a shared endeavor.[13] Tony Lawson's strategy has been to articulate what he sees as the foundations of heterodoxy's "unity within difference."[14] It is difficult to escape the fact, however, that some of this unity derives from a sense of mutual estrangement from the orthodoxy, one that represents more than just an intellectual mainstream, but also a bastion of gatekeeping and management functions, with implications for access to disciplinary resources, status, and other forms of recognition.[15]

There are several levels of irony at work, however, in the heterodox habit of assembling itself in the mirror of orthodox economics, not least in that the dissenters have proven to be rather more adept at portraying the theory-culture of the orthodoxy than the (mostly unreflexive) mainstream itself. Hardly a mere inversion, there is no such sharpness of focus in the rather blurry, kaleidoscopic figure that is to be found on the heterodox side of the looking glass. A common complaint, more ironically still, is that heterodoxy's galvanizing critique of orthodox economics ascribes an exaggerated degree of unity and coherence to the mainstream neoclassical project. Conventionally, this is defined by more or less strict devotion to the holy trinity that is atomistic self-interest, rational optimization, and general equilibrium. It is well known, of course, that many in the orthodox camp have strayed from this path, even if only rarely does this mean falling under the spell of genuinely heretical influences. There have been deviations, for example, into experimental and behavioral economics, into evolutionary game theory, and into the study of information asymmetries that raise, and do not neatly resolve, some quite troubling and even sacrilegious questions for the orthodox belief system. Some claim that mainstream economics is fragmenting under these centrifugal dynamics.

One does not have to be a card-carrying splitter, then, to notice a series of deviant tendencies within the neoclassical program. Where mainstream economics demonstrates a strikingly monist intellectual culture, however, is in the field's resolute commitment to formalistic-deductive methods, in the pervasive tendency to equate theory building with modeling, and in the veneration of the theory-language of mathematics. What Lawson calls the "mathematising inclination" of orthodox economics, reinforced by a preference for formalistic representation and deductive modeling, amounts to more than an innocent methodological choice; it implies (indeed imputes) the existence of a closed-system economy, the most pertinent features of which are not only measurable but modelable, and therefore establish the foundations of known coordinates and event regularities: "the formalistic-deductive framework that mainstream economists everywhere adopt and insist upon," Lawson remarks, "is so taken for granted that it goes largely unquestioned."[16] This robustly positivist orientation, grounded in a predisposition toward mathematical modeling, substantially (pre)determines what orthodox economics can see, and how that which is rendered visible is subsequently valued.

Where they respond to challenges deriving from heterodox economics, mainstream economists will often do so by finding closed-system substitutes, in effect to model or remodel these challenges into digestible (or manageable) form. Such is their taken-for-grantedness, mathematical modes of knowing and communication are considered to be practically synonymous with "serious work" in mainstream economics, as in the notorious declaration, "If it isn't modeled, it isn't economics."[17] Critiques and alternatives that fall "outside the net of mathematical formalism" tend to be filtered out if they cannot be expressed in modeling terms; they may "not even [be] recognized as economics."[18]

There are differences and debates around many issues within mainstream economics, but rare indeed are instances of dissent from the monoculture of modeling. According to Diana Strassman, for the "mainstream economist, theory means model, and model means ideas expressed in mathematical form":

> Mainstream economists believe proper models—good models—take a recognizable form: presentation in equations, with mathematically expressed definitions, assumptions, and theoretical developments clearly laid out. . . . [It is understood] that the legitimate way to argue is with models and econometrically constructed forms of evidence [but] that no model is perfect. Indeed, students learn that it is bad manners to engage in excessive questioning of simplifying assumptions. Claiming that a model is deficient is a minor feat—presumably anyone can do that. What is really valued is coming up with a better model, a better theory. . . . In this way economists learn their trade.[19]

When the leading growth theorist, Paul Romer, raised some troubling questions about the economics profession's apparent tolerance for analytical and political sleights of hand enacted under the cover of modeling and quantification—a form of sophistry that he chose to portray as "mathiness"—the pattern of responses spoke to an entrenched culture of methodological conformity. The advice from his friends was "don't make waves," while younger colleagues were especially anxious that if they "deviate[d] from what's acceptable, they [would] get in trouble."[20]

Among the social sciences, economics stands practically alone with its insistence on the maintenance of a "unitary disciplinary core," based on a disciplined intellectual culture that tends to be self-regarding and deferential to internal hierarchies, such that when economists venture into other fields, they seem inclined more to teach than to learn, their rigorously defined models being mobilized with the intent of "set[ting] other disciplines straight."[21] As Marion Fourcade and colleagues have written, this only reinforces the commonplace perception among "sociologists, geographers, historians, political scientists, [and] even psychologists, [that] economists resemble colonists settling on their land."[22] After Clifford Geertz, one might peer behind the strongly centered theory-language of orthodox economics to conceive of this as a culturally specific domain of "sacred symbols," one that has been defined by the integration of a widely shared worldview (a model *of* reality) with a particular ethos (or model *for* living). Orthodox economics reads the world through its model *of* a price-directed market system populated by rational actors living under circumstances of scarcity, but this is bolstered, sometimes almost unconsciously, by adherence to a scheme of normative valuation, a model *for* competitive modes of existence and methods of minimalist governance.[23] Crucially, the latter maps onto significant sources of ideological and institutional power within contemporary capitalist societies:

> Economics as a profession is prominently intertwined with public administrations, corporations, and international organizations; these institutions not only provide economists with resources and collect their data, they also foster a "fix it" culture—or, as sociologists would put it, a particular "habitus," a disposition to intervene in the world.... Economists, particularly modern economists, want to fix things, which is both a product of their theoretical confidence and of the position of their discipline within society.[24]

The normative power of economics, coupled with this "disposition to intervene," takes a particular historical form under the economizing hegemony of neoliberalism: even while mischaracterizing the social world, neoliberalism works with performative force and persuasion, as Wendy Brown argues, to "disseminate the *model of the market* to all domains and activities." Under this distinctively neoliberal rationality, she continues, "human capital is both our 'is' and our 'ought'—what we are said to be, and what we ought to be, and what the rationality makes us into through its norms and construction of environments."[25]

It is important to emphasize that heterodox economists do not find it necessary to disavow either normatively based argument or the value of mathematical modeling (both of which have significant and constructive roles to play within pluralist and reflexive theory-cultures) in their repudiation of the orthodox variety of formalized market reductionism. If much of the monism of orthodox economics is epistemological in nature, the pluralism of heterodox economics finds different expressions. Heterodox practices are orthogonal to those of the mainstream in the sense that the embrace of (and respect for) pluralism is axiomatic, not marginal, exceptional, or temporary. The limited pluralism of orthodox economics may involve some splintering around the edges, but the central tendencies in its resolute theory-culture are such that pluralism can only be a "temporary position," en route to an anticipated synthesis.[26] Heterodoxy, on the other hand, is based on recognition that all scientific enterprises are conducted by and within scholarly communities (usually revealed as "research programs"), each of which operates according to internally sanctioned paradigms and methodological practices, the premises of which are somewhat variably recognized and respected in other communities, and which in principle are always open to revision. The criteria for recognizing and rewarding "progress," in turn, are also governed by scientific communities themselves, proceeding according to "local" understandings of normal science and achieving wider influence in accordance with their "persuasive" efficacy. Since facts do not speak for themselves, and neither is there a universal yardstick of scientific validity, "progress" across the heterodox economic sciences is characteristically governed by more or less compelling arguments, always positioned among other arguments, and backed by various forms of documentation and evidence; persuasion is not simply a narrow matter of "science," but also a rhetorical, ideological, institutional, cultural, and sociological issue.

Reflexive and self-aware heterodoxies will often internalize a challenge to the imperialist claims of orthodox or ruling paradigms (this is the measure of more-than-normal science, or "extraordinary science" in the Kuhnian sense), but in the case of economics at least, the effectiveness of these challenges to mainstream supremacy has (so far) been limited. Heterodox knowledge cultures are defined by an active embrace of pluralism and by the simultaneity of alternative ways of knowing (along with their own modes of representation), as different paths are followed in a parallel and overlapping fashion. It is in this sense that heterodoxy's "unity within difference" takes the form of a "*coming together* of separate ... heterodox projects or traditions," not into a unified science, but as a diverse community of practices within a polycentric culture of dialogic and contested coexistence.[27]

Heterodox economics defines a loosely bounded and decentered field that (just about) hangs together despite its enduring internal differences, its multiculture of coexisting research programs being fortified not just by a shared rejection of reductionism and monism, but by fundamentally different conceptions of economic ontology. Heterodox economists tend to read "economy" as a processual, porous, and open-ended system, subject to transformative social agency and enduring patterns of institutionalization. Along with virtually all of the human sciences, with the notable exception of orthodox economics, they characteristically see social forms and processes *preceding* the formation of individual preferences, rather than the other way around.[28] Heterodox economists also reject the notion that the economy (or, in its reduced form, the market) can be conceived as an hermetically separate or functionally autonomous domain, understanding this to be embedded in and co-constituted with the more-than-strictly-economic world. In such open and leaky systems, the universe of relevant relationships and variables is somewhat unbounded and not comprehensively knowable, with the result that knowledge-building initiatives, research programs, or theoretical formulations, are always partial and contestable. The formalistic-deductive methods of the economics mainstream, in contrast, typically presuppose relatively high degrees of closure, in the sense of a known array of variables and relationships rendered mathematically commensurate, demarcated from (or subordinating) the spheres of culture or politics or nature, closed-system qualities that are imputed to the market as a self-regulating domain, coterminous with economy, with its own rationality, logic, and characteristic patterns of behavior.[29] The orthodox economic ontology is premised on a singular economy, which is encountered and read in a similarly singular fashion, the variability of which over historical time and concrete space being deemed for the most part trivial or transitory.

If Tony Lawson is one of those who represent orthodoxy's orthodoxy as a fundamentally epistemological one, he portrays the foundations of economic heterodoxy in ontological terms. On this basis, he rejects any claim to the existence of a legitimately separate, let alone superior, science of the economic:

> [T]he materials and principles of social reality are the same across economics, sociology, politics, anthropology, human geography, and all other disciplines concerned with the study of social life. Hence I think we must accept that there is no legitimate basis for distinguishing a *separate* science of economics. Rather, economics is best viewed as at most a division of labour within a single social science.[30]

Among the (critical) social sciences, heterodox economics is duly defined by its substantive concerns with the material conditions of well-being (along with their constitutive cultures, social relations, and recurrent practices and processes), and *not* by a determinate or exclusive methodological or theoretical canon, while the various branches and sub-branches of heterodox economics (ecological economics, economic sociology, economic anthropology, and so on) are likewise defined by their respective substantive foci, and by a sustained concern with particular problematizations, knowingly coproduced not as universal modes of explanation but alongside (and in conversation with) other heterodoxies. In contrast to orthodox economic formalism, economic heterodoxies are defined *substantively*, more by what they do than by how they do it, and by what they seek to problematize, rather than the parameters that they choose to impose.

Theory-Cultures in Economic Geography

According to the (admittedly forgiving) criteria by which economic heterodoxy has defined itself, economic geography—at least in its post-1970s Anglo-American form—surely qualifies as a heterodox project. But what are the positive features of economic geography's theory-culture? On what grounds might the field be said to "hang together,"[31] or travel together, despite its manifestly disparate concerns, its theoretical and methodological diversity, and its occasionally argumentative disposition? The following are some situated and experiential observations concerning the patterning and diversity of analytical practices in economic geography, which in their nature are open to challenge and correction. They derive not from a systematic study per se, but more from participant observation. More systematic inquiries, however, do tend to confirm them, at least in broad outline.[32]

First, "space matters" for economic geographers, in the most basic sense of an ontology founded on the principles of open-system complexity, social and institutional variegation, uneven development, and more-than-contingent geographical difference. Relative to other branches of heterodox economics, moreover, space tends to come first for economic geographers, not only in the sense that spatial variation is understood to be constitutively significant, but also in the field's belief system and modus operandi. Second, economic geography is characteristically engaged with the real and the now, with studies of actually existing economies, mostly conducted in real time; it is for the most part a "dirty hands" enterprise, in which researchers collect and construct their own data (working alone or in small teams), typically in direct dialogue with economic actors. "Being there," on the scene, matters in experiential and methodological terms for economic geographers, as well as for their claims to credibility. Third, there is a leaning toward richly contextualized, contingency-laden, and often cluttered modes of explanation, married with a degree of suspicion about highly parsimonious, heavily stylized, or overly deductive reasoning; intolerant of both grandiose theorization and pedantic description, this is a field that both attracts and produces small-scale lumpers, the manipulators and modifiers of (generally midlevel) theories, and more skeptical splitters, working between the deconstruction of coarse conceptual categories and the development of alternatives. In this vein, Gordon Clark once characterized the prevailing methodological norms in economic geography this way: "a fine-grained, substantive appreciation of diversity, combined with empirical methods of analysis like case studies," involving the utilization of mostly "qualitative and speculative [modes of inquiry] in the hope of representing the spatial scope and diversity of economic life."[33]

This methodological orientation is reflected, fourth, in a robust culture of critique, featuring alternating currents of deconstruction and reconstruction, as well as periodic "turns," but also in a lower level of priority assigned to methodological triangulation and verification. The disciplinary temperament is one of eclecticism, skepticism, and impatience, would-be orthodoxies, or research programs, rarely being allowed to reach the stage of calcification but often failing to develop to the point of thoroughgoing codification either, progress being measured more by change than consolidation. To summarize, the prevailing theory-culture in contemporary (Anglo-American) economic geography is, among other things, precocious, unruly, vigorous, inconsistent, anti-canonical, erratic, restive, improvisational, selective, forgiving, unsystematic, fickle, creative, impatient, and forgetful.

In this respect, economic geography's internal culture is noticeably different even from those of its closer relatives in the non-nuclear family of heterodox economic studies, such as economic anthropology and economic sociology. Somewhat impressionistically, in relation to these peers, economic geography is characterized by a relatively uninhibited degree of eclecticism in the choice of theories of methods; by elevated levels of theoretical and normative display, broadly distributed across the field; by a porous and inclusive intellectual community with open borders and low barriers to entry; and also by less exacting expectations with respect to methodological specification and codification.[34] If the various branches of the heterodox family are defined not by a singular parentage but by self-determined foci of substantive concern, however, then the domain of economic geography is unusually sprawling and practically boundless, perhaps even in comparison to sociology and anthropology. Economic geography's wide-ranging beat stretches over the horizon itself; in principle, it encompasses all aspects of the geographical variegation of economic processes, practices, and phenomena—in other words, the inherent patchiness and lumpiness of the economic world. At root, economic geography problematizes (and frequently privileges) the explicitly spatial dimensions of economic diversity, a more than ample remit that has been grasped and signaled, in a wide variety of ways, including: the recognition of basic notions of uneven geographical development and unequal exchange; the production of positive theory claims around logics of agglomeration and (regionalized) cumulative causation; the anti-essentialist validation of alternative economic imaginaries and community economies; attentiveness to the relational positioning of regional economies, with reference to spatial divisions of labor, regulatory orders, global production networks, and such like; the development of evolutionary and institutionalist formulations like path dependency and developmental lock-in; and methodological orientations tending to favor local case studies (nominally or explicitly) located within worlds of economic difference. The heterodox conversation in economic geography persistently turns on these and other issues concerning the nature, extent, and form of economic spatiality—and how to capture, explain, represent, and respond to it.

Neither eternal nor universal understandings of the economic have much currency in the field of economic geography, which instead is attuned to distinguishing and dealing with kaleidoscopic difference as its always moving object. From the austere perspective of orthodox-economic monism, this may look like a state of permanently contingent distraction, or a splitter's charter, but in fact relatively robust currents of both lumping and splitting coexist in the field of economic geography, the heterodox conversations between which, rather than flowing toward some equilibrium resolution, tend to be perpetually destabilized under conditions of continuing turbulence or "chop." There are precious few smooth or entirely predictable passages through the shifting currents and countercurrents of economic geography. The field's lumpers and splitters are passing and engaging one another all of the time.

Economic geography's lumpers are drawn toward bigger, connective categories, variously trimming in the direction of emergent prototypes like new industrial spaces, hegemonic formations like neoliberal governance, or widely encompassing concepts like financialized capitalism. They will rarely go to the stake for an absolutist interpretation of these categories, which invariably recognize difference and diversity on the "inside," instead tending to favor their adaptive (re)use and ongoing modification, on the basis of productive frictions and tensions with grounded empirical evidence. The discipline's splitters, on the other hand, are wont to identify significant exceptions to these and other overarching formula(tion)s, to demand recognition for alternative configurations and visions of the economic, to draw the practically neglected and ostensibly marginal into the spectrum of the theoretically and politically visible, and to value exuberant difference over tendentially dominant patterns. Crucially, the splitters and lumpers in economic geography do not exist as warring factions, separated by an unbridgeable divide, even if they oscillate around a conspicuously absent center. Most economic geographers will be inclined to work more in one register than the other, while acknowledging that the terrain is shared, and not likely ever to be monopolized. There is cohabitation and communication, and even if there is not consensus, there is mutual recognition and a fair amount of mutual adaptation.

Economic geography's distinctively heterodox formation is characterized by a climate of mostly pacific coexistence (in that a wide range of intellectual projects and programs function as neighboring clusters or loci of activity), although this is marked, according to some observers, by a centrifugal pull toward a multiplicity of solitudes.[35] This means that coexisting projects and the "cellular" communities with which they are associated only rarely chafe against one another, and only sporadically contest the same explanatory turf. While Allen Scott once remarked that the field is predispositionally "quarrelsome," today's economic geography seems to be rather less about a few Big Arguments and instead more of a continuing cacophony. There is more talking past than taking on, more live-and-let-live than there is active raking over of divisions.[36] With some exceptions, economic geography's theory-culture consequently is marked by broadly tolerant cohabitation, amid varying degrees of ambivalence, (mis)communication, and mutual (in)compatibility, coupled with an unruly accretion of habitual orientations, unevenly shared sensibilities, and loosely taken-for-granted positions, many of which are only really remarked upon on occasions of noticeable breach. Its quite particular brand of heterodoxy has been shaped by a diverse array of sedimented perspectives and practices, or what Scott aptly calls "traces," including a knot of propositions, premises, and practices derived from various forms of political economy, institutionalism, feminism, management theory, poststructuralism, and so on, such that the field's somewhat cumulative but heterogeneous culture of emergence is shot through with webs of continuity and commonality.

Having properly issued all of the necessary caveats, Eric Sheppard has sought to gather this particular configuration of unity-within-difference under the capacious banner of "geographical political economy," a relatively big-tent edifice shaped at least as much by corralled dissensus as by settled consensus.[37] There have been occasions when geographical political economy has paused to look at itself in the mirror of neoclassical economics, but this has hardly been a preoccupation for an unplanned research program that has largely made its own tracks, mostly by walking them. There has been an uptick in engagements with neoclassical alternatives of late, although more as a response to the resuscitation of orthodoxy's own version of "geographical economics" than as a locally grown initiative. For quite some time, orthodox economics has existed as a "lost continent," with few cross-channel connections to economic geography's island.[38]

In as far as geographical political economy represents a prevailing current within contemporary economic geography, this speaks to the character of a discipline that remains, to varying degrees, "haunted by Marx,"[39] even if sometimes this means little more than positions being defined outside or against various strands of (neo)Marxian political economy. A similar point might be made about numerous branches of heterodox economics, where Marx and Marxism remain significant (if not defining) points of reference. Again, the contrast with the orthodox mainstream—within which Marxian economics is somewhere between invisible and irrelevant—is particularly stark. In economic geography, followers of high-church Marxism are few and far between these days, in the loose congregation that is geographical political economy, although there are some articles of the old faith that have passed, in diluted form, into the field's own ecumenical mainstream. It is true that some have taken a more orthodox path (albeit rarely beyond the precincts of conventional institutionalism), while more have embraced various forms of poststructuralism (as a more reflexive style of political economy in some cases; splitting away from geographical, political economy in others). But even across these differences, Eric Sheppard finds that something approaching a critical commonsense can be discerned:

> [T]he consensus among economic geographers is that capitalism is conflictual and unstable, incapable of solving its own internal problems and productive of the very socio-spatial inequalities that its proponents believe it can (at least in principle) overcome. . . . Beyond conceptualizing capitalism as an unstable economic system, characterized by uneven geographical development, geographical political economists insist [that] capitalism is just one way of organizing the economic imperatives of any society (i.e., production of a surplus, transforming

"nature" into objects of use, exchanging such products, distributing the surplus among participants, setting aside surplus for accumulation and/or reproduction, improving technical knowhow and waste creation and disposal). While capitalism may be hegemonic, it is neither necessarily superior to alternatives nor the only form of economy worthy of serious consideration.[40]

Economic geographers devote considerable energy to understanding how contemporary capitalism works, and periodically fails, across its many forms and formations. Much of the field operates in "restructuring time," being particularly attuned to emergent dynamics of capitalism(s), studied in real-time motion and through methodological optics like regional clusters or global networks, its constantly reassembled project tending to move with the rhythms of (selected features of) the actually existing economy, often at the breaking edges of change. This brings with it the virtues of contemporary relevance, occasional novelty, and almost spontaneous renewal, but economic geography remains vulnerable to the critique that its attention span is both restrictively short and myopically focused. The dominant gaze remains a largely presentist one, being drawn to the (current) frontiers of capitalist restructuring, with both more deeply historical and substantively expansive inquiries remaining for the most part minority enterprises. The time before Fordism or developmental-statism, for example, is not especially well charted, and while the more-than-capitalist nature of economies is (now) widely recognized in theory, rather more isolated have been significant adaptations of practice. If economic geography lays claim, in principle, to a rather larger waterfront, its effective coverage of that waterfront is far from complete or comprehensive. It might be said to be somewhat haphazard, rather than systematic, and defined as much by significant gaps as by the well-documented sites that prevail in the literature. There is detailed knowledge, and commonsense understanding too, of the global cities and major industrial regions that make up the archipelago of "advanced capitalism," with its deep roots in Europe, North America, and parts of Asia. On the other hand, the same cannot really be said (for received knowledge or active research programs) about Russia, India, much of Africa and Latin America. If economic geography's calling card is knowledge of the world and its diverse geographies, then it is important to acknowledge that the documentation and calibration of these differences is incomplete, or more forgivingly, a work in progress.

It is another measure of economic geography's critically oriented heterodoxy that one of the principal lines of internal contention in recent years has concerned the character and consequences of capitalist hegemony. Here, though, something like an impasse has been evident. Telling critiques developed by feminist and poststructuralist scholars have called into question the presumed centrality of advanced-capitalist dynamics, as well as the analytical priority conventionally assigned to production, to wage-labor, and to the formal sphere of economic relations. The charge is that sprawling theories of capitalist restructuring are overgeneralized, constraining, and unproductive metanarratives—yielding totalizing conceptions that tend to look "down" from what are cast as commanding heights or "out" from the presumed center of driving processes—essentializing visions that are deemed equally problematic in conventional globalization theories *and* neoMarxist formulations. It was Gibson-Graham who first articulated the complaint that "depictions of capitalist hegemony deserve a particularly skeptical reading," notably for the way that these tend to relegate non-capitalist or anti-capitalist worlds, lives, and visions to the margins of the barely visible, credible, and perhaps even believable, while acting as a self-applied "brake on the anticapitalist imagination."[41] This is the extra-capitalist universe that is submerged under the waterline of Gibson-Graham's now-famous iceberg metaphor, a diverse and fecund undersea world that languishes out of sight in "capitalocentric" readings. The latter tend to assign vitality, centrality, and dynamism to the rationalities of capital accumulation, enterprise competition, and class struggle around the (waged) workplace, it is argued, in a manner that devalues or obliterates the actually existing diversity of economic processes and practices, rendering subordinate and inert the noncapitalist economy.

Having portrayed "the beast"—of an omnipresent and all-consuming capitalism—in this way, Gibson-Graham could see little to no purpose in efforts to tame or domesticate the creature, to be distracted by the elaboration of its taxonomic varieties and adaptive mutations, or to be taken in by superficially sophisticated accounts of its confounding and contradictory evolution. They have sought instead to starve the beast, depriving it of the oxygen of attention, "muzzl[ing] and silenc[ing] it," and then pretty much exiting the jungle altogether in order to engage in alternative forms of cultivation. Gibson-Graham chose, in other words, to ask different questions:

> What difference might it make [to] allow an anticapitalist economic imaginary to develop unrestricted? If we were to dissolve the image that looms in the economic foreground, what shadowy economic forms might come forward? In these questions we can identify the broad outlines of our project: to discover or create a world of economic difference, and to populate that world with exotic creatures that become, upon inspection, quite local and familiar.[42]

As a strategy for recognizing and working with economic-geographical difference, this is not one satisfied with the extension or refinement of conventional registers of (capitalist) diversity; it seeks instead to occupy new (or reconstituted) positions beyond and outside the political economy of contemporary capitalism, rejecting received frames of (critical) analysis for their alleged conflation of "capitalism" and "economy," and for an endemic and debilitating capitalocentricity. (The analytical sin of capitalocentricity attributed to radical political economy can be considered to be broadly analogous, in principle, to that of "marketcentricity" in orthodox economics, since these are each world-reading devices that assign priority and pertinence to a systemic nexus of predefined forces and relations.)

Gibson-Graham's alternative strategy, since adopted as the programmatic ethos of the community economies collective, has been to construct new frames and formulas for economic vision and action linked to alternative models of (and for) ethical living, to experiments in neocommunitarianism, and to projects of self-organization.[43] This is about more than establishing a new project-position within the always emergent heterodoxy that is economic geography, or raising an awning alongside the big tent of geographical political economy. Rather, it represents an internally delivered but virtually external critique (if not repudiation) of significant elements of the theory-culture of economic geography. The serious charge, leveled especially at the discipline's political-economic lumpers, is that their expansive, system-like, and integrative categories of analysis—such as capitalism, financialization, or neoliberalism—are irresistibly prone to slide down the slippery slope to totalizing, over-encompassing modes of analysis; by accident or design, they tend to temper or trivialize extra-capitalist diversity, imposing self-limiting methodological constraints and stunting the political imagination. A preoccupation with the sticky categories of capitalist restructuring is seen to obscure the actually existing, granular diversity of economic life. According to this critique, there is a price that must be paid for a process-oriented worldview—for visualizing financializing and neoliberalizing capitalism as a mutating grid or moving matrix of forces, rules, and dynamics—which comes in the form of a truncated analytical and political outlook, variously marked by intellectual conformism, incremental reformism, and preemptive closure or fatalism. Those transfixed by the matrix, it is said, are unable to see beyond it, or to think outside its categories. Worse still, in recounting tales of the prodigious power, menacing rationalities, and tentacular capacities of the beast, these analytical lumpers risk becoming complicit in the reproduction of extant (or imagined) structures of dominance. In this vein, Gibson-Graham has equated the critical study of neoliberalization with "an ethical choice to participate in constituting neoliberalism."[44]

The stock defense, such that it has been fully articulated, is that political-economic *geographers* are to some degree inoculated against the diseases of totalization, homogenization, and universalization, by virtue of a deeply socialized recognition of sociospatiality, uneven development, variegation, path-dependency, and embeddedness. (They work with smaller lumps, at least.) This does not really wash with those who have leveled the charge of capitalocentric reductionism and essentialism. The critique of capitalocentrism stands, apparently itself as something like a total one. Defenses, such as they have been mounted at all, tend to be regarded as manifestly insufficient (or even delusional), on the grounds that, for political-economic lumpers, difference is still often gathered at the margins or in gestures of concession, under the smothering signs of global connectivity or capitalist articulation, and typically in the shadows of dominance or hegemony. The pluralization of capitalism, for example, is seen as a sleight-of-hand method of "represent[ing] capitalism's chameleon qualities as an aspect of its sameness," merely stretching the same big-lump category into subtypes, rather than transcending or trashing the totalizing category itself.[45] Furthermore, anti-essentialist critics maintain that the ingrained habit of equating context-spanning political-economic processes with power, dynamism, and agency functions inevitably to privilege some sites, spaces, sinews, and subjects over others, therefore serving to resurrect or legitimize already dominant hierarchies of recognition, pertinence, and valuation. Against these oppressive structures, anti-essentialist and anti-capitalist alternatives require both analytical and political autonomy.

Consistent with basic precepts of heterodoxy, the anti-essentialist program has established its own codes of performance and communities of practice, along with largely independent criteria for evaluation, critique, and progress, according to internally validated principles of localized normal science. As such, the program exists in a space of intellectual self-determination, alongside but not answerable to others. This is not, however, a receipt for passive cohabitation. The anti-essentist project reciprocates, as it were, the allegedly imperial (over)reach of capitocentrism (which by definition does not keep to itself, but blunders into other domains) by projecting its critique across much of the extant field of economic geography, or at least the expansive dominion that would be geographical political economy, raising mostly unanswered questions about the very foundations of its "heterodoxy as orthodoxy." Insofar as it is possible to summarize the responses to this critique across economic geography's heterodox mainstream, one might say that these have typically been accommodative, absorptive, or additive. There has been some degree of incremental adaptation across the field, at least in terms of common language and framings, running the spectrum from quite profound poststructuralist turns, and the repudiation of big-picture, big-story categories, to the more superficial adoption of less deterministic modes of exposition, explanation, and phraseology. There have also been efforts to extend the spectrum of the economically visible, and to validate an expanded array of alternative, community, social, and non-capitalist economies, in action-oriented interventions and performative projects as well as in more conventional research initiatives. So there has been some accommodation and adaption to anti-essentialist critiques. But there remain, nevertheless, basic and quite stubborn differences between those (lumpers) that are convinced that they can both see *and see beyond* the matrix of political-economic power relations, acknowledging that it works in mysterious and mercurial ways, and those (splitters) that either do not recognize the matrix, and its hegemony, or who prefer to focus their attention and energies elsewhere.

While across economic geography and related fields there has been a fair amount of splitting and refinement of received, big-process categories of analysis (from globalization, capitalism, and neoliberalism on down), and some degree of lateral augmentation of these (in an incremental, "and/also" fashion), it is undeniably the case that the categories themselves are still very much in circulation. For Gibson-Graham, this represents more than methodological inertia, but a troubling attachment to debilitating versions of "strong theory"; her diagnosis of this situation goes beyond the suggestion of a stubborn reluctance to change (or to listen), to the more disconcerting claim that parts of the field may have succumbed to a kind of intellectual paranoia, symptomized by the (bad) habit of marshaling "every site and event into the same fearful order [such that e]verything comes to mean the same thing, usually something large and threatening."[46] Here, the recognition of a matrix-like order becomes its own disorder. Appropriately enough, the Rorschach test (which has its own place in the annals of rudimentary psychodiagnosis) has been invoked as a heuristic device by Gibson-Graham and her colleagues, a scheme of pattern recognition that in this context serves as a metaphor for the propensity to perceive the (same) economic world in either foreboding or emancipatory ways: the paranoid subject remains in the thrall of shadows of the devilish form, while those able to see with new eyes are drawn to the open spaces of economic possibility.

> In economic geography ... the dominant topic of research over the past decade or more has been neoliberalism and neoliberal capitalist globalization. This has been represented as needing study for the apparently self-evident reason that "it is the

most important process of our age, transforming geographies worldwide"... In the face of what has become "normal science" for economic geography—studies of neoliberal this and that—many geographers are making other choices, contributing to new performances by bringing economic diversity to light.... Through devoting academic attention to hidden and alternative economies they have constituted new objects of study and investigation, making them visible as potential objects of policy and politics.[47]

A stark (indeed binary) choice is duly presented, between the shadowlands of the neoliberal night, with its fatalistic and deterministic embrace of strong theories of corporate hegemony, disciplinary statecraft, and market rule, and the sunlit horizon of experimental alternatives, with its left-libertarian ethic of self-realization, supplemented by deliberately "small," autonomous, or local categories of analysis and practice. In relation to economic geography's loosely articulated pluralism, with its laissez-faire culture of live-and-let-live cohabitation, this represents a notable impasse, if not an invitation to pick a side in what has become a more polarized theory culture.

All heterodoxies are contested, of course, and this is certainly not the only line of fracture (or communication failure) in the heterogeneous universe of contemporary economic geography, in which the degree of inter-referencing and mutual dependency between different intellectual projects may be eroding over time. Barnes and Sheppard, after all, described a condition of "multiple solitudes," marked as much by detached monologues as by genuinely responsive dialogue.[48] But if economic geography's almost absent center lies somewhere between, or at the confluence of, various political-economic, poststructuralist, evolutionary, feminist, and institutionalist currents, then this apparent rupture in the conversation may have consequences for the field's heterodox theory-culture more generally. There is arguably little to be gained by reiterating what by now are fairly well-articulated positions—between, on the one hand, that variant of qualified lumping in which diversity is recognized around a dominant axis of relational difference (what can be portrayed as the problematic of variegation), and on the other, that version of principled splitting in which extra-capitalist difference is validated and valued more unilaterally and on its own terms (the posture of alterity, perhaps). But instead, might there be different ways of staging this conversation, drawing on different methodological axioms, and calling upon a different grammar of heterodox dialogue? Might it be possible, in other words, for economic geography's lumpers and splitters, rather than parting company or agreeing to differ, to engage in different ways? The remainder of this chapter, and indeed much of the book, is concerned with an exploration of this contention, not out of some forlorn effort to save economic geography, *qua* discipline, from itself, or to defend this tenuous position in the academic division of labor for its own sake, but instead to hold on to lumper-splitter relations as the source of creative, and often productive, tension. The case is made from a position closer to that of a lumper (should the disclosure be necessary), although hopefully not as a partisan exercise.

Substantivist Imaginaries

What economic anthropologists call *substantivism* can be seen as a mode of methodological framing that is, at one and the same time, broadly consonant with prevailing patterns of practice in economic geography yet also a provocation to think and do things somewhat differently. The origins of substantivism go back to Karl Polanyi's protest against what he perceived as the "economistic fallacy," the tendency to (super)impose, as a normalized analytic, "the market shape of things."[49] The economistic fallacy is an act of selective seeing, carrying with it a diagnostic and normative privileging of market rationalities and forces. By the same token, it is also a form of myopia—relegating nonmarket (or "irrational" or "cultural") phenomena to the blurry margins. Polanyi defined the economistic fallacy as

> the practice of analyzing all economic systems through a theoretical gaze that presumes that the horizons of the economy are fully comprehended by a map that includes *only* market exchange and the calculative behavior couplet. . . . [G]iven the methodological and ontological standpoint that it embraces, the neoclassical theory constitutes the paradigmatic case of the economistic fallacy, analyzing as it does both market and non-market economic activities *indiscriminately* through a formal choice-theoretic framework built upon the postulate of rational individual calculative behavior.[50]

This, in other words, is to question the indiscriminate projection of the market pattern (and presumptions of market-like behavior) onto all economies, past and present, a problem compounded by a singular reliance on methodological formalism (based on a choice-theoretic framework that privileges economizing behavior under conditions of scarcity, governed by prices). Polanyi did not believe that the apparatus of mainstream economics was inherently and necessarily problematic; his point was that its domain of applicability was far more circumscribed than was conventionally acknowledged; that perhaps it made (some) sense for actually existing market economies, but certainly not for *all* economies.[51] Polanyi's wide-ranging explorations of ancient and contemporary economies, including so-called primitive societies, had convinced him that the market was neither a universal phenomenon nor the civilizational future of society, but a "special case."[52] In his more polemical moments, Polanyi railed against the devastating effects of commodification and marketization, of course. His quarrel was not with the recognition of the system of regularized exchange as one (albeit *only* one) form of economic organization, but with the implicit or explicit claims that were (and are) made to analytical universality (or as he might have otherwise put it, marketcentricity), and politically, with the elevation of the logic and ethic of the market to the status of a governmental program and reigning social principle. This marked the birth of what Polanyi called "market society," the historical threshold after which the "formerly harmless market pattern expanded into a sociological enormity."[53] Polanyi may be most famous for the elusive metaphor of embeddedness, which despite its limitations as a rigorous analytic nevertheless signals in a blunt fashion that market-exchange systems are never exclusive or autonomous, since in practice their existence depends on legal and institutional frameworks, while their operations are always and everywhere infused by cultural predispositions and preconditions. It is more than ironic that actually existing markets (must) coexist with, are codependent on, and are enabled by other socioeconomic forms and modes of regulation, even as the latter are commonly (mis)represented, in market *ideologies*, as anathema, as alien, inferior, and anachronistic, as meddling interventions, and as "interferences" with otherwise freely and efficiently functioning systems.[54]

So markets—*qua* regularized systems of exchange—are out there, even if they are not everywhere. And they may be dominant under some circumstances, but they can never be coterminous with "the economy" and neither do they define, teleologically, an ultimate stage. Formalistic methods may grasp some of the pertinent features of markets, even as they tend to understand these in methodologically reductive and socioinstitutionally impoverished terms. However, in what amounts to an orthodox version of totalization, essentialism, or "economics imperialism," the market optic is often rendered as a universal, a first and foremost source of causality, an all-encompassing diagnostic, or as a one-size-fits-all "map" of (rational) economic behavior. In anthropological terms, this projection of the market model represents a kind of ethnocentricity analogous to the study of comparative religions from the perspective of Christianity, or the judgment of alternative political systems according to some idealized template of Western democracy.[55] It also amounts to a profoundly inaccurate reading of the ethnographic and archaeological record, which displays a qualitatively rich geography of socioeconomic forms while giving lie to the "myth of the individualist savage" as some direct ancestor to *Homo economicus*.[56] "In the beginning, there were markets . . ." will not do; neither will market teleologies, or contemporary conceptions of blanket marketization.

Rather than hewing toward a monist interpretation of the economic—based on a deductive and singular model of the perfect market and rational calculation—the substantivist alternative is constructed between, and across, grounded readings of *real economies*, leveraging the actually existing heterogeneity of economic forms, subjectivities, cultures, institutions, and structures as concretely revealed time and space, "the fount of . . . substantive concepts [being] the *empirical economy itself*."[57] Substantivism is a means of bringing into the field of the analytically visible the full spectrum of (institutionally stabilized) social means that have been developed for the satisfaction of material needs (this is what Polanyi called the other meaning of the economic—its human, material, and substantive meaning). It is a receipt for an analytically polycentric and empirically grounded "cross-cultural economics," a searching and creative program of "comparative economy," or what from a slightly different angle might be called economic geography.[58]

The heterodox group of economists, anthropologists, and historians with which Polanyi surrounded himself in the postwar phase of his career, some of whom would later style themselves as "comparative economists," was collectively motivated by the (negative) question of whether the postulates of economic formalism—with its underlying science of choice—were relevant for the so-called ancient and primitive societies.[59] Their extensive (if necessarily exploratory) surveys of the historical and ethnographic record convinced them otherwise. They knew markets when they saw them, but they also encountered many other socially durable ways of organizing economic life. As the young scribe Abe Rotstein wrote in the introductory note to the Polanyi group's *Trade and Market in the Early Empires*:

> It is an impoverished economic history that narrows its concern to markets or market antecedents, for these may only be fragmentary aspects of the economy. The economy would then seem to be in unilineal evolution to our own day, whereas in fact other economies need not be miniatures or early specimens of our own, but may be sharply at variance with it, both as to individual motives and organization.[60]

Yet the Polanyians were determined not to get bogged down by indigestible levels of complexity, or to fall into an empiricist rabbit hole by conferring unique, sui generis status on each and every localized socioeconomic formation.

The comparative economists were lumpers, yes, but definitely not of an indiscriminate kind, since they saw a vital methodological purpose in splitting too: they endeavored to work *across* revealed economic difference, carefully formulating their categories in relatively small lumps, in order to develop and revise operational concepts along with appropriate tools of analysis.[61] Having rejected the monism of market ontology, their lever would be the expressed diversity of economic life, not with a view to capturing this photographically, in some fixed and final way, but to work across and relativize economic difference as an integrated empirical and theoretical strategy:

> In order ... to see what is analytically important in Trobriands' economy, [we] must first understand the structure of industrial capitalism; to understand the special usage of pig-tusk and cowrie money, [we] must first understand the organization and usage of dollars and francs.[62]

On the basis of a wildly ambitious attempt to document the principal lines of diversity across "all of the empirical economies past and present," the comparative economists identified, verified, and then interrogated three or four organizational species (or what they termed modes of economic integration), which *always in combination* occupied a socially contingent if institutionally stabilized presence in the accumulated record: exchange, reciprocity, redistribution, and (less consistently) householding.[63] For present purposes, the details of this particular schema are less relevant than the epistemological principles upon which it is based, including, first, the recognition of enduring and irreducible diversity (substantive economic systems are understood as compounds of durably distinctive forms, found side by side, in many somewhat interdependent combinations); second, an appreciation of the historically and geographically contingent nature of the resulting hybrids (one or other mode of organization may be dominant, but these are nevertheless constituted relationally); and third, the absence of presumptions of historical teleology, universal or central tendencies, or incipient homogenization (all such hybrid formations being socially made and open to politically guided change, not structurally preordained).

On these grounds, Polanyi and his followers can be counted among the original theorists of the hybrid economy, the constitutive elements (or moving parts) of which were defined and refined through transductive dialogue between, on the one hand, an extremely wide range of concrete cases identified from the historical and contemporary record (the many moving parts), and on the other, creative forms of mid-level theory building involving the continuous interrogation of categories and concepts (relating to the emergent and heterogenous "whole" that is the economy). Exchange, reciprocity, redistribution, and householding were identified as the principal sources of economic diversity to which the comparative economists repeatedly returned, as the basic organizational building blocks of real economies. It has been said of the Polanyian style of qualified, principled lumping, which directs attention toward institutionalized patterns and socially stabilized forms of coordination, that

> [a]ll economies, that is, all the material aspects of human cultures, involve the provisioning of human purposes by the technological interaction and transformation of nature. In all but the most primitive [sic] societies, there is also a division of labor with the concomitant necessity of integrative institutions to coordinate economic activities. These institutions have at least superficial similarities—marketplaces, trade, monetary objects, and accounting devices.[64]

Similar principles of substantive economic diversity might just as easily apply to other well-known schematics—such as markets, hierarchies, and networks; capitalist, alt-capitalist, and non-capitalist economies; state, market, and third sector, and so forth—all of which ought to be deemed revisable through "lateral" interrogation, amidst and *in relation to* their others, and in dialogue with culturally and analytically situated interpretations of the facts on the ground.[65]

Now, a quite reasonable observation would be that some aspects of this kind of approach can be found in currents of extant practice in economic geography, especially those involving the formulation and refinement of midlevel concepts, attuned to broader theory claims, through case-study investigations. This is partly true, but with an important qualification: substantivist epistemologies call for programs of inquiry and research designs that are demandingly comparative in a double sense. First, there is a minimum requirement for cross-cultural, cross-contextual, cross-site, or cross-local comparisons, as means to render the near-familiar newly strange, as a means of moving recursively between moments of lumping and splitting, and as a guard against (implicitly or ignorantly) ethnocentric theorization. Within economic geography, norms of lone-scholar production, sometimes extending to small-group collaborations, raise some obvious practical problems in this regard—perhaps one reason for the ongoing paucity of comparative work in a field that otherwise (and somewhat paradoxically) trumpets its commitment to geographical contextualization and spatially sensitive explanation—but the methodological and interpretive point nevertheless stands. The injunction is boldly to work across economic-geographical difference (comparing sites and cases, working across borders, and so on), with the aid of research designs that embrace, problematize, and provide a potential basis for explaining that diversity. There are a great many ways of doing this, including the conventional approach of side-by-side comparison of (like or contrasting) economies, but any honest assessment would have to conclude that the productive execution of such research designs in the field has been sporadic at best.[66] In explanatory terms, economic geography's "island" has been smaller (and sociologically cozier) than some might like to think.

This first dimension of comparativity (comparing places), while demanding, is at least conventionally understood and occasionally realized, but otherwise worked around or compensated for. The same cannot be said, however, of the second substantivist axiom: this is an injunction to extend analyses across the "internal" divisions and discontinuities that comprise the heterogeneous, diverse, hybrid, and variegated economy itself—in situ, as it were. This means working at the interstices of, as well as between and across, revealed economic difference within social formations, for instance, between community economies and the state, or firms and households, coexisting however contingently and asymmetrically within the "same" economy, no matter how that might be defined. It means striving to exceed, say, "market only" or "network only" methodological optics, and transcending (or at least thoroughly positioning and contextualizing) modes of analysis that prioritize just one dimension or site, such as the wage-labor process, an industrial or service sector, the state, or the cooperative economy. In the Polanyian lingo, it demands an analytical reach across, as well as into the various creases and crevices of what were determined to be the bare-minimum signifiers of economic difference (redistribution, reciprocation, exchange, householding). As a matter of methodological principle, these or other dimensions of durable economic difference should be afforded parity of analytical esteem, sans binding or a priori expectations of hegemonic dominance, functional centricity, or prevailing trajectory. (This is a preemptive caution against built-in and self-affirming assumptions of capitalocentricity or marketcentricity or statecentricity, or the dominance of finance or the efficacy of production networks, or the social integrity of community economies; instead, it is to be expected that asymmetrical relations, political autonomy, or hegemonic dominance, where evident, should be documented empirically, not presumed.) There is a concern, in other words, to specify both the "shifting place" and the shifting, multifaceted form of the always compound, always hybrid economy,[67] by working across its diverse parts while also addressing the emergent whole. This calls for research designs that bring to light and problematize internal diversity and geographical difference, and that expose and explain the relationally interconnected, heterogeneous makeup of actually existing economies. It entails a maneuver that is less like "adding diversity on" and more akin to embracing diversity as a methodological objective—and then verifying, stress-testing, and accounting for that diversity.

The goal of exposing and diagnosing hybridity, of working laterally across diversity within local and regional economies, need not always entail exhaustive, holus-bolus modes of inquiry, but at a minimum there is a call for more-than-monological encounters, such as those that travel in from (or out to) the constitutive outsides of market-exchange, the state-governance nexus, or corporate-hierarchical systems; or alternatively, those that problematize interstitial formations or boundary objects, like varieties of market regulation associated with different state forms, or those third-sector or social-economy experiments that exist somewhat outside, but not exactly beyond, the market and the state. The injunction, in other words, is to problematize the cocktail itself, rather than focusing on just one of the ingredients, or in more methodological language, to problematize the conjunctural or intersectional analysis of heterogeneous social formations over one-sided modes of abstraction and inquiry.[68] A guiding principle here is that each and every economic site, institutional formation, pattern of subjectivities, and such like, is understood not as some hermetically sealed domain, but through its relational connections to, and hybrid fusions with, other spheres, near and far, and according to their relative positioning within constitutively diverse economic landscapes. Once again, research designs that explicitly work *across* difference, diversity, and discontinuity *within* regional or local settings can be found in economic geography, although they are hardly commonplace.[69]

Economic geographers tend to find themselves working amid thickets of contingent, contextual, and conjunctural effects, many of which—notably those deemed to be connected to space, place, and spatiality—are assigned higher levels of explanatory significance than would otherwise be the case in other branches of the heterodox economic sciences. However, it is notable that only sporadically have research designs in the field been sufficiently compelling to persuade *other* heterodox economists of the "difference that space makes," a (defining) feature of economic geographer's own belief system (and remit) that has won no more than limited recognition on the "outside." Diversity-embracing "Polanyian comparisons" represent one way to address this. Exhortations to engage in more comparative work, even of the conventional sort, are liable to be treated in the same way as other varieties of eat-your-greens advice, being recognized as almost uncontestably a "good thing" and yet often out of reach for practical reasons, but beyond their contribution to healthy methodological lifestyles they serve a more particular purpose in substantivist economics: difference-spanning comparisons, either between spatially discrete sites or across the realms and registers of economic diversity within heterogeneous formations, necessarily place an analytical premium on robust methodological designs and lucid exposition, and the simultaneous parsing of both evidentiary and theory claims. Furthermore, the promise of *substantively comparative* economic geographies is that they might set up, constructively, different kinds of conversations between lumpers and splitters, courtesy of a demanding repertoire of relational methodologies in which the utility and reach of categories of analysis are persistently stressed and always open to revision.

Comparatively Different Economic Geographies

Economic geography has for some time been in possession of a heterodox and dynamic theory-culture, perhaps as much by accident as by design, one that tends productively to favor the experimental and the emergent. More than this, the discipline places a premium on moving with the shifting tides and currents of the real economy, which is properly recognized as a source of both vitality and relevance, and which with more mixed results fosters a persistent "churn" across much of the field. These are surely features of a quite deeply socialized but constantly evolving theory-culture that many in the field will want to preserve. At the same time, if there is truth in the observation made by Trevor Barnes and Eric Sheppard that intensifying dynamics of fragmentation and dissipation are at work in the discipline, in what they interpret as a less-than-productive form of centrifugal or disengaged pluralism, then those concerned with the combined or social productivity of the field *qua* field and scholarly community, its more-than-the-sum-of-the-parts contributions, have no grounds for complacency.

Heterodox disciplines are in their nature undisciplined, unsettled, and resistant to unification. Yet if they are to flourish as heterodox communities, they must develop ways actively to cultivate, and periodically to reinvigorate, internal codes and modes of dialogue and debate, sustained across difference. It has been suggested here that a distinctive facet of economic geography's theory-culture is the always unresolved tug-of-war between its lumpers and its splitters, between the staking of broad (but not universal) theory claims and the restless search for telling exceptions and revelatory anomalies, between the construction of umbrella concepts and overarching frameworks and their purposeful critique and contestation. The discipline's lumpers habitually engage with prevailing categories of analysis, working toward their refinement and reconstruction, while its splitters prefer to work against (or outside) such tacitly accepted categories, often entailing their deconstruction and displacement. If there is a necessary relation at the heart of economic geography's theory-culture, it is that lumpers and splitters each benefit from the presence of the other. They tend to see and do things that the others do not, and the presence of each is a check on the potentially wayward tendencies of the other. One of the occupational hazards of lumping is that of *singularism*, the shortcut taken to monocausal explanation (an extreme expression of which is universalism); an occupational hazard of splitting, on the other hand, is that of *separatism*, and the dead end of idiosyncratic explanation (the extreme form of which is particularism). The contested explanatory spaces in between are invariably more productive.

Perhaps it is true that lumpers and splitters are never entirely comfortable in one another's company, but neither should they be allowed to live apart. Unsettled cohabitation seems to be a feature of economic geography's internally disruptive theory-culture; hence the relevance of calls for "engaged pluralism," and for the development of "new vocabularies" for communication across difference, including the making of creole languages around so-called trading zones. Beyond this, the field may also need to work on the collaborative development of new methodological rules and routines, especially where these have the potential to break down some of the walls around those explanatory comfort zones that understandably tend to grow up around particular research programs and approaches, which can become self-affirming if they end up privileging their own, sequestered, modes of inquiry and objects of analysis. Substantivism, with its culture of situated theorizing and engaged comparativism, might be one way to do this (among others), one that resonates with extant practice in some respects, but which also draws out both lumpers and splitters onto the always contested terrain of connectivity and diversity, difference and interdependence. The field would do well not just to acknowledge, but to actively engage this heterodox theory-culture, and to make a virtue of the fact that, as Darwin had it, "It is good to have hair-splitters and lumpers."

3
Socioeconomic Geographies
Networks, Embeddedness, and More

This chapter began life as a long article in the journal *Economic Geography*.[1] It was written during what was a restive period for me, institutionally as well as intellectually. During my time at the University of Wisconsin-Madison, I had a cross-appointment at the graduate level between geography and sociology. For me, this proved to be enormously energizing, and I was repeatedly struck by the potential complementarities between economic geography and economic sociology, as well as by their continuing differences in theoretical and methodological culture. In Britain during the 1980s, especially productive collaborations had developed between these two fields, linked among other things to the spatial turn in the social sciences and more purposefully to the research program around what became known as "restructuring," when some of the most important interlocutors included Doreen Massey, John Urry, Andrew Sayer, Ray Hudson, Huw Beynon, Alan Warde, and Linda McDowell, among others. There had been little evidence of parallel developments in the United States, however, where the disciplines appeared to be further apart, both formally and in temperament. There had been some important examples of "crossover" work, though, perhaps most notably Saxenian's (1994, 2001) pioneering study of regional industrial networks.[2] But in some respects this exception illustrated a more general rule. One of the reasons why the book struck a chord, apart from its exemplary execution of the comparative research method, was because it resonated with what had become the dominant intellectual project in U.S. economic sociology, the "new economic sociology" (NES), which had become largely defined by its concern with the phenomena of embedded networks.

Now, in Wisconsin, where my affinities in sociology were with Erik Olin Wright, Jane Collins, Gay Seidman, and an outstanding group of graduate students including Mark Harvey, Erin Hatton, Brent Kaup, Greta Krippner, Steve McKay, Amy Quark, Landy Sanchez, Matt Vidal, and Josh Whitford, the NES had little traction. There was economic sociology, but it was an economic sociology of a more heterodox and indeed radical stripe. It was rigorous and creative, to be sure, but there was not the same animating interest in the networks-and-embeddedness paradigm, which to some extent was recognized in constructive coexistence, but which was also subject to critique. Also rather notable was that the stronger connections, historically, between sociology and geography at Madison had been via environmental sociology and political ecology, rather than heterodox economic studies per se. Yet there were certainly compatibilities on this latter front, grounded in shared interests and overlapping commitments. I remember Gay Seidman saying to me once that there were striking family resemblances between the kinds of projects undertaken by economic sociologists and economic geographers, but for one notable difference: geographers were more inclined to include the names of places in their titles! As a matter of fact, this was almost certainly true, but the joke also captured a subtler point, that while sociologists and geographers were both concerned to contextualize economic behavior, it was the latter group, mine by training and outlook, who were more likely to attach proper-noun particularity to their analyses. The diagnosis did not stretch all the way across the board, however, as among the sociologists there was an often-unexamined methodological nationalism, so explanations pegged to national differences were commonplace, in a manner hardly warranting acknowledgment or comment. Economic geographers, for their part, seemed to have a rather skittish attitude to analyses pitched at the national scale, preferring to work at the regional scale, or through local-global connections, often in ways that did not entirely "translate" across to sociology.

Some of these might be regarded as surface differences, and in many respects they are. Both fields recognized the constitutive role of (institutional, social) context, even as one tended to spatialize while the other would instead stylize. And both were alienated, albeit in different ways, from orthodox economics. In contrast to the clean, abstract, and parsimonious modeling tradition of the dismal science, economic sociology and economic geography both have "dirty hands."[3] In contrast to mainstream economics, they each favor empirically rich accounts of concrete and socially situated economic processes; they each emphasize the essential diversity of economic phenomena, valuing (somewhat different styles of) context-rich explanation, in which history is deemed to matter, even if it is not always problematized; they each attach greater significance to plausibility and explanatory power than to elegance and predictive power; and they each strive not only to explain, but also to improve the characteristically messy, unequal, and unjust economic worlds that they encounter. Getting past the titles of their books and articles, economic sociology and economic geography share a similar language and, apparently, have things to talk about. Not least, neither has reason to be comfortable with relative positions in the scholarly division of labor that defer to orthodox economics on the so-called fundamentals and the operations of "the" market, while they get to deal only with supposedly deviant formations, local curiosities, and various institutional leftovers. As David Stark once said, in a critical reflection on some of the self-limiting proclivities of the NES, "we would be spinning our wheels if we leave the analysis of markets and economic relations to economists while focusing our efforts on the social relations in which they are embedded."[4]

The focus of this chapter is a critical engagement with the NES, not as an end in itself, but as a means to open up the space for a different kind of dialogue between geography and sociology. It asks, in effect, what a spatialized form of socioeconomics might look like. While mainstream NES tends to lean toward the microsociological, augmented by a rather benign understanding of embeddedness, more direct complementarities can be found between economic geography and historical or macroeconomic sociology, as well as with institutionally inflected heterodox political economy, reflecting shared concerns with the socially constructed, politically mediated, and variegated economy. Subsequent chapters in this book will identify other stepping stones in this direction; this one makes a start.

A New Economic Sociology

The term "new economic sociology" was coined by Mark Granovetter in 1985, the year that his seminal article on the "problem of embeddedness" was published in the *American Journal of Sociology*. Granovetter's work was distinctive in the explicit rhetorical challenge that it made to the accepted division of labor between economics and sociology. Since Talcott Parsons, this intellectual boundary had been effectively institutionalized. Parsonian sociology left the determination of economic rules to the economists, which it combined with a certain deference to the methodology of neoclassical economics. Parsons had insisted on a clear division of labor between economics and sociology, with the former being the proper domain of abstract work on rational actors in market settings and the latter being concerned with cultural norms, social values, and economic institutions.[5] At the time, Parsons had been especially critical of one of economic sociology's potential allies in exile—institutional economics—for its disdain for analytical abstraction and its overconcretized view of economic "reality."[6] In fact, the next half century would see both institutional economics and economic sociology recede into insignificance, while economics—having been granted "the market"—bowled along its independent course.

Against this background, Granovetter took issue with the marginal role that was assigned to sociology in economic analysis. He was not content to leave the big questions of economic rationality to the economists, while sociologists busied themselves with the secondary tasks of studying ostensibly irrational actions, cultural deviations, and suboptimal institutions. The NES would no longer passively cohabitate with economics, so the argument went, but would instead seek to *contest* economic explanations: the defining difference between the old and the new economic sociology, in this respect, would be its relationship with economics. According to Swedberg and Granovetter, the task of the NES was to mount a challenge to the privileged claims of orthodox economics "by elaborating the sociological viewpoint as forcefully as possible."[7] In practice, the bite of the NES would turn out to be less than its bark, even as the project sought to define and refine itself in opposition to (orthodox) economics. And out of this opposition, the NES's programmatic purpose would be defined around a variegated set of ostensibly "extra-market" concerns: networks, institutions, organizations, and culture.

Granovetter revisited Polanyi to develop a set of arguments concerning the social embeddedness of economic action. Yet Granovetter's insistence that economic behavior is inescapably "embedded in networks of interpersonal relations" represented something of a departure from Polanyi's use of the conpcet, which referred to the organic relationship between economy and society under different historical configurations.[8] In fact, new theoretical constructions were being developed under loosely defined Polanyian labels. According to Granovetter, by "embeddedness I mean that economic actions, outcomes, and institutions are affected by actors' *personal relations* and by the structure of the overall network of relations."[9] The pertinent contrast here is with that essentially antisocial character, *Homo economicus*.

To a reworked understanding of embeddedness, Granovetter added the second "master concept" of the NES—the notion of the socially constructed economy. This refers to the process by which economic institutions are produced, how they "lock in" patterns of sedimented or habituated behavior, and how they become normalized.[10] For Granovetter, network forms often represent proto-institutions, in the sense that many will subsequently "congeal" into more stabilized and regularized configurations with the passage of time. This, essentially, is how they assume norm-making capacities. In contrast to the impersonal play of market forces, the NES draws attention to the essentially social processes of norm making and institution building, which, in turn, are connected in significant ways to the patterning of "economic" behavior.[11]

It was Smelser and Swedberg's *Handbook of Economic Sociology* that first began to codify the project and program of the NES, defined at the time as "the application of the frames of reference, variables, and explanatory models of sociology to that complex of activities concerned with the production, distribution, exchange, and consumption of scarce goods and services."[12] This underlined the fairly explicit claim that was being laid upon the territory of economics. Economic sociologists would no longer be content with the "leftovers" after economists had finished theorizing rational, market behavior, what Williamson characterized as the residual "tosh" of unsystematic social and institutional phenomena.[13] This said, in a more than trivial sense, the NES was defining itself in the mirror of economics, and it may be that, in this reflection, it would look its most coherent and distinctive. Certainly, the distinctions are sharp ones, to the point that many of economic sociology's defining features are antonyms of those of orthodox economics: inductive and grounded theory development is favored over deductive and axiomatic model building; multiplex social groups, rather than narrowly rational individuals, tend to be the objects of analysis; contingency and specificity are taken seriously; there is skepticism about "universal" economic laws, while orthodox economics privileges abstracted forms of synchronic reasoning; the flesh and blood of economic life receive more attention than the bare bones of mechanistic relations; and so forth.

According to Guillén and colleagues, the NES is substantially defined by its attempts to avoid three traps of conventional economic analysis.[14] The first is the fallacious separation of the economic from the social. While this separation may facilitate the deployment of formal techniques of reasoning, it does so at the expense of a grounded, contextualized, and integral understanding of economic processes. Economic sociologists contend that all forms of economic behavior (including "market" behaviors) are socially constructed, socially grounded, and socially enabled. The analytical privileging of the market, coupled with the reductionism that is implicit in assumptions of economically rational behavior and perfect knowledge, means that orthodox economics has a blinkered conception of the economic, dismissing social and institutional relations as marginal sources of "interference" in what would otherwise be smoothly functioning, orderly, and equilibrating markets. Economic sociologists insist on widening the field of the visible in the analysis of economic relations, not simply to produce more complex and contingent arguments, but as a means of exposing and probing the fundamental motives and "ground rules" of economic behavior, many of which can be traced to institutionally regularized modes of conduct and to constitutive social and legal norms. In other words, market actions are constituted and shaped by the social relations, institutional norms, and interpersonal networks in which they are embedded—which, among other things, provide the glue of "trust" and mutual understanding that, in the final analysis, makes many markets workable and sustainable. Social relations, in this sense, exist prior to the fact of markets; they do not merely disturb their operation ex post facto. This view represents an inversion of Williamson's vivid but historically incorrect assertion that "in the beginning there were markets."[15] One of the central tropes of economic sociology is the Polanyian insight that markets are *made*; they do not spontaneously arise from some instinctive imperative to truck, barter, and exchange.[16]

The second mainstream economic fallacy to which economic sociology reacts is the related tendency to reduce decision-making behavior to the working out of a rational, utility-maximizing calculus, shaped by exogenously determined preferences. Economic sociologists insist, in contrast, that "preferences and actions [are] fundamentally connected to and affected by cognitive biases, limited powers of reasoning, nonconscious and ambivalent feelings, role expectations, norms, and cultural frames, schemata, classifications, and myths," the cumulative consequences of which are that "social forces affect reasoning in ways that defy a strict rationality assumption."[17] *Homo economicus*, from this more socialized perspective, exhibits the characteristics of a "reckless selfish monad," the Pavlovian actions of which bear little resemblance to "normal" human behavior, even in markets.[18]

The third point of difference is economic sociology's qualified rejection of methodological individualism. Even though a great deal of the NES, including the work of Granovetter, has microsociological roots, there is widespread acceptance of the view that explanations of economic phenomena that are constructed by "aggregating up" individual behaviors are at least problematic, if not fundamentally flawed. Economic sociologists typically invoke a range of structural, or at least mediating, factors in discussing the relationship between individual actions and "aggregate" or system-level outcomes, paying more attention to class, race, and gender relations. Not even instrumentalist behaviors are context-free. Self-interest is typically defined, economic sociologists insist, within the parameters of larger contexts of social action, while relations like trust, cooperation, power, and compliance act to drive a wedge between individual action and the overall configuration of the social networks in which they are embedded.[19] Their skepticism about methodological individualism leads economic sociologists to be more careful about theorizing the connections between economic action at different scales or at different levels of abstraction, yet they lack any consensus on *how* context matters.

Although there have been continuing attempts to systematize and "clean up" sociological explanation, one of its defining features remains a (perhaps necessary) level of complexity and indeterminacy. Dominant approaches to theory building are certainly different, as Baron and Hannan observe:

> Economics, at least in its neoclassical micro variants, relies on a highly simplified model of individual action (rational choice) and a simple mechanism (market equilibrium) to aggregate individual actions to derive system-level implications. Most sociology uses complicated models of individual behavior (including effects of values, prior experience, commitments, location in social networks, and context), and complicated mechanisms to aggregate interests and actions.[20]

An expositional fact of life is that the alternative positions that economic sociology has established are never going to be as singular and coherent as those that are defined by neoclassical economic theory. Economic sociology does not have the luxury of such absolutist, reductionist, and essentialist forms of theory construction, which contribute so much to the *aesthetic* force of blackboard proofs and the austere elegance of economic reasoning. While the economists have their "clean models," the economic sociologists seem destined always to have "dirty hands."

Beneath the surface of economic sociology's loosely constructed theoretical-methodological consensus, however, lie ambiguities, tensions, and contradictions. Economic sociology labors with a persistent theoretical identity crisis, reflecting the fact that it "lacks one dominating tradition."[21] It counts among its founding figures Weber, Durkheim, Polanyi, Parsons, Schumpeter, and Marx. The tensions, inconsistencies, and flat-out contradictions among these theoretical traditions have been impossible to reconcile within the NES. Smelser and Swedberg's exploration of the theoretical lineages led them to conclude that this is a "fundamentally eclectic and pluralistic" field of inquiry: while "the influence of Weber and Parsons can be seen," Polanyi represents little more than a "presence," albeit a symbolically significant one, as Marx, Schumpeter, and, to a lesser extent, Durkheim fade into the background.[22] Significantly, Granovetter's account of this intellectual movement does not refer to Polanyi (although in Polanyi's stead there is a stylized discussion of embeddedness), while sociological work that is conducted in a "Marxist key" (such as industrial sociology, before and after Braverman) is characterized as effectively outside the NES project.[23] Swedberg concedes that "economic sociology is currently characterized by several theoretical approaches [but] a firm theoretical core is missing."[24] Yet the absences and silences are distinctively patterned. Bourdieu portrayed the NES as a "reappropriation of Polanyi and Weber in U.S. sociology [along with] the development of 'network' analyses designed to move away from an atomized conception of economic agents."[25] Moreover, in substantive terms, the search for a rigorous and distinctive center has been associated with a "tendency to see network patterns as a distinctive organizing motif of economic life."[26]

Both a precursor to and an aggravating factor in the rise of the NES was the reawakening of interest in economic institutions within mainstream economics. Beginning in the 1970s, neoclassical economists have become increasingly concerned with extensions of conventional economic reasoning to ostensibly "non-economic" spheres of social life, such as religion, crime, and marriage. Many have traced the origins of this movement to Gary Becker's audacious treatise, *The Economic Approach to Human Behavior*, where it was declared that "the economic approach is a comprehensive one that is applicable to all human behavior [which] can be viewed as involving participants who maximize their utility from a stable set of preferences and accumulate an optimal amount of information," the rationale for the imposition of an orthodox interpretative framework based squarely on "the combined assumptions of maximizing behavior, market equilibrium, and stable preferences, used relentlessly and unflinchingly."[27] This effectively marked the end of the "gentleman's agreement" struck by Talcott Parsons and Lionel Robbins in the 1930s, which had demarcated the territory of economics in terms of the rational choices of means in the service of given (and narrowly defined) ends and that of sociology in terms of institutional and cultural explanations of these ends.

This ungentlemanly behavior on the part of some economists and the "territorial overconfidence" that it reflected certainly helped to galvanize the revival of economic sociology. Yet while the rhetoric of the NES can be confrontational, its practice has been more conciliatory. "Network sociology," in particular, has involved a reworked accommodation with orthodox economics. The microsociological bent of mainstream NES sometimes has enabled (and perhaps encouraged) a complementary (if not complimentary) and reformist relationship with economics. As Granovetter noted:

> Many [social network] analysts are mathematically inclined and thus not scared off by the techniques of microeconomics; and since network analysis often takes the individual as a fundamental unit of analysis, it is methodologically more individualist than some other sociological traditions. But the underlying conception of

network arguments lends itself to a fundamental critique of the atomized conception of action in neoclassical theory. Thus, this group, close enough to appreciate economic arguments but different enough to offer a basic critique, has been in a structurally strategic position.... [N]eoclassical theory [is] flawed in [a way] that a sociological perspective can highlight and help remedy. The brilliant achievements of neoclassical arguments in illuminating the efficient pursuit of well-defined preferences must be accompanied by an appreciation of the extent to which such pursuit is intertwined with noneconomic goals, and deeply embedded in structures of social interaction.[28]

Granovetter went on to express a desire to see orthodox economic theory "strengthened," rather than overthrown, emphasizing that "I share with its proponents the positivist quest for general, universal explanations."[29] Speaking for the project as a whole, Smelser and Swedberg optimistically hoped that the zone that is defined by "economic institutions" might be one of interdisciplinary engagement, echoing Parsons in their desire to see the disciplines "cooperat[ing] and coexist[ing]."[30]

While there may have been coexistence, there has been precious little cooperation, since mainstream economics has remained largely oblivious to these sociological attentions. Citation studies have revealed that the traffic has largely been in one direction, with economic sociologists engaging selectively with the economics literature, while mainstream economists have largely remained in their own world.[31] Perhaps it is the case that, as Steve Keen caustically remarked, "economists have no ears."[32] Although parts of the NES have sought to initiate a reformist dialogue with economics, reciprocal influences on orthodox economic practice have been negligible. It is important to recognize that orthodox economics is not a singular enterprise, but at least in comparison with most of the alternative worldviews that it confronts, an overriding priority is placed on integrity and coherence, coupled with the colonizing belief system that "[e]conomic really does constitute the universal grammar of social science."[33] A side effect is that alternative ways of reading the economic world are typically rendered, in comparison, as decentered, disorganized, undisciplined, messy, ad hoc, and opportunistic. Yet this is where economic sociology lives.

A strategic objective of the NES, according to Granovetter, has been to insist upon the existence of and then document the effects of "the mixture of economic and social purposes that motivate people while they are engaged in production, consumption, and distribution."[34] This microsociological perspective is typically complemented with a searching set of questions concerning the nature of the various contexts that shape "economic" behavior. If action frameworks are not reducible to the aggregated outcomes of individual actions, as the critique of methodological individualism would suggest, then as Granovetter points out, "the problem of how contexts of action arise remains unresolved."[35] And not only is the question an open one, it is one that is considerably beyond the reach of conventional economic theory, the central postulates of which presume the deep-freezing of such contextual factors.

Once thawed, so the economic-sociological argument goes, these contextual factors melt into and fuse with ostensibly "economic" relations in a way that makes it impossible to parse out rational-instrumentalist motivations from those that are related to, say, sociability or trust. In this context, Granovetter draws a telling distinction between "horizontal" and "vertical" social relations—in which the former are largely nonhierarchical and concern issues like trust, cooperation, and solidarity, while the latter relate to hierarchical issues like power, domination, and compliance. He went on to concede that the NES has, in practice, been preoccupied with horizontal or nonhierarchical relations, although in principle, vertical or power relations are no less significant in shaping socioeconomic behavior and economic institutions. The horizontal inclination of much of the NES is hardly accidental, however, since it reflects a fairly systematic tilt against the underlying principles of political economy and a great deal of macroeconomic sociology.

Randall Collins pointedly characterized Smelser and Swedberg's *Handbook* as a "triumph for network sociology," while Samuel Bowles contrasted its indebtedness to Williamsonian transaction-costs economics with an apparent indifference to the question of class—"once the organizing principle of much work on economy and society," class and class analysis had become "virtually absent."[36] Viviana Zelizer makes a parallel point about gender relations, which when they emerge at all in the NES tend to be read through the lens of network relations: "The result is to treat gender as one more attribute of single, decisionmaking economic actors instead of an organizing principle of economic life."[37] In network sociology, networks become (relatively concretized) condensates of *both* social agency *and* social structures: social agents act in the context of network relations, and the same relations mediate—albeit in a displaced and muted way—structural forces.[38] In other words, network sociology has its own way of freezing contextual relations, even as it insists on thawing out more of them than does orthodox economics.

Granovetter did not go as far as to deny the causal significance of deeper social structures, but he was more concerned with the intermediating mechanisms of the social embedding process and their associated "proximate" sources of causality.[39] Having cut an intermediating path between under- and oversocialized conceptions of social action and having focused on midlevel understandings of market structure, it is notable that much of the subsequent dialogue in the NES has been unidirectional—it has been a dialogue with economics, a dialogue about how to embed *Homo economicus*, how to make him a somewhat more socially adept individual. This view was evident in Granovetter's initial concern with "social structure *in the market*" and, in the context of the subsequent theoretical research agenda, with "how the larger social setting determines the parameters within which interest is defined."[40] This approach unfreezes some, but not all, of the social context, and the outcome is correspondingly slushy. And *Homo economicus* has more of a social life, but he certainly has not been put to death on the altar of feminist theory or class analysis.

In a telling commentary on the field of economic sociology, Zelizer identified three categories of work: first, there is the *extension* of standard or modified forms of economic analysis to issues that are rendered marginal in mainstream economics, such as household behavior; second, there are the various explorations of the *contexts* of economic action, which, for the most part, are seen to be embedded in interpersonal networks, organizational structures, or differentiated market forms; and third, there is an eclectic group of *alternative* explanations of economic activities and structures, which, by definition, are inconsistent with neoclassical economic principles and range far and wide in terms of subject matter and theoretical foundations. These categories may be regarded as, respectively, one, two, and three steps away from orthodox economics. As Zelizer noted, the "first two approaches, extension and context, have predominated" in the NES.[41] For the most part, the field has therefore been one or two steps away from economic orthodoxy, and much of it faces in that direction. The focus has been on those relatively plastic social networks that are located in and around the market and are amenable to concrete analysis.

Capitalism and patriarchy, as historically constructed and geographically differentiated social systems, largely fade into the background in mainstream NES. It was Granovetter's goal to "produce a theoretical argument [that is] consistent with the high level of contingency operating in the actual construction of economic institutions, but to do so without sliding down the slippery slope into historicism."[42] Instead, he found himself on another slippery slope—this time toward a new kind of Parsonian appeasement. Bernard Barber contends that Granovetter "shows no understanding of the importance of the larger social systems in which all economies are located. Where have the social structures of kinship, stratification, age, gender, the economy, the polity, organizations, education, and communications disappeared to?"[43] These social structures are typically collapsed into the proximate and overconcretized notion of networks, which in turn are only contingently related to concrete outcomes, just as they are only loosely connected to macrostructural forces.

According to Samuel Bowles, the NES "takes a more horizontal view: Class has been subsumed by networks, organizational ecology, reciprocity, asset specificity, and other more benign concepts."[44] And as Arrighi observed, what makes the NES

> "new" in relation to the old is its emphasis on "networks" and "embeddedness." The thesis that markets are embedded in social networks has been the main weapon in the critique of the economists' belief in self-regulating markets.... Less recognized but more fundamental is another difference: the distinctly "micro," "social-interactionist" approach of the New Economic Sociology in comparison with the distinctly "macro," "social-systemic" approach of the old economic sociology. With rare exceptions, the networks that are investigated link individuals or small groups over relatively short periods of time. In any event, any investigation of "big structures" and "large processes" ... lies almost completely outside the realm of the [NES], and so does anything resembling Braudel's *long durée*.[45]

Although Polanyi's name is often invoked in the NES, its constrained remit sits somewhat uneasily with Polanyi's more expansive project.[46] Polanyi's approach was not confined to the intramarket configuration of institutional relations, but began from the conception of markets as political constructions, requiring significant and continuing state intervention.[47] Moreover, Polanyi regarded stylized conceptions of institutional effects as inherently suspicious, advocating instead the careful historical analysis of institutions in their concrete complexity: "Let us beware of the abstract generalizations in things economic that tend to obscure and oversimplify the intricacies of actual situations, for these actualities alone are our concern. Our task is to divest them of generalities and grasp them in their concrete aspect."[48] Even though Granovetter declared his intention to move away from a "focus on the mechanics of networks alone," his embrace of a more abstract and synthetic notion of relational sociology seems oblivious to Polanyi's cautions.

The traction of the NES has been severely undermined by a pervasive tendency to conceptualize the market as somehow outside, beyond, or external to the variously "more embedded," "more social," or "more institutionalized" spheres of economic life that represent the substantive concerns of the subfield. The NES has made no more than relatively timid claims on the market itself, as a fundamentally political construction, too often making do with a series of suggestive, though partial, contextualizations of market behavior. In some form or another, the "pure" market and the instrumentalist behaviors with which it is associated continue to provide the more or less explicit foil against which contemporary accounts of the networked or embedded economy have been developed.

The tendency to refer (and defer) to an idealized market, to place the market at the other end of the spectrum of more socialized versions of the economy, or to rely in other ways on the abstract market as an analytical foil is widespread, even in ostensibly heterodox economics. The implications of this tendency are more than semantic, for they imply a continuing naturalization of some presocial market, even as they ostensibly seek to deconstruct this very formulation. This kind of slippage is clearly evident in network sociology, just as it is in Williamsonian economics and the associated strands of economic governance theory; it even appears in some neo-Polanyian work, in which various degrees of "marketness" or disembeddedness are countenanced, and in approaches that sequester networks as a third, distinctive form of economic organization. The argument that begins by asserting that markets are socially constructed and then goes on to discuss the manner in which "more" or "less" socialized economic forms exist *alongside* the forces of supply and demand has apparently become as commonplace as it is logically incoherent. Yet the statement that markets are embedded is surely a *qualitative* and *relational* one, not a matter of degree.

Greta Krippner has persuasively argued that, "every transaction, no matter how instantaneous, is *social* in the broader sense of the term: congealed into every market exchange is a history of struggle and contestation that has produced actors with certain understandings of themselves and the world which predispose them to exchange under a certain set of rules and not another."[49] It follows that nominally extra-economic factors relating to the state, politics, culture, and so on, are effectively "*contained* in every market act," Krippner continues, and their influence cannot be pegged to some sliding scale, as if to be more pertinent in some market settings than others, or present here but absent there. *Socio*economic theorizing therefore cannot start with the idealized market and then work outward to progressively "less marketlike" variants of the same; neither should it meekly accept that context-free economic action is simply a "rather special case," as Granovetter put it.[50] This is what Williamson did by visualizing markets in an axial relationship with certain hierarchical forms and the immediate "institutional environment" within which the economy operates, beyond which there is only "tosh." And while tosh may indeed be a "source of interesting variety [which] adds spice to life," he insisted that it must not be confused with the "core features of institutional environment," like legal rules and market regulations.[51]

Benign interpretations of embeddedness can be seen to be part of the problem here, rather than an interim solution or mere heuristic. For Krippner, a rather truncated reading of the

> embeddedness concept has led scholars to layer a social economy on top of a pre-social and untheorized market. In contrast, network theorists explicitly examine the market, but the social content is distilled away from social structure. It is both telling and troubling that, given the way in which the paradigm of economic sociology has been formulated, sociologists have only been able to study markets by stripping them of the features that most make them social. The concept of embeddedness posits that the world of the market exists apart from society even as it attempts to overcome that divide.... [A]s long as the market is treated as alien to social, political, and cultural forms, it will be in a position to pre-empt more tenuous understandings of social practices.[52]

Paradoxically, the NES project may have contributed to the very naturalization of markets that it set out to transcend, theorizing context and embeddedness in such a way that it has proved relatively easy to decant them off from an ostensibly presocial market.

"The major downfall of the network approaches," Fligstein and Mara-Drita argue, "is that they are such sparse structures that it is difficult to see how they can account for what we observe.... [T]hey contain no model of politics [and] no social preconditions for market exchanges."[53] Within the NES, networks are often placed in some parallel conceptual universe, sequestered both from markets, on the one hand, and power relations, on the other hand. Ironically, this process confers on networks some decidedly "marketlike" properties—floating, decentered, spontaneous, self-organizing, objects of analytical deference.[54] Network-centric analyses therefore share certain features with the market-centric analyses they purport to transcend: politics and power are rendered contingent and contextual, and, as a result, they are only haphazardly theorized; the bloodless, over-endowed, and underspecified concept of the market is replaced with, or complemented by, the anemic, over-endowed, and underspecified concept of the network.

Zelizer maintained that economic sociology must commit more fully to the "theoretical challenge" that, implicitly at least, lies at the heart of the project: "Instead of huddling in the corner designated for them by conventional economic analysis, economic sociologists should move freely through the whole range of economic life."[55] Fundamentally, this statement surely means taking on the market and its theorization, not eking out strategies for respectful coexistence. It means once and for all rejecting the Parsonian pact that has implicitly shaped the parameters of the NES. This is where economic geography has a potentially positive role to play, at least if it can be rooted in some way in a principled rejection of market essentialism and universal rationality. If the promise of a more robust economic sociology entails embracing Fred Block's concept of the "always embedded economy," then a complementary task in economic geography may involve explorations of the *everywhere* embedded economy.[56] If the first tends to privilege the historical contextualization of actually existing economies, the latter would take it one step further—analyzing the historical geographies of variegated, hybridized, and unevenly developed economies.

Spatializing Socioeconomics

Understandably, the NES project has been preoccupied with issues that it may potentially make its own: embedded networks. Increasingly, though, the limitations of "pure" network approaches are becoming evident.[57] The network optic has shed new light on variegated forms of social relations beyond markets and hierarchies, although it must be acknowledged that these are not mutually exclusive *but mutually constitutive* spheres of economic life. The logical implication of this position is an antagonistic attitude toward orthodox economic theory, yet the reformist wing of the NES seems, in practice, reluctant to acknowledge this implication, focused as it remains on the (distant) prospect of a rapprochement with the neoclassical mainstream. Against this strategy, the remainder of this chapter makes a case for moving beyond weakly contextualized networks, which necessarily entails transcending the restrictive dialogue between network sociology and orthodox economics. Instead, the move here is to engage those interdisciplinary literatures that have been attending to the (social) construction of markets and the diversity of capitalisms. In this vein, as Fred Block has observed:

> [T]here are many varieties of capitalism and there are many different ways that these varieties can be articulated together into a global system. Some systems of articulation—like the ones favored by neoliberals—operate to reduce varieties of capitalism that are possible at the national or regional level; but other systems of articulation are consistent with much greater variety at the national or regional level. It also follows that just as different varieties of capitalism can have dramatically differing levels of inequality or of economic insecurity for poor and working people, different systems of international articulation might be more or less consistent with reforms favoring subordinate classes.[58]

Although these observations provide an intriguing point of departure, Block readily concedes that "it is not enough to say that capitalism is a constructed system. The task is to illuminate *how* it is constructed: to see how a diverse and often contradictory set of practices are welded together to produce something that has the appearance of being a natural and unified entity."[59]

Certainly, the objective cannot be to proliferate variants of capitalism or constructions of the market willy-nilly. It must extend to the production of causatively significant accounts of economic variegation, both in space and through time. "Speaking of '*guanxi*' or 'predatory' or 'diaporic' capitalism," as Blim remarks, "is not to trade metaphors but to create a possible field and vocabulary for describing variation in a constructive, causally interesting way."[60] So it is clearly not enough simply to state that capitalism is a locally constructed system. The task is to illuminate how these local constructions have evolved, how they intersect and (co)evolve, and how such a geographic sensibility makes a difference to the form and functioning of variegated capitalist economies.

Deconstructing markets, market relations, and market ideologies means confronting the messy reality of economic behavior and economic structures, not assuming them away. "Market actors," as Fligstein notes, "live in murky worlds," in which information never flows freely, rules vary, actions are mutually interdependent, and motivations are always mixed.[61] Granted, the analytical task is likely to be messier and more inconclusive too, for it must confront the fact that actually existing economies are hybrid, mongrel structures. This is what Hodgson calls the "impurity principle," that *all* economic systems blend and fuse "market" and "nonmarket" elements, such that this binary distinction—which the NES may have inadvertently helped to sustain—is rendered defunct.[62] As Polanyi famously put it:

> The human economy . . . is embedded and enmeshed in institutions, economic and noneconomic. The inclusion of the noneconomic is vital. For religion or government may be as important for the structure and functioning of the economy as monetary institutions or the availability of tool and machines themselves that lighten the toil of labor. The study of the shifting place occupied by the economy in society is therefore no other than the study of the manner in which the economic process is instituted at different times and places.[63]

It makes no sense, in this context, to categorize economic formations in terms of their supposed deviation from the utilitarian abstraction that is the pure market economy, or for that matter some standard-issue rendering of liberal capitalism. Polanyi's contributions can be criticized on this score, too, for at times he also engaged in a discussion of *degrees* of embeddedness and disembeddedness, pointing to an apparent historical tendency for market systems to become relatively disembedded from societal structures, in contrast to the more deeply embedded alternative economies of redistribution and reciprocity. Those who would otherwise seek to build on Polanyi's insights usually find it necessary to clarify, correct, or contextualize this flawed historical-theoretical interpretation.[64] Barber complains that the placement of the (free) market on a supposed spectrum of economic forms affords the market "a false kind of analytic as well as concrete independence," in turn leading to "a further common error: that the market is not only disembedded and independent but also that it is the part of society that determines all the rest."[65] These errors are compounded, of course, when the market is equated with American capitalism and when this, in turn, is represented as the normative ideal against which "transitional," "unfree," "developing," or "sclerotic" economies are judged.[66] This is, of course, not just a neoclassical but a neoliberal conceit.

In contrast, a social-constructivist conception of the market draws attention to the ways in which markets, even idealized American markets, operate in the context of, *and are infused with*, particular configurations of cultural, legal, political, and institutional relations, not the least among which are shared understandings of the "contractual" nature of market exchanges themselves. The market therefore ceases to be the privileged, Archimedean point around which alternative, "more social" systems are arrayed; there *is no* Archimedean point. It is difficult to exaggerate the significance of this position for an economic geography that is even loosely wedded to the concept of an uneven, variegated, hybrid economy.[67] Although it may yet to have been formalized as such, the *spatially variegated economy* ought to be one of the fundamental constructions of heterodox economics. And even if they have yet to state it forcefully in this context, economic geographers have had a great deal to say about this variegated economy, both theoretically and empirically. The challenge is to make sense of *both* the macro *and* the micro sources of variation—or, as Massey put it, to hold on to the general as well as the particular—without falling into the "thousand capitalisms" trap of indiscriminate cultural theorizing (too messy) or the "two capitalisms" trap of sociological formalism (not messy enough). Theories of uneven spatial development and concepts of local institutional specificity should not be seen as irreconcilable alternatives, but as different sides of the same phenomenon—the variegated economy.

This said, the attendant methodological and theoretical challenges are anything but resolved, as some of the debates around postsocialist economic transformations, for example, have clearly demonstrated. Stark and Bruszt's analysis of the "recombination" of capitalisms in Eastern and Central Europe, and their associated forms of path-dependent restructuring, provides a sharp critique both of "one best way" neoliberalism and of "one inevitable way" structuralism. They have also connected a variety of institutional and network forms to a series of relatively "structural" features of this variegated capitalist landscape by way of comparative analyses of actually existing capitalisms.[68] "As sociologists with a disciplinary disposition to exploit variance," Stark and Bruszt stated, "we see real analytic leverage in taking the diversity of capitalisms as an object of study and comparing *capitalisms* vis-à-vis each other."[69] For his part, Michael Burawoy was not convinced by these arguments, countering that they privilege (superstructural) institutional manifestations of capitalism while failing to problematize questions of diversity rooted in the (base) conditions of class relations and forms of production:

> Even though capitalism may diverge in its expression from sector to sector, from country to country, from region to region, these divergences are interconnected—the result of common underlying economic processes. To study such *sui generis* economic processes, one must subordinate the study of historical paths and trajectories to careful *in situ* analyses of actual social relations. It is difficult to talk of independent national or regional capitalisms—as is implied in "comparing capitalisms"—when the global order is so inter-connected. We need to understand how the global, whether through supranational institutions, transnational connections, or post-national discourses, has mediated effects on what has come to be called the "local."[70]

Burawoy would apparently wish to cut through many of the institutional layers that are so often afforded explanatory weight by both economic sociologists and economic geographers, seeking to uncover the generalized capitalist dynamics that lurk beneath the much-vaunted varieties. Although Burawoy's method also calls attention to global-local articulations, these articulations are viewed from the other end of the telescope from those that *begin with* diversity. Stark and Bruszt resisted what they characterized as Burawoy's "unitary model of capitalism [and his analytical] standpoint outside capitalism."[71] At the same time, Burawoy's skepticism calls attention to the risks of a relativist analysis of capitalism, given that what different models or varieties of capitalism that there might be must exist in the context of deep transnational connections and structural interdependencies. Declarations of hybridity, after all, presuppose interconnection and family resemblance, as well as local variation, the explication and theorization of which may be viewed as a *particularly* economic-geographical task.[72] As Burawoy rhetorically asked, "how many advanced capitalisms can there be in the world?"[73]

Making sense of the uneven terrains of capitalism means taking "embeddedness" seriously in a macrosociological sense. Social constructivists insist that economic relations must not be reduced to market relations, that the two are not coterminous. Even the most "marketized" transactional environments fuse what may be conventionally understood as market and nonmarket elements, just as they often imply extensive—not to say deepening—roles for the state. The projects of state building and market building are continuous ones, and they are deeply interpenetrated.[74] Especially vivid contemporary illustrations of this situation can be found in the extensive market-building projects that are under way in Eastern Europe, the former Soviet Union, China, and the European Union,[75] while neoliberalism can also be understood as fundamentally a state project.[76] Yet, of course, this situation is anything but new. After all, the vision of the free market itself began life as a utopian construct, as Polanyi powerfully argued; its transformation into a prevailing ideology and an associated set of institutional technologies involved decades of concerted political action. In this sense, as Polanyi ironically observed, "The road to a free market was opened and kept open by an enormous increase in continuous, centrally organized and controlled interventionism. While laissez-faire economy was the product of deliberate state action, subsequent restrictions on laissez-faire started in a spontaneous way."[77] Moreover, this road is still being traveled, in that the process of installing and maintaining markets is a continuous one, beset by failures of governance and unforeseen perturbations, rather than one that is focused on a predetermined and realistically attainable destination. As Barber observes, even the fabled economic theorists of the nineteenth century lacked a fully formed and coherent

> vision of the market system that was gradually coming into being. It was not for them the explicit, full-blown "utopia" that Polanyi called it. Since the sociohistorical process created what we now know as the market system in a bits-and-pieces, incremental, unintended way, the theorists and ideologists who were among the significant actors in that process likewise created only theoretical bits-and-pieces of what gradually coalesced into a highly structured intellectual creation that still has its scientific and ideological functions.[78]

Something similar might be said about the always incomplete and contradictory project of neoliberal globalism. Despite suggestions to the contrary (on the part of both critics and advocates), this has never been a singular or coherent project. It has been stitched together from various "bits-and-pieces," including Chicago School economics, the projects of conviction politicians like Reagan and Thatcher, experiments around the world with "shock therapy" and structural adjustment, reconstructions of cold war geopolitics, the ideological realignment of various multilateral institutions, the increased reach of think-tank networks, and so forth.[79] The point is that neoliberal ideology was not simply "out there," waiting to be invoked, but instead had to be *constructed*, and its rise to contemporary dominance was not preordained, but has involved incrementalism, trial-and-error experimentation, and encounters with a series of fortuitous or path-altering conjunctures. It is a measure of the relative success of this concerted ideological and institutional project, of course, that neoliberalism has the *appearance* of a monolithic, omnipresent, and inevitable "force of nature." Under the surface, neoliberalism is a more fragile creation than these appearances suggest: its political-economic narrative has been stitched together from a series of partially overlapping fragments, and there has been a need for several midcourse adjustments. In fact, the project of neoliberalism seems increasingly to be preoccupied by, if not mired in, the management of its "own" contradictions, since institutional flanking mechanisms are repeatedly invoked as a means of supplementing and sustaining flawed programs of marketization and "deregulation."[80]

If the ideological project of neoliberal globalism indexes a (powerful yet misleading) vision of a flat-earth economy, comprising free-trading, flexible agents, then a critical economic-geographic counterproject would seek strategically to survey the uneven landscape, to expose the cracks and fissures—what Block called "welds"—in this supposedly unitary system. It would draw attention to the ways in which uneven spatial and social development disrupt this universalist narrative; it would map out the command centers and constitutive networks of the project; and it would explore its vulnerable flanks, its fissures of stress and contradiction, its sites of localized failure and frontiers of active extension, and the alternative economic geographies that are being made both in its wake and in its stead. Indeed, there are signs that some movement in this direction is occurring, although progress has so far been only fitful.

Conclusion: Heterodox Conversations

Appropriately, this chapter ends with a discussion of openings, and glimpses of an interdisciplinary agenda yet to consolidate. Research programs keyed into the potential of spatialized socioeconomics would surely retain some affinities with the NES, which itself has continued to proliferate, but they would also need to work across a considerably broader canvas. Themes in this heterodox conversation might include the following. First, there is scope to draw energy and direction from critiques of the theoretical worldview of orthodox economics. On its own, of course, oppositionalism can never be enough. As the previous chapter argued, an agenda defined principally in reaction to, or as an inversion of, orthodox economics is sure to be both distorted and partial. Yet something can also be said of strategies of passive coexistence, as the experience of the NES shows. Any alternative project worth its salt will need to contest the terrain occupied by neoclassical economics. But a spatialized socioeconomics would have its own positive program too. If economies are indeed embedded in qualitatively different ways not only always but *everywhere*, then there is a massively challenging task at hand, that of mapping the hybrid formations of real economies in movement.

Second, in contrast to the rather timid treatments of "context" in the NES, there is scope to stake out more forthright arguments about the contextual embedding of economic life. Making a strong case for context is consequently not just an empirical position; it is a theoretical and methodological stance. One of the striking features of the various ways in which the NES took steps to unfreeze the "non-economic" parameters of economy life, and to highlight the social and institutional embeddedness of market processes, is that they have done so, for the most part, without theorizing the simultaneously *spatial* constitution of these phenomena. The typically undertheorized ways in which labels like "regional," "local," and "national" are casually applied to phenomena, such as industrial districts, modes of regulation, learning systems, governance regimes, systems of innovation, varieties of capitalism, and so forth, have prompted criticism, particularly from geographers. Yet there is still much to do to convert this skepticism into a positive research program and to convince the other heterodox economists that these concerns are substantive, rather than secondary, or, worse still, merely semantic distinctions or articles of (geographic) faith. Fundamentally, this is the challenge of *explaining* the spatial dimensions of economic variety and uneven development, including where it comes from and why it matters, rather than taking this as a pregiven and unquestioned point of departure. The majority of heterodox economists are convinced that history matters in this respect; few have seriously engaged with the question of how geography and uneven spatial development may matter. Demonstrating *how* geographic context matters, of course, involves dispensing with the notion that the effects of, say, gender regimes, production cultures, or governance systems are merely "contextual" in the first place. Instead, their *constitutive* effects must be demonstrated, not merely asserted or assumed.

Third, a parallel set of arguments can be made about scale and rescaling, the creative theorization of which has largely been confined to political-economic geography and critical urban studies, but which has much wider implications. There is a telling resonance between geographic critiques of conventional globalization narratives—which take issue with the frequent invocation of an ostensibly "out there" zone of unregulated, universal, and unmediated market forces—and sociological critiques of orthodox economic narratives—which take issue with the idea of an ostensibly separate sphere of undifferentiated and purely rational action. Both of these orthodox constructions recycle the myth of a disembedded, placeless economy. If, as Barber, Block, and others have insisted, *all* economies are embedded, then the global economy is no exception, but there is much work yet to be done convincingly to pull apart the commonplace binaries of global/abstract/disembedded market versus local/concrete/embedded market. Strategically useful in this respect is work that sets out to uncover the local and sociospatial constitution of ostensibly "global" processes, or that problematizes explicitly transnational and extralocal forms of economic embedding and institutionalization. There is also work to be done in denaturalizing received terms like "national economy" and "regional system of production," to reveal the constructed (and repeatedly reconstructed) nature of such categories.

Fourth, in terms of the substantive content of work that may facilitate a widened interdisciplinary dialogue, much more may be done to explore the historical geographies of market making and state building, both comparatively and across scales, and to examine the social (re)construction of economic institutions more generally. Economic sociologists have produced many of the seminal contributions on market making,[81] although issues concerning the spatial and scalar constitution of these market-building projects tend to play no more than trivial roles in these accounts. Strangely, markets (even socially constructed ones) have not been objects of sustained, critical attention in contemporary economic geography. If this means that the big questions about markets and their theorization are being handled elsewhere, then it is troubling. To the extent that research programs around actually existing markets and processes of marketization are underdeveloped, then orthodox conceits and neoliberal articles of faith are being sanctioned through non-engagement.

4
Rascal Concepts
Tangling with Neoliberalism

The precursor to this chapter was the *Antipode* lecture, given in London in 2011, which itself was one of several articles written around that time which revisited the concept (and the facticity) of neoliberalism in the wake of the global financial crisis of 2008–2009.[1] These were by no means my first kick at this particular can. A decade later, it is quite remarkable that neoliberalism retains its dogged presence, as an unstable and persistently contested "rascal concept," after countless invocations and "applications" (some rigorous and definitive in their use of the concept, many more invoking the term in a looser or more ambient sense), accompanied by a fluctuating chorus of denunciations. The concept of neoliberalism is hardly any less troublesome and controversial today than it was decades ago, when it first began to circulate (as a critics' term) in the 1980s. Critical theorizations of neoliberalism have had a bumpy ride from the start, never really securing either stability or widespread acceptance. To some extent, this has echoed the wayward and contradictory process of neoliberalization itself, which has represented, all along, something of a moving target—never to be "fixed," never to take a standard form, never to trend unequivocally in the direction of completion or for that matter toward terminal crisis. The lexicon of neoliberalism has never achieved much mainstream currency (say, in everyday political discourse, or in the social-science orthodoxies of fields like political science or sociology; certainly not in economics, of course), even if it has become part of the critical commonsense in some quarters. To the extent that there has been recognition of the concept across the social sciences, this has been somewhat grudging, while from time to time it has been suggested that the idea should be banished altogether. Among the alleged misdeeds are that it misattributes agency and causality; that it misrepresents history and flattens out geographical differences; that it is too loose and capacious, serving as a catch-all for all manner of contemporary ills; that in explanatory terms, it does more harm than good; that it is too structuralist, as an overarching concept, or not structuralist enough, in obscuring the effects of capitalism; and so forth.[2]

Although I have found myself working on questions relating to neoliberalism and neoliberalization over the long haul, I have never thought of this in terms of a particular theory claim, or the defense of some predetermined position in back-and-forth debates. Rather, it found its way into what I do, and stuck around, by virtue of its explanatory salience and conceptual utility, making connections that needed to be made, not least across a series of quite different research projects concerned with concrete problems and situations. Sometimes this has been concerned with the medium- to long-term movement of policy norms and institutional orientations (in fields like welfare reform and urban development), sometimes it has been focused on particular moments of transformation or crisis (such as early to late-stage Thatcherism), and sometimes in situations where currents of neoliberalization appear to be dominant or otherwise normalized, as in the United States or England, but on other occasions where this is not necessarily the case, such as in Japan or China. This said, from time to time, the combination of conjunctural circumstances and the movement of academic debates has called for a more explicit engagement, tangling with the always emergent concept itself, its (ab)uses, and its discontents, such as during the near-death moment for neoliberalism (both in theory and in practice) triggered by the global financial crisis, and the subsequent flurry of debates around "post-neoliberalism" and the political economy of austerity.[3] The origins of the present chapter date from this latter period, around a decade ago, a period which has since sprawled into its own kind of interminable impasse, or interregnum, and in various ways the arguments continue to bear that time-stamp. In a different sense, though, the discussion speaks to challenges of conceptualization and interpretation that are ongoing and in some ways quite intractable ones, and which in a variety of ways continue to find echoes and refractions. And not least, the discussion speaks to the practice of situated theorizing which is an animating concern of this book.

In retrospect, my own (long-term, cumulative) encounter with neoliberalization seems to have evolved through three or four phases, which were hardly planned, needless to say. My first encounter, in the 1980s, was a Polanyian one, via Claus Offe and institutional economics. This was primarily concerned with the persistent contradictions and enduring "regulatory dilemmas" embedded in the operations of capitalist labor markets (and relating to unemployment, socialization, wage-setting, workplace control, and so on). Labor markets do not "clear." They are not self-regulating. The supply of and demand for labor are not simply governed by quantities and prices. And if real-world labor markets do not regulate themselves, then they can be expected to be the source of endemic challenges and dilemmas of regulation (including how to regulate wages and working conditions, how to prepare and socialize rising generations for waged employment, how to regulate and restrict access to non-wage sources of income). Many of these involve the less-than-perfect actions and reactions of the state, (re)actions that are politically mediated and institutionally intractable. These uncoordinated but variously induced responses are not functionally determined, even if in a sense they are effectively necessitated, or rendered imperative, *in some form or another*. In practice, the contradictory and always somewhat contingent presence of the state will often become patterned and institutionalized in various ways. So it was that there was a discernible nineteenth-century English pattern of labor regulation, for example, and a postwar German one too, while real-time observation during the 1980s gave credence to the claim that a distinctively neoliberal pattern might be taking shape, revealed in the form of family resemblances between experiments in Thatcherism and Reaganomics, marked by overlapping ideological critiques of "interventionism" and "welfare," and by the deployment of programmatic projects and strong discourses relating to markets, "flexibility," and competition. When working on these questions in the mid-1980s, I do not recall that recourse to a ready-made theory of "neoliberalism" was really an available option, although there were some that were beginning to develop arguments along these lines.[4] For the most part, the vagaries of contemporary labor regulation seemed to present themselves more in the form of empirical and political questions, freighted with all manner of contingencies, none of which could be readily put aside. In this context, notions of neoliberalism and neoliberalization, as modalities of "applied" market rule, were embryonic at best. And they were never "generic" theory claims, but context-specific conceptual framings, worked and reworked around different purposes and problems. Neoliberalization, in this context, served as a real-time device for capturing and characterizing patterned processes of change. It arose as a provisional label for a particular kind of state restructuring, studied across the terrain of design, implementation, and reform.

Layered on top of these "grounded" and real-time explorations of the nitty gritty of de facto neoliberalization, for me at least, would somewhat later come a regulation-theoretical reorientation, or rethink, beginning at the start of the 1990s. In this literature, too, there was no off-the-shelf concept of "neoliberalism" to be had per se, the emergent form and facts on the ground of which presented somewhat awkwardly in relation to regulationist precepts— which after all were never intended to be predictive, even if they were sometimes misused in this way. On the one hand, there were concerted challenges to and moves away from the established norms of Fordist-Keynesian labor regulation that might be interpreted as the first signs of a putative successor regime, as a neoliberal mode of regulation coevolving and interdigitated with "post-Fordist" dynamics in the economy. On the other hand, these same developments could be read as something almost like the very opposite, as indicators of a continuing and unresolved crisis. What these early-stage neoliberal projects *did* seem to be doing, however, in advancing various forms of pro-market and pro-corporate (de)regulation, was to perform their own styles of targeted anti-statism (focused in particular on the social state and on industrial interventionism), while at the same time remobilizing state power to their own ends. This said, "neoliberalism" remained rather difficult to compute from a regulationist perspective, since it failed to satisfy the theoretical criteria captured by the notion of a mode of social regulation structurally coupled with a (moderately) sustainable model of growth. Falling short on these "reproduction" measures, neoliberalism seemed to be presenting, instead, as the patterned politics of extended crisis management, while at the same time threatening to be(come) more than this. In this context, a question was also raised about the extent to which a certain set of mid-twentieth-century conditions (and Eurocentric assumptions) were effectively baked into some of these regulationist concepts,[5] with the result that while regulation theory was the source of a series of demanding questions about neoliberalism and its compatibility (or otherwise) with emergent growth models, it was less well equipped to parse and evaluate the (range of possible) answers.

By the first decade of the twenty-first century, my own evolving approach to the neoliberalism question had become more explicitly processual (even if it had been tacitly so since the beginning). This was coupled with a growing sense that this increasingly hegemonic *modality* of regulation was displaying not only persistence but capacities for reinvention and reproduction, never mind that this interpretation seemed to straddle (or muddle) the nominally either/or conceptions, derived from regulation theory, of mode of regulation *or* conjunctural crisis. Out of this processual approach, developed in the interstices of established concepts, came a working definition of neoliberalization: a dominant pattern of regulatory transformation, invariably initiated by or implicating the state, anchored in the contradictory reproduction of market(-like) rule in the face of abiding antipathies to socioeconomic redistribution, social entitlements, and collective institutions. As such, this was a way to name and characterize the *process of transformation itself*, and the qualitative form(s) of regulatory restructuring with which it was associated; it was not a label to be applied to an era, a "system," or an order per se.[6] It consequently did not describe (and was not a name for) an end state, but rather a distinctive pattern of transformative restructuring.

With this came the idea that neoliberalism embodied its own kind of creative destruction, being shaped both by the reactionary impulse to "roll back" antithetical forms and power structures (notably those anchored in the social state and sources of collective resistance) *and* by the proactive imperative to "roll out" institutions and infrastructures somehow capable of sustaining its failure-prone projects of market-centric, anti-labor, and corporate-centric *re*regulation, or at least muddling through.[7] This means that projects and programs of neoliberalization, while often displaying family resemblances and constitutive connections, were in another sense always and everywhere contextual. There was no blanket condition of "neoliberalism in general," because each and every transformation was forged through its own reactions and struggles against what went before (like a reactionary form of path dependency), with the politically mediated outcomes of those struggles, and with its own experiments and adaptations. Across contexts, neoliberalism could apparently "multiply," but it did so more through politically mediated contagion and interaction, not by the imposition of some Grand Design. This is why neoliberalization is in many ways a quintessential geographer's problem: made out of multiple contextualizations, its uneven spatial development is not a secondary issue but an integral one.

So there would never be a pure form, an ideal type or a moment of completion; just a rolling and contradictory historical geography. But back to the conjunctural context: the global financial crisis of 2007–2009, for all its endogenous causes, had not proven to be neoliberalism's terminal moment of reckoning, despite some prominent predictions to this end. Instead, there had been new rounds of austerity-based social-state degradation and public-budget purging, the rationalizations and justifications for which had many a familiar ring. This not mean, however, that some prefabricated rendering of "neoliberalism" only needed to be dusted down and repurposed, as an indicator of business as usual. New rounds of empirical work would be required, but also more than that. What was becoming an iterative process of theorizing neoliberalism would have to be rejoined anew. Not least, there was a need to account for the complex interdependencies between neoliberalizations in their plural form and the emergent properties of this more-than-the-sum-of-the-parts condition. This underscored the need, in other words, to address the *variegated* nature of neoliberalization in its uneven developed, adaptive, and polymorphic form.[8] While it had evidently not done so though the demonstration of coherence or stability, neoliberalism nevertheless appeared to be generating its own modality of reproduction, endemically crisis prone but repeating the feat of "failing forward" (into ideologically and budgetarily constrained responses), while evidently continuing to cater to entrenched and elite interests in not one but many social formations. This is not to position neoliberalism as some eternal default setting, but to recognize the character of its contradictory reproduction. The critical analysis of neoliberalization, it follows, is not about the cumulative revelation of some "general form," since not only must the analysis continue to be contextual and conjunctural, but there is an increasingly pressing need to work *across* these interdependent "localizations." For these reasons, the problematic of variegation has to become a central concern.

My own approach to neoliberalism, then, has been pieced together, not from some "whole-cloth" theoretical position, but in a more incremental and dialogic fashion, linked to a range of empirical research projects and problems, extending over several decades now. These have brought to light a multiplicity of configurations, manifestations, and mutations, which would often rhyme and resonate with one another, even if they never seemed to repeat or replicate. This has called for an approach analogous in some ways to that associated with the earlier wave of "restructuring" studies in industrial geography, tracing differences "in connection," and exploring one-to-many relations between transformative tendencies and locally mediated outcomes. Methodologically, it suggests an orientation not against but positioned *between* those emphasizing ethnographic or institutional particularity, on the one hand, and those that identify broad, political-economic rationalities or logics, on the other. It would have to learn from and respond to both modes of analysis and both ways of "seeing" neoliberalization, being dismissive of neither but also refusing to privilege one over the other in a definitive fashion. Over time, this contributed to a reading of neoliberalization as a variegated and unevenly developed phenomenon, the power and reach of which might exceed the sum of its individual parts, but which was certainly not reducible to any particular one of those parts. Those skeptical of the utility of political-economy approaches to neoliberalism and neoliberalization, in contrast, have often taken the view that the phenomenon was actually *less* than the sum of the parts, and that these theories were making something big and connected out of something that was much smaller and much less articulated, if indeed there was any "there there" at all. Yes, there was—for all to see—a rash of experiments with projects like privatization and market-oriented audit systems, going back a generation in fact, but the skeptics maintained that these were not to be yoked to some master narrative of neoliberal transformation, because every case told a contingent story, while few, if any, resembled textbook conditions. On the other hand, those of us who found utility in midrange theories of neoliberalization countered that these were surely not random incidents or coincidences, and neoliberalism need not (indeed could not) work as a replicating machine. To the extent that these amounted to lumper-versus-splitter differences—with one side interpreting differences and distinctive localizations with reference to an encompassing conception, while the other interpreted these differences as evidence of overreach and mis-specification—they were discussions often conducted at cross purposes.

My own view has been closer to that of a lumper in the sense that I have been less inclined to disaggregate, disembowel, or disown the concept of neoliberalism/neoliberalization on the grounds that its realizations and manifestations are (but *can only be*) diverse and always contextual, that they never complete and never resemble the ideal type, but are routinely thwarted, derailed, and redirected. There are ample grounds for rejecting (quite correctly) totalizing, essentialized, or mechanical conceptions—such as a model of top-down convergence entrained on a destination resembling the small-state stereotype—but in reality this caricature tends only to circulate as an advocates' pipe dream or skeptics' foil. These are not the grounds, however, on which to reject processual and contextualized interpretations of variegated neoliberalization. And they were not grounds for dismissing invitations to explore the messy and mongrel forms of neoliberalism in the wild, extending to their complex lines of connection and coevolution across diverse sites and situations, cases, and contexts. This said, the persistent undercurrent of scholarly grumbling about "neoliberalism," with its promiscuous applications and alleged foreclosures, has at various times called for some sort of response, and a response that went beyond a simple defense or reiteration of the concept of neoliberalization. Constructively, a response might instead seek to articulate how neoliberalism's very conditions of existence (and contradictory reproduction) imply a different kind of research program.

These were among the original motivations for the chapter that follows, which presents a reading of variegated neoliberalization in which uneven spatial development is not some empirical anomaly, unexplained variable, or confounding complication, but rather, a defining characteristic of the process itself. The dynamics of neoliberalization are not moving inexorably toward completion or unification or even coherence; neither is the diversity of their actually existing forms captured by a simple discrepancy between ideational purity and messy realization. Instead, the argument here is that neoliberalism, and especially projects of later-stage neoliberalization, are being reproduced through "multi-conjunctural" means, through deep interdependencies and relays, through polycentric adaptions across *many* sites of (re)production, and through all manner of crisis-assisted adjustments. The resulting conception is quite some distance from regulation theory's "primacy of internal causes," even as it remains animated by some of the same questions and problematics. It implies a rejection of an exaggerated choice between a "global" conception of neoliberalism, *qua* singular, one-world order within which sites and subjects are enrolled (or steamrollered), and a "disintegrated" understanding in which neoliberalism represents no more than a scattered presence, living mainly on the "inside" of states, societies, or institutions, here and there. The arguments that follow refuse this mutually negating binary, between a catch-all conception of "big-N" Neoliberalism, as a solid-state condition of epochal proportions, stamping out replicas of itself around the world, and a more timid and noncommittal take on "small-n" neoliberalizations of a jurisdictionally contained or site-specific kind, and studiously agnostic about the more-than-local nature of the beast. Instead, this approach means grappling with neoliberalization in its necessarily plural and hybrid forms and with its ramifying and super-emergent capacities. Importantly, it also means confronting questions of uneven spatial development, variegation, and what might be called "path interdependencies" in ways that are fundamental to the ontology of neoliberalism itself, not just downstream matters of contingent, "empirical" variation. This is the work that the current chapter sets out to initiate, and to which the remainder of the book, in various ways, is substantially dedicated.

Deflating Neoliberalism?

For some, neoliberalism is the spider at the center of the hegemonic web that is worldwide market rule. For others, it is a bloated, jumbo concept of little utility, or worse, a cover for crudely deterministic claims tantamount to conspiracy theorizing or closet structuralism. Poststructuralist critics, even those who use the term, are wont to argue with some justification that the concept of neoliberalism is too often "inflated" or "overblown," and that it is frequently deployed in a manner that less than convincingly "accelerates," in explanatory terms, from specific circumstances to large claims.[9] Premature declarations of the death of neoliberalism, in the thick of the global financial crisis, proved to be variously wishful and misleading, although the crypto-regulationist contention that neoliberalism was lurching into its zombie phase—spasmodically advancing in roughly the same direction, anti-socially pursuing many of the same warm-blooded targets, but largely dead from the neck up, as a program of intellectual and moral leadership—seems to have retained a certain morbid currency.[10]

In the political-economic twilight world "after" the crisis, it appears that neoliberalism—both as a fact of life and as an explanatory concept—did not go away, but neither did it remain the way it was. The sobering failure, to date anyway, of post-neoliberal "alternatives" to gain much meaningful traction has meant that neoliberalism appears to have scored a most audacious (yet at the same time hollow) victory.[11] It now sits as a lonely occupant of an ideological vacuum largely of its own making. In this afterlife, the arch-advocates of market reform in the global power centers have taken to sounding rather more circumspect and less emphatic, their rhetorical hubris, intellectual cant, and technocratic self-assurance having been tempered, but for the most part they and their ilk remain in post. As Centeno and Cohen concluded their 2012 assessment of the perplexing arc of market rule, "[t]he crisis and ensuing Great Recession may have shaken neoliberalism's supremacy, but it remains unchallenged by serious alternatives and continues to shape post-2008 policy."[12] Many of these policies—hewing toward the familiar line of regulatory restraint, privatization, rolling tax cuts, and public-sector austerity—were in fact pursued in an even more sternly necessitarian fashion than before. After doubling up, neoliberalism went on to double down. This apparent staying power itself commands a certain kind of attention, even for those who might have preferred just to be rid of the concept. But in truth, explanations of neoliberalism have been evolving along with their mutating *explanandum*. Evidence of what looked like an ideological resurgence of a brusquely renovated version of neoliberalism, coupled with the roughly simultaneous arrival of probing intellectual histories that have leavened the old conspiracy theories with some new conspiracy facts,[13] prompted some to contemplate a recuperation of the concept. More skeptical than many of "leftist Don Quixotes tilting at ideological windmills," Mitchell Dean's perceptive tour of the postcrisis horizon arrived at the conclusion that neoliberalism must now be correctly seen as "a militant thought collective, many of whose innovations and ideas have become embedded in the techniques of various regimes of national and international government over the last thirty years."[14] And as Stuart Hall reflected, also in this ideological "hangover" period:

> The term "neo-liberalism" is not a satisfactory one. . . . Intellectual critics say the term lumps together too many things to merit a single identity; it is reductive, sacrificing attention to internal complexities and geo-historical specificity. I sympathize with this critique. However, I think there are enough common features to warrant giving it a provisional conceptual identity, provided this is understood as a first approximation. Even Marx argued that analysis yields understanding at different levels of abstraction and critical thought often begins with a "chaotic" abstraction; though we then need to add "further determinations" in order to "reproduce the concrete in thought." I would also argue that naming neo-liberalism is

politically necessary to give the resistance to its onward march content, focus and a cutting edge.[15]

The fact that the meaning, and in some quarters the very existence, of neoliberalism continues to be debated, several decades after its ascendancy as a (euphemistically styled) governmental project, and almost as long after the term's lagged emergence as a social-scientific signifier, must be telling us something. It points to the need to understand neoliberalism's longevity and adaptability, despite so many near-death experiences and declarations of irrelevance.[16]

Is neoliberalism, as more "inflationist" accounts tend to have it, an expansive and adaptable ideological project, jointly constituted with prevailing forms of financialized capitalism, a project that variously frames, legitimates, and necessitates a paradigmatic package of policies? (Here, neoliberalism represents a codification of the prevailing rules of the globalizing-capitalist game.) Or does it designate but one strand of a diffuse complex of individualized post-social governmentalities, a never more than "small-n," flexible assemblage of technologies, routines, and modes of conduct, as more "deflationist" and particularized analyses are more inclined to argue? (Here, neoliberalism is but one transformative pulse among many, and not necessarily the dominant one.) Does it really define the principal ideological power grid of the contemporary world, or is it some figment of the left-structuralist imagination? Prompted by these questions, the chapter proceeds in four steps. First, some of the conditions of "actually *still* existing" neoliberalism, in this post-crisis afterlife, are briefly examined. Next, by way of a retro-methodological reflection on the politics of Thatcherism, and contending accounts of those politics then and now, some critical questions are raised about "catch-all" explanatory maneuvers, even under conditions of neoliberal hegemony. Third, moving toward the definition of more positive methodological (pro)positions, an argument is sketched for situating processes of neoliberalization within and among "discrepant" formations—which, it is suggested, more closely resemble their normal, rather than exceptional, conditions of existence. A fourth section takes this a step further, proposing that neoliberalism, whether or not it is understood to be hegemonic, must be theorized among its others—that is, among others *of* neoliberalism that are not only elsewhere and "out there," but also right here, side by side, in mixed-economy forms of market rule, and theorized "heterogeneously" and therefore among others *to* neoliberalism, its various competitors, would-be successors, and alternatives. This entails some rethinking of neoliberalism "inside/out." Finally, the chapter is concluded with a comment on the longing to get over neoliberalism, which might be considered to be a scholarly as well as social condition.

Neoliberalism: Undead

On some counts, it lasted barely six months. That was the length of the ideological service interruption experienced in the global power centers, when the Wall Street crash of 2008 shorted out some of the primary circuits of financialized capitalism. For a while, this temporary power failure was deeply disorienting, not least for those corporate, financial, and media elites whose actions were among the proximate causes of the overload. There followed a brief fling, in some mainstream circles, with alternative rationalities, ruses, and remedies, as even Keynes was exhumed, if not entirely rehabilitated, as a justification for once again saving capitalism from the capitalists.[17] The "system" duly saved, almost entirely at public expense and with precious few strings attached, it was not long before business was being conducted almost as usual, including in the epicenters of the crisis in Washington, New York, and London. The moment of ideological free-fall, which had begun in the fall of 2008, quickly passed into a normalized crisis, managed in the barely reformed terms of a neoliberal *resettlement*. By the time of the London G20 summit in April 2009, as the *Guardian*'s Larry Elliot later observed, the "flirtation with alternative thinking was over," global elites having "returned to the pre-crisis mindset with remarkable speed."[18] Never mind that internal assessments would not only reveal, but effectively *confess to*, debilitating levels of "groupthink" and "intellectual capture" in multilateral agencies like the International Monetary Fund,[19] very little had changed. The social and economic fallout of the crisis would endure for years, but the regulatory regime seems only to have been reset.[20]

What might be incautiously labeled "the system" was brazenly rebooted with more or less the same ideological and managerial software, complete with most of the bugs that had caused the breakdown in the first place.[21] And in the midst of another neoliberal reincarnation, there were signs that its post-crisis mutations might be yet more antisocial than their predecessors, imposing the rule of markets in more intensely disciplinarian ways, and substituting still more coercive and necessitarian strategies for the politics of consent and compromise. A new normal was taking shape, as the costs of restructuring and insecurity were visited (once again) on the poor and the marginalized, as austerity programming, entitlement cutbacks, and radical reforms of the public sector were again raised to the status of non-negotiable imperatives. There was a wide array of social-movement responses to these conditions, including Occupy, the Indignados, and a resurgence of left parties in Southern Europe, which Don Kalb would portray as a "global mass upheaval in fragments."[22] But none was able to gain traction in the shape of a sustained, anti-systemic program. While the diverse forces of neoliberalization seemed to gain energy and impetus from extended conditions of crisis, these same conditions sapped the resources of oppositional movements.

These highly asymmetrical conditions, of hegemonic rearmament on the one hand and inchoate resistance on the other, seemed to broadly affirm those first readings of the initial fallout of the Wall Street crash and the Great Recession that followed, that the conjuncture was unlikely to be propitious for ideological regime change—for all the evident culpability of the bankers and (de)regulators. Rather than an imminent, post-neoliberal turn to the left and to renewed social-statism, the crisis seemed set to play into the hands of established corporate, financial, and political interests, setting the stage for a host of reactionary responses and presentational makeovers.[23] Second readings may have been somewhat more circumspect, though the optimism of the progressive intellect would remain distinctly tempered. When Colin Crouch rhetorically asked, three years after the Wall Street crash, "what remains of neoliberalism after the financial crisis," his blunt answer was "virtually everything."[24] Neoliberalism's rude return from what was widely interpreted, for a time anyway, as a terminal event—a very public financial crisis, striking at its central nervous system—represents a sobering lesson about both the persistence of market rule and the challenges of effecting various kinds of progressive turn. Perhaps neoliberal policy preferences are now just too deeply entrenched in the dominant circuits of corporate, financial, and political power? Perhaps the array of progressive alternatives is destined to remain, in the short to medium term at least, too disparate and isolated, advocated by social forces generally short on political leverage, strategic capacity, and institutional resources? Recurring questions such as these, it must be said, have yet to find conclusive answers. In the meantime, neoliberalism has once again ratcheted to a different version of its own normality.

What Thatcher Did

"I blame Thatcher" was an almost reflexive retort on the British left in the 1980s, since passing into cliché status. Beyond its function as a mobilizing slogan, the phrase also performed explanatory work, of a kind. It pointed unambiguously, of course, to a root cause, personalizing and politicizing at the same time. By implication, it suggested a remedy for various ills that (at least in principle) was simple: remove Thatcher and then. . . . Whatever the depressing *explanandum* (the deindustrialization of northern Britain, management failures across the underfunded public services, or the social breakdown of inner-city communities), "I blame Thatcher" could serve as a universally applicable and pithy *explanans*. However, setting aside for the moment the question of the proper positioning of Thatcherism in the long and geographically checkered history of transnational neoliberalization, its meaning and salience as a political-economic and cultural phenomenon divided even the most astute analysts of the time.[25] Stuart Hall and Bob Jessop would later agree that Thatcherite neoliberalism has been the dominant, if not defining, force in British politics since the 1970s, although they continued to differ on the extent of its cultural hegemony (Hall characterizing Thatcherism as "epochal," in its establishment of a new political stage; Jessop maintaining that British neoliberalism has been more unstable, less consensual), and to disagree over the role of historical and external constraints on the effective availability of governing strategies, which Jessop underscores and Hall tended to downplay.[26] They also diverged on the question of whether the New Labour project of Blair and Brown represented an asymmetrical hybrid of neoliberalism and social democracy, in effect an attenuated form of Thatcher's "full-blown" neoliberalism, or the contradictory consolidation of neoliberal accumulation strategies and ameliorative socioinstitutional "flanking," secured in conjunction with a deformed resurrection of Christian socialism. Decades later, the question of what Thatcher did remains contested.

What does seem to be clear, however, is that neither she nor her successors were acting alone. Neoliberalization, even when it is dominant, never secures an absolute monopoly. As a frontal political project, it always exists among its others, usually antagonistically. So Thatcher forged a governing strategy across the fault lines of neoliberalism and traditional British Toryism along with little-Englander anti-Europeanism; Blair reworked the interface between an inherited neoliberal settlement and social democracy or Christian socialism (take your pick), while separating from the labor movement; Cameron's coalition after 2010 offered a volatile cocktail of Blairism and Thatcherism, remixed in the context of weak leadership, deepening financialization, and rising insecurity; and Brexit and its aftermath have witnessed an apparent normalization of late-neoliberal crisis management, arguably in a more incoherent and chaotic form than ever before. Meanwhile, the institutions of the British welfare state (and its allies) did not disappear altogether, even if they have been relentlessly eroded and restructured for more than four decades now. Neoliberalism has evidently been much more than a sinewy presence here, but its shapes have kept shifting and it has never been the *only* occupant of the social stage. It may have become entrenched, but there is no sense of a path to completion or even stability.

As a result, although this may be analytically inconvenient, neoliberalism can only be found among its others, in mobile states of messy coexistence. Likewise, the contemporary cry, "Neoliberalism did it," should never be taken at face value as an omnibus "first cause," since it will always be found among other causes, not to say other culprits, while both its form and consequences can *only* be revealed in conjuncturally specific ways.[27] During the long 1990s, the catch-all concept of "globalization" would often perform an analogous (and equally misleading) function, as an ostensibly first or primary cause, a form of reductionist reasoning that Frances Fox Piven memorably critiqued as "globaloney."[28] There can be no excuse for propagating parallel forms of "neoliberaloney," as a kind of all-determining super-cause, bluntly attributed. Establishing causality necessitates the *specific* consideration of cases, conjunctures, and contexts, no less in situations where neoliberalism is understood to be incipient or subordinate, as in some analyses of contemporary China, for example,[29] than in those where it is considered to be dominant, normalized, or to occupy a leading position.[30] To reference "hybridity" in this context is more than a poststructuralist caveat; it is an indicator of the inescapably mixed and impure contexts in which neoliberalizing tendencies are found.

Since neoliberalization is always an incomplete process (and a frustrated yet frontal project), these circumstances of contradictory cohabitation represent the rule, rather than the exception. Chronically uneven spatial development, institutional polymorphism, and a landscape shaped by opportunism, serial policy failure, obstacles and oppositional pushbacks of different kinds, and stuttering forms of malregulation—these are all consequently par for neoliberalism's zigzagging course. Incomplete or partial neoliberalization is not some way-station on the path to complete neoliberalism, so it represents a category error to evaluate neoliberalism against some notional yardstick of absolute market rule, or against the utopian ideal type that is the free market/small state.[31] Explaining with neoliberalism is about accounting for its variable copresences, always in context. As a result, cities, regions, or countries must not be classified in the wrongheaded terms of "degrees" of neoliberalization, as if lined up on a historic (down?) escalator to "total" neoliberalism. Neoliberalism may be present in this or that regional formation. Its traces may even be almost *omni*present. But it can only be present in conjuncturally hybrid forms. Statistically, there may be a good chance these days that "neoliberalism did it," where this historically specific mode of market rule is hegemonic or dominant, but the contextual circumstances of such acts are more than background scenery, since neoliberalism is never found alone, cannot exist alone, and it never acts alone. Even hegemonies, Stuart Hall reminds us, are incomplete and contradictory.

> [I]s neo-liberalism hegemonic? Hegemony is a tricky concept and provokes muddled thinking. No project achieves a position of permanent "hegemony." It is a process, not a state of being. No victories are final. Hegemony has constantly to be "worked on," maintained, renewed and revised. Excluded social forces, whose consent has not been won, whose interests have not been taken into account, form the basis of counter-movements, resistance, alternative strategies and visions ... and the struggle over a hegemonic system starts anew. They constitute what Raymond Williams called "the emergent"—and the reason why history is never closed but maintains an open horizon towards the future.... Neo-liberalism is in crisis. But it keeps driving on. However, in ambition, depth, degree of break with the past, variety of sites being colonized, impact on common sense and everyday behaviour, restructuring of the social architecture, neo-liberalism does constitute a hegemonic project.[32]

The manner in which neoliberalism has kept "driving on," at least so far, is in this respect never preordained. And in real-time analyses of urban and regional restructuring, an (analytical) context in which "neoliberalism" is now regularly invoked—clearly *too regularly* for some—if and how *particular* events, actions, or movements are connected to the contradictory reproduction of neoliberal hegemony must always be empirical and political questions. The establishment of straight-line, unmediated connections to a singular global Neoliberalism are not just innocent analytical shortcuts; they misrepresent the constructed and contradictory nature of neoliberalization as a transformative process.

Even those skeptical of the claim that neoliberalism represents a globally hegemonic "common sense" can perhaps accept the proposition that what Hall calls a "common thread" has been identifiable for some time, across a whole swath of political-economic, social, and cultural (trans)formations.[33] This would include the somewhat cumulative ideological/institutional realignments of the kind seen in the United Kingdom after Thatcher, or in the United States after Reagan, in which the strategies of each successor borrow selectively from and react selectively against those before them; but it would also extend to the relational interpenetration of governing logics and routines, across sites and territories, through such means as structural adjustment, normative isomorphism, and competitive discipline, across transnational space.

Whether one leans toward heavily qualified readings of neoliberalism-as-exception ("splitting"), or bolder notions of neoliberalization-as-common-process ("lumping"), many of these lines of connection and "cross-formation" are widely recognized.[34] Analytically, however, the next steps can be quite divisive.

In fact, it is almost as if there were a fork in the road, between those who would take a political-economic or macro-institutionalist path and those pursuing more particularized approaches, often in a poststructuralist and/or ethnographic vein (with the latter being *different* paths to the usually more-provisional recognition of neoliberal influences or inflections in particular or localized settings). The former are inclined to emphasize extra-local disciplines and (always) "out there" forces, expressed through structurally unequal power relations and sometimes through dominant institutions, like those of the Washington Consensus. The latter will tend to find neoliberalism, if at all, as just one of many pulses, in more frail and provisional forms, in closely observed "in here" situations. For the former, neoliberalism possesses a structural and more-than-the-sum-of-its-parts quality, even as attention is duly paid to "the diversity of 'actually existing' neoliberalisms," as John Gledhill puts it, and to why and how "the diffuse system of power that lends them a certain unity has managed to implant itself with such apparent success in such a wide range of circumstances [across] both neoliberalism and its counter-movements."[35] For the latter, pertinent questions are more reflexively defined, often self-consciously *against* those "paradigms that envision neoliberalism as a coherent, unitary force or treat it as a monolith acting upon the world [and] the project of identifying neoliberalism's unifying strands across disparate contexts," as Tretjak and Abrell put it, instead favoring difference-finding approaches that foreground the "contingent, contradictory, and unstable character of neoliberal processes, examining historically and geographically contextualized situations through grounded studies of concrete places, people, and institutions."[36]

There are sound reasons to take the latter cautions seriously, just as (for different but in some cases overlapping reasons) there is an indispensable role for investigations in various ethnographic registers. But if there is a recurring analytical fault line here, this is exposed when more nuanced and contingent accounts are counterposed to an appreciation of the commonalities and connections across ("local") neoliberalisms; if they are positioned at an ironic distance from the more-than-local ideational and ideological constitution of neoliberalism *qua* hegemonic formation; or if they are detached from the normative networks, policy frames, and power relations that recursively secure the parameters for (or limits on) local or national action. Surely few critical analysts would seriously dispute the claim that neoliberalism exists as a "*thwarted* totalization," and that the vagaries of neoliberal policy depart, routinely and raggedly, from the pristine vision of neoliberal ideology.[37] Indeed, Kingfisher and Maskovsky characterize their approach, constructively, not as the antithesis but the "flipside" of Gledhill's stated project of tracing connections and commonalities across different cultural formations, seeking to place these analytical traditions in conversation rather than simply in opposition.[38] In other situations, however, this can flip over into more practiced ambivalence, invoking neoliberalism effectively as a foil, at arm's length and in scare quotes, where exceptionalist-particularist readings of "small-n" neoliberalism are set up as weakly contingent manifestations of an underspecified other, in a field of unpatterned difference, *against* the (mis)conception of a "uniform global condition of 'Neoliberalism' writ large," sometimes concretized as American capitalism.[39]

The comparative advantage of close-focus, experience-near, low-flying methods is their facility for finding and placing neoliberalism where and how it lives, in muddy hybrids, in fraught and often frustrated forms of partial or distorted realization. They bring neoliberalism to earth, in all kinds of ways, both literally and metaphorically.[40] Here, pulses and traces of neoliberalizing tendencies are deeply contextualized, often in quite idiosyncratic "local" formations. On the other hand, such accounts typically have less to say about the (more macro and translocal) context of this (more immediate and usually local) context. They are unable readily to address (and sometimes actually demur from) issues related to the spatial patterning and historical evolution of neoliberal strategies and fronts *across* cases and contexts; though they differ on the question of whether such macro-analytical work is a different but complementary exercise, or a worrisome symptom of residual structuralism. Partly conceding this point, Collier quite reasonably counters that to say that poststructuralist approaches "fail to grasp the 'context of context' . . . or the 'macro-spatial rules' that structure neoliberalisation processes" is only an argument against doing so in a rather tautological sense, since it restates "the fact that a non-structural approach is a non-structural approach."[41] But if supposed islands of hybrid neoliberal practice exist, at least in part, in mutual relation to one another, and if the reproduction of neoliberalism as a more-than-local regime of rules, disciplines, and incentives occurs, at least in part, through "out there" circuits, domains, and logics (such as competitive pressure, ideational normativity, prescriptive policy modeling, and fiscal constraints), then a non-structural approach, for all its other virtues, will be missing something if it is *anti*-structural, either by commission or omission.

In this respect, while there is a great deal to be gained from deeply contextualized and methodologically skeptical investigations that purposefully set out to put neoliberalism in its place (among other forces, formations, dynamics, and tendencies), there is much to be lost if such analyses reflexively spurn more abstract and/or macro formulations. It is not sufficient to stereotype analyses of the recurring, structural forms of neoliberalization processes—their more-than-the-sum-of-the-parts and more-than-local qualities—as no more than another invocation of the Big Picture. Problematizing the issues of how local neoliberalizations articulate with one another, of how family resemblances run through hybrid formations, of how midlevel and higher abstractions can be generated and interrogated, and of how macro patternings emerge across multiple cases and conjunctures is not merely a matter of "staging the totality," as Latour maintains; it is not just a matter, simply, of preemptively positioning every "local neoliberalism" in a preconceived box, shackled to an unchanging Master Narrative.[42] Rather, it is a matter of confronting the question of how, in practice, processes of neoliberalization are continuously remade through uneven spatial development (not instead of it), and of recognizing the ways in which all such local formations are jointly constituted, not only with distant others but also with formative networks (e.g., of technocratic expertise and policy norms) and differently scaled relations (e.g., of a fiscal or geopolitical nature). Methodologically, it is unhelpful to be "voluntarily blind" to such cumulative, multi-locale rationalities and to the constitutive outsides of neoliberalization processes, or to pass them off as merely Big Picture fantasies.[43]

Just as it is never adequate to characterize neoliberalism only in reference to its fanciful self-representation, it is also misleading to position supposed deviations and exceptions only in relation to some imagined, overbearing norm (of Neoliberalism as rigid monolith or mechanically imposed Global Hegemon), the very existence of which is effectively denied. The fear seems to be that the incautious capitalization of the phenomenon invites structuralist foreclosure, consuming and smothering everything in its path, so protection is sought in the methodological swaddling of hyper-contingency. In the process, self-consciously "small-n" treatments of neoliberalism tend to render their local objects of analysis into conceptual and political orphans, separated from all of their "relatives." Against such maneuvers, which are more likely to obfuscate the meaning and consequences of neoliberalism than they are effectively to *position* it, process-based interpretations of neoliberalization seek to specify the *patterning* of contingencies across cases, with no expectation of imminent regulatory monopoly or incipient socioinstitutional convergence, just as they problematize uneven development as a fundamental characteristic of this process. These approaches do not, however, presume that neoliberalism resides exclusively "up there," in quasi-global settings, where it operates deterministically from the top down. Rather, they propose, as a central methodological challenge, the problem of empirically connecting and dialectically relating "in-here" conditions, projects, struggles, and alternatives with "out-there" rule regimes, disciplinary pressures, competitive constraints, and so forth. Rather than floating offshore as a detached but all-determining superstructure, "out-there" neoliberalism is seen to be jointly constituted through all of the various "in-heres," even as this more-than-local phenomenon can be shown to be disproportionately animated by certain centers of calculation and sites of conjunctural power.

An additional aspect of this dialectical commitment, to *always* positioning the local, is an abiding skepticism concerning attempts to detach or bracket off—for whatever reason—the "in here" from the "out there." As a restructuring paradigm and frontal ideological project with a global reach, neoliberalism cannot be separated from those extra-local domains that contribute to and facilitate its reproduction, nor is it advisable to imply that neoliberalization is natural and normal in some places but an alien or aberrant presence in others. Neoliberalism is found, almost overwhelming empirical evidence now shows, in all manner of forms and formations, but it can *never* be found in a pristine state, implemented on a *tabula rasa*, in a fashion that is entirely unobstructed or unmediated. And there is no ideal type, original form, or institutional template against which hybrids can be singularly evaluated. Instead, the problematic of variegated neoliberalization—while hardly a receipt, admittedly, for an easy methodological life—entails the relational analysis of hybrids among *other* hybrids.[44] More like an ideological parasite, neoliberalism both occupies and draws energy from its various host organisms—bodies politic ranging from post-Soviet states to East Asian developmental regimes and European welfare states—but it cannot, ultimately, live entirely without or outside them. (So again, the "out there" and the "in-here" are jointly constituted—pretty much inescapably.) Understanding the effects of such "parasitical" infections and mutations must involve the diagnostic study of many patients, not just a few of the more (or less) susceptible to the deregulatory bug.[45] This also necessitates an understanding of what Jessop calls the "ecological" conditions and preconditions that have enabled the emergence and spread of such viral forms, their favored sites of incubation, their swarming behavior, their modes of reproduction, and their various mutations.[46]

Discrepant Formations

As a discrepant, contradictory, and shape-shifting presence, found in a wide range of political-economic settings, governance regimes, and social formations, neoliberalism will not be fixed. Ontologically, it cannot exist monolithically or in a "standard" configuration. In some respects, it is more appropriate to define neoliberalism—or the process of neoliberalization—through its recurring contradictions and uneven realization than in reference to some presumed, transcendental essence. At its contradictory heart, as an ongoing process of regulatory transformation, lies the discrepancy between the galvanizing utopian vision of freedom through the market, discursively channeling competitive forces that are far from imaginary, and the prosaic realities of earthly governance and its twin, endemic governance failure. Hence the now well-understood gulf between neoliberalism as ideology, as a strong discourse of market progress, and the much less prepossessing array of actually existing neoliberalisms.[47] In abstract terms, this gulf exists because the neoliberal worldview rests on the fundamentally mistaken understanding that it is possible somehow to "liberate" markets from their various institutional moorings and social entanglements, to dis-embed and purify social life as (if) a projection of utilitarian rationality. In concrete terms, the gulf exists because neoliberal restructuring schemes, while often damagingly consequential, will always be incomplete. They are inescapably associated with negative externalities and with downstream consequences that prompt their own counterflows, resistances, recalibrations, adjustments, alternative mobilizations, and occasional U-turns. And in their tendency to overreach and overflow (in the absence of a theoretical "brake" on what are rolling programs of marketization, privatization, dispossession, deregulation, commodification...) will inadvertently prompt double-movement counteractions and recoils of various sorts. These counteractions and recoils, however, may be either regressive or progressive; and they may impede neoliberalization or enable its (nonlinear, adaptive) reproduction. In practice, the course of neoliberalization almost never describes a tidy arc from regulated to deregulated markets, or big government to smaller states, but is more likely to result in a plethora of gyrations across the terrains of social regulation.

The messiness of these revealed outcomes should not be taken as grounds on which to dispense with theories of neoliberalization; on the contrary, it means that they are all the more necessary, and that they are necessarily contextual. But of course, *critical* theories of neoliberalization must not be confounded by what the neoliberal medicine doctors choose to write on their own bottles ("Miracle cure: shrinks the state, grows the economy, frees the people!"). Neoliberalization cannot be reduced to a unidirectional process of enacting a master plan cooked up by Hayek and friends at the mountain-top resort in Mont Pèlerin, deviations from which stand as variants or refutations of "neoliberal theory." Neither should it be expected that processes of neoliberalization are working inexorably toward the "destination" of a particular institutional formation, or that they express an incipiently coherent institutional logic.[48]

Damien Cahill has identified three recurring anomalies in neoliberal statecraft, where revealed practice diverges, time and time again, from the official script—that the aggregate "size" state has not significantly been reduced since the 1970s; that the scope or reach of the state has been extended in some realms; and that there has been extensive recourse to coercive and authoritarian powers.[49] His means of addressing this apparent paradox is a Polanyian one: "the discrepancy between neoliberal theory and practice," Cahill explains, stems from "the failure of neoliberal theory to recognize the inherently socially embedded nature of the capitalist economy."[50] The contradictions, in other words, are part of the package. Furthermore, they are not randomly distributed but distinctively patterned.

The fact that all neoliberal experiments are antagonistically embedded means that they can only exist as unstable, mongrel formations; in practice, there can be no "purebred" neoliberalisms. Critical theories of neoliberalization must therefore be purposefully addressed to the contradictory dynamics *between* neoliberal theory and practice, design and delivery; neither purely abstract-ideational nor purely concrete-institutional analyses will alone suffice. Neoliberal theory will always be frustrated, yet at the same time it has the (demonstrated) capacity to inspire, direct, and prioritize programs of socioeconomic transformation and state restructuring; the effect is to invoke a utopian destination, even if this is unattainable, as a means to sustain a strategically transformative *direction* in reform and restructuring efforts. (Insofar as neoliberalism "works," as a frontal ideological program, this appears to be its *modus operandi*.) Neoliberal practice necessarily diverges from this same (flawed) theory, yet it does not merely exist "downstream" from the ideological commanding heights; neoliberal nostrums have been perpetually adjusted, strategically, in dialogue with the vagaries of practice and comingled with others, even as they continue to resound to a certain matrix of idealized commitments. The contradictions, again, are part of the package, and they are patterned too.

On these grounds, one can support Hilgers's assertion that neoliberalism "can never be understood in radical separation from historical configurations," even while questioning his earlier claim that it is only when neoliberalism touches down, in particular grounded formations, that it becomes properly the subject of anthropological investigation.[51] As Collier has countered, not only is it a self-limiting error to sequester ethnographic practice in such a way, there is "no reason that an anthropological investigation of neoliberalism as an original movement of thought ... could not be linked to policy programs, to trans-local channels of circulation carved by powerful institutions or peripatetic experts, [and] to patterns of adoption and adaptation in various countries and sectors," even if these extra-local concerns have not been of paramount concern in the field to date.[52] It is not that neoliberalism only becomes sociologically complex in grounded, local, and lived settings, while its founding principles and global logics can be somehow cordoned off as an ethereal realm of iron-clad economic laws and philosophical principles. There is a need for *no less* situated and sociological analyses of the origins, tenets, and imperatives of neoliberalism—before, "above," outside, and beyond this or that "local" configuration, actually existing neoliberalism, hybrid assemblage, and so forth—and although Collier, for his part, is skeptical that these are "reconcilable" with more structural accounts of neoliberalism, ruling out what could be a fruitful conversation.[53]

Analyzing neoliberalism is never "quite as simple as lining up a list of attributes of neoliberalism, such as privatization, deregulation and the limited state," Dean points out, and then "showing whether or not they correspond to the current 'institutional reality' of state."[54] As a rolling, reactionary, and somewhat revolutionary program of macrosocial and macroinstitutional transformation, neoliberalization *acts on and through* these institutional landscapes; this is not a static neoliberal*ism*, a classificatory category that can be cleanly determined to be more or less commensurate with different state or social forms. It follows that theorizing more or less exclusively within the domain of concrete state or social forms, or in the realm of hybrid assemblages, can only generate partial explanations. It may indeed be wise to heed the Foucauldian injunction that neoliberalism should not be *presumed* to display unity or coherence as a governing doctrine-cum-political program; yet a reflexive presumption of disarticulated *incoherence* hardly stands as a meaningful methodological axiom.

For all its mixed achievements on the ground, the hegemonic grip of neoliberal ideology continues to be manifest in the form of unrelenting political pressure for market-oriented and voluntarist modes of governance, based on the principles of devolved and outsourced responsibility, along with a correspondingly circumscribed regulatory solution space. (This is how neoliberalism frames, brackets, and preemptively narrows the field of the politically visible and tractable.) It follows that invocations of (dynamic) neoliberalization rather than (static) neoliberalism represent more than analytical sophistry. Rather, they seek to capture the underlying character of this transformative process, as a "directional" and not a "destinational" mode of regulatory restructuring. (This is one reason why the Gramscian metaphor of the hegemonic front seems appropriate in this context.) The unreachability of this utopian destination may also help account for the typical mood, or temper, of the neoliberal reformer—endlessly frustrated, impatient, seeing (potential) setbacks at every turn and socialist-interventionists under every bed, and as a result always (re)targeting obstacles to, and opponents of, the rolling program of market-oriented transformation. History may ultimately judge neoliberalism, as a result, as rather more efficacious in dismantling and disabling alien and contesting social formations (like collective provisions, systems of social redistribution, planning regimes) than in effectively securing its alternative vision of a small-state order based on market freedom. Denied their utopian destination, pathways of neoliberalization invariably describe a vagarious and crisis-strewn course, markedly away from preceding social formations, such as the developmental state or Keynesian-welfare state, but hardly describing some beeline to the neoliberal nirvana. Hence the significance of Hayek's portrayal of neoliberalism as a "flexible credo," and Milton Friedman's recurrent complaint that the aggregate size of government has proved to be extremely difficult, historically speaking, to shrink. In practice, neoliberal reformers have been condemned to dwell in the purgatories of piecemeal reform and improvised governance. Their guiding philosophy provides a framework for action in these circumstances (which is why they repeat many of the same mistakes), but it delivers few (if any) sustainable solutions.

For some considerable time now, it has been an article of faith on the left that neoliberalism would eventually succumb to its own contradictions.[55] There would of course have been poetic justice in the terminal crisis of neoliberalism being incubated in New York City and London, the project's staging grounds, but this was not to be. It would have been a fitting bookend to the neoliberal era if this project so often advanced through shock treatment were to end with its own big bang, but this was not to be. In fact, it may be that neoliberalism will never "end" in such a singular and total way, simply because it has never existed in such a way. Local failures—even "big" ones—will no doubt continue to animate the moving and somewhat chaotic landscape of neoliberalization. Analytically, single-site case studies, either of an affirmative or a dissenting character, cannot properly capture what is a multi-sited, relational process of reproduction, frequently operating at the cusp of crisis or indeed in its throes. The persistence of neoliberalism, despite it all, and the unmistakable patterning of regulatory responses to its practically predictable crises, all stand as an explanatory challenge to those who would have preferred to do away with the concept of neoliberalism altogether. Refusing to use the word or invoke the concept, even *sans* capital-N, did not make these conditions go away.

Neoliberalism Inside/Out

The awkward reality, perhaps, is that it is difficult to live either with, or without, macrological concepts such as neoliberalization.[56] On the one hand, the concept's apparent promiscuity, and its ready availability as a plausible source of all-purpose causality, means that it is readily prone to inflation into a blunt, omnibus category. On the other hand, dismissing neoliberalism (or Neoliberalism) as a structuralist fantasy, while instead taking recourse to the "exceptionalist" analyses deliberately detached from the consideration of macro-scale constraints and incentives, hegemonic formations, translocal rules of the game, cross-case connections, family resemblances, and so forth, is to privilege localist-particularist forms of explanation over relational-conjunctural ones. What Collier poses as a choice between a more hierarchical, political economy-style reading of neoliberalism as "macro-structure or explanatory background" and flatter, more poststructural and horizontalist approaches to "neoliberalism as though it were the same size as other things," is not one that is amenable to reconciliation in some happy, friction-free synthesis.[57] There are real tensions between what are different ontological and epistemological understandings of neoliberalism, but this does not mean that there is no scope for dialogue, interactions, and even mediation between these positions.

The potential contribution of variegated neoliberalization approaches, in this context, lies in their overlapping concern with "how neoliberalism is specified in a variegated landscape of institutional, economic and political forms."[58] In the terms summarized in Table 4.1, this means embracing a conception of neoliberalism based on the twin principles of relationality and connectivity. Relational approaches can be distinguished from gradational ones in that they call attention to the mutual constitution and qualitative interpenetration of "local" neoliberalisms, rather than drawing more/less distinctions of a quantitative kind between supposed "degrees" of neoliberalization, or measuring near/far distances relative to some imagined "heartland." And approaches that emphasize (global) connectivity over (local) exceptionality likewise problematize the linkages, interconnections, and more-than-local

96 Variegated Economies

Table 4.1 Between Neoliberalism as Exception and Neoliberalism Inside/Out

	Gradational neoliberalism	*Relational neoliberalization*
Localized exceptionality	Attenuated neoliberalism: local exceptions, defined against foil of normalized and naturalized market rule; sampling on contingency; inside optic: unpatterned difference set against a monolithic norm *a*	Varieties of neoliberalism: multiple forms of market rule; "inherited" difference through strong path dependence, weak family resemblances *b*
Globalizing connectivity	Hybrid neoliberalisms: variable intensities of deep versus shallow market rule, weakly articulated through globalizing flows and vectors *c*	Variegated neoliberalization: polymorphic; mutual and multi-scalar interdependence of local formations, deeply articulated "horizontally" and hierarchically; inside/out optic: patterned difference across a moving and unevenly developed landscape *d*

patterns revealed by neoliberalization processes; they work between internalist treatments of neoliberalism (as a characteristic of, say, particular institutions or territorialized political regimes) and externalist conceptions of global hegemony, instead to problematize what might be called inside/outside relations.

From a Foucauldian perspective, Collier recognizes that neoliberalism "is a concept we cannot do without," and therefore that the operationalization of this concept implies definitional coordinates. While the position that "neoliberalism can be just anything" is manifestly indefensible, wary of inflationary tendencies, Collier is equally concerned that expansionist conceptions can become indiscriminate theories of "everything."[59] These are sensible (if not commonsensical) admonitions. Even though they only represent a first step toward methodological operationalization, the fact that such propositions (still) need to be stated is itself revealing. If a minimalist point of departure is that neoliberalism is never everything—either "within" a particular social formation, governance regime, or territorial space, or in the realm of extra-local relations—then it is clearly imperative that neoliberalism must, inescapably and in every situation, be located among its others. Even where neoliberalism is demonstrably hegemonic, it is never the *entire* story, never the *only* causal presence; it never acts alone. Furthermore, friction, double movements, resistance, alternatives are ever-present. While a case can be made that neoliberalism possesses an inherent expansionary logic (since it actively targets new spaces and fronts for marketization, while unleashing loosely bounded projects of commodification, privatization, and deregulation), 100% monopoly status is impossible, even in theory.

Globally, neoliberalism exists among other world-changing forces and conditions, such as uneven processes of financialization, the rise of China, and the tripling of the size of world proletariat since 1989. That these global conditions were in part enabled by earlier rounds of neoliberalization (such as the selective deconstruction of "barriers" to the flows of trade, capital, and labor), and that they also establish conditions for the further entrenchment of neoliberal regulation (for instance, in terms of exacerbation of interjurisdictional competition, inducing more "entrepreneurial" postures on the part of local actors, coupled with downward pressure on taxes, wages, and costs, which in turn redouble pressures for entrepreneurial responses and competitive adjustment), clearly does not mean that all these phenomena should be rolled into an all-inclusive catch-all notion of Global Neoliberalism, at which point the quest for explanation ceases. The indiscriminate cry that "Neoliberalism did it" belongs in the same family as the "I blame Thatcher" denunciations of old; who did what, to whom, where, and how must be specified in social, economic, and institutional terms. In the global or extra-local realm, this means teasing out neoliberalizing tendencies (again, among their others) in particular settings, circuits, and fields—such as decision-making cultures within multilateral agencies; channels of policy learning and mobility; the rules of regulatory regimes in investment, trade, and finance; the operations of epistemic communities and technocratic networks; governance at a distance through financial instruments, indexing and benchmarking systems, model-building and best-practice emulation, and so forth. Neoliberalism has different valences, registers, capacities, and contradictions across these (and other) fields, circuits, and settings; they are not all the neatly fitting components of a singular, global template. Theoretically informed, and informing, empirical work on these issues is consequently essential for the refinement even of relatively abstract understandings of neoliberalization, which cannot be divined unilaterally from founding theories, germinal texts, or paradigmatic events.

Because neoliberalization <u>can</u> only exist among its others (as well as among counter-tendencies), even where it is dominant, properly conjunctural analyses must take account not only of "internal relations" and characteristics but external connections and contradictions too. This cannot be reduced to a binary choice between situations in which neoliberalism is allegedly "exceptional" and those where it is supposedly normal and unexceptional, for this implicitly naturalizes neoliberalism in some settings, while preempting questions of its contextualization and trajectory in others. Likewise, all "local" neoliberalizations exist in a relational global field, not as islands. And furthermore, as an especially crisis-prone pattern of social regulation, neoliberalism might be considered somewhat deviant wherever it is found.

This calls for methodological strategies that are pitched somewhere between, on the one hand, those finely granulated studies of local neoliberalizations, that are characteristically light on extra-local referents or invoke the concept only ambivalently, and on the other hand, those sweeping accounts of neoliberal hegemony that are largely abstracted from any kind of social or textural specificity and which gloss over uneven development and contradictory hybridity. Operating in between (and in and between) these methodological poles means turning neoliberalism, as a real-world process, inside/out. There are no "abracadabra" solutions to be had here; indeed, a plurality of strategies is called for, rather than anything singular. But some of the well-established rationales for (extended) case selection seem appropriate in this context: selecting and theorizing cases in an orthogonal or awkward relation to emergent explanatory conceptions, in order both to interrogate and reconstruct those conceptions.[60] This means positioning local cases in relational and conjunctural terms, rather than on the terrain of typicality or exception. It means striving to make part-whole connections, while recognizing that this more-than-the-sum-of-the-parts phenomenon only exists by dint of its parts. It means uncovering local constitutions of global forces, rather than resorting to top-down "impact" models. And it means rendering the moving landscapes of neoliberalization as theoretical problematics in their own right (rather than placing these in the shadow of presumed convergence), probing power centers and vulnerable flanks, mapping the spatialities of consent and conflict, and tracing interdependencies through hierarchies and networks. In this context, the functioning of neoliberalism as an operational matrix, as a form of regulatory hegemony always in the (re)making, would not reside, unquestioned, as an article of critical faith, but would be rendered anew as an object of sustained, reflexive, and dialectical interrogation.

In this respect, there may be scope for different kinds of conversation between lumpers and splitters, between approaches to variegated neoliberalization rooted in geographical political economy and more situated treatments of neoliberalism found in some stripes of Foucauldian and poststructural scholarship. In rather different terms, a parallel conversation might also emerge between analysts of neoliberalism as an ideological and/or macro-institutional phenomenon, on the one hand, and those on the other hand who have been more concerned with its more granulated, grounded, and provisional forms, often unearthed ethnographically or through intensive case studies. For Collier, the "significance of neoliberalism must be sought, at least in part, in the disparate experiences in which neoliberal styles of reasoning, mechanisms of intervention, and techniques have played a significant role in shaping the forms of government."[61] Where he registers a concern, understandably, is with those analyses that do not "pay the full price" of establishing the interconnections and commonalities to which their definitions implicitly adhere. Quite right. But there is a price, too, to be paid for invocations of neoliberalism that are *only* local, which are distanced and detached from extra-local domains, referents, conditions of existence, and spaces of reproductive circulation. "Interior" manifestations of neoliberal logics—a privatization program in Macedonia, say, or a conditional welfare initiative in Indonesia—are locally embedded and constitutively contextual, to be sure, but they must not be shorn of their constitutive outsides, such as the actually existing and imagined "reform families" to which they belong, as near or distant relatives to other and earlier projects, experiments, and models. This underlines the need for a continuing concern with neoliberalism's *family* misfortunes.

Conclusion: Getting over Neoliberalism

To say that neoliberalism is still with us is not the same as saying that this is a permanent condition or that neoliberalism is always, transcendentally, the same. This is one reason why simple invocations of neoliberalism as an all-purpose, omnibus explanation for the contemporary condition can never be sufficient. Citing the process of neoliberalization must not be a substitute for explanation; it should be an *occasion* for explanation, involving the specification of particular causal mechanisms, modes of intervention, hybrid formations, social forms and foibles, counter-mobilizations, and so forth. It might be said that the concept does define a problem space and a zone of (possible) pertinence, and as such represents an entry point for critical analysis. But it is here that the task of excavating contextual forms and connective flows really begins; it is here that analysts really have to "pay the full price" of invoking this more-than-local concept.

If "neoliberalism did it" should never be a fig leaf for preemptive explanation, neither should invocations of neoliberalism be a prelude to unbounded analytical (or indeed political) fatalism, of the "we're all doomed to endless market rule" variety. As an always thwarted totalization, the neoliberal circle is never squared. Even hegemonies have their outsides and others; their construction is a continuing and contradictory process, not a fixed condition. Those skeptical of the utility of the concept of neoliberalism sometimes complain that its deployment, even the dropping of the name, somehow throws gasoline on the flames while effectively denigrating alternatives, both actual and potential. Some of this skepticism, clearly, stems from a deeper concern with all forms of explanation that invoke structural rationalities, big processes, and hegemonic forces, but quite often these are stereotyped as mechanistic forms of template theorizing rather than for what they actually are. Process-based approaches to neoliberalization, in fact, work explicitly with *and across* difference, problematizing the (re)production of that difference, and they are no less attentive to the contradictions and limits of neoliberalism in both theory and practice. These approaches do not necessitate the automatic or preemptive dismissal of non-neoliberal alternatives or post-neoliberal trajectories, but they do require that such (emergent) developments are understood, in the current context at any rate, *in relation to* neoliberalized fields of power and their associated domains of transformative practice. Searching questions are therefore likely to be raised about one-sided projections of enclavist alt-models, if the advocacy of these is detached from an assessment of the challenges of scaling up or networking out. "Alternatives" must be analyzed relationally too, not in utopian isolation.[62]

Squaring up to neoliberalism, in such a context, need not mean genuflecting before the altar of limitless market rule.[63] Applying the principles of relationality "all the way down" (or all the way out), however, calls for an understanding of the ways in which hegemonic forms of neoliberalization both inhabit, and tendentially remake, the field of difference. There are few bright lines, these days, between neoliberalism and its others, irrespective of whether these others are progressive or conservative, liberal or authoritarian. So it is ill-advised to code the world "beyond" neoliberalism in blanket terms, as a space of somehow untouched alternatives or as a generalized zone of resistance. Two conditions of neoliberalism's contradictory existence— its apparent facility for shape-shifting survival and the fact that perhaps its signal, enduring achievement has been the incapacitation of bases for ideological opposition—suggest that it may be less likely to meet its ultimate end in some epic, dialectical contest between a muscular Neoliberalism in the blue corner and plucky Resistance in the red. Perhaps it is still likely that the contradictions of neoliberalism will get it in the end, but the end may well be a protracted one—maybe one in which the complex of neoliberal projects and programs is eventually exhausted, and incrementally outflanked, worn down, or exceeded. Meanwhile, if no big-bang failure of neoliberal rule is imminently expected, then what are currently styled as alternatives will have to do (even) more than stand their ground in local enclaves; they will have to stake claims on enemy territory while rewriting the rules of extra-local redistribution, reciprocity, and competition.

Doing away with the concept of neoliberalism will not do away with the conditions of its still hegemonic existence; neither, on its own, would such an act of denial render alternatives any more realizable. Rather, it is imperative that the array of alternatives—from the reformist though to the radical—are positioned relationally in ideational, ideological, and institutional terms. This is not, then, a plea for a relentlessly "neoliberalocentric" perspective, for it is arguably more important than ever to ensure that the reach and ambition of critical endeavors—methodological, theoretical, and political—extend across the *entire field* of socioeconomic difference, a task in which Polanyian forms of comparative socioeconomics, for instance, have constructive roles to play. Consistent with such an approach is the observation that the necessary incompleteness of the neoliberal program of free-market reform means that it must always dwell among its others, along with the rather cold comfort that its ultimate destination is unattainable. Actually existing alternatives (progressive and otherwise) will never be completely expunged. The residues of preexisting social formations will never be entirely erased or rendered inert. Double movements against the overextension of market rule will not only continue, but can be expected to intensify, presenting new challenges but also opening up new opportunities for social action. Crises, in forms old and new, will recur. Realistically speaking, it is on this uncertain and uneven terrain that all forms of post-neoliberal politics will have to be forged.

5
Relocating Variety

Toward Variegated Capitalism

with Nik Theodore

The varieties of capitalism (VoC) approach, with its signature concern for institutionally mediated (macro)economic diversity, together with its stylized distinction between the liberal capitalism of the American way and German-style coordinated capitalism, rose to canonical status in the late 1990s, at least in heterodox circles, after which it would become a common reference point for followers and skeptics alike. What was attractive about the VoC framework, and what allowed it to travel, was the way that the approach "packaged" a set of clearly articulated claims about institutions, growth, and economic difference, bundling these into tidy categories labeled "liberal market economies" (LMEs) and "coordinated market economies" (CMEs), as a bulwark against mainstream arguments in favor of one-best-way global convergence and neoliberal deregulation. The VoC school told a different story, about the durability of distinctive national capitalisms rooted in path dependencies and cultures of governance, which had both a commonsense resonance and a normative appeal to defenders of "more regulated" and socially sustainable models of development. At the same time, the VoC approach was limited by its methodological nationalism, by a reliance on static, cross-sectional analysis, and by latent traces of institutional functionalism. It was also difficult to reconcile the emphasis placed on national specificity, path-dependency, and relative institutional stability with cross-cutting and often disruptive tendencies in capitalist restructuring.

The origins of this chapter are in a European Commission-funded research program called DEMOLOGOS (Development Models and Logics of Socio-Economic Organization in Space), which aimed to construct and then apply a new methodology for the study of socioeconomic development, allied to case studies in a variety of countries, regions, and cities. This heterodox methodology was explicitly comparative, historical, and multidimensional, working across scales as well as across the various dimensions of socioeconomic development (such as capital accumulation, state regulation, sociocultural dynamics, and strategies for growth, development, and social cohesion).[1] An early phase of the research program called for a series of discussion papers dealing with different aspects of the DEMOLOGOS agenda, for which Neil Brenner, Nik Theodore, and I wrote an article on neoliberal urbanism, while Nik Theodore and I worked on an article concerned with the comparative analysis of capitalism.[2] The latter project, which involved a sympathetic critique of the VoC thesis-cum-position and an initial attempt to assemble an alternative and more relational approach linked to the problematic of variegation (and differences in connection), is the basis of this chapter.[3]

One of the motivating questions, shared with but not limited to the VoC school, had earlier been articulated by Robert Boyer: "Is there a single brand of capitalism or can a significant variety of capitalisms coexist even in the long run?"[4] Economic geographers would likely respond in the affirmative, and almost reflexively so, and yet with very few exceptions they had been on the sidelines of "varieties" debates, which had mostly been conducted in an interdisciplinary space between political science, economic sociology, and institutionalist economics.[5] VoC approaches were for the most part explicitly comparative and pitched at the national scale, they were focused on formal institutions, and the inclination was for systematic and stylized modes of analysis. All of these, on the other hand, can be said to be minority pursuits in economic geography, with its inclination to work in, out from, or between more "local" (and usually extra-national) sites, with its more eclectic approach to institutions, and with its preference for more cluttered, grounded, and less formalized modes of analysis. This had meant that economic geographers and VoC scholars had generally been talking past one another, notwithstanding a number of overlapping affinities and commitments which positioned both in the larger (and not exactly tightly knit) family of heterodox economic studies. VoC scholarship has been animated by a concern to compare in order to codify, while economic geographers tend to contextualize and to complexify; VoC scholars value crispy formulated taxonomies, while economic geographers typically work against or around such formulations, seeing them as foils, chaotic conceptions, or stereotypes, and often favoring deconstruction, disaggregation, or even debunking. Furthermore, the (defining?) concern in economic geography to go beyond the documentation of spatial difference in order to demonstrate relationality, mutual constitution, and interdependence reserves little space (or value) for the development of "clean" models, parsimoniously portrayed.

One of the consequences of this state of near-incompatibility between theory cultures and methodological orientations was that the road toward a "variegated" conception of capitalism was bound to be a somewhat winding one, just as it seemed unlikely to produce a tidily demarcated "alternative." While the varieties rubric handled questions of geographical variability in an extremely disciplined, contained, and even blunt fashion, with the foot effectively hovering over the brake, "variation" signaled an approach to spatial difference, specificity, and scale with much more open-ended implications, moving the foot from over the brake to the accelerator. By implication, it entailed a more expansive (and perhaps less "manageable") engagement with the uneven and combined development of an "always embedded" capitalism riddled with complex interdependencies and riven by enduring contradictions. The promise, though, was an approach to the problematic of variegation that was anchored in the distinctive perspective and practices of heterodox economic geography, an approach that did not freeze and compartmentalize spatial difference, decanting it into taxonomic categories, but instead sought to expose dynamic differences in relational connection. The present chapter begins this task, working through a critical assessment of VoC scholarship before offering a preliminary take on variegated capitalism.

Rediscovering Variety

The antecedents of what became the VoC approach are many and varied, but one of the most important tap roots was David Soskice's comparative analysis of national economic institutions, which initially spawned the conceptual distinction between CMEs ("coordinated" market economies like Germany, Japan, Sweden, Austria, and Norway), within which the strategies of employers are shaped by dense regulatory networks and long-term, structural relationships, and the LMEs (the liberal market economies classically modeled on the US, but also including the UK, Canada, and Ireland), in which economic relations and contracts tend to be decentralized and short term.[6] Soskice elaborated these models through rather synthetic, but concretely rooted, examinations of the behavior of firms in capital markets, drawing contrasts between the shareholder-driven systems of the liberal countries and the patient-capital approach of the coordinated economies, distinctions echoed in spheres like wage-setting, training, competitive strategy, employment contracts, and innovation policy.

Far from being assigned analytical primacy, the liberal market model was often defined according to its deficits, in some cases with pejorative undertones. As Soskice told it, the liberal model is definitionally *un*coordinated, reflecting a "lack of coordinating capacity," the "absence of long-term stable cross-shareholding arrangements," and an "inability to act collectively" on the part of companies, which in turn erodes the state's strategic capacity.[7] There was, then, a measure of dissention in such arguments, pitched as they knowingly were "against the full weight of Anglo-American liberal economic theory," as Albert saw it, the sway of which was already being acknowledged as "considerable (if not totally dominant), from the canteen to the boardroom, from the classroom to the economic think tank."[8]

In contrast to previous conceptions of capitalist diversity—which placed the constitution of welfare regimes or predominant forms of labor organization in the analytical foreground,[9] utilizing measures such as degree of labor commodification or union density in the generation of cross-sectional taxonomies of capitalist systems—the VoC school privileged the organization and regulation of *production* in its classificatory and explanatory schema. At the center of this schema lies a relational conception of the firm as a social institution—not merely a legal entity, a transactional nexus, or a bundle of competencies, but a social institution that draws deeply on, and is constituted by, institutional and cultural resources derived from its (national) environment.[10] Enterprises are seen to be embedded in "production regimes" or "social systems of production," generally taken to comprise five interlocking elements: industrial relations, vocational education and training, corporate governance, inter-firm relations, and workplace regulation. Extensively tracking gradual, path-dependent shifts in these various spheres, and the forms of firm behavior with which they are reciprocally embedded, has become the staple activity in the varieties literature.

Hollingsworth and Boyer argue that "nation-states have different trajectories of capitalist development, in which there is considerable variation in the role of markets and other institutional arrangements as coordinating mechanisms."[11] This diverse array of coordination mechanisms both shapes, and is shaped by, a no-less-variant set of social systems of production, in this instance conceived in broad terms, and with a distinctly regulationist flavor:

> By a social system of production, we mean the way that the following institutions or structures of a country or region are integrated into a social configuration. The industrial relations system; the system of training workers and managers; the internal structure of corporate firms; the structured relationships among firms in the same industry, on the one hand, and on the other firms' relationships with their suppliers and customers; the financial markets of a society; the conceptions of fairness and justice held by capital and labor; the structure of the state and its policies; and a society's idiosyncratic customs and traditions as well as norms, moral principles, rules, laws, and recipes for action. *All these institutions, organizations, and*

social values tend to cohere with each other into a fully-fledged system. While each of these components has some autonomy and may have some goals that are contradictory to the goals of other institutions with which it is integrated, an institutional logic in each society leads each institution to coalesce into a complex social configuration. This occurs because the *institutions are embedded in a culture* in which their logics are symbolically grounded, organizationally structured, technically and materially constrained, and politically defended. The institutional configuration usually exhibits some degree of adaptability to new challenges, but continues to evolve within an existing style.[12]

Individual institutions are therefore each ascribed distinctive features and logics, though in turn these are located within a matrix of macroinstitutional relations that itself displays an incipient form of unity, coherence, and even logic. Furthermore, these macroinstitutional orders are seen to be embedded in idiosyncratic but relatively enduring sociocultural environments—"national cultures." This strand of the VoC literature rejects functionalist explanations of the existence and persistence of such distinctive institutional configurations, instead conferring on the institutional sphere a degree of relative autonomy from the imperatives of the accumulation process, even while drawing attention to their symbiotic connectivity and coevolution. The ultimate source of these enduringly distinctive institutional configurations therefore remains something of a puzzle: "Why these configurations occur within a particular place and time," Hollingsworth and Boyer readily concede, "is a complex theoretical problem which has yet to be solved."[13] Geographical differences in institutional cultures and logics are, in effect, inherited.

While there was, at this time, no consensus among varieties scholars as to the *way* in which institutions mattered, their loosely shared conviction that they did matter placed them in varying degrees of tension with the neoclassical paradigm. At the reformist end of the spectrum lay extensions of transactions-costs analysis, which comprehended the resort to non-market models of coordination, like corporate hierarchies, as a rational response to the costs of market relationships under specific circumstances. At the radical end of the spectrum, regulation theorists were arguing that institutional forms reflected a series of class compromises fashioned in response to the enduring contradictions and patterned regulatory dilemmas of advanced capitalism. The extensive zone in between contained a range of other, no less distinctive, approaches, variously focusing on forms of institutional production relating to corporatist bargaining, rule systems and constitutional settlements, challenges of regional economic governance, and so forth.

Across this literature there is a common concern with the (more-than-singular) logics of social systems of production, coupled with a shared sense that not only do these production regimes tend to be associated with different modes of economic coordination, but that these distinctive couplings result in "different kinds of economic performance" and distinctive, or even diverging, patterns of long-run development.[14] The fate of different national capitalisms had, from Hollingsworth and Boyer's perspective, analytical as well as substantive implications. While the national scale had been, during the Fordist-Keynesian period, the principal site for securing institutional cohesion, this contingent primacy was now being challenged by, on the one hand, "more competition between interdependent markets and ... the building of supranational rules of the game" at the global scale, coupled on the other hand with the emergence of new "sources for competitiveness [at] the regional or even local levels where under some circumstances trust and tacit knowledge are better nurtured within communities and networks."[15]

The market retains a strong presence in this literature, both as a polemical foil and as a formal abstraction, but varieties analysts are theoretically and normatively inclined to cast doubt on (prevailing) claims as to the omnipotence, superiority, and exclusivity of market mechanisms. "Some degree of market conformity might be good for societies," Boyer and Hollingsworth concede, "but too much of it may be very destructive for economic efficiency and social justice as well."[16] This was precisely the threat posed during the 1980s and 1990s, when Fordist-Keynesian regimes encountered a series of terminal challenges in the form of an unprecedented "surge of market mechanisms," the self-perpetuating consequences of which included, for Boyer and Hollingsworth, the dissolution of a range of "national and regional institutions in which market activity had been embedded."[17]

New developmental trajectories, however, were emerging in a context of complex, contradictory, and sometimes countervailing political-economic dynamics. On the side of fixity and institutional resilience, "the superiority of any system of social production [was seen to be] context-dependent," while modes of institutional regulation and economic coordination were described as "deeply rooted" in geo-societal conditions, limiting the extent to which coordinating systems—like the rudely ascendant market models—might be "transferable from one country to another."[18] The European social model, in other words, seemed to be relatively safe, at least for the time being. On the side of motion were the (ostensibly more dynamic) forces of market-led adjustment, which in the face of the prevailing sentiment of "Hayekian optimism about the efficiency of markets" was more likely to generate socially *and economically* perverse forms of institutional selection, with "intrinsically superior institutions" being eroded, undercut, or even "ruled out by market mechanisms."[19]

Formalizing Variety

The VoC research program took a more orthodox turn with the publication in 2001 of Hall and Soskice's edited collection, *Varieties of Capitalism*. In contrast with the "more sociological" treatment of institutions in some previous varieties work, Hall and Soskice made the case for firm-centric style of institutional political economy. They advocate a single-minded analysis of national institutions as reciprocally adjusting shapers of economic action at the firm level, arguing that "the most important institutions distinguishing one political economy from another will be those conditioning ... interaction."[20] A correspondingly limited array of national institutions—relating to corporate governance, labor-market regulation, and education and training—is afforded analytical primacy. And through processes of strategic interaction, these are seen to be *both* outcomes of routinized economic behavior *and* conditioners of this behavior. In an approach apparently designed to conform with, but at the same time revise, orthodox economic postulates, rational actors are positioned in the center of analysis—individuals, governments, producer groups, and business associations, but above all *firms*—the strategically calculating behaviors of which are simultaneously shaped by, and give rise to, institutional environments. In the attempt to make these arguments work, and to "connect the new microeconomics to important issues in macroeconomics," the institutional environment is drawn in broad-brush, stylized forms: Hall and Soskice "look for national-level differences and terms in which to characterize them that are more general or parsimonious" than earlier varieties-school work.[21] This rational-choice variant of the VoC approach does not go so far as to deny the importance of regional or sectoral institutions, which evidently also shape firm behavior, or international institutions, which rather recede from view. Instead, it focuses on a limited set of national institutions in order to establish a parsimonious rendering of the regulatory landscape.

The firm, as the central actor in this rather artificially uncluttered institutional environment, is conceived in relational terms. In order to sustain profitable production, firms must develop sets of competencies and capabilities that enable the effective resolution (or at least management) of a set of quite intractable coordination problems.[22] Most germane to this analysis are the coordination problems relating to five spheres of firm behavior:

- industrial relations, notably the coordination of wages and working conditions;
- vocational training and education, especially the return on investments in skills for individuals and firms;
- corporate governance, with an emphasis on access to capital markets and firm-investor relations;
- inter-firm relations, including upstream relationships with clients, downstream links with suppliers, and connections with other firms in each sector, and their implications for issues like innovation and technology transfer;
- and employment, with specific emphasis on the efficient social organization of the workplace, and the management of knowledge and competence.

The analytical gaze here is located within the firm, looking out. And institutions are comprehended through the behavior of firms, in effect as arenas for the resolution of coordination problems. Geographical differences in, for example, economic performance are not attributable to institutions per se, but rather, institutions are themselves second-order outcomes of patterned searches for coordination solutions, through which actors tend to reveal a (national) culture. Institutions, in this respect, are "created by actions," actions that both reflect and recursively reproduce common cultures and shared understandings. "Institutions, organizations, and culture enter this analysis," Hall and Soskice somewhat cautiously state, "because of the support they provide for the relationships firms develop to resolve coordination problems."[23]

Ultimately, this is the basis upon which capitalist diversity is seen to rest, since Hall and Soskice conclude that "national political economies can be compared by reference to the way in which firms resolve the coordination problems they face in these five spheres."[24] The analytical trammeling is taken one step further when Hall and Soskice boil down the problem of coordination to a single axis, running from an ideal-typical LME at one end, where coordination largely occurs through hierarchical and competitive market arrangements, through to a mirror-image ideal type, the CME, where there is much greater reliance on non-market modes of coordination like networks and collaborative relations. The liberal end of this hypothesized continuum is characterized by almost textbook neoclassical conditions: impersonal, arm's-length relations prevail, hierarchies are resorted to only when markets will not do, and actors respond to price signals "often on the basis of the marginal calculations stressed by neoclassical economics." The coordinated economy, in contrast, is partly defined in terms of its deviation from this putatively hegemonic ideal-type, but rather than the market alone establishing equilibria, these derive from "strategic coordination among firms and other actors." Germany and the United States represent the critical cases that are subsequently invoked to exemplify each typical formation, establishing what Hall and Soskice portray as "the poles of a spectrum ... along which many nations can be arrayed."[25]

Empirically, these arguments are typically advanced by way of comparative national case studies, though they are also abstracted to the level of ideal-typical constructions like CMEs and LMEs. In this context, perhaps the most far-reaching stylized fact of this branch of the VoC literature is that the preference for market-oriented institutions within LMEs induces a distinctive pattern of corporate behavior—investment in "switchable assets," such as general skills or multipurpose technologies, since these do not tie up corporate resources in the long term, instead facilitating short-run realization of value if higher returns can be secured elsewhere. Meanwhile, in CMEs, there is a much higher propensity to sink corporate resources into specific or "co-specific" assets, the value of which cannot be realized rapidly, but which is instead predicated upon both the availability of patient capital and open (rational) expectations of complementary, cooperative behavior on the part of other firms. In this conception, corporate behavior is reciprocally embedded in (variable) institutional logics, themselves the outcome of relays and interactions between different institutional spheres.

These maneuvers enable Hall and Soskice to make the case for parity of esteem—in both functional and ideological terms—between the LME/American model and the CME/Euro-Japanese model of capitalism, a rare accomplishment in the VoC literature. "Although each type of capitalism has its partisans," they concede, "we are not arguing here that one is superior to another."[26] Both are seen to be capable of sustaining high levels of economic performance, albeit in the context of divergent distributional outcomes within the domestic sphere—with LMEs exhibiting a high employment/high inequality pattern, while CMEs tend toward the opposite configuration. And in the international sphere, too, a form of functional coexistence is visualized, with each system trading on its *comparative institutional advantages*. Likewise, each national capitalism will respond to "external shocks" in distinctive ways, reflecting national cultures and institutional settlements, and which may ultimately entrench geographical variety rather than erode it. Even where corporations engage explicitly in institutional arbitrage, such as when Nissan locates a design facility in California, or General Motors an engine plant in Düsseldorf, convergence is not a likely outcome. In fact, "corporate movements of this sort should reinforce differences in national institutional frameworks," Hall and Soskice remark, "as firms that have shifted their operations to benefit from particular institutions seek to retain them."[27]

Subsequent empirical testing has lent some credence to this twin-peaks vision of capitalism,[28] with countries tending to crowd around one of the two poles, rather than occupying intermediate positions: "productive advantage comes from being all fish or all foul," as Goodin puts it.[29] However, others have discovered a larger number of distinct clusters,[30] much weaker associations between institutional configurations and macroeconomic performance,[31] and growing internal differentiation and divergent behavior within the national "models."[32]

While challenging simplified notions of market-led or neoliberal convergence, Hall and Soskice recognize that the threats posed to the two principal varieties are somewhat asymmetrical. Put simply, in the face of international economic integration, much of which is market mediated, it may be easier to take the low road than the high road: market-oriented de/reregulation is held to be a more viable and available option within CMEs, all else being equal, than is the mirror-image of this situation, the strategy of enhanced social coordination within an LME context, because here economic actors lack the "requisite common knowledge" to make such strategies work, while "market relations do not demand the same levels of common knowledge."[33] Hall and Soskice add that the continuing liberalization of international financial relations might remove an essential foundation stone of the CME model: "Financial deregulation could be the string that unravels coordinated market economies."[34] There is a real danger, albeit an easily overstated one, that the offshore threat of neoliberal globalization could undermine the once-robust institutional equilibria that have underpinned coordinated models of capitalism. So while analytical parity may have been asserted in *Varieties of Capitalism*, there is a distinct subtextual fear that the low road is beckoning.

Most subsequent engagements in the varieties debate, both critical and constructive, tend to deal centrally with the claims of Hall and Soskice. But if this stands as perhaps the most elaborate formulation in the mainstream varieties literature, by no means is it alone. Some important alternative strands in this recent literature include the fusion of regulationist and varieties frameworks, resulting in novel combinations of historical and macroinstitutional modes of analysis and less parsimonious conceptions of capitalist variety.[35] The tendency for orthodox varieties approaches to reify neoclassical economic theories is rejected in favor of an approach that combines the inductive and deductive analysis of actually existing capitalist formations: "From a regulationist perspective," Boyer writes, "it is difficult to accept that the dichotomy of two polarized models can account for an entire distribution of modern economies."[36] Yet regulationists will not label capitalisms willy-nilly; the regulation approach has established demanding criteria for the determination of "models" of capitalism. Localized varieties are also positioned in relation to more structural accumulation-regime dynamics—in particular the emergence of financialized capitalism.[37]

Developments in a different direction are to be found in Sorge's closely argued and multi-scalar analysis of the German "inter-nation," focusing on the dialectical relations between internationalizing forces and "societal effects" at the local level, refracted through relatively durable "meta-traditions" or political-economic cultures.[38] This complex rendering of a path-dependency argument evokes the metaphor of the Ho Chi Minh Trail as a means of illustrating the intersecting pathways and routing options characteristic of Germany's long-run development trajectory. Here, the interplay between "international incursion and local assertion" results in a historically and geographically uneven "layering" of social space, institutional landscapes reflecting the "recombination of internationally and locally given practices."[39] If Sorge opened up questions of scale, Kathleen Thelen has made the case for more dynamic conceptions of institutional change, better able to handle the differentiated form and outcomes of ostensibly "common" challenges to national capitalisms like (neo)liberalization.[40] In this vein, Streeck and Thelen underscore the need to transcend "tendenc[ies] in the literature to understate the extent of change, or alternatively to code all observed changes as minor adaptive adjustments to altered circumstances in the service of continuous reproduction of existing systems."[41]

After Variety

The VoC school made a mark in the defense and productive agitation of arguments around the *socially and spatially differentiated character* of actually existing capitalist formations, and the roles of social choice and institutional agency in guiding and sustaining these systems, all of which was achieved against the less-than-supportive backdrop of American economic triumphalism, the ascendancy of globalization as a strong discourse, and the progressive deepening of neoliberalization. In stoutly defending the contention that "institutions matter," and that they matter in systematic and sustained ways, this literature has been something of a fly in the ointment for flat-earth visions of globalized, turbocapitalism,[42] advancing both normative and analytical arguments around viable *alternatives* to the free-market pathway. What began as a muted celebration of the German and Japanese models has matured into robust assertions of alternative pathways, logics, and rationalities of capitalist development, explicated through rigorous, comparative analysis.

These nontrivial achievements are reflected in the prominent place that the VoC approach has rapidly secured within the wider research programs of institutional economics, political science, sociology, and comparative political economy. It is also important to recognize, however, that serious limitations and distortions have also followed from the manner in which capitalist variety is conceptualized in this literature. In some respects, the project's strengths can all too easily flip over into weaknesses. Its location on the borderlands of Polanyian sociology, institutional economics, and rational-choice political science, for example, has enabled some degree of interdisciplinary dialogue, but it has also meant that the project's theoretical foundations have remained unstable, contested, and eclectic. The laudable attempt to explore how economic behaviors are variously embedded in, and constituted through, institutional relations has given license, in some cases, to excessively narrow, firm-centric, and rational-action models of variation. Its generally productive concern with institutional logics and rationalities can bleed off into implicit functionalism and fetishism, when such superstructural phenomena are afforded exaggerated normative and explanatory weight. The holistic treatment of institutional ensembles is analytically demanding, but it can also generate false impressions of coherence and complementarity. Its welcome recognition of geographical variability in capitalist systems, and in their institutional regulation, is marred by a pervasive tendency to methodological nationalism and spatial archetyping, in which the coherence of national regulatory configurations is presumed rather than demonstrated.

Furthermore, the concern to identify and validate alternatives to American-style liberal capitalism rather perversely raises this very model, *qua* model, to the status of analytical pivot and normative foil, while conferring perhaps unrealistic levels of coherence on the conglomeration of alternatives, which coalesce into a singular "coordinated model," when viewed in this idealized mirror. Its resort to analytical binaries like market/non-market and liberal/coordinated capitalisms likewise can be credited, on the one hand, with legitimating heterodox and more socially regulated alternatives, but on the other hand has the effect of shoring up some of the very categories of orthodox analysis—particularly the normative standard of the liberalized, deregulated market—that otherwise the project seeks to transcend. Its inclination not only to recognize, but to crisply systematize, capitalist variety across space has been conceptually productive, but has tended to yield increasingly parsimonious taxonomies, rather than causal analysis, thereby also narrowing the spectrum of economic variation to a single, privileged continuum of difference internal to the advanced capitalism of the Northern Hemisphere. Its appropriate skepticism concerning convergence arguments often takes on an exaggerated, reactive form, in a principled (but weakly substantiated) insistence on necessary divergence. And its programmatic and sometimes instinctive recognition of institutional resiliency and strong path dependency can lead to the radical underestimation of transformative and path-altering change.

So, while the VoC project can be said to have opened up distinctively new analytical, and perhaps political, opportunities, representing as it does one of the more prominent dissenting narratives in a climate generally more inclined toward global convergence arguments, at the same time there are some serious open questions about whether this is an appropriate way to comprehend economic variegation. Taking some limitations of the varieties approach as its starting points, the remainder of this section considers some of the ways in which these might be transcended, in the service of a richer conceptualization of the geography of advanced capitalism. Three themes are taken up below: first, the implications of the kind of ideal-typical reasoning deployed in the varieties literature are examined; second, attention is turned to the question of institutional change and problems of dynamizing varieties accounts; and a third section considers the rise of neoliberalism and the awkward issue of potential convergence in models of capitalism.

Less than Ideal Types

There is some irony in the commonplace association of the varieties approach with the argument that "institutions matter" in the functioning of advanced capitalist economies. It is undeniably true that the CME model is saturated with, indeed defined by, institutional relations, structures, and effects. The model is predicated on the concept of "non-market coordination," which is achieved through a range of institutional means (including networks, governmental regulation, social bargaining), but the recourse to institutional "solutions" is its defining feature. This is the Polanyian face of the varieties approach: markets are deeply embedded in institutional and social relations, such that adequate explanations of, say, the structure of corporate financing or labor-market dynamics must necessarily take serious account of institutional logics. "These non-market modes of coordination," write Hall and Soskice, "generally entail more extensive relational or incomplete contracting, network monitoring based on the exchange of private information inside networks, and more reliance on collaborative, as opposed to competitive, relationships to build the competencies of the firm."[43]

Problems begin to arise, however, when one moves to the liberal end of this continuum. If the CME model represents a stylized description of the actually existing economies of countries like Germany, Japan, and the Netherlands, the LME model is a curious mashup of neoclassical economic theory and an idealized form of American capitalism. Hall and Soskice see LMEs as sites where "firms rely more heavily on market relations to solve coordination problems," and where "competitive markets are more robust."[44] Here, markets are "fluid" and they are characterized by "high levels of transparency," in the words of Hall and Gingerich, and the resulting market-like behavior yields "equilibrium outcomes dictated primarily by relative prices, market signals and familiar marginalist considerations."[45] While Hall and Soskice continue to issue the (quite appropriate) disclaimer that "markets are institutions," it would seem on this reading that some markets are more embedded than others; that institutional regulation varies in intensity, not just in kind; that markets can work in a more fluid and less mediated way in some places than others; that some economies are less institutionally cluttered than others.[46] The United States is therefore anointed as the locus of pristine market relations, the place where orthodox textbook conditions prevail and competitive systems work under their own steam, without heavy-handed regulation: "Market coordination," the defining characteristic of LMEs, "is a familiar concept in neo-classical economics," one that requires little further elaboration, according to Hall and Gingerich, while the earthly manifestation of these conditions is found in the "typical liberal market economy," the United States.[47]

Not only does this conception recycle the bad abstraction of the disembedded, self-regulating market, it compounds this problem by characterizing the coordinated or un-American economies as a composite "other" to this questionable theoretical construction, as the repository of all of advanced capitalism's least market-like phenomena, and as the sphere of uncompetitive acts like networking, intervention, negotiation, and so forth. Far from dethroning those market-centric conceptions of economy that occupy such a central role in the analytical framework of orthodox economics and in discourses of neoliberal globalism, the varieties approach runs the risk of reinscribing the very same flawed construction. In seeking to substantiate a definition of a singular, un-American form of capitalism, the varieties approach effectively reifies the market while also idealizing American capitalism. Processes of institutional coordination are then defined, at least in part, in this mirror, with the result that refined versions of the LME/CME continuum begin to resemble quite orthodox conceptions of more/less market or more/less intervention.

Even while seeking to validate an alternative to this model, then, the varieties approach tends to confer a misleading coherence on an idealized reading of American capitalism which, in turn, is elided with the market, market coordination, and market capitalism. To be certain, any adequate account of contemporary capitalist variegation must deal centrally with the US case, but to sequester this concrete case with a series of ideologically laden neoclassical precepts is to establish a quite inappropriate Archimedean point around which to theorize variety. The problem of market essentialism is hardly resolved by placing a utilitarian abstraction of the market at one end of a continuum, with a chaotic conception of "non-market coordination" at the other end, since this separates the very elements that must be (problematically) *combined* in any actually existing capitalist or "market" system.[48] While markets, of varying kinds, are invariably constitutive elements of such systems, their inability to function autonomously, in disembedded form, calls attention to their *necessary* articulation with coexistent social, institutional, and political structures. In fact, actually existing American capitalism is arguably no less reliant on extra-economic conditions and "flanking" institutions—including, most conspicuously, the country's unique geopolitical position, its distended prison system, and its massive defense sector—than its ostensibly "more regulated" European cousins. On the other hand, German capitalism may also be diverging from the stylized model of the CME, as German employers increasingly defect from the very institutions that define the model.[49]

The (necessary, yet indeterminate) blending of the economic and the extra-economic within different "local" formations of capitalism is not adequately captured in the kind of bipolar model that positions a "pure" economy at one extreme. This artificial construction is, in effect, a Ricardian "either/or world."[50] In fact, the principles of distinction are more appropriately conceived in terms of *qualitative variegation* than quantitative variation (more or less market), as is suggested, for example, in Hodgson's "impurity principle" as a means to denote the messy institutional hybridity of capitalist development, or the regulationist analysis of "structural couplings" between distinctive patterns of accumulation and diverse modes of social regulation.[51] The varieties literature has made the case that economic coordination represents the primary dimension of difference between national capitalisms, but it must be recalled that these are differences in (institutional) form, not degree. Correspondingly, national economies are not simply engaged in a kind of unidimensional, neo-Ricardian regime competition, played out on a level playing field; the complex historical trajectories that they display are both diachronic and mutually interpenetrating—they are a product of *joint* evolution.

Dynamizing Variety

The search for national-level differences in modes of economic coordination, which has been the principal preoccupation in the VoC literature, has usefully focused attention on linkages and complementarities between spheres of coordination within national economies. Rather than conceiving spheres of economic coordination (e.g., systems of corporate governance, industrial relations, and vocational training) as entirely autonomous institutional realms, the varieties school calls attention to their "supermodular" interconnections and logics. For example, much is made of the ways in which the "German model" is predicated on patient capital in financial markets, which in turn fosters a longer-term perspective on the part of employers. This enables a collectivist orientation among these employers (which is expressed and achieved through "non-market" institutions), undergirding coordinated wage formation, reducing employee poaching, and aiding long-run skills development.[52] The resultant regime of corporate governance makes product and process innovation a priority, holding in check any tendency toward cut-throat price competition in key national industries. In short, the German model is lauded not simply for its competitive superiority in leading sectors, but as much for its distinctive institutional architecture.

Such stylized portrayals of "established" national institutional-economic systems are hallmarks of the VoC school. But how do these deeply embedded and closely interwoven institutional matrices respond to change? Hall and Soskice, for their part, invoke the concept of general equilibrium: conditions of institutional stability will prevail, absent an external shock that disrupts the established order. "Institutional complementarities should play an important, if ambiguous, role in . . . processes of adjustment," they explain, raising the "prospect that institutional reform in one sphere of the economy could snowball into changes in other spheres."[53] It follows that under conditions of general equilibrium, economic actors (firms, to be more precise) will "attempt to sustain or restore the forms of coordination on which their competitive advantages have been built."[54] The analysis here rests on a punctuated equilibrium model in which extended periods of stability are unsettled only by shocks from "outside" the economic system, setting in motion adjustment processes that culminate in the restoration of equilibrium. Hall and Soskice's strong claims about institutional complementarity lead them to assume not only that harmonious clustering is normal, but that eclectic institutional mixing is economically dysfunctional—the fish *or* foul scenario. In reality, however, there remain several perplexingly "mixed" cases, which expose such simplifying assumptions for what they are.[55]

To assume, rather than demonstrate, equilibrium is problematic for other reasons. Mere inertia may be mistaken for equilibrium, consequently generating misplaced expectations of institutional durability. This form of theoretically induced complacency is only compounded by the tendency to comprehend institutional change in binary terms. In another manifestation of the either/or world, it would seem that there can only be steady states (with incremental, stabilizing, and reinforcing change) or systemic change (following radical, disruptive, and crisis-inducing shocks). But this misses entire registers of (potentially significant) institutional change, including cumulative transformation and experimentation. Binary, system-centric conceptions of institutional change also underestimate the extent to which institutional regimes are hierarchically organized, given that some institutional fields are likely more important than others, as initiators or exemplars of reform dynamics. This is now being actively debated inside the varieties project. Streeck and Thelen, for example, take Hall and Soskice to task for "ignoring the possibility of endogenously generated change that is more than just adaptive," particularly in light of the fact that "an essential and defining characteristic of the ongoing worldwide liberalization of advanced political economies is that it evolves in the form of gradual change that takes place within, and is conditioned and constrained by, the very same postwar institutions that it is reforming or even dissolving."[56] Analyses of capitalist variety that underplay incremental yet transformative change run the risk of misinterpreting the extent and scope of non-adaptive, incremental adjustments that can fundamentally alter the underlying logics and performance of institutions.[57]

The politics of institutional defense and transformation are also decisively shaped by power relations. Powerful actors and blocs may be able to mobilize sufficient resources to impose or defend an institutional order, even when the outcomes of these arrangements are suboptimal, inefficient, and inegalitarian. Exalting such arrangements as (necessarily) "efficient" radically underestimates the contentious politics and power plays that invariably accompany institution building and maintenance. Moreover, the ongoing processes of trial-and-error searching and political conflict sit awkwardly with the notion of equilibrium. Varying degrees of institutional discordance and disequilibrium are much more commonplace than many varieties scholars seem prepared to concede.

Equilibrium notions also pervade the categories used to typologize national economies, which strongly imply long-run stability and internal coherence. Such conceptions underplay the dynamic nature of modes of economic coordination within these models, and they take insufficient account of the fact that the same institutional "shell" can be used for different purposes. (The example of corporatist institutions being re-tasked around neoliberal goals is a well-known example.) As a result, "a national system may 'appear' stable due to the persistence of formal institutional differences," Deeg and Jackson argue, "but still undergo functional change that alters the 'logic' or complementarities behind the model."[58] A key strength of varieties-style analysis therefore turns out also to be a weakness: the concepts of complementarity and coordination are analytically demanding, setting the bar high for institutionally oriented forms of explanation, but the strong focus on national, system-wide changes and the preference for dual equilibrium modeling tends to narrow the field of vision. Some forms of institutional change barely even register, while others are reduced to unthreatening noise within reassuringly equilibrating systems. Deeg and Jackson's sympathetic critique concludes that the analytical routines inherited from the VoC school are too static, while they also fail to capture important forms of contemporary institutional change that are occurring beyond the national-system optic:

> [I]mportant limits have been reached to the notion of national varieties of capitalism as institutionally complete, coherent and complementary sets of institutions, which achieve and maintain stable sets of characteristics. A growing wealth of empirical literature has shown that national forms of capitalism to be more institutionally fragmented, internally diverse and display greater "plasticity" with regard to the combinations of institutional forms and functions. These trends are not entirely new, but their implications have not been fully taken on board within existing theoretical frameworks.[59]

The elephant in the room here is neoliberalization, which in a perplexing sense exists *simultaneously* as a set of "internal" characteristics both of the liberal model and of key multilateral institutions; as an "offshore" threat to, and internal undercurrent within, coordinated capitalist systems; and as the prevailing "rules of the game," structuring relations between national models.

Neoliberal Convergence?

Since its inception, the varieties approach has been preoccupied with the threat of neoliberalism. Initially, the tone was a confident one, since the normative preference for coordinated, Euro-Japanese strategies was apparently being validated by patterns of national economic growth. But as the US and British economies surged in the 1990s, while Germany and Japan faltered, the tables were turned. The coordinated models, having been praised for their socioeconomic sustainability, were now under siege; the threat of neoliberal institutional degradation was a real and present one. And now, even the strategy of placing LMEs and CMEs on an equal analytical footing smacked of normative wish-fulfillment, if not political-economic nostalgia. Increasingly, varieties analysts will acknowledge that a generalized and concerted trend toward neoliberalization is in evidence, with marked consequences for the coordinated economies in particular, while continuing to point to the *relative resilience* of national models, the often-incremental nature of institutional change, and continued variability in economic outcomes.[60] As the global financial crisis would reveal, however, neoliberalization may have been more of a threat to the archetypically (neo)liberal economies, the LMEs, than it was to the CMEs: the "internal" threat was at least as significant as the supposedly external one.

This said, the varieties literature has been associated with the argument that neoliberalization is a threat from "outside," with especially foreboding implications for trust-based CMEs. According to Robert Goodin:

> [T]he relationships of trust that are so central to the CME way of organizing an economy are hard to build and easy to destroy [which] explains why CMEs are always at risk, in ways that LMEs are not. That explains why countries in the middle ground between a CME and a LME should naturally be expected to slide in the LME direction: each pole is equally rewarding, economically, but the polar LME model can be achieved and start paying economic dividends much more quickly.... The logic underlying the *Varieties of Capitalism* project seems to suggest that CMEs are naturally doomed to extinction, and LMEs ultimately to prevail. That is so, not because LMEs necessarily yield better outcomes, but merely because CMEs are highly sensitive to disruption in ways that LMEs are not.[61]

Hall and Soskice read this as "a striking and neo-Darwinian conclusion," loosening their rational-choice position to argue that efficiency considerations alone are unlikely to drive institutional change—politics still matters. They concede, however, that the logic of the varieties approach may indeed suggest "a long-term historical bias leaning in the direction of liberalization," countering somewhat defensively that CMEs "are not as fragile as many suppose."[62] This is a familiar formulation in varieties circles, positing the relative robustness of inherited institutional ensembles in the face of ostensibly more dynamic (if generally destructive) contemporary institutional challenges: like sand castles on King Canute's beach, the CMEs should be capable of withstanding waves of neoliberalization by virtue of their solid foundations. Yet the sobering conclusion of Streeck and Yamamura's historical inquiries into the origins of "nonliberal capitalism" is that even though the unique kinds of state capacities found in Japan and Germany have deep-rooted political preconditions, these may be subject to "permanent dismantling" in the face of gradual "liberal erosion."[63]

To rework the oceanographic metaphor, the rising tide of neoliberalism could actually sink some of the best-engineered boats, whose sluggish steering is ill-suited to navigating such choppy waters. Hall and Thelen do not deny that the tide may have turned, but they take issue with the concept of (neo)liberalization, since the "crudeness of this category . . . obscures more than it illuminates."[64] They raise three objections. First, neoliberalization is a multidimensional process—comprising an array of specific reforms like privatization, welfare retrenchment, labor-market "deregulation," financial liberalization, and so on—not all of which necessarily accompany one another in every instance. As a result, the concept of neoliberalization needs to be "disaggregated." Second, even specific reform measures, such as the adoption of international accounting standards or the empowerment of minority shareholders, are associated with not a singular outcome but a range of effects. And third, the impact of neoliberal reforms will be shaped by the wider institutional environment and its associated interaction effects. "Even when identical institutional reforms are being examined, to assume they will have identical effects in all nations is a mistake."[65]

This, it must be said, is a rather convenient caricature of neoliberalism. It recalls Hirst and Thompson's straw-man critique of globalization *as if it were* a unified, totalizing, end-stage phenomenon.[66] Such overdrawn, monolithic conceptions of globalism and neoliberalism are easily dismissed, merely by pointing to exceptions and inconsistencies. But process-based conceptions—sensitive to conjuncture, contingency, and contradiction—are less vulnerable to such blunt critiques, since they are explicitly concerned with the manner in which (partially realized) causal processes generate uneven and divergent outcomes.[67] Likewise, concepts of neoliberalization that call attention, inter alia, to its historical and geographical specificities; its often contradictory discursive and governmental moments; its context-specific yet interconnected form; its plasticity, polymorphism, and porosity; its capacity for creative adjustment in the face of internal limits and contradictions; and its crisis-driven and hybrid character are difficult to reconcile with the flat-footed, flat-earth rendering invoked by Hall and Thelen. Certainly, one would not want to presuppose high degrees of monolithic unity in the project/process of neoliberalization, which is always provisional and partial, in comparison to the all-or-nothing caricature presented by Hall and Thelen. Neither would one anticipate one-to-one, functional correspondences between policy interventions and outcomes, since these are always mediated and contingent. It is inescapably true, of course, that adequate, operational conceptions of neoliberalism are necessary, if the term is to be used in the critical analysis of institutional change. Yet it may be more, not less, difficult to visualize this process through the VoC optic, since this tends either to sequester (and naturalize) neoliberal impulses *within* the LME model, placing them at one end of a singular analytical spectrum, with an ostensibly non-liberal "other" at the opposite pole, or to position them as extraterrestrial, *offshore* threats.

Regulationist-inspired conceptions of capitalist variation are less constrained in their handling of the process of neoliberalization. Boyer, for example, declares *both* a programmatic concern to "unsettle [the] deceptive unanimity" of neoliberal fatalism/triumphalism, through the searching analysis of crisis, contradiction, and nascent alternatives, together with a worldly recognition that "bad *régulations* are driving out good," by virtue of the apparent short-term compatibility of neoliberal institutional forms with transnationalizing and financialized capitalism.[68] Future maps of capitalism, it follows, will be shaped by complex forms of dynamic transformation, mutual adaptation, and crisis-driven change, such that even common pressures will (continue to) produce diverse outcomes. Reducing this process to an either/or choice between liberal and coordinated capitalism runs the risk both of misconstruing the processes of change and reducing/polarizing the set of future options.[69] Visualizing complex, polycentric transformations through a monochromatic lens will therefore result in distorted images of the future.

Finally, there is the question of scale. Here, the monoscalarity of the VoC approach again emerges as a serious obstacle, since this tends to privilege the notion of a "smoothly functioning, self-adjusting political economy" operating at the national scale, while processes of change are seen to reverberate through these relatively cohesive national systems in ways that further accentuate national differences.[70] Such static conceptions stand in various degrees of tension with those approaches that emphasize the far-reaching "rescaling" of contemporary political economic relations and state forms, which, among other things, is fostering new connections and relays between increasingly incomplete and porous national "systems," spawning "models within models" at the local scale and network-style "models between models" in translocal space, while generating new forms of externally oriented adaptation, learning, and hybridity.[71] Approaches that reify the "cages" of distinctive national institutional systems, and which go as far as to confer on these self-sustaining, equilibrating tendencies, are therefore likely to be inattentive to *new forms* of capitalist variety, realized at different scales and across different registers.[72] The tendential "ecological dominance" of neoliberal restructuring strategies is a case in point, since these have profoundly disrupted inherited scalar hierarchies, while setting in train new rounds of creative institutional destruction across multiple scales.[73] Of course, neoliberalization will not mean the death of variety, but it certainly represents a profound challenge to *old forms* of institutional variety.

Economic Geographies of Variegated Capitalism?

Economic geography and the varieties school ought to have had plenty to say to one another. But the conversation between the two fields never really ignited. In some respects, there may have been a basic lack of "fit" between the two research programs, though in principle a closer engagement might yield benefits in both directions. To briefly recap the affinities, there is a shared sense that institutions matter; there is a mutual interest in various branches of heterodox economics and in the development of midlevel theories; and there is an overlapping concern with the spatial variability of economies in general and economic governance in particular. But analytical norms vary quite significantly in other ways. While the varieties school practically fetishizes the national scale, and the cluster of formal institutions that are anchored at that scale, economic geographers have been more inclined to pursue various forms of multi-scalar analysis. The varieties project has been quite explicitly programmatic in nature, doggedly pursuing (and refining) a core set of propositions, while in contrast the "new economic geographies," as the name suggests, have tended to be proliferative. International comparative research is, in effect, the methodological modus operandi of the varieties program, but remains rather surprisingly rare in economic geography. In much of the VoC literature, a premium is placed on parsimonious analysis, crisply summarizing "essential" sources of geographic difference; meanwhile, economic geographers tend to opt for contextually rich forms of documentation and explanation, adopting a relatively open and permissive attitude to claims concerning the causes and consequences of spatial differentiation. While the former is rigorously focused on the demonstration of geographical differentiation within a single register (that of the national institutional spaces of advanced capitalism), among the latter, spatial variegation is problematized across multiple registers, even if in many cases the *fact* of that variegation seems almost to be accepted as an article of faith. And while the ontological status of *national economy* is accepted as more or less given in VoC scholarship, this is problematized quite explicitly in economic geography, where the spaces and scales that are constructed by circuits of value and regimes of valuation are no longer assumed to be pregiven.

Varieties scholars are much more inclined to deal with "big geographies." They have found considerable utility in the rather generalized construct of national capitalism, being content to "live with" quite high degrees of variability at the regional or industry-sectoral level. Economic geographers seem more inclined, in contrast, to deconstruct, disaggregate, or even dismiss national "models" as overgeneralized archetypes, opting instead to work closer to the ground—at the subnational scale or through transnational networks. And the VoC school's penchant for "big picture," structural forms of analysis, spanning multiple institutional domains, contrasts with economic geography's concern with more "grounded," if not localized, specificities of economic relations and formations, revealed through close-focus analyses of "singular" phenomena like networks, institutions, sectors, and discourses, rather than macro-scale systems, conjunctures, or ensembles.

Economic geographers have, broadly speaking, been on the same side as varieties scholars in globalization debates—emphasizing continuing geographical variability, refuting market teleology, cataloguing resilient institutional forms at the local and national scales. The broad formulations and bold claims of varieties scholars have certainly been more visible in these debates. Economic geographers are arguably more attuned to the complex array of multi-scalar transformations that have been associated with "globalization" processes.[74] But a case can also be made, in this context, that *both* fields could benefit from a more explicit engagement with processes of combined and uneven development.[75] From the varieties side of the debate, Howell has argued that

> [t]he [Hall and Soskice] approach . . . is middle-level theorizing at its best, but, in the absence of an articulation with theorizing about the uneven and interdependent development of national capitalisms and the contradictory elements, crisis tendencies, and propensity for perpetual reinvention within capitalist economies, the danger for institutionalist analysis is always that it will become too static, able to explain stability but not rupture, and will render invisible the exercise of class power that underlies coordination and equilibrium in the political economy. Recognizing that the economy in which transactions are being coordinated is capitalist and that the actors whose actions are being coordinated are class actors goes a long way to restoring dynamism, conflict and power to the center of comparative political economy. What is required, in other words, is not simply an institutional theory, but an institutional theory of capitalism. The intellectual promise of the varieties of capitalism approach opens up exciting new research agendas. The next

step is to place its distinctive institutional analysis within a wider theoretical framework that incorporates historical trajectories, class relationships, and the development of capitalism as a global system.[76]

What is called for, one might otherwise say, is an enriched analysis of the temporality *and spatiality* of capitalist development, on the face of it one of economic geography's bread-and-butter concerns. Long skeptical of descriptive labeling and typologizing approaches to capitalist development, and reluctant to sequester causal processes to particular scales or locales, economic geographers might indeed be well placed to help make sense of the kinds of relationally combined, multi-scalar hybrid forms of restructuring that tend to confound formalized, system-centric analyses. This means moving beyond the routine pluralization of capitalism, and the alternating proliferation and pruning of a reified set of "models," to probe the principles, sources, and dimensions of *capitalist variegation*, understood as a more explicitly "relational" conception of variety. In other words, it means coming to terms with the causes and forms of capitalism's dynamic polymorphism.

Different strands of the varieties school have found "analytical leverage in taking the diversity of capitalisms as an object of study and comparing *capitalisms* vis-a-vis each other," Stark and Bruszt point out, while problematizing various "recombinant" forms of capitalist governance and growth.[77] In doing so, they have suggestively placed institutions, and institutional ensembles, in the analytical foreground, often reading off relatively simple—patchwork or bipolar—geographies from their subsequent theoretically informed empirical investigations. The result has been a rudimentary geography of two-plus capitalisms, with a binary model defining the most parsimonious form of diversity, and the maximum degree of variability apparently being set only by the number of national cases.[78] The more excessive forms of geographical reductionism trammel variety down to a dubious, unidimensional continuum—running more or less directly from Germany to the United States. Where should we locate China, India, and Brazil in this picture? And what do their modes of growth reveal, not only about the bandwidth of contemporary capitalist "variety," but also about the interpenetrating nature of capitalist development at the global scale?

Granted, the varieties project has been productive, and it has established some of the most suggestive stylized facts in the burgeoning field of heterodox economics. Yet it has barely scratched the surface of deeper forms of geographical differentiation and spatial dynamics, as they pertain to the transnational *combination* of modes of capitalist development. This calls for the calibration of connections, as well as the documentation of differences, in capitalist development paths. Reading differentiation primarily through the lens of (national) institutional coordination runs the risk of exaggerating and reifying some forms of geographical difference, while obfuscating threads of commonality and interdependence. Critical of the institutional fetishism in the VoC rubric, Burawoy has questioned the tendency to privilege the "diversity of *superstructural* manifestations of capitalism . . . rather than [explicating] an underlying diversity of economic forms of production and corresponding class relations."[79]

Hence the need to transcend the cataloguing and labeling of *variety* according to institutional criteria, to probe the meaningful forms of *variegation*. For while the VoC "literature has a great deal to say about 'varieties,'" Pontusson points out, it has "surprisingly little to say about 'capitalism,'" since it tends to reify institutional differentiation, while dismissing evidence of systemic interdependence and contingent convergence on the misleading grounds that this represents nothing more than a backdoor form of structuralist monologism.[80] Economic geography's acute analyses of local formations of capitalism have much to contribute here, though to date there has been very little dialogue around this part of the heterodox project. To do so would reciprocally challenge some of economic geography's long-established practices and stylized understandings. Even though it is by now a staple position that unprincipled declarations of local uniqueness are indefensible, and even though the differentiated space economy remains one of the discipline's principal analytical objects,[81] the criteria for determining the scope and character of economic variegation across space have—perhaps surprisingly—not been subject to sustained interrogation. Indeed, despite now-routine invocations of "multi-scalarity," there seems to be a growing reluctance explicitly to "embed" analyses of localized economic practices within wider structural contexts, the gaze of economic geography having shifted during the 1990s toward mesoanalytical and microinstitutional questions.[82]

This said, many of the analytical inclinations and commitments for what might be provisionally styled as a variegated capitalism approach are relatively well established in economic-geographical practice, even if these are hardly subjects of explicit consensus. Table 5.1 seeks to bring some of these to the surface, by way of a series of stylized contrasts with varieties-school positions. It must be acknowledged that the two "projects" outlined here are not nearly as symmetrical as this device may make them seem. Not least, the varieties school—for all its eclecticism—tends to cohere around a number of programmatic concerns and shared problematics. Economic geography,

Table 5.1 Varieties of Capitalism versus Variegated Capitalism

	Varieties of Capitalism	Variegated Capitalism
Problematique	Understanding institutional variability among advanced capitalist economies	Explicating processes and forms of uneven development within, and beyond, late capitalism
Case study rationale	Comparative cases positioned relative to the privileged axis of LME ↔ CME	Individual cases selected according to their theoretically generative properties
Method	Tendency for parsimonious institutional political economy with strong rational-choice component; ideal-typical theorizing; reliance on secondary sources and game-theoretic procedures	Relatively ecumenical institutional/cultural political economy, elaborated through qualitative case studies; post-positivist theorizing; inclination to urban and regional analysis; rejection of methodological individualism
Privileged agents	Firms, business associations, and policy entrepreneurs	Agents generally afforded relatively weak analytical status, as bearers of prevailing modes of restructuring or nascent forms of resistance; agents embedded in constitutive network relations
Analytical gaze	Privileging of national institutional archetypes and relatively bounded national economies; emphasis on lead firms, dominant industries, and formal institutions	Emphasis on decisive moments of economic transformation and institutional restructuring; real-time analysis of regulatory projects and experiments in the organization of production; multi-scalarity
Temporal dynamics	Presumption of equilibrium within selected institutional fields (absent exogenous shocks); emphasis on relative stability, incremental change reinforcing institutional settlements, punctuated by occasional disruptions	Dynamic analysis, concern with endemic restructuring; presumption of disequilibrium and persistent crisis-proneness
Scalar dynamics	Methodological nationalism; presumption of high degrees of endogenous institutional coherence and a unified national-economic space; supermodularity registered at the national scale	Social construction and relativization of scale; potential for supermodularity and conjunctural effects at multiple spatial scales (e.g., "locality effects"); concern with multi-scalarity (e.g., "glocal" hybrids and cross-scalar networks)
Historical trajectory	Dual convergence or "twin peaks"; static-comparative analysis of archetypal development models	Combined and uneven development; embrace of contingency; rejection of the necessity of either convergence or divergence; concern with path-shaping and path-altering change

(*continued*)

Table 5.1 Continued

	Varieties of Capitalism	Variegated Capitalism
Typical levels of abstraction	Micro-analytic accounts of firm behavior embedded within meso-level institutional architectures	Meso-analytic interpretations of relatively concrete institutional conjunctures located within unevenly developed (capitalist) system
Normative project	Defense of European- and Japanese-style social democracy and corporatist regimes; concern to explicate non-neoliberal modes of development	Revealing internal contradictions of neoliberal globalization; identification and promotion of alternative (and/or progressive) forms of local development

in contrast, tends to be even more polyglot, and may even have entered a "post-programmatic" phase. The place-holding label of variegated capitalism therefore attaches less to a self-conscious project than to a bundle of complementary practices and mutual orientations within the field of economic geography. It is, however, suggestive of an alternate, if somewhat inchoate, take on the question of capitalist variety, carrying implications for potential points of engagement with the varieties project itself.

The nascent problematic of variegated capitalism invites a more concerted engagement with "macroeconomic geographies"—more work of a holistic nature, concerned with macroeconomic patterns and trajectories, longue-durée processes, the restructuring of institutional ensembles (including those at the level of the nation-state, one of economic geography's less fashionable scales of analysis), and with those "big geographies" of capitalist restructuring. Crucially, this should involve *holding together* questions relating to the uneven development of capitalism and co-constitutive/coevolving forms of institutional restructuring, for instance at the interface of neoliberalization and financialization. On the economic side of this agenda, this would mean focusing rather less on "islands" of emergent economic practices per se, rather more on structural formations and extralocal conventions, and the patterned relations between "local" capitalisms. On the institutional side, one of the conspicuous missing links in this research agenda likewise concerns the relational geographies of economic institutions (embracing both the uneven development of regulation and the regulation of uneven development), complementing well-established lines of work on localized forms of governance with explorations of the evolution of institutional landscapes at the international scale and the production of new (inter)state spaces.

Conclusion: From Variety to Variegation

Since its consolidation as a research program in the late 1990s, the VoC approach has delivered a lot. It has established a plausible analytical counternarrative to one-world visions of globalization; it has called attention to the institutional embeddedness of economic systems and transformations, in the face of a prevalent free-market discourse; and it has reminded heterodox economists "that there are particular geographies of production and consumption."[83] The VoC rubric has been useful in problematizing the systemic institutional logics of a range of national capitalisms, indeed in spawning the concept of national capitalism itself. And it has been successful in inserting geographical questions, of a certain kind, into circulation within mainstream heterodox economics, while breathing new life into the field of comparative political economy. The project has had less to say about the reconstitution of capitalist structures and relations at scales other than the national, or through institutional domains and modalities beyond the formally defined sphere of nation-state institutions. But its bold claims about the meta-geographies of contemporary capitalist restructuring have certainly made waves.

There is a sense in which the VoC program has been a project of economic geography, albeit one practiced for the most part by economic sociologists, institutional economists, and political scientists. Operationalizing spatialized concepts in its own ways, the varieties school has been busily making its own economic geographies. Clearly, proper-noun Economic Geography has no proprietary rights over this conceptual territory, though at the same time its absentee status ought to occasion some reflection. The causes and consequences of spatial-economic restructuring have long been economic geography's stock-in-trade, but the discipline may have been vacating the territory first sketched out by Michel Albert in his widely read *Capitalisme contre capitalism* just when interdisciplinary debates around globalization and varieties of capitalism were taking off.[84] In the ensuing period, economic geographers have developed new bodies of work on localized, network, cultural, and alternative economies, forging new insights and alliances along the way, but in the process they may have ceded some of the questions of macro-economic geography and larger-scale theorizing to other fields, which have subsequently paid little attention to what they seem to regard as provincial or contingent theorizing. On the other hand, economic geography clearly has more to say, if it can find its voice in this conversation. A somewhat provisional position on "variegated capitalism," as it has been outlined here, draws on languages that are one part established, one part embryonic. Furthermore, they have been developed, so far, more through critique and deconstruction than through substantive reconstruction. The task for the remainder of this book is to move these arguments further in the latter direction, to explore a more positive and forward-looking case for critical analyses of variegated capitalism.

6
Confounding Variety?

Neither Mao nor Market

with Jun Zhang

The previous chapter concluded that while the varieties of capitalism (VoC) framework can be credited with stabilizing the signature claim that capitalism comes in varieties, rather than in a standard or singular form, the manner in which this claim was advanced and stabilized ultimately proved to be constraining. Critiques of the VoC framework are now almost as well known as the framework itself, and will often travel together in what has become (yet) more heterodox and open-ended research programs on comparative capitalisms and capitalist diversity. From a range of more or less sympathetic perspectives, what came together as a VoC orthodoxy is conventionally faulted for its preoccupation with limited, formal registers of (national) institutional variety, to which the (re)production of difference itself is rather singularly indexed; for its hardwiring of jurisdictionally bounded inquires combining methodological nationalism with methodological internalism; for its turn to rational-choice, firm-centric methods, and formalized institutional analysis; for its failure to account for the deep interpenetration and mutual interdependencies between "varieties" of capitalism, which may indeed be distinctive but do not stand apart; for its habit of taking capitalism itself for granted, placing (formal) institutions in the foreground while directing attention away from cross-cutting dynamics, historical evolution, and shared contradictions; and for its tendency to privilege typological elaboration over causal explanation.

For some, these critiques are ultimately unanswerable. There are those that take the view that the VoC framework can be credited with posing some important questions (e.g., concerning the geographically variable constitution of capitalism and the persistence of uneven spatial development), but it has been tackling these the wrong way, from the wrong point of departure, or in too timid a fashion. The previous chapter took a somewhat similar tack, crediting the approach for carving out a space for the recognition of constitutively significant geographical difference and against economism, universalism, and orthodoxies of market-oriented convergence, but finding the approach to be self-limiting. Nevertheless, critical engagement with the VoC approach served as a spur to the development of an alternative, albeit a somewhat inchoate one. To this end, an orientation to variegation rather than variety provided an initial remit for the exploration of differences-in-connection. A variegated-capitalism approach, it was argued, might be animated by the following methodological concerns: first, an embrace of multi-scalar rather than mono-scalar modes of analysis; second, an emphasis on contradiction and disjuncture rather than on (nationally scaled) institutional coherence; third, an expressly relational perspective, emphasizing the mutual interdependencies between "local" economies over endogenous logics and separatist treatments; fourth, recognition of the need to balance situated analyses of capitalism(s) with the constitutive role of cross-cutting and connective processes, such as neoliberalization, not just as carriers of convergence tendencies but as drivers of combined and uneven development; and fifth, a commitment to extend the field of the analytically visible beyond Eurocentric capitalism while at the same time confronting the ecological dominance of neoliberal globalism.

Implicit in this emergent variegated-capitalism approach is a commitment to the substantivist exploration of actually existing economies, more often than not in the throes of transformation and restructuring. This is not just a matter of classifying and codifying cases according to some alternative schema; it is an invitation to theorize with and through cases, indeed conjuncturally positioned cases. The present chapter, originally written in collaboration with Jun Zhang, seeks to take a step in this direction with the aid of the often-confounding case of China, the post-1970s economic transformation of which has few parallels in world history and the current role of which in the world system effectively demands attention, both theoretically and politically. The apparently sui generis nature of China's development path and mode of economic governance is sometimes taken as an alibi for theoretical defeatism, or dissent from so-called Western conventions of analysis. Alternatively, its conspicuous presence as an ostensibly "more statist" counterpole to US-style liberal capitalism has given license, particularly in the past few years, to a new generation of Cold War–like theorizations, which like their predecessors tend to exaggerate the role of (free) markets and liberal governance in the West, while sequestering the more corrupting and overbearing functions of the state to the East.

This chapter makes a different kind of move, seeking to make a virtue of the "frictions" between theoretical frameworks on the one hand and actually existing governance styles and socioeconomic conditions on the other, while examining the Chinese case as a source of constructive provocation and reflexive opportunity.[1] This is a case, after all, that stretches and strains received conceptions of *both* capitalism and variety, in ways that ought to prompt some rethinking of both. With this as its charge, the chapter proceeds in two stages. The next section situates the Chinese case in conversation with received VoC-style categories of analysis. Then the subsequent section explores China's political-economic transformation in more detail, drawing on some of the problematics of VoC analysis, but moving also to operationalize the principles of a variegated capitalism approach. Working in a Polanyian spirit, particular attention is called to contradictory tendencies and awkward articulations in this heterogeneous development pattern. The chapter's conclusion reflects on how the substantivist interrogation of vexing cases like Chinese capitalism might assist in the development of variegated-capitalism approaches.

Beyond Variety?

China has been a white space on the map of the VoC debate, scarcely warranting a mention—even as an external threat—until quite recently. Indeed, there are continuing debates over whether the Chinese economy can even be considered to be functionally capitalist, let alone its own "variety," or some newfound variant of the already polycentric Asian model.[2] Beyond this, critical observers remain divided over whether China should be celebrated as a bulwark against neoliberal globalism or condemned for executing an unforgiving "capitalist restoration."[3] The meaning of the Chinese "model" often lies in the eye of the beholder: while Arrighi was able to determine post- or alt-capitalist possibilities in China, the *Economist* was until recently dismissive of claims that the country's development might represent an "object lesson in state capitalism," in favor of an affirmation of its own worldview, that "China's remarkable success [is attributable to] an odd and often unappreciated experiment in laissez-faire capitalism."[4] The magazine has since changed its tune, however, maintaining that what it now calls "state capitalism," epitomized by China, "represents the most formidable foe that liberal capitalism has faced to date."[5]

The restrictive register of the VoC framework, reduced to its classical form, does not permit too many options, but reconciling the Chinese case with its binary schema tends to divide even well-informed opinions. Witt carefully weighs each of the VoC approach's principles of analytical pertinence before concluding that Chinese capitalism "looks much more like a LME than a CME" (with the notable exception of its sui generis financial regime).[6] Meanwhile, Fligstein and Zhang's version of the same thought experiment leads them to "safely reject" parallels with US-style LMEs, in favor of a historically unprecedented configuration of CME-adjacent "organized capitalism" most closely related to France![7] To take the VoC framework to what is arguably its most ill-fitting global site, that of contemporary China, is therefore more than an empirical exercise, since the Chinese case raises distinctive challenges for the style of methodologically nationalist, firm-oriented, and boundedly comparative political economy practiced under the VoC banner, troubling settled understandings of both "variety" and "capitalism" along the way.

The problematic of "Chinese capitalism" does indeed seem to represent not only a provocative but also a productive case. It places stress on established VoC nostrums (such as institutional integrity at the national scale and the evaluation of institutional forms according to the singular LME-CME yardstick), but it likewise opens up some challenging questions concerning multi-scalar governance, socialist-capitalist hybrids and the political management of endemic contradictions, such as those arising from uneven growth and sociospatial inequalities. After all, for three decades after 1949, actually existing "Chinese capitalism" was a strictly offshore, *extra*-territorial phenomenon, more or less coterminous with the vibrant, diasporic economies of the "overseas Chinese,"[8] but entirely absent from the People's Republic of China itself. A historically unparalleled hybrid of reformist Leninism and insourced capitalism has since been forged. In the process, it has been claimed that not one, but in fact several, "indigenous" capitalisms have been cultivated in China, through a unique blend of central orchestration and local devolution,[9] many of which have profited from neoliberal globalism while at the same time spurning some of the most cherished policy prescriptions of the Washington Consensus.[10] For these and other reasons, the problematic of "varieties of capitalism with Chinese characteristics" opens up some searching questions about the sociospatial constitution and geographical (re)formation of capitalism.

As a first take, Table 6.1 presents a heuristic reading of Chinese capitalism according to orthodox VoC criteria. Here, the Chinese model is located in a "triangular" relationship with the two established ideal types. The quasi-CME face of the Chinese model is revealed in the extensive reach of the All China Federation of Trade Unions (ACFTU), which has a membership footprint extending across half of the workforce; a reliance on bank-based financing; continuing dominance of state-owned enterprises (SOEs), especially in the

Table 6.1 Varieties of Capitalism versus the Chinese Model

	Coordinated Market Economies	Liberal Market Economies	A Chinese Variety of Capitalism?
Industrial relations	Coordinated of wage determination across key industries (involving employer associations and unions) Employee-elected bodies and representative bodies play key roles in company decision-making	Company-based, uncoordinated wage bargaining Institutionally weak unions with limited workplace presence	Company-based, uncoordinated wage bargaining Party-controlled unions Sharp urban-rural divide
Education and training	Strong systems of vocational education and training, with stakeholder involvement Limited post-compulsory/higher education	Market oriented; weak systems of vocational training; limited company involvement Strong post-compulsory/higher education	Emphasis on general skills, weak vocational training; skills mismatches Low enrollment rates in further and higher education Brain drain/circulation
Interfirm relations	Consensus-based standard setting Business associations regulate relational contracting Close relations between business associations and research/education institutions Mitigated of competition in domestic markets; open competition in export markets	Market-based standard setting Strong anti-collusion policies Underdeveloped institutional framework for technology diffusion Weakly regulated relational contracting	"Managed competition" in strategic technological sectors favoring "national champions" Foreign dominance and open-competition in export-oriented sectors Dominance of family and *guanxi* networks, plus patron-client ties, in private economic coordination Weak legal enforcement and limited protection of intellectual property rights

(continued)

Table 6.1 Continued

	Coordinated Market Economies	Liberal Market Economies	A Chinese Variety of Capitalism?
Corporate financing and governance	Stable stakeholder arrangements, with banks playing monitoring role Reluctance to finance higher risk ventures and technologies Industry-based monitoring Hostile takeovers difficult	Unstable shareholder arrangements Orientation to higher risk capital markets Hostile takeovers permitted	Corporate financing dominated by state-owned banks Financially starved private firms coexist with "spoiled" state-owned enterprises Soaring overseas stock market listing of domestic firms Large-scale FDI in technologically advanced sectors
Examples	Germany (paradigmatic case); Japan, Austria, Switzerland, Italy, Belgium, the Netherlands, Denmark, Sweden, South Korea	United States (paradigmatic case); United Kingdom, Canada, Australia, New Zealand	China (extra-paradigmatic case)

strategically significant "pillar" sectors, which account for around one-third of GDP; state prescription of minimum wages and a post-2008 labor contract law that offers de jure employment protections sometimes even exceeding CME norms. In practice, however, the ACFTU functions in more of a bipartite than a tripartite fashion; as a political instrument of the Chinese Communist Party (CCP), it aligns with the interests of management rather than workers. Likewise, de facto employment protections, and provisions for unemployed and marginalized workers, remain only minimal. The enforcement of Chinese labor law, like its intellectual property laws, has been notoriously loose and arbitrary. The challenges of achieving meaningful business accountability, in a legal sense, also hinder collective coordination and the formation of horizontal linkages for employers and workers alike. However, partly as an imperfect substitute in this regulatory vacuum, the use of family and kinship ties (*guanxi*) to coordinate intra- and inter-firm relations is widespread, especially among China's small, private firms. It is these deficits in actually existing, CME-style non-market coordination that prompted Witt to locate China in the family of LMEs.

China's economic and institutional structures diverge considerably from the prototypes advanced in the VoC approach. State-led industrialization and export-oriented production, commonly found in China and other Asian economies at various stages of emergence and transition, are difficult to shoehorn into the LME-CME dichotomy.[11] China's marketization project has been paradoxically prosecuted by a communist party-state, largely on the basis of unevenly applied policy directives. As in other (post-)communist economies, it is the state, rather than the firm, that defines the principal locus of coordination, while the party-state also performs crucial (though always flawed and partial) roles as a transformative agent.[12] Given the transitional and hybrid nature of the Chinese economy, one would search in vain for a singular, emblematic firm. The country's mixed industrial system is characterized by the *copresence* of monopolistic SOEs, with ready access to finance, arrayed across the "commanding heights" of the so-called pillar sectors; foreign-owned firms with dominant positions in many export-oriented manufacturing sectors, and a plethora of township and village enterprises (TVEs) and small family-run private firms.

China's institutional matrix, which has enabled blistering economic growth for over three decades, alongside (new and old) forms of sharply uneven development, has hardly displayed any significant degree of system-level complementarity. Meanwhile, the country's "institutional comparative advantage" has yet to be translated into sustained technological innovation, either radically or incrementally. China's global competitiveness has been constructed through a feat of self-transformation into a new "workshop of the world," on the basis of a labor-intensive, export-oriented production system, deeply integrated through global value chains into offshore economies. The Chinese model has been forged as a profitable, "external" complement to extant varieties of Western capitalism, with which it has evolved through a combination of competition, complementarity, and coexistence. It is not simply a new model, additively introduced to a level playing field occupied by discrete, "horizontally" competing capitalisms.

No matter whether the analytical preference is for two, four, five, or more varieties of capitalism, the fact remains that existing VoC formulations have not made space for the Chinese variant of capitalism, notwithstanding its global significance. Christopher McNally, having noted the potential utility of the VoC approach as a framework emphasizing "marked differences amongst capitalist institutions on the national level," is ultimately unsure how to handle the "odd case" of China, opting "consciously [to] eschew a map of institutional variations among capitalisms, especially since in China capitalist institutions are merely in the process of forming."[13]

Sino-Capitalism?

Sinologist Gary Hamilton once posed what for a long time has been one of the most demanding negative questions in historical sociology and comparative political economy: How could it be that a country that had been a driver of world development for millennia—and which had played pioneering roles in the early evolution of trade, finance, and technological innovation—was reduced to the status of a capitalist backwater by the beginning of the twentieth century?[14] Historically, discourses of absentee capitalism revealed more about the presumptions of Western observers than they did about China itself, Hamilton averred. As he knew full well, however, the tide had recently been turning in China, most markedly since the inauguration of Deng Xiaoping's "second revolution," its economy being progressively "opened up" after 1978. Setting aside the question of whether China might one day be "officially" designated as a capitalist country—highly unlikely, as long as the CCP retains its grip on power—the contention that it is even functionally capitalist continues to exercise controversy. While many Asian neighbors now recognize China as a fellow "market economy," the United States, Europe and Japan pointedly do not—nominally on the grounds of the weight and character of the state's presence in economic life. Arrighi preferred to leave open the question of whether there might be another form of socialism, as opposed to capitalism, at the end of China's long transformation: the (decisive?) fact that private control over the means of production remains far from fully secured in China being taken to imply that, "despite the spread of market exchanges in the pursuit of profit . . . the nature of development in China is not necessarily capitalist."[15]

This, however, is now a minority view. There is a growing consensus that China has become functionally capitalist—albeit far from comprehensively or unambiguously, and certainly not either "classically" or officially. Yet profound differences remain over just about every aspect of the qualitative form, and the ultimate destination, of this great transformation. Among the many flashpoints in these debates, there are questions around whether the Chinese state should be characterized as socialist-developmentalist, tendentially neoliberal, or something else altogether, with Baum and Shevchenko counting no fewer than seventeen contending labels in the literature.[16]

Bearing in mind the ambiguities and contradictions of the Chinese development path, rather than by attempting to fix (or to force) a singular reading of Sino-capitalism, the discussion instead proceeds by exploring some of the principal fields of contention in the contemporary debate around the form and indeed the fact of "capitalism in the dragon's lair."[17] The following discussion focuses on three themes, each of which has been a locus for divergent interpretations: first, the oxymoronic formation of China's "socialist market economy" is problematized; second, the chapter turns to the character of the Chinese state and its variegated mode of governance; and third, the power circuits of "Chinese capitalism" are explored.

Market Socialism or State Capitalism?

It has been enigmatically stated that "China is both far away from socialism and far away from capitalism."[18] While this may be somewhat representative of the kind of double-speak that pervades official economic discourse in China, where the CCP can apparently embrace capitalism in deed but never in word, it sheds little light on the actual character of transformative change in the country. The winding path from Maoist state socialism has been navigated with incremental caution (and more than a few reversals), in the interest of maintaining social stability and party power, while averting political crisis. Continuing intolerance of public dissent, or even society-wide debate, has meant that the reform process has taken the form of a protracted, and ongoing, intra-party struggle.

Correspondingly, the enabling concept of the "socialist market economy" has been assembled only gradually. Chen Yun's opinion that "planned economy is primary, the market economy supplementary" had been enshrined at the Party's 1980 Central Work Conference. But this was rejected at the Third Plenum of 1984, where the "Decision on the Reform of the Economic Structure" endorsed an official conception of the "commodity economy," in contrast to the "planned economy"—a significant ideological breakthrough that served to justify further liberalization.[19] In 1987, Zhao Ziyang, then the general secretary of the CCP, reaffirmed that China remained in the "initial stage of socialism," facing a decades-long challenge of improving material living standards for the majority of the population. Zhao also proposed a dramatic curtailment of central planning, advocating the further development of labor and financial markets, while putting both pricing policies and political reform on the agenda.[20]

The Tiananmen incident, however, resulted in the purge of Zhao and other liberal leaders, and Deng's status within the Party plummeted. Chen Yun's interpretation of socialist economics was restored as orthodoxy, being powerfully reaffirmed by General Secretary Jiang Zemin. In 1992, however, the eighty-eight-year-old Deng began to fight back. His famous southern tour of market-oriented hotspots, married with robust rhetoric and a willingness to deploy the military in the service of intra-party struggle, was indication of a new determination. Deng's ultimate victory was proclaimed by the Fourteenth Party Congress in 1992, where "the chief architect of our socialist reform" was credited with the historically fateful "theory of building socialism with Chinese characteristics."[21] The congress adopted the most liberal economic document in CCP history, sanctioning sweeping economic reforms under the rubric of the "socialist market economy," although a more liberal stance on economic affairs was matched with an undiluted commitment to political control. Nevertheless, socialism remained the official ideology, the CCP continuing to claim legitimacy under the sign of Marxism-Leninism, with significant political consequences.

A long-suppressed interview with Deng Xiaping, conducted in 1979, revealed some of the intentionality here, which was to appropriate the *methods* of the (capitalist) market economy, though not its ethic. As Deng rhetorically asked,

> Why can't we develop a market economy under socialism? . . . Taking advantage of the useful aspects of capitalist countries, including their methods of operation and management, does not mean that we will adopt capitalism. Instead, we use those methods in order to develop the productive forces under socialism. As long as learning from capitalism is regarded as no more than a means to an end, it will not change the structure of socialism or bring China back to capitalism.[22]

During the early years of China's reforms, the device of the market (or commodity) economy was adopted as a means of complementing, rather than a substituting for, the plan. For example, the CCP's 1984 Resolution on Economic Reform rather tortuously stated that while China possessed a "planned commodity economy [this was] not the market economy which is completely regulated by the market."[23] This characteristically abstruse party line therefore carried an unintended Polanyian irony. As a principle of economic coordination, markets would be formally subordinated to the logics of the socialist state and to the long-run goals of revolutionary transformation; the market would not rule, it would be embedded within a socialist-state integument.

It follows that state socialism remains a defining feature of the Chinese model, even if the point may have since passed where China can be considered to be functionally socialist, at least in terms of actually existing political-economic structures and priorities.[24] Affirming at least one VoC axiom, China's transformation has been a profoundly path-dependent one, such that its unique experience of "capi-communism" has been jointly constituted not only with "external" forms of globalizing capitalism, but also with a unique state-socialist trajectory, in an extended and reciprocal process of recombination.[25] If there is a fire-and-water quality to this contradictory hybrid, then this perhaps explains how it is that interpretations of contemporary China tend to be so ideologically polarizing. It may be more appropriate to define Chinese capitalism in terms of its long-lasting contradictions, rather than search for some submerged source of logical coherence and through its paradoxical admixtures rather than in terms of some purified essence.[26]

Such a strategy is plainly at odds with the overriding emphasis that is placed, in the VoC literature, on (national) institutional complementarities, on medium-term equilibrium, and on relatively orderly rationalities. Instead, the improbable combination that is socialism and capitalism in China can be seen as simultaneously contradictory and complementary. Its "productivity" very much depends on how the reform process is phased, paced, and channeled and how its attendant contradictions and externalities are managed. This out-of-equilibrium hybrid is clearly on a transformative path of some kind, but this should not be construed as a simple, linear transition from one system to another. "China's economic development has not followed any predetermined economic strategy," McNally has argued, "but might be more appropriately conceptualized as a process of upward spiraling virtuous cycles of induced reforms."[27] Such diachronic and open-ended dynamics are hardly alien to capitalism, of course, which exists in a perpetual state of disequilibrium. If China has been oscillating in the social space somewhere between socialism and capitalism for several decades, how might its shape-shifting position be calibrated? Might it even be improvising a developmental form of its own?

A first cut at these questions must consider the enduring residues of China's socialist formation. According to Szelény, there are three fields in which the socialist legacy is most strongly evident in the contemporary Chinese setting.[28] First, unambiguous private property rights, while conventionally regarded as an essential precondition for capitalist development, are anything but typical in China. In marked contrast to the post-socialist countries of Eastern and Central Europe, where abrupt transfers from public to private ownership were prioritized in the earliest applications of "shock treatment," gradualist China has steadfastly ignored Washington's advice on the question of property rights. Initially, the legally permissible zone of private (and typically foreign) ownership was strictly circumscribed, and reports of "discrimination" against private and corporate interests have been commonplace.[29] Most analysts, with the notable exception of Huang, agree that the *direction* of reform has, however, been toward increasingly privatized and regularized property rights, even as the legal system remains underdeveloped and opaque, as SOEs retain a significant presence, as land and natural resources are not yet privatized, and as both party functionaries and labyrinthine rules (many unwritten) continue to extend significantly into the (sometimes only nominally) "private sector."[30]

Second, the Chinese state retains a massive presence in the national economy, with a reach into increasingly global spheres too, far beyond the question of control over property rights. Extensive bureaucratic and party involvement in corporate governance—the defining feature of Victor Nee's concept of "politicized capitalism"—has been presented as a peculiarly Chinese hybrid, marked by the extensive "overlap of political and economic markets and the absence of clearly defined state-firm boundaries," together with "institutional arrangements patched together in ad hoc improvisations to address the needs and demands arising from rapid market-oriented economic growth."[31] For Naughton, retaining, reinventing, and redistributing patronage resources, partly through state-dominated sectors and state-run corporations, are crucial to the continual survival of the authoritarian regime.[32] Today, the official list of strategic sectors and pillar industries that are monopolized (or at least dominated) by SOEs includes the following: banking; power generation and distribution, oil, coal, petrochemicals, and natural gas; telecommunications; armaments; aviation and shipping; machinery and automobile production; information technologies; construction; railroads; insurance; grain distribution; and the production of iron, steel, and non-ferrous metals.[33] State-owned banks are especially dominant, with economy-wide implications, a situation that recent reforms have done little to change.

Third, the CCP remains a deeply secretive body, sitting outside and above the law, which continues to exercise a far-reaching form of political monopoly.[34] Private entrepreneurs have been welcomed as party members since the inauguration of the "Three Representatives" policy in 2001, an option that approaching half of all CEOs is estimated to have exercised, while in practically every sphere of life the CCP remains "a major force shaping national, local, and firm-level policies and through the *nomenklatura* system, controls appointments to crucial positions even in the business world."[35] For example, after decades of supposedly pro-market reform, the career prospects of SOE executives continue to depend on decisions by the Organization Department of the CCP, which is charged with the task of maintaining party discipline.[36]

If it is impossible, then, to dismiss Chinese socialism as an inert historical force, what can be said about the country's tendential form of capitalism-with-no-name? Notwithstanding the important qualification that received understandings of capitalist development reflect distinctly Eurocentric histories,[37] which of course have strong echoes in the VoC literature itself,[38] the question of the degree of "fit" between capitalism-as-abstraction and the presently existing Chinese conjuncture is clearly a crucial one. One of the most rigorous responses to this question has been provided by Christopher McNally, drawing on the generic model of capitalism elaborated by Heilbroner.[39] The defining features of capitalism, in these terms, are essentially threefold. First, what might be called the Marxian face of capitalism is the driving force of the accumulation process, wherein the profit motive and the extraction of surplus value represent both fundamental dynamics and organizational principles of the system. Here, the picture is uneven, at least spatially. Deng's incremental reforms rested heavily on the principles of devolution and experimentation, opening up selected enclaves for profit-driven accumulation at the local level, often in conjunction with "overseas" Chinese capital and deploying "zoning technologies" like special economic zones (SEZs) as means for trialing new business arrangements and governance models.[40] According to Gallagher, SEZs have served as localized "laboratories for capitalism, introducing new and destabilizing reforms of employment, social welfare and enterprise management."[41] The private-sector contribution to overall economic growth in China has risen markedly over time, to more than 50%–70% of GDP, and the profit-oriented segment of the economy has also been the most dynamic.[42] These logics also permeate the state itself, as SOE executive bonuses are tied to financial performance, while inter-local competition and "GDPism" have each played roles in resource allocation and party advancement.[43]

A second dimension of capitalism, which might be considered its Polanyian face, concerns the rise of the market as the dominant regime of economic coordination and cultural identity. In China, the once-elaborate system of price controls has been almost completely dismantled, enabling market pricing on everything from rice to Rolexes.[44] Exceptions to this general rule are those aforementioned strategic sectors still dominated by SOEs—although market impulses and pressures are increasingly important here too. The most decisive Polanyian move, of course, is the commodification of labor and land. Since 1986, there has been a progressive shift in the direction of labor contracts; a 1988 bankruptcy law terminated the guarantee of lifelong employment, while a 1994 labor law normalized the status of wage labor, partially decoupling welfare from the state, although the socialist *hukou* regime continues to segment the labor market.[45] In a parallel process, Shenzhen's pursuit of foreign investment led to the establishment of an inventive model of quasi-privatized land-use rights, managed under a nominally socialist tenure regime.[46] By separating usage rights from ownership, pragmatic leaders effectively legitimized the transfer of land for commercial uses in the absence of de jure privatization. Furthermore, China seems to be spawning its own version of a "market culture," according to some accounts often more vulgar and unvarnished than its counterparts in the West, but certainly with highly distinctive features.[47]

The third and final dimension of capitalism is its Gramscian face: this concerns the advance of capitalist *class* interests, incorporating yet at the same time exceeding those of the (capitalist) state. Although McNally is generally convinced that "China is generating a form of capitalism," he emphasizes that this is most clearly expressed in the first two of Heilbroner's criteria, the dominance of profit motives and market relations; when it comes to the third, "the bifurcation of secular authority," the situation is considerably more mixed, since pro-capitalist developments are more embryonic.[48] While the Chinese bourgeoisie has acquired some degree of "independent" influence, the extent to which this is meaningfully autonomous from the party-state is highly debatable.[49] In fact, it has been argued that the political power of capital in China remains fundamentally embedded in, and interlaced with, the infrastructure of the party-state and the political tentacles of the CCP.[50] While there has been considerable growth in business associations and chambers of commerce, most of these exist in the shadow of the party-state. Dickson's conclusion is that it "may be more appropriate to see red capitalists as a symptom of changes underway in China, rather than their cause."[51]

If McNally's argument is extended to the question of class structures, however, the story is unequivocal. Perhaps the strongest evidence of China's postsocialist form is the spiraling level of inequality. In the space of a few decades, the Chinese social structure has lurched from one of the world's most egalitarian to one of its most polarized.[52] Deng once reasoned that "[w]e permit some people and some regions to become prosperous first, for the purpose of achieving common prosperity faster. That is why our policy will not lead to polarization, to a situation where the rich get richer while the poor get poorer. [We] shall not permit the emergence of a new bourgeoisie."[53] But decades of market-oriented reforms have indisputably led to the rise of an economic elite, deeply interwoven with the party-state *nomenklatura* system, while the degree of socioeconomic polarization has reached alarming levels.

Socialist-Developmental State or State Neoliberalism?

Some of the most intractable paradoxes of China's monumental economic transformation concern the role of the state, which manages, at the same time, to be a source of near-ubiquitous power and daunting opacity. The apparent success with which the CCP has fabricated a unique style of transformative market-Leninism—balancing the imperatives of globalizing capitalism and the demands of explosive, market-led growth with the maintenance of virtually total political control—has continued to confound academic analysts and political commentators far and wide. Irrespective of whether the VoC framework is embraced or spurned, the regulatory form and orientation of the state remain a key concern. VoC debates sometimes slide into wrongheaded discussions of capitalism with "more or less" of the state—one that the CME/LME polarity may inadvertently sustain, while there are also readings of the notion of "state capitalism" that recycle the red-herring question of the state's absence/presence (as if zero-state capitalisms were something other than a libertarian utopia). On the face of it, China might be located in the Asian family of "strong states,"[54] but its trajectory can hardly be reduced to a (mere) variant of those exhibited, for example, by Japan, Singapore, or South Korea. At issue, clearly, is not the quantitative size or "weight" of the state, but its qualitative form, role, and posture.

An influential line of work in the 1980s portrayed China as an exemplar socialist-developmental state, animated by the failures of Maoism and by the imperatives of political self-preservation, which embraced strategically targeted market measures—not as a preconceived path to capitalism or indeed to neoliberalism,[55] but as a historically unprecedented experiment in socialist modernization. According to White and Wade, instead of

> the classic Soviet-derived perception of the gradual triumph of planned economy over markets, of state over cooperative or individual forms of production, another model of transition has arisen which to some extent returns to Marx's original position that true socialism could only be built on the basis of an advanced commodity economy developed by capitalism. In effect, the reform project envisages a "replay" of the original Marxian analysis of the transition from pre-capitalist modes of production to capitalism to socialism *within a socialist integument* [. . .]. What the reforms represent, at their deepest level, is an attempt to reproduce, within a socialist framework, the social, economic and psychological dynamics advanced commodity production which have been achieved elsewhere within a capitalist framework.[56]

This active, developmentalist posture positioned China as an outlier among the post-socialist "transition" states, since it was not bounced into radical regime change in the context of systemic ideological-institutional rupture or externally administered "shock treatment," as was the case in the Soviet sphere.[57] While in the former Soviet bloc, "reform-economics was [rapidly] replaced by transitology" and the saturating ideology of inevitable (but painful) capitalist modernization, Szelény observes that in "China the reconstruction of economic institutions was not labeled as either transition or transformation [just as] the meaning of reform changed slowly and gradually."[58]

China's socialist developmental-statist path toward capitalism has been negotiated more on its own terms—albeit within the opportunity structure of globalizing capitalism—being typical neither of the post-socialist pattern nor for that matter of the trajectories of the classic developmental states of Asia. The latter were grounded in a productive nexus between technocratic expertise and bureaucratic rationality, exploiting connections between government and leading industrial sectors in the context of an all-consuming (often nationalist) "will to develop."[59] While China's economic development may have been state led, or at least significantly state facilitated, it can hardly be said to have been "plan rational" in the manner of the earlier generation of (Asian) developmental states.[60] Again, it would appear that the Chinese case is "just too different" to be shoehorned into extant state-theoretic categories, as Deans puts it; having rapidly evolved "from a socialist-developmental state into a hybrid system which is no longer socialist but which cannot be properly understood as capitalist either: a post-socialist developmental state."[61] This said, the pattern of China's policymaking practice across its state-dominated strategic and technological sectors—including cultivating national champions, fostering indigenous innovation, and forging national technological leadership through large-scale science and engineering projects, or what Suttmeier and Yao dub "neotechno-nationalism"—bears a resemblance to those pursued by East Asian developmental states.[62] Beyond the narrow concern with the national state and industrial policies in the developmental state literature, China scholars typically call attention to the crucial significance of central-local relations and the wide array of roles assumed by localized state agencies under the guiding influence of the local revenue generation regime. For example, Qian, Weingast, and colleagues have documented the rise of what they term "market-preserving federalism" with Chinese characteristics,[63] arguing that the fiscal decentralization and intergovernmental resource-sharing system introduced in the 1980s effectively bound the center and the provinces into long-term and relatively stable fiscal relations, generating strong (but bounded) incentives for inter-jurisdictional competition at the local level. Likewise, what have been labeled as "promotion tournaments" have pervaded the CCP's *nomenklatura* system, rewarding those local officials most successful in facilitating local economic growth and melding the calculus of the party state with a style of centrally incentivized local entrepreneurialism known as GDPism.[64]

In a similar vein, Xu argues that the Chinese reform and development project is being driven by a regionally decentralized authoritarian (RDA) system, combining political centralization with economic regionalization.[65] On the one hand, centralized political control remains substantial, in that subnational government officials continue to be appointed, evaluated, and disciplined from above. On the other hand, subnational governments effectively manage much of the economy through their multifaceted roles in initiating, negotiating, implementing, diverting, and resisting various reforms, policies, rules, and laws. This style of decentralized governance seems to alleviate the degree of exposure to economy-wide coordination failures resulting from external macroeconomic shocks, while also fostering a decentralized ecology of ongoing institutional experimentation, at least partly insulated from internal political opposition or macroeconomic risks.[66] The RDA system also facilitates the CCP's adaptive rebuilding of the political hierarchy, with promotion opportunities and patronage resources flowing from the top, reciprocated with allegiance and loyalty to the leadership from below.[67] Nevertheless, Xu also points out that China's RDA system is by no means immune from the intrinsic deficiencies of an authoritarian regime, such as the lack of an independent judiciary, rent-seeking behaviors, and indifference to citizens' needs and preferences.[68]

A very particular form of authoritarian decentralization, fusing political and economic interests across the state system, has animated Chinese growth during the reform era. Notable here has been the rise and re-tasking of the TVEs, which were in various analyses taken as emblematic of the Chinese model, in its early 1980s vintage. The developmental enthusiasm of local states was enabled/encouraged by fiscal decentralization, which selectively devolved decision-making power to local governments, tying revenue growth to the career progression of local officials and spawning a unique form of "local state corporatism."[69] TVEs, known as commune and brigade enterprises during the Mao era, were originally managed by local governments, concentrating on the production of fertilizers, iron and steel, agricultural tools, and cement. Redesignated as TVEs during the first decade of the reform era, this sector soon experienced explosive growth, accounting at its peak (in the mid-1990s) for almost one-third of national GDP growth—significantly beyond the initial expectations of central planners.[70] Indeed, Arrighi goes as far as to speculate that "TVEs may well turn out to have played as crucial a role in the Chinese economic ascent as vertically integrated bureaucratically managed corporations did in the US ascent a century earlier."[71] The rapid growth of TVEs occurred effectively outside the state planning process,[72] fortuitously sidestepping the challenge of a big-bang downsizing of the SOE sector, as in the former Soviet bloc, while generating both positive momentum and the financial means for subsequent rounds of reform.

The political and institutional environment favored these "public" enterprises during the early years of reform, since private businesses faced severe restrictions and indeed discrimination in terms of access to resources and favorable regulations. The problem of soft budget constraints was partly sidestepped by virtue of China's massive size, because each township or village would be forced to compete with thousands of counterparts.[73] As local governments rushed to develop their own enterprises, however, regional protectionism resulted in duplication, fomenting serious problems of industrial overcapacity and mounting pressure for restructuring.[74] With rising competition from the urban sector, official discrimination against TVEs and a growing preference for foreign-owned enterprises, the dynamism and profitability of the TVE sector declined markedly after the mid-1990s, causing many enterprises to be privatized or converted into shareholding cooperatives.[75]

Long-running struggles over taxation powers and revenue sharing between Beijing and the provinces eventually resulted in the fiscal reform of 1994, which substantially reduced the subnational government share of national tax revenues, from 70% to 40%, while further decentralizing public-expenditure responsibilities.[76] While augmenting the budgetary and patronage resources of the center, this fiscal reversal made TVEs immediately less attractive as cash cows for local states, but it duly spawned a new form of real-estate developmentalism. Local governments were compensated for revenue losses with new rights over land sales within their jurisdictions, together with monopoly control over the conversion of farmland to commercial uses. As a result, the primary role of local states shifted from that of shareholder of state-owned firms, including TVEs, to that of a land developer and tax collector, competing for mobile private and foreign investment, with the aid of heavily subsidized infrastructure and a broad (but substantially concealed) capacity to strike "deals."[77] According to You-tien Hsing, it was the rise of land rent as a primary source of local capital accumulation and political leverage that inaugurated a far-reaching "urbanization" of the Chinese state: "urban modernity, more than industrial modernity, now captures the political imagination of local state leaders."[78]

This "land-infrastructure-leverage paradigm" rests on a specific kind of institutional complementarity.[79] First, the enduring "socialist" land tenure system, together with the huge gap between land acquisition costs and leasing prices, allowed local governments to exploit lucrative, simultaneous roles as land owner, regulator, planner and developer, capturing windfalls from land conversion and development, typically at the expense of farmers.[80] In the process, land became a key instrument in the interjurisdictional competition for mobile investment and the basis for new "zoning technologies." Second, the windfall land revenues that have become the lifeblood of local public finance were predicated on the renegotiation of central-local fiscal arrangements and the scalar redivision of the tax-and-revenue pie. Third, the demand for massive, upfront financing to defray the initial costs of land requisition and site preparation continues to be met by the half-reformed, state-controlled bank system. Under the current corporate-governance structure, state-dominated banks are predisposed to such "politically safe" deals with SOEs and quasi-governmental agencies, channeling massive capital flows in the direction of ever-more extravagant infrastructure projects. Fourth, the *nomenklatura* system and "promotion tournaments" drive local party-state leaders to propagate development megaprojects, like high-tech parks, enterprise zones, and even "new cities," as visible affirmations of political prowess.[81]

Correspondingly, China's industrial relations "system" is also riddled with contradictions. Authentic forms of labor-union mobilization continue to be suppressed, under the disguise of the nominally socialist ACFTU. The industrial relations regime remains predicated on a regressive and piecemeal welfare system and on the political deprivation of workers, especially the peasantry. The land seized for industrial parks, enterprise zones, and new cities is largely requisitioned from the peasants. The migrating peasantry is the principal labor supply for urban megaprojects, as well as for the fast-growing manufacturing and service sectors of the cities. The socialist *hukou*-cum-land regime renders this "floating" workforce exceptionally vulnerable to workplace exploitation and social discrimination. In the countryside, this same *hukou* system, while offering rudimentary protection against the extremes of deprivation, exposes disenfranchised farmers to the arbitrary power of local officials, developers, and managers.

Heterogeneous local-state configurations and strategies have proliferated in an environment marked by deep (but inherent) contradictions in the country's "transitional" institutional system, the enormous regional disparities that have characterized all stages of the reform process and high levels of devolution, decentralization, and interjurisdictional competition across this unevenly developed, continental-scale economy.[82] In turn, these unevenly developed state structures have been interdigitated with an equally wide array of regionalized varieties of statist capitalism, dirigiste developmentalism, and market socialism.[83] China's vast interregional differences in historical legacies, resource endowments, leadership capacities, and local politics significantly shape both local-state behavior and economic-development models more generally. While localities along the coast have generally enjoyed better circumstances for economic development, reflected in localized state forms like "market-preserving federalism" and "local state corporatism," local states in resource-stressed and more agriculture-based regions have tended toward predation.[84] Saich suggests that there are, in fact, multiple models of state-society relations operating at the same time both within and between administrative jurisdictions, yielding distinctive sociopolitical outcomes.[85] Predatory and developmental state behaviors therefore coexist, even at the local scale.

The combined outcome of these conditions is a Chinese state formation that is not only heterogeneous in form but in some ways both doggedly effective and perpetually on the cusp of crisis.[86] For Howell "what remains of the socialist developmental state is an increasingly isolated central policy elite," confronted by formidable implementation constraints and a range of "fragmenting, eroding and hyper-rivalistic pressures." These pressures "in turn lead to an increasingly complex tapestry of local state formations, exhibiting overlapping and contradictory features of developmentalism and predation; of relative autonomy and clientelism; of efficiency and inefficiency; of regulation and anarchy; of facilitation of and excessive interference in the private sector."[87] Indeed, the Chinese state seems to be moving in several, contradictory directions at the same time, being characterized by Howell as "polymorphous" and by Chu and So as "multiorganizational."[88]

If there has been a successor concept to the (socialist) developmental state, it has been that of neoliberalism, although again this term has been only cautiously deployed by China scholars—often more as a foil than a framework. The best-known account is David Harvey's, where the Chinese case is handled as a contradictory instantiation of globalizing neoliberalism (as a state-assisted project for the restoration of capitalist class rule), shaped by conjunctural opportunism and pervasive inconsistencies: "While there are several aspects of Communist Party policy that were designed to frustrate capitalist class formation, the party has also acceded to the massive proletarianization of China's workforce, the breaking of the 'iron rice bowl,' the evisceration of social protections, the imposition of user fees, the creation of a flexible labour market regime, and the privatization of assets formerly held in common."[89] Alvin So largely affirms Harvey's account, at least for the 1990s. During that time, while spurning unpalatable features of the "neoliberal internationalism" advocated by Washington-Consensus agencies, China was moving decisively toward the deeper neoliberalization of its domestic sphere.[90]

In some respects, this Chinese version/vision of neoliberalism may be even bleaker than its Western counterparts. As Qin has argued, the Chinese population has less welfare than those in LMEs and less freedom than those in CMEs; yet ironically, these very miseries constitute the foundations upon which China has secured its formidable competitiveness in low value-added, labor-intensive activities—what Qin labels the country's "low human rights advantage."[91] But does this represent an evolution from state socialism, through the transitional stage of the socialist-developmental state, to neoliberalism with Chinese characteristics? Not according to Alvin So, who contends that a pattern of development since the late 1990s—prompted by the costs of soaring inequality and by a groundswell of social protests across the country—has led to a series of double movement-like "departures from neoliberalism."[92] These arguments remain controversial, but So seeks to sustain his case by reference to a series of developments: the strengthening of state capacity (and local control) through a more elaborated cadre performance evaluation system and through redistributive tax reforms; a redoubling of Keynesian-style infrastructure spending (which would surge again after the global financial crisis); a renewed emphasis on "harmonious" development, including rural reinvestment and transfers to the "new socialist" countryside; economic upgrading, away from low-road, low-skill, and low-wage production in favor of value adding; the continued subordination, or "dependency," of the capitalist class to the state; the carefully calibrated reconstruction of nationalist sentiments and a steadfast refusal on the part of Beijing to accede to the dictates of international finance capital, manifest in continued restrictions on investment and banking. On these grounds, So draws the conclusion that China has now "moved *beyond* the neoliberal mode and closer to the pattern of state developmentalism in East Asia," a transformation that (characteristically) has been an "adaptive process without a clear blueprint [accomplished through] trial and error, with frequent midcourse corrections and reversals of policy."[93]

The oscillations that China has made between market-led and state-led development and its attendant transformative multiplexity seem repeatedly to frustrate even the most sophisticated attempts at conceptual categorization. As a result, there is increasing resort to what might appear to be openly oxymoronic (not to say willfully contradictory) formulations like "neoliberal developmentalism," and "state neoliberalism," while others prefer to dissent from the trope of neoliberalism altogether.[94] Whether or not "neoliberalism" is the most appropriate way to characterize the coexistence of these evolving state (and party) forms with endemic, uneven, and conflictive processes of deepening marketization will no doubt remain a hotly contested question among Sinologists and comparative political economists. This represents yet another way in which Chinese capitalism is more appropriately defined *through* its dynamic contradictions and certainly not as some static social form or institutional matrix. It displays little functional coherence, either as a socialist-developmental or as a neoliberal state, and neither does it display a tidy transition between the two. Instead, China *combines* contradictory forms.

Guanxi Transnationalism or Power-Elite Capitalism?

The fact that China's market transition was never technocratically prescribed from the center, according to some fixed developmental blueprint, nor was it unilaterally imposed from outside, Washington-Consensus style, but instead progressed, in Deng's memorable phrase, by "feeling for stones," seems also to have proved to be fortuitous in the longer run—at least for economic growth. Crucially, it has meant that endogenous state capacities and centralized party control have been maintained through China's developmental transformation. In contrast with other post-socialist states, China has not had to contend with shock treatment or systemic institutional failure; it has preserved formidable powers in the "steering" and sequencing of the reform process, while propagating a diverse ecosystem of subnational economic-governance regimes through orchestrated experimentation. In this socialist market economy, the state's hand is nearly always visible (or failing that, palpable), sometimes "guiding" and sometimes "grabbing."[95]

This gradualist transformation was initially enabled by the presence of "offshore" cells of Chinese capitalism, notably in Hong Kong and Taiwan, prior to the reform era.[96] The Chinese party-state therefore had hands to hold as it felt for stones. The reform process was initiated by a business-like marriage of convenience between the CCP and overseas networks of *guanxi* capitalists, which has been enormously profitable for both parties.[97] Between 1982 and 1994, Hong Kong and Taiwan investors contributed more than 70% of the $107.4 billion total of realized foreign capital inflows to China.[98] The subsequent proliferation of diasporic networks enabled what Arrighi portrays as a "matchmaker" function, a historic "encounter of foreign capital and Chinese labor, entrepreneurs and government officials."[99] In this respect, the (re)formation of Chinese capitalism was a cross-border and in some senses extraterritorial phenomenon from the start, as diasporic capital exploited a range of localized (and liberalized) openings, mostly in coastal enclaves, subsequently to spawn not so much transplanted replicas of Hong Kong, Taiwanese, or Singaporean capitalism,[100] but substantially new hybrids of state-facilitated, "insourced" capitalism—actively predicated on the exploitation of massive and highly disciplined internal labor reserves by "repatriated" Chinese capital. The availability of preexisting kinship and friendship relations and the exercise of reciprocal gift exchanges played a key role in enabling and facilitating these investments,[101] lubricated by government appeals to the latent loyalties of émigrés.

The conspicuous role played by overseas Chinese capitalists has prompted some to resume the search for a cultural essence of Chinese capitalism, grounded in supposedly transcendent values and common practices (as opposed to structural capacities and conjunctural conditions). Some formulations of *guanxi* (or family-kinship) capitalism have been fashioned in these terms, and they are echoed in Jacques's reading of China as a culturally distinct "civilization-state."[102] Whyte believes that familialism and kinship loyalty constitute the social roots of a geographically unique economic-development model, perhaps the most important distinguishing factor between the successful Chinese reform project and the protracted problems of its Soviet counterpart.[103] He goes on to wryly observe, however, that many of the same cultural traits that were once portrayed as obstacles to development (such as enduring kinship ties; the embrace of non-scientific rationalities; and reverence for tradition, stability, and harmony) have since been rediscovered, in revisionist histories of the Chinese-capitalist present, as supposed secrets of growth.[104]

The emphasis that is placed, in VoC scholarship, on formal state structures and institutional logics, almost exclusively at the national scale, is ill-suited to the challenge of understanding the complex, multi-scalar, and deeply networked constitution of political-economic power in China. Endogenous institutional capacities at the national scale certainly have a role here, but it is crucial also to attend to those diverse "relationalities" that exceed this singular frame, for example between those onshore and offshore Chinese capitalisms marked by mutual dependency; between those more liberal and more coordinated regional models that exist within China, not as islands but as conjunctures within a wider pattern of uneven spatial development and between local economic-development strategies on the one hand and the shifting matrix of opportunities/constraints presented by globalizing supply networks and overseas markets on the other. Perhaps most notably, among these relational characteristics, is what many consider to be the essence of Chinese relationality, the distinctive network capacities of *guanxi* capitalism.[105] These are difficult, if not impossible, to explain according to the monochrome distinction between market and coordinated relations, since they are different in kind.

In fact, several varieties of "network capitalism," which draw in various ways on long-term, reciprocal relations between kinship groups, have been identified in Asia; although it should be noted that networks barely figure in Amable's seriously underdeveloped construction of the "Asian variety of capitalism."[106] For McNally, Wenzhou City represents the "quintessential capital" of this pattern of development, where the density of network ties across small, family enterprises has been such as to generate an economically functional form of social capital, propelling an almost entirely private network of family enterprises into the realm of world markets and globalized supply chains.[107]

Proponents of network capitalism maintain that, in an environment characterized by weak legal infrastructures, limited property-rights protections, deficient capital-market structures, and extreme institutional uncertainty (none of which, it should be noted, are conditions remotely typical of mainstream varieties of capitalism), social-network ties have effectively filled some of the attendant institutional voids, working around some of the obstacles of the old command system in making critical information, resources, and opportunities accessible to firms and entrepreneurs.[108] Significantly, however, these same culturally charged social-network ties have also been instrumental in the development of a more malign pattern of reciprocal exchange between commercial wealth with bureaucratic power in the post-Mao economy, between private entrepreneurs and state cadres. This combination of concentrated power and weak accountability has meant that party officials at all levels have been in a unique position to parlay professional relationships and personal connections into financial gain. The rampant commodification and capitalization of political power, manifest in the growth of power-for-money deals among elites, has fueled a form of "power-elite capitalism" or "crony communism," according to some observers.[109]

Systemic conditions of distorted public-private reciprocity have also transformed many SOEs into de facto fiefdoms.[110] Members of this unique "state capitalist class" tend to be both consummate party insiders *and* avid readers of the Chinese edition of the *Harvard Business Review*. State cadres and a new breed of "red capitalists" (former party and government officials who defected into private business, *xiahai*, often following the "insider privatization" of SOEs), have been (ab)using their connections to convert political privilege into economic wealth.[111] Capitalizing on personal and familial ties, many such cadres (along with their kin and protégés) have succeeded in amassing private fortunes, morphing into what has been characterized as a first-generation "cadre-capitalist class."[112] The so-called princeling party, comprising the children and grandchildren of China's revolutionaries, continue to dominate the country's political and economic markets.[113] This other face of *guanxi* yields significant and continuing distributional consequences, while also shaping China's distinctive class structure, as disparities grow between those "inside" and "outside" the system of party-state favors.

The political foundations of China's power-elite capitalism are also rooted in the *nomenklatura* cadre management system. This weaves formal hierarchies with *guanxi* networks, vesting in so-called commanders-in-chief (*yibashou*) enormous discretionary power—to appoint lower-level state officials and

SOE managers and to approve projects or contracts—with very little external scrutiny.[114] For example, land development across China has become a key instrument of discretion for local cadres, enabling the construction of durable political coalitions, while enriching friends and relatives, through the manipulation of lucrative business opportunities.[115] This, in turn, has become a major force behind the maintenance of high property prices, fueling the country's extended construction boom. According to Wang, economic inequalities are further stretched by related flows of unreported, hidden or "gray" income (amounting to 30% of China's GDP), which primarily accrues to the wealthiest decile of urban households in the form of bribes, kickbacks, and other monopolistic rents associated with *guanxi*-mediated land and financial deals and other abuses of state power.[116]

Economic growth, rather than facilitating the emergence of democracy, has instead spawned exclusionary networks of vested interests, based on patronage, co-optation, and the appropriation of economic resources.[117] This is neither a desirable nor a stable configuration. The disproportionate enrichment of those with privileged backgrounds and connections, coupled with flagrant acts of political repression directed at dissenters, has not only been disincentivizing productivity-enhancing innovations but is fueling widespread resentment on the part of deprived workers and farmers.[118] It may be that, on balance, the political incentive structure confronting Chinese citizens continues to favor the maintenance of authoritarian rule, as long as economic growth can be sustained.[119] Yet the fact that government spending on internal security (policing and domestic surveillance) has exceeded the size of the country's defense budget calls attention to the costs and challenges of "stability maintenance."[120] The persistence of power-elite capitalism has nevertheless been facilitated, so far, by its decentralized and diffuse form and its expansive web of beneficiaries, in a manner that echoes the mode of reproduction of Chinese-style decentralized authoritarianism.[121] Its symbiotic nature creates a strong, self-perpetuating tendency, as the parties capture mutual gains; meanwhile, incentives to challenge the rules of the game are generally weak. The regime's success in co-opting the population in one historical period, however, does not preclude quite different outcomes in subsequent phases, the seemingly "fixed, fast-frozen relations" of the society may prove to be more transitory and fragile than is commonly assumed.[122]

The pervasiveness of *guanxi* ties in structuring exchange relations in China's burgeoning political-economy affirms the Polanyian lesson that the many faces of reciprocity are more than mere vestiges of primitive societies. Personal and particularistic connections, coupled with informal norms governing trust and authority relations, are crucial in all economies, especially in situations where trust- and contract-guaranteeing formal institutions are weak or unreliable.[123] These irreducibly social relations may sometimes substitute for, but can also hinder the growth of, those exchange relationships normally governed by formal procedures and institutions. Richard Whitley, in his discussion of capitalist variety beyond the West, has highlighted the analytical importance of the overall cohesion, prestige, and autonomy of the state executive and bureaucracy and its "strength" vis-à-vis social-interest groups and economic elites.[124] From this perspective, it must be concluded that China's mode of networked, power-elite capitalism marries prodigious capacities with potentially fatal flaws. In this, as in other spheres, its achievements in economic development and growth have been secured in the face of deeply contradictory circumstances.

Apparently, the merits and demerits of China's gradualist transformation represent two sides of the same coin. The gradualist transformation, pragmatically managed by the old regime, conferred overwhelming advantages on the ruling elites relative to potential sources of opposition. As political and economic power fused ever more deeply, party elites would come to read any opening up of the political system as a threat to their accumulating privileges and benefits,[125] effectively reinforcing the primary circuits of power. While political monopoly affords party elites tremendous advantages in the rapid mobilization of resources and policy capacities for favored projects, the unseemly mélange of GDPism, rent-seeking, corruption, and unchecked tendencies for overproduction represent ever-present threats to whatever "integrity" this system possesses. As the sustainability of the China model has been called into question, not least due to the juxtaposition of market bubbles, audacious cronyism, and suppressed dissent, there are many who are beginning to wonder whether the elite-based ruling coalition that has—so far—managed this unprecedented marriage of a single-party Leninist state and an escalating program of market reforms can keep all of the plates spinning. Should they stop, the interdependencies of the global system are such that the reverberations will certainly overspill far beyond this unparalleled new "variety" of capitalism.

Conclusion: Karl Polanyi in Beijing

The question of contemporary China's transformation, it has been suggested here, presents a formidable challenge to extant theories of capitalist development, growth, and variety. Rising to global prominence largely outside the field of visibility defined by the VoC literature, the Chinese case in many ways echoes the earlier, category-contesting ascendancy of Japanese capitalism, located as it was in a distinctly "offshore" position relative to the regulation-theoretic heartlands of Atlantic Fordism.[126] If the awkward formulation of "state capitalism" reveals anything, it is that the recombinant Chinese state, which somehow holds together an unlikely marriage of entrepreneurial developmentalism with Leninist party discipline, remains the principal orchestrator of the country's development path.

If this is indeed a "model," it is a complex and heterogeneous one, and one that is maybe better appreciated by way of its paradoxes and contradictions than by reference to some singular logic or form of institutionalized equilibrium. China's internal heterogeneity and its profoundly constitutive, mutual relations with other capitalisms, far and near,[127] speak to the futility of searches for an "essential" form of institutional-cum-macroeconomic coherence at the national scale. Its idiosyncratic "socialist market economy," moreover, is quite clearly an "instituted" market, to invoke another Polanyian concept,[128] and it is one with few peers, even among the near-relatives of the post-socialist and developmental states. The role of a comparative methodology, in this context, is not to grant "exceptional" status willy-nilly, but instead to position such cases in relation to their others.[129] Chinese capitalism may indeed display a "hybrid" or "alloyed" form, but some of its constitutive elements (like *guanxi*) are absent from the mainstream varieties of capitalism. This, however, is no excuse for atheoretical, case-by-case explanation: there is much to be gained, in explanatory terms, from placing capitalisms among their others—even, or perhaps *especially*, the rogue cases. This stands as a challenge radically to rethink received readings of "variety," to continue to extend the registers of the Polanyi project of comparative economy, and to position both anomalies and affirmative cases within a reflexive and relational explanatory frame. This is one of the promises of variegated-capitalism approaches.

Crucially, these theorizations of capitalism must remain in a state of reconstruction, always being available for empirical "stress-testing."[130] This implies that a special place is reserved for ostensibly discrepant or disruptive cases in particular and for economic-*geographical* investigations more generally. Some degree of common cause (or critical dialogue) might be forged with VoC scholars here. The Chinese experience can be seen to affirm at least one of the central tenets of VoC scholarship, concerning the entrenched nature of institutional path-dependence, even if it does so in a way that overflows the usual tolerances of VoC analysis. The path dependencies of the Chinese case plainly transcend capitalism itself. The success of post-1978 reforms was partly predicated on prior achievements in social development under Mao, while even the excesses of the Cultural Revolution generated spaces of political opportunity for reform elements in the CCP—to experiment with, rather than hold doggedly onto, Maoist-Leninist doctrines.[131] This is not, however, to simplistically glorify or demonize China's socialist past: during the Maoist era, the state effectively stripped the underprivileged of their political agency, under the sign of socialism.[132] The peasantry was sacrificed by Mao to support the country's historic urban-industrial catch-up, thereby institutionalizing an urban-rural divide that to this day is profoundly constitutive of the unevenly developed Chinese "model."[133] This comprises more than an array of subvarieties of capitalism, since the islands of dynamic development in China remain in a sea of relative underdevelopment.[134]

One of the many paradoxes of China's distinctive development path—even as it has become increasingly engaged with capitalist logics in general and by the imperatives of neoliberal globalism in particular—is that the origins, the productivity, and possibly even the sustainability of its "model" must be understood to be substantially anchored in its state-socialist past. Furthermore, the Chinese experience raises the question of whether it is possible for some (socialist) states to engage selectively with capitalist development, rather than buy the full "package."[135] As Michael Burawoy has argued:

> Today, in China, markets are ... creating a dynamic if unstable society, leading in as yet unclear directions—a new form of socialism, or more likely a new form of capitalism (state capitalism)? This reflects China's specific strategy of transition in which markets were incubated by the party state—so different from Russia's strategy of shock therapy. Indeed, one might say that Russia replicated the Bolshevik strategy of War of Movement, which aimed to destroy the old socialist order as the precondition for the spontaneous growth of a new capitalist order. The Chinese strategy, on the other hand, has been a War of Position from above, a passive revolution—transformation as a way to avoid revolution.[136]

Given the soaring economic inequalities and undercurrents of social unrest that are characteristic of contemporary China, however, whether it is a revolution avoided or just delayed, must remain a radically open question. Nevertheless, Burawoy's inventive melding of Gramscian and Polanyian concepts here can be seen as a necessary corrective to the relatively narrow analytical bandwidth of more conventional VoC approaches and the constrained institutionalism that this has engendered. It also calls to mind Arrighi's provocative reinterpretation of Chinese economic development in *Adam Smith in Beijing*.

It could be said, instead, that Karl Polanyi may be more urgently needed in Beijing. It may be going too far to conclude, as some neoPolanyian readings of contemporary China have been doing, that the country's "reform variant" should be seen as a stalwart member of the dwindling family of "embedded socialisms," or that the country's turn to sociospatial redistribution represents a historic "double movement" in the direction of social re-embedding,[137] but on the other hand the Chinese case certainly does call to mind the injunctions of Polanyi-the-comparative-economist.[138] What if, instead of positioning the principle of market coordination in a *sequential and historical* relationship with social regulation and institutional embeddedness, in a temporal reading of the double-movement metaphor (as if marketization and socialization only see-saw against one another, in a zero-sun fashion, through time), this was replaced with a *simultaneous and geographical* conception of the contradictory coexistence of the integrative principles of market exchange, reciprocity, and redistribution within fundamentally heterogeneous economies? This conception, in which variegated capitalisms necessarily (co)exist with their others, in contradictory and often crisis-prone hybrids and in webs of mutually constitutive relations, might enable a critical but theoretically "positive" understanding of China's development path. Rather than flatten out this model's Janus-faced complexities, contradictions, and countertendencies, different kinds of explanations might be generated by confronting these disjunctures more directly.

It is insufficient simply to "add" China to the existing catalogue of VoC cases, as if these were merely self-contained, mostly independent systems engaged in "pacific" forms of lateral competition,[139] because they each represent conjunctural locations within an unevenly developed global system. If nothing else, China's globally proportioned square-peg case has rightly earned the status of exhibit A in a far-reaching reconsideration of the singular development blueprint associated with the Washington Consensus,[140] though arguably more as a negative lesson or corrective, than as a source of unambiguous, "positive" alternatives. At the very least, it can be said that the distinctiveness of China's transformation conclusively demonstrates that "there is no single development strategy or set of institutions that have to be adopted everywhere to foster" economic growth.[141] China's mode of residually socialist market-developmental statism might be considered to be not so much an alternative *to* market rule but rather an alternative modality *of* market rule. And like all forms of marketization, it is prone to overreach, to overflow, and to overheat, since marketization defines a direction, not a destination. Whether this ultimately takes us back into, or beyond, the Polanyian territory of transnationally scaled double-movement style crises must remain to be seen.

7
Mapping Economies
Substantivism in Space

I can remember, quite vividly, the first time that I encountered Karl Polanyi's distinctive approach to (socio)economics. It was as a graduate student trying to find a footing, with an emergent project on the state and (local) labor markets. Early on, I had been disabused of the notion that there was any constructive bridge to be built to mainstream labor economics. At the same time, though, it also seemed to be the case that geographers had little to say on the subject of labor markets, beyond arid discussions of travel-to-work patterns and commuting sheds, where workers became data points while homes and workplaces were rendered as little more than trip nodes.[1] This sense of disorientation changed when I read Claus Offe's *Disorganized Capitalism*,[2] in part for its own productive take on work, welfare, and capitalist transformation, but in larger measure due to the extensive discussion of (and debt to) Polanyi in the book. I was prompted to read *The Great Transformation* not long after and remember finding it provocative and suggestive, if somewhat difficult to digest (let alone "apply").[3] Had it not been for Offe's "introduction" (a notable contribution to the secondary literature on Polanyi which would remain rather sparse until quite recently), I am not sure that I would have had much idea what to "do" with Polanyi, beyond referencing the obvious takeaways about fictitious commodities, double movements, and embeddedness. "Doing" this kind of thing seemed like a very tall order. Polanyi seemed to be doing his own thing, and it was a thing that had drifted in and out of visibility in the critical social sciences in the decades since the publication of *The Great Transformation*, his magnum opus, in 1944 and the author's death twenty years later. With enough exceptions to just about prove the rule, it had remained mostly on the margins, an idiosyncratic outlier.

This state of affairs did not change all that much until the early 1990s, by which time Polanyi had become a talismanic figure for the (new) economic sociology (despite often being read, via Granovetter, in rather restrictive, microsociological terms). Polanyi would also be a touchstone for the literatures on varieties of capitalism and developmental states, as well as for (some) second-wave regulation theorists and world-systems scholars.[4] Across this somewhat scattered and uneven pattern of take-up and influence, something of a divide was evident between those who chose to read Polanyi with or against Marx, and in dialogue with Marxism or as an alternative project, but for the most part the invocations were positive and constructive, if far from singular or consistent. In some respects, these different readings reflected the fecund and multidimensional character of Polanyian socioeconomics, but they also spoke to some of its ambiguities (if not contradictions).

Polanyi's presence in geography echoed several of these different readings, although in some respects it was more liminal still. Largely forgotten is the fact that David Harvey drew rather significantly on Polanyi for important sections of his *Social Justice in the City* (where he found the notion of modes of economic regulation to be a useful supplement to the Marxian concept of modes of production), perhaps because this particular trail then went cold, not to be picked up again in any significant way until his *Brief History of Neoliberalism*, three decades later, when Polanyi returned as the original critic of free-market fundamentalism.[5] Yet if Harvey's early 1970s reading of Polanyi was countercultural, the same could not be said of his millennial revisit, since following the reissue of *The Great Transformation* in 2001 (with a new foreword by Joseph Stiglitz), the book had found its widest audience ever, as something approaching an urtext for the anti-globalization movement, from Seattle to Porto Alegre and beyond. In between these two engagements, three decades apart, Polanyi appeared as a different kind of presence in economic geography, particularly during the 1990s, in the form of two principal currents. One of these was more sociological, tracking into an influential body of work on nodes, networks, and embeddedness.[6] The other was framed around questions of institutional political economy, centering on the (de)regulatory development of neoliberalism.[7] This having been said, perhaps reflecting the magpie propensities of economic geography, it was unusual for discussions of Polanyi (and explicitly Polanyian approaches) to extend beyond a handful of pages, or the occasional reference to the concept of embeddedness, in the vast majority of cases, reflecting a pattern of citational engagement that may have been relatively wide and in some ways persistent but, with a few notable exceptions, not especially deep.[8]

To be clear, though, somewhat fickle engagements with Polanyi are by no means the exclusive preserve of geographers; this might be closer to the norm in the social sciences. At least some of the reason for this, it logically follows, lies on the supply side, and with the author rather than the audience. Polanyi's, after all, was anything but a conventional academic career, being defined by a succession of displacements (institutional, geographical, and professional). On the positive side, this conferred an organic quality to his conjunctural theorizing, which was practiced on (or across) a momentously moving terrain, with a keen eye for the deep play of historical events and shifting circumstances. Less positively, in both style and purpose, Polanyi's research and writing program was an unsettled, staccato, and incomplete one, at times lucid and remarkably incisive, but also sometimes wayward and cryptic. Indeed, as two of his foremost interpreters, Fred Block and Peggy Somers, have remarked, "understanding Polanyi's arguments calls for significant interpretive work."[9] Something similar can be said about Polanyi's methodology, only perhaps more so. Seen in this light, it is anything but surprising to find that Polanyi tends to be read selectively and somewhat instrumentally. This was not, for all its other strengths, a systemic or neatly cumulative corpus. Reading across it does indeed require a significant interpretive effort, often with results that are anything but convergent or conclusive.

This chapter is also interpretive and instrumental in its own way, but it is less concerned with the pursuit of some "correct" or fixed reading of Polanyi, or with ironing out inconsistencies and ambiguities, than with an attempt to read the project as a whole for its methodological purpose *and potential*. And it does so with a more explicit goal in mind, too, of exploring the complementarities between Polanyian socioeconomics and economic geography (and more specifically, geographical political economy).[10] It is not too much of an exaggeration to say that the two fields-cum-projects share the same objects of inquiry—culturally inflected, institutionally mediated, politically governed, socially embedded, and heterogeneous economies, understood in the plural. They have recourse, moreover, to an overlapping methodological repertoire, generally favoring the qualitative analysis of grounded and contextualized economic formations. And they might both be said to be engaged in "the search for general principles of economic organization in our world," as Hann and Hart have put it, given "the need to explain not only the common form, but also its infinite variation."[11] True, in (neo)Polanyian hands, "variation" tends to be associated with a much wider ambit of socioeconomic difference than has typically been the case in contemporary economic geography, running as it has done from Ancient Babylon through rural Java to Wall Street. This said, in their somewhat different ways, geographical political economists and Polanyians are concerned with a shared problematic—that of situating, contextualizing, and *placing* economies.[12]

But this can also be seen as one of the ways in which a constructive (re)engagement with the Polanyian project—in all its breadth, complexity, and only partially realized potential—might be a spur to methodological innovation in and around economic geography. Anticipating some of the conclusions of the chapter, a number of axiomatic principles might be associated with specifically Polanyian economic geographies. First, they demand a more forthright commitment to historical and comparative analysis, reanimating the lost heterodox project of "comparative economy." Second, they seek to interrogate and stretch registers of difference *within* local economies, across what Polanyi called modes of integration, like exchange and reciprocity, exploring not only their distinctive logics, but their intersections, interactions, contradictions, and complementarities as well. Third, they are institutionalist all the way down, being skeptical of economic reductionism in all its forms, exposing social constructions and institutionalized patterns, while seeking to enrich the political imaginary through the exploration of alternative socioeconomic arrangements. And, fourth, they explicitly confront, and work with, the tensions between holistic, integral modes of analysis and those difference-finding methodologies that yield exceptional or disruptive cases (rather than rendering these as somehow irreconcilable approaches).

Exploring how substantivist economic geography might be specified, as a reflexive methodology, rather than a fixed framework or template, this chapter proceeds in two steps. The first section positions Polanyi, calling attention to the social and intellectual context of his work. Given that Polanyi's was a life of dislocations, it was almost inevitable that the programmatic potential of his intellectual and political endeavors would never be fully realized; hence the need to understand what remains an emergent methodological framework in the context of its constrained production. Next, the chapter turns to a (re)reading of the Polanyian legacy, positively and purposively, with an eye to its methodological potential for geographical political economy and economic geography. Here, four methodological principles are considered—substantivism, variegation, dialectics, and comparativism—each opening up opportunities for the extension and elaboration of that practice. Admittedly, these are hardly available in off-the-shelf form; instead, they emerge from a relatively forgiving assessment of Polanyi's project of substantivist economics, read for its capacity for catalyzing methodological productivity gains. The chapter concludes with a comment on the distinctiveness and potential of substantivist economic geographies.

Man Out of Time

Those that have attempted to detach the Polanyian method from the context of its production have invariably been frustrated. In practice, the derivation and application of Polanyi's central concepts and modes of analysis are difficult, if not impossible, to separate from their author's mostly extra-disciplinary, transnational biography. They are embodied practices, forged in the course of a life profoundly shaped by the tectonic twentieth-century movements of fascism, liberal capitalism, state socialism, and cold warfare. They were produced by a restless polymath who always "defie[d] academic pigeon-holing," one who improvised a career out of less-than-freely chosen transitions between political journalism, workers' education, academic instruction, and even a little poetry.[13] There is some irony in the fact that the symbolic father of embeddedness (to invoke one such occasionally misappropriated concept) should have led such a disembedded life, displaced from Vienna, and the "functional socialism" that was his lifelong inspiration, to liminal existences forged between England, Canada, and the United States. Polanyi's was a life and a "pattern of thought," as his daughter once recalled, persistently positioned "against the stream."[14]

The achievements of Red Vienna, the Russian revolution, and early twentieth-century failures of liberal capitalism together constituted the "mainspring" of Polanyi's life and thought,[15] his subsequent work in journalism providing critical, real-time interpretations of the always emergent present, including the wavering fortunes of British socialism, the rollout of the New Deal in the United States, and the descent into fascism and war in Europe. Polanyi's writings from the turbulent 1930s served as the working notes for *The Great Transformation*, while also reflecting a tension characteristic of all his work, "between a certain utopianism and an acute sensitivity to the actual historical and political context."[16] Polanyi saw historically reflexive opportunities in the crises of his times (which he would style in terms of "double movements"), especially once the manifest inability of orthodox economics to explain or contain the great economic dislocations of the interwar years "opened the field to eclectic searches in comparative economics for new doctrines."[17] These eclectic searches continued to animate Polanyi's work during and after the Second World War, along with his evolving analytical framework, yet they too would remain somewhat idiosyncratic creatures of context.

Polanyi lived out the final years of his life in North America, in an environment decidedly "less liberal" than his previous existence in Europe.[18] Teaching economic history at Columbia University in New York, he commuted from a modest house in rural Ontario, due to the intolerance, south of the border, of his wife's communist party associations.[19] Working (appropriately) as a *visiting* professor of economics, but engaging extensively with anthropological materials, Polanyi cut his own postdisciplinary path. Along with a coterie of junior collaborators, he spearheaded a Ford Foundation project on "economic aspects of institutional growth," the ambitious goal of which was a cross-cultural, historical analysis of the "place of economy" in a wide range of social systems, from Ancient Greece to more contemporary, but usually non-Western or "tribal" societies.[20] Conspicuously absent in the research program of the postwar Polanyi, especially for one whose previous work—both as a journalist and in the luminous pages of *The Great Transformation*—pivoted so powerfully around the critique of liberal capitalism, was any serious engagement with the advanced capitalist economies of the time. Fatefully, many (mis)took this to mean that Polanyian concepts such as embeddedness, substantivism, instituted economy, and non-market forms of economic integration like reciprocity and redistribution, applied only to antique, non-Western, or "primitive" economies. Yet more pernicious was the flipside implication: that the apparatus of formal economics could suffice for the capitalist, liberal-market economies.

Polanyi was skeptical of formal economic theorizing, derived only from the "logical character of the means-ends relationship" and the singular problem of choice under scarcity, opting instead for what he portrayed as a substantivist alternative: grounded in a more ecosocial understanding of the economic, rooted in "man's [sic] dependence for his livelihood upon nature and his fellows," this proceeded from the contention that "[p]rocess and institutions together form the economy."[21] Born under constrained circumstances, the potential of the substantivist alternative was never fully realized. The debate over formalist (or neoclassical) versus substantivist (or realist-institutionalist) approaches to economic analysis, which Polanyi triggered, would be largely conducted in defensive terms, on the terrain of the premodern economy, soon being reduced to a forlorn objection to neoclassical imperialism, whispered from the (geographical) margins.[22] Analytically, Polanyi's postwar project ended up provincializing itself, while barely disrupting the dominant project of neoclassical universalism.[23] Affinities with radical critiques of modern, market economies, especially Marxian ones, were left untended by Polanyi, only to be more actively spurned by his immediate successors, who themselves would be attacked from some Marxist positions in the 1970s. In the space nominally reserved for Polanyian analyses of the modern, market economies of the 1950s and 1960s, there had been mostly silence.

Why did Polanyi himself apparently stop short of applying his pancultural analytical schema to a radical critique of *contemporary* capitalism? Rhoda Halperin's explanation is persuasive, if circumstantial and for some still controversial. Holding to the view that the Polanyian apparatus must not be sequestered either geographically (as if the toolkit were designed only for pre-capitalist economies), or epistemologically (as a mode of analysis distinct from other forms of radical heterodoxy, especially Marxism), Halperin's explanation for the blindspots in Polanyi's postwar research program, and indeed for the obtuseness of so much of his writing in the 1950s, is traced to the ideological climate of McCarthyism:

> Polanyi was extremely careful to avoid the terms capitalist, precapitalist, and noncapitalist in his post-1950 writing. He systematically substituted the word market for capitalist. [His advocacy of substantive over formal methods of economic analysis] was interpreted to mean that Polanyi was merely objecting to conventional economic analysis on the grounds that it is ethnocentric in its imposition of particularistic, market concepts and categories upon precapitalist economies. Indeed, Polanyi objected to the imposition of the "market shape of things" upon essentially nonmarket economies. However, Polanyi's was not a simple rejection of capitalistic analytical categories. The aim of the rejection was twofold: (1) to mask his critique of capitalism per se; and (2) to continue his cross-cultural analysis of human economies. [Hence the] critique of capitalism appears in Polanyi's [postwar] writing primarily as a critique of economic concepts.[24]

As a result, it is hardly an accident that the postwar, analytical Polanyi is a much more "difficult read" than the prewar, polemical Polanyi; after *The Great Transformation*, he had learned to write "in a sort of code, so as to avoid any association with Marx during the 1950s," gripped by a visceral awareness that he was "walk[ing] on political eggshells."[25] Lewis Coser, who counted Polanyi among the foremost intellectual "refugees" in the United States, likewise observed that the "witch-hunting atmosphere during the Cold War" had consigned him to a life "perpetually in transit" between New York and his home in Canada; by the 1950s, the "instinct for the jugular" that had been revealed in *The Great Transformation*'s radical reinterpretation of the Industrial Revolution, the hearth both of free-market capitalism and classical economics, had been subsumed beneath a more cryptic and circumspect style of engagement.[26]

Polanyi's "masked" critique of contemporary capitalism, Halperin went on to explain, obscured both his continuing commitment to socialism and his complex affinities to, and differences with, Marxism.[27] For a time, however, these claims of Marxian affinities and complementarities in Polanyi's "humanistic" economics were controversial and divisive arguments, not least because Polanyi's leading disciple, George Dalton, fought a rearguard action against them for the remainder of his career—to the extent of allegedly suppressing the publication of Halperin's exposé for nine years.[28] To be sure, Polanyian substantivism had been subjected to some robust Marxist critiques in the 1970s, no doubt stiffening Dalton's resolve that these were "rival" theories.[29] Barry Isaac concludes, however, that Polanyi would have been "deeply shocked" at the self-administered methodological exile of the Dalton group, long after the McCarthyite moment had passed, since his programmatic goal had been to establish "a truly universal framework for comparative economics."[30] As Gareth Dale has recorded, Polanyi's wife and daughter were shocked too; the man that they knew was not one for reformist bromides, and neither was he inclined to strike a Cold War pact with neoclassical economics, especially if that ceded the analysis of economies of the "free world" to Milton Friedman and the Chicagoans.[31]

For Fred Block, the more expansive Polanyian framework finds its ultimate, if still subdued, methodological expression in the notion of the "always embedded economy," one that he associates with an alleged trimming away from (at least orthodox) Marxism, more or less from the second half of *The Great Transformation* through to the end of his life.[32] But this post-Marxist reading of Polanyi is mainly extrapolated from his principled rejection of economic determinism, crude materialism, teleology, and automatism—perhaps a receipt for the rejection of vulgar structuralism, but hardly a cause for estrangement from all forms of (neo)Marxian theory.[33]

Taking a different tack, Michael Burawoy enlists Polanyi and Gramsci as co-progenitors of a sociological Marxism. This reconstituted mode of political economy is based not on a historical stage model of capitalism, but on the problematization of those deeply variegated, relationally interpenetrated economic formations that have become characteristic of the sprawling complex of global capitalism and its (actual and potential) others:

> Sociological Marxism dispenses with historical materialism—laws of motion of individual modes of production and the linear succession of one mode of production after another—and replaces them with the coexistence of multiple capitalisms and emergent socialisms within a singular world economy.[34]

It may be true that, in his later years, Polanyi's "prophetic voice . . . gave way to more innocuous academic propositions,"[35] but this need not be taken as a refutation of the radical potential of his approach. Perhaps Polanyi can be forgiven for thinking, in his retirement and after the long freeze of McCarthyism had finally begun to thaw, that the prospect of a Hayekian restoration of free-market economics was not only a distant but a receding one.[36] His view was that, "[a]side from [Senator Barry] Goldwater and his followers [there was] no serious concern . . . that the steady departure from the unregulated market system" across the advanced capitalist countries would be disrupted by a pro-market political resurgence.[37] At the time of Polanyi's death, in 1964, it may indeed have appeared that the flow of history had belatedly vindicated his wartime prognostications, rendering redundant those Hayekian dreams of a free-market counterrevolution, such that the world had at last "caught up" with the displaced Hungarian.[38] Ideologically, the economic world of the early 1960s was rudely multipolar (though maybe bipolar), while even the most dynamic capitalist economies were quite unapologetically "mixed."

Paradoxically, it was the rise of neoliberalism that afforded the Polanyian legacy a new but unwanted relevance, albeit (initially) as a source of antimarket polemics, rather than as a methodological rubric for a substantivist mode of comparative political economy. And while it may be true that the "anti-capitalist edge in Polanyi's work," best represented by his trenchant critique of laissez-faire capitalism's Satanic Mill in nineteenth-century England, had been rather "blunted by his belief, most apparent in his postwar writings, that its iniquities [could] be overcome through institutional reform,"[39] his most abiding convictions remained both more radical and more expansive. The "primacy of politics" is an enduring Polanyian principle; "the future," he maintained, "is constantly being remade by those who live in the present."[40] It had been to her father's dubious advantage, Kari Polanyi-Levitt reflected in the late 1980s, that he had never been "fashionable."[41] Worse than that, by the end of the Reagan/Thatcher decade, his voice had seemed almost irretrievably "faint."[42] This economic historian had apparently himself been consigned into history, although his contributions were not entirely overlooked in retrospective treatments. In one such assessment, Coser observed that, even though Polanyi's influence had waned to insignificance by the Reagan years, he nevertheless deserved an honorary mention as one of that "small band of heretical economic thinkers, from Veblen to Galbraith, who have been perturbers of the intellectual peace in traditional economics departments."[43] It was not until the 1990s, the decade of free-market globalization, that Polanyi was to be rediscovered, by just the kind of broad audience that he had been denied in later life.

In the past two decades, the Polanyian inheritance has become both newly relevant and newly contested, for the most part productively. Following the reissue of *The Great Transformation* in 2001, the man even became fleetingly fashionable. The Daltonistas may have driven their circumscribed version of substantivism onto the rocks off the Trobriand Islands, but there is ironic justice in the fact that Polanyi should be rediscovered in the "globalization decade" of the 1990s, a time once again of definitive declarations of the ultimate victory of free-market capitalism, as an expression of society's supposedly highest form of development. Polanyi's work has been extensively mined, in this context, for rhetorically sharp rebuttals of market-fundamentalist claims. Meanwhile, his almost accidental appearance in Mark Granovetter's microsociological manifesto for network economics was a major spur to the development of the new economic sociology, although the Polanyian influence in this work has remained highly stylized.[44] Beyond these selective borrowings, however, there have been relatively few attempts, at least until recently, to excavate the wider methodological potential of substantivist economics. In this sense, Polanyi's programmatically ambitious yet practically incomplete project—for a postdisciplinary, institutionally holistic, comparative economics, global in reach but anti-universalist in form—has still to truly find its moment. Responding to this opening, the remainder of the chapter explores how a more proactive reading of the Polanyian legacy might serve the evolving project of geographical political economy.

Substantivism as Method

It follows from the preceding discussion that there are many ways to read Karl Polanyi, so no amount of textual literalism should be expected to yield decisive, final-word interpretations. This is neither a tidy nor a complete corpus. The uneven and truncated nature of Polanyi's intellectual program means that even forensic attention to the letter of his lifelong writings is just as likely to spark new disputes and counter-readings as it is to stabilize a definitive account.[45] Yet there is plenty of inspiration here, nonetheless. While it is easy to find gaps and inconsistencies in Polanyi's oeuvre, it can also be read, more constructively, with an eye to its programmatic purpose, methodological potential, and guiding spirit. As Stephen Gudeman has argued, "Perhaps Polanyi did not write with the erudition of Mauss, the grace of Malinowski, or the force of Lévi-Strauss, but he is persuasive for his ideas if not his data."[46] According to Block and Somers, his was an expositional style that "move[d] back and forth between metaphor and metatheory," but which nevertheless articulated "a series of constant causal arguments" across an impressively wide array of cases and conjunctures.[47] This entailed a distinctive methodology, a means of articulating emergent theory with the reflexive (or "retroductive") analysis of multiple *and intentionally* varied cases, working between the recognition of heterogeneity and the ambition of holistic explanation.[48]

Rather than cherry-picking or essentializing Polanyi, the approach in the remainder of the chapter is to read his substantivist program openly and forgivingly, for positive methodological injunctions. It will dwell less on silences, inconsistencies, or loose ends, but instead will endeavor to work positively with those retrievable methodological insights that might resonate with extant, emergent, or realizable research practices in geographical political economy. In this spirit, the ensuing discussion calls attention to four potentially productive dimensions of the Polanyian analytic. The first of these concerns substantivism. Polanyi's substantivist approach was forged, on the one hand, through critiques of the orthodox economic practices of market-centrism, analytical formalism, and methodological individualism, and on the other hand, by advancing an alternative grounded in the principles of holism, institutionalism, and realism.[49] Second, a case for the relatively open-ended, empirically informed, and theoretically pluralist analysis of hybrid, more-than-capitalist, and variegated economies is made on the basis of this rejection of economizing monism.[50] Third, Polanyi's well-traveled conception of the double movement is interpreted in methodological terms as a rationale for a form of dialectical analysis, strategically centered on those (social and institutional) reflexes triggered by marketization and commodification that are never singular and predictable, but always variable and politically animated.[51] Finally, this section ends with a discussion of the methodological principle of comparativism, building on the demonstrable "strength of [Polanyi's] approach," the coupling of "methodological originality [with a] wide range of comparisons," both historically and geographically.[52] This recalls the ultimate ambition of his analytical program, which was to establish space for the interdisciplinary project of comparative economy.

For Substantivism

The debate between formalism and substantivism may have been initiated by Polanyi but it only caught fire after his death. Fought by the Dalton group,[53] what became a defense of a restrictive reading of substantivism would unproductively ossify a binary divide between a bundle of more inductive, ethnographic, and substantive approaches on the one hand, and the idealized and singularly market-based abstractions of neoclassical economics on the other, projecting this onto an ultimately defeatist division of methodological labor in which substantivism was allegedly *only* suited to the purpose of studying the extra-capitalist world (or pre-capitalist, ancient societies), while neoclassical economics was implicitly assumed to be well adapted to conditions in modern market societies. This was a door that Polanyi himself had left open, in part by his postwar neglect of contemporary capitalist economies per se (to some extent due to the political calculations emphasized by Halperin and Coser) and in part by misleading (or defensive) programmatic statements, such as his observation that the apparatus of neoclassical economics, rather than being flawed in principle, was one applicable (only) to "an economy of a definite type, namely, a market system."[54]

Halperin's claim that Polanyi's arguments against formalism were, in effect, a politically necessitated proxy for his "masked" critique of capitalism becomes increasingly persuasive the further one follows the logic of his institutionalist counterargument.[55] Polanyi's objection was not to formal methods, such as modeling and quantification, the role of which he defended.[56] Rather, it took the form of an attack on methodological individualism, mechanistic reasoning, and rational-choice monism. Holding to the Aristotelian position that the whole precedes the part, Polanyi vigorously contested both the concept of *Homo economicus* and its downstream consequences, challenging the orthodox view that invariant and individual, if not *primal*, rationalities established enduring (micro) foundations for universal economic logics. Instead, social institutions effectively come first. "Acts of exchange or barter on the personal level produce prices only if they occur under a system of price-making markets," Polanyi argued, "an institutional setup which is nowhere created by mere random acts of exchange."[57] Working across various levels of abstraction, he deliberately "chose to focus his analysis at the level of concrete institutions," the "main methodological instrument" of this bespoke style of substantivism being "institutional analysis."[58]

Polanyi's position was that methodological institutionalism should be favored over methodological individualism, an axiom in principle applicable to both market and non-market societies. Institutionalist analyses must duly attend to those organized (or "instituted") patterns of valuation, understanding, and behavior that are culturally stabilized and contested within different socioeconomies. Conceptually and methodologically, the foundational sociological principle here is that institutional formations preexist the patterning of individual behaviors.[59]

Polanyi took methodological as well as political issue with the universal, orthodox imposition of the "market shape of things," challenging the proclivity of neoclassical "formalists . . . to see an abstract individualism everywhere."[60] He concluded that the resulting "web of preconceptions" had produced "a tendency of *seeing markets* where there are none."[61] According to Kaplan, this market optic renders visible (only) a world in which

> individuals act with complete information and foresight; in which all action issues from economically rational decisions and is directed towards ends that are always maximized; in which there are no cultural or psychological restraints on translating decision into immediate action; and in which all individuals make choices and act wholly independently of one another. Within this idealist world, economists have

been able to move with logical consistency, deductive certainty and, frequently, mathematical elegance. In responding to criticisms that this idealized world seems to bear little relationship to any concrete empirical economic system, economists have replied that this is the way of science.[62]

There are, however, other ways of science, and Polanyi's alternative path was substantivist in the sense that it called for an iterative engagement with actually existing (or formerly existing) *real economies*, understood in terms of their prevailing patterns of institutionalization, applying, interrogating, and refining midlevel concepts along the way. This is a receipt for reflexive theorizing with, and between, concrete cases in a manner especially sensitive to socioinstitutional context. "The substantive economy is situated in both time and place," Halperin remarks; "The formal economy, by contrast, operates in a time and space vacuum."[63]

Polanyi would sharply (and unfavorably) contrast the formal economics of the rational-choice logicians with the substantivist economics of the institutionalists, approaches that he likened to "opposite directions of the compass," with the singular and deductive model of the former being derived purely "from logic," while the variegated conceptions of the latter were shaped "from fact."[64] The "fount of ... substantive concepts" was duly held to be "the empirical economy itself," while the programmatic task for substantivist economics should be concerned with "the shifting place occupied by the economy in society [and] the study of the manner in which the economic process is instituted at different times and places."[65]

This substantivist concern with the plurality of real economies was combined with an embrace of methodological institutionalism. Polanyi's approach represents a distinctive form of heterodox institutionalism, positioned not only at the opposite end of the compass to neoclassical economics but also some distance from more structural forms of Marxism. On the other hand, as Table 7.1 suggests, his approach might be seen to occupy a broadly similar position in the universe of economic theory as geographical political economy, eschewing formalism and individualism in favor of substantivism and institutionalism.

Polanyi's substantivism may be less deductive than neoclassical economics, but it is certainly not naïvely inductive or blindly empiricist; its "transductive" sensibility resembles some of the methodological routines characteristic of critical realism, or indeed global ethnography, in tracking back and forth between (revisable) theory claims and a plurality of deeply contextualized cases.[66] While formalist approaches emphasize "the regular operation of ... the universal claims of neoclassical economics," understood as relatively

Table 7.1 Mapping Economic Methodologies

	Individualism	Institutionalism
Formalism	Neoclassical economics, new institutionalism, analytical Marxism, new (orthodox) political economy	Classical Marxism, structuralist macroeconomics, evolutionary game theory
Substantivism	Austrian economics, network sociology	Polanyian economics, anti-essentialist Marxisms, institutional economics, heterodox feminism, geographical political economy

Source: Developed from Adaman and Madra (2002)

unmediated positivist laws, substantivism "gives priority to the empirical content of material circumstances and disputes that diversity can be adequately grasped through just one set of concepts."[67] For Polanyi this took the form of a programmatic investigation (across multiple cases, contexts, and indeed centuries) of what he portrayed as institutionalized modes of economic integration: "I prefer to deal with the economy primarily as a matter of organization, and to define organization in terms of the operations characteristic of the working of [those] institutions."[68]

It follows that the "substantive definition of the economy necessarily serves to place the economic back in the context of the social whole."[69] This entails a close methodological engagement with a range of actually existing economies (past and present), in a fashion attentive to the various social and institutional ways in which provisioning for material wants have been (and can be) organized. It calls, moreover, for grounded and granulated forms of analysis, in which the inductive moment is taken seriously (although not privileged in a one-sided manner), as a component of polyvalent explanations that draw creatively on an array of heterodox theoretical resources. The multifaceted complexity of real-world economies is seen to be such as to militate against the imposition of universal or monological explanatory schema, such as those of neoclassical economics (or, for that matter, vulgar Marxism). While substantivist explanations are crafted in context-rich and institutionally saturated settings, formalism implies a preference for parsimonious reasoning, prefabricated models, and singular logics, like the rational-choice paradigm.

While it is rarely stated so bluntly, this echoes prevailing practice across much of the field of economic geography, which can be considered to be substantivist in spirit if not in name. In comparison with the historical and geographical reach of Polanyi's analysis, the empirical reference points of economic-geographical inquiry seem somewhat unadventurous, being skewed in favor of "advanced capitalist" cases, although this has been (belatedly) changing. Contrarian interpretation and the embrace of countervailing cases are also both commonplace in economic geography, a field that remains generally skeptical of dogmatic or mechanical theorizing. This said, economic geography's mostly arm's length relationship with neoclassical economics (and its favored mode of reasoning) tends to go largely unproblematized, rather than being actively addressed or contested. A culture of disengaged antagonism (or systematic indifference) prevails. The experience of mainstream economic sociology shows, however, that a posture of acquiescence (or passive coexistence) can come at a price; it can become a self-limiting position.[70] To do otherwise, to adopt a more active posture, has to amount to more than issuing ever more frontal challenges to market-centrism and methodological formalism; it calls for reconstruction as well as critique. Here there is a case to advance substantivism as a positive and reflexive methodological program. This should not be mistaken for some excuse for dressed-up empiricism; it is not a second-best method. Reflexive and exploratory, substantivism remains somewhat resistant to codification as a singular and readily replicable approach. Yet in a programmatic sense it entails not only a robustly pluralist contestation of neoclassical imperialism and market essentialism, but the foundations for an alternative.

For Variegation

"[O]nly the substantive meaning of 'economic,'" Polanyi maintained, "is capable of yielding the concepts that are required by the social sciences for an investigation of all the empirical economies of the past and present."[71] Since economic understandings and actions are always mediated by institutional forms, these (variable) institutions can provide entry points for understanding variegated economic formations. Polanyi's instituted economy was a multilogical one. He identified three (and occasionally four) distinctive "modes of economic integration" on the basis of his historical and comparative researches—reciprocity, redistribution, and exchange, with the fourth being householding—thereby extending his critique of market monism to a pluralist ontological principle. These modes of integration are found in a wide array of heterogeneous combinations; and even where one is clearly dominant, that dominance may be codependent on other forms (therefore calling for analyses that exceed single or separate modes of integration in order to explore their relational interdependencies and mutual tolerances and frictions). As such, modes of integration (often in hybrid combinations) establish the basis for the organization of (re)productive and (re)distributive capacities in different societies, which reflect and normalize patterns of belief and behavior, and which are stabilized through processes of acculturation and institutionalization. In tandem (and really only in tandem), they govern the ways in which real economies work, as combinatory sites of multiple rationalities, interests, and values, rather than as spaces governed by singular and invariant economic laws.

At root, the Polanyian economy takes the form of an "instituted process of interaction serving the satisfaction of material wants," a less than determining but nonetheless "vital part" of every society: "Man [sic], though he may not be able to live by bread alone, cannot exist without bread."[72] All economies comprise a matrix of material movements and relations that Polanyi summarized in terms of "locational" and "appropriational" dynamics, his oblique code words, it has been suggested, for those near-relative processes that are the Marxian concepts of forces and relations of production.[73] Locational movements involve the production and transportation of material goods, including the flows of resources, energy, labor, and final outputs. Appropriational movements refer to the dynamics of economic organization, control, and rights, especially the rights to land and property, and the design of labor processes. Defined at the highest level of abstraction, in Polanyi's multilayered conception of economy, locational and appropriational movements represent analytical criteria applicable to all economies, capitalist or otherwise. It also reflects his plenary claim that all economies are "more than capitalist" economies.[74]

At the next level down in the model come those modes of integration that refer, in essence, to institutionalized patterns of economic organization—reciprocity, redistribution, exchange, and householding (see Table 7.2). *Reciprocal* modes of integration are embedded in recurring, social logics of give and take; they can be seen as community or gift-giving economies, being predicated on broadly symmetrical social relations, such as those rooted in kinship networks. *Redistributive* systems, on the other hand, are typically marked by appropriational movements to and from a recognized central authority, tribal or governmental. Next, the most familiar mode of integration, *exchange*, has as its locus the market, but hardly in its textbook form; it is associated with polydirectional, short-term, and more random social relations, organized under price-making markets that are variably institutionalized. Finally, *householding*, the least formalized of Polanyi's categories, is organized around the principles of "own-use" or group provisioning, in its various domestic, kinship, or family forms, the dominant characteristic of which is circularity.

176 Variegated Economies

Table 7.2 Contrasting Modes of Economic Integration

	Reciprocity	Redistribution	Exchange	Householding
Locus	Community	Central authority	Instituted market	Closed group
Dynamic	Symmetrical	Centric	Multidirectional	Introspective
Motive	Mutual sociality	Dues/obligations	Individual gain	Self-provision
Governance	Societal	Custom or law	Price	Circulation
Subjectivity	Give-and-take	Allegiance	Bargaining	Group
Object	Gift	Tax-tribute	Commodity	Own-use resources
Loci classici	Trobriand kula rings	Babylonian storage systems	Nineteenth-century capitalisms	Rural economies; patriarchal family

Polanyi's forms of integration should be seen as midlevel concepts, developed in dialogue with a diverse array of concrete cases; they are not descriptive categories. Their invocation serves a number of analytical purposes within the Polanyian schema. Economies are understood to be "internally" heterogeneous; real markets do exist, but in variegated and always (pre)institutionalized forms; particular modes of integration should not be expected to secure monopoly positions within actually existing economies, which are and can only be "mixed" and hybrid; economic logics and rationalities are plural, warranting parity of analytical esteem across modes of integration. The Polanyian notion of markets, ironically, may have been the most incomplete, since for the most part the market was analyzed historically and in a manner that left open multiple (mis)interpretations: for example, concerning whether markets might be "more" or "less" embedded.[75] It is fair to conclude, however, that a Polanyian take on markets (like other modes of integration) has to be grounded in a social ontology: markets are constituted through instituted processes; markets coexist with other forms of integration, usually in awkward and contradictory ways; and to the extent that markets display disembedding tendencies, far from being the prelude to equilibrium or the attainment of "purity," these are by definition disruptive, provoking a range of social and institutional responses (or "double movements"). In this respect, "the" market is neither singular nor is it a stable form, and it is certainly not self-regulating. Rather, a plurality of market(-like) forms may be present within actually existing, heterogeneous economies. Instead of existing above, beyond, or outside politics, markets exhibit an inescapably political form (since they are institutionally embedded and socially regulated), being subject to recurrent political contestation and multiple modes of governance.

Polanyi repeatedly emphasized that a "*wide variety of combinations* [is] possible,"[76] the clear implication being that economies are not simply differentiated by degree (say, of marketization or modernization, as if these were singular dimensions), but *in kind* and in qualitative form. Real economies are variegated, mixed, and combinant formations (the number of combinations being large, though less than infinite). Polanyi was emphatic that the different modes of integration should "not [be taken to] represent 'stages' of development. No sequence in time is implied. Several subordinate forms may be present alongside of the dominant one, which may itself recur after a temporary eclipse."[77] This position is consistent with his rejection of both Marxian teleology and neoclassical equilibrium. However, the fact that Polanyi and the Dalton group concentrated their efforts on non-capitalist societies practically invited the misinterpretation that this was a framework designed explicitly and exclusively for the others of the modern, market economy—contributing to its subsequent marginalization. This was certainly the line of attack seized upon by neoclassical formalists like Scott Cook, who parodied the Polanyians' "obsolete anti-market mentality," smugly consigning their analytical framework to a shrinking field of application defined by not only non-capitalist but "primitive" and indeed "moribund" economies. While the substantivists held to the position that the differences between primitive-subsistence and advanced-market economies were differences in kind,[78] for formalists like Cook they were differences only of degree, and differences amenable to lining up on a Rostovian conveyor belt leading from the "peasantization of the primitive [to] the *proletarianization* of the peasant," with the market system representing its ultimate form.[79]

Having painted themselves into this very corner, the Dalton group had access to only the weakest of replies, further reifying the unhelpful binary association that had emerged between, on the one hand, formalism, capitalism, and contemporary market economies, and on the other hand, substantivism, extra-capitalism, and marginal or ancient economies. And while some Marxian anthropologists continued to work creatively with concepts like modes of integration,[80] others became quite dismissive, citing the absence both of a theory of articulation between (coexistent) modes of integration and of a plausible account of historical transformation.[81] In the past two decades, though, the tendency has been to read Polanyi less dogmatically (and in more careful, genealogical terms), especially among those with a greater distance from the polarizing anthropological debates of the 1960s and 1970s, which according to most accounts resolved only into a "dead end."[82] In particular, the notion of a variegated, heterogeneous, and hybrid economy, the structures and dynamics of which include but exceed those of both capitalism and the market, has gained traction across an array of heterodox traditions, from feminist economics to regulation theory, and from institutionalist sociology to international political economy.

By definition, Polanyi's framework is not monological; so it makes space both for plural economic forms (combinations of integration modes, variably institutionalized) and for heterodox modes of economic explanation (as opposed to theoretical monopolies of various kinds). This said, the scope for analyzing *spatially* variegated economies in such terms has only been fitfully realized. The Polanyian injunction is that explorations of unevenly developed, heterogeneous economies should be conducted systematically, with a view to theoretical recalibration and reconstruction; furthermore, this should not be confused with an invitation to the shallow celebration of surface-level economic-geographical difference, effectively for its own sake, or for the unprincipled declaration of extra-theoretical "exceptions." Rather, the purpose of this pairing of reflexive theorizing and substantivist methodology is to probe underlying logics and rationalities, together with characteristic forms of social embeddedness and institutionalized combination, *through and across cases*. It should not lead, therefore, to the proliferation of freely relativized "local" models of economy (or enclave sub-models within these), since variegation must be explored in the context of rigorously cross-cultural and comparative methodological matrices.[83] It calls for iterative explorations of local specificities, cross-local patterns, and mixed economy "wholes." And as Halperin goes on to explain:

> That ethnocentrism and romanticism should be avoided at all costs goes without saying, but without concepts that deal with non-market economies and non-market economies and non-capitalist forms of resistance to capitalism, *as well as with* the basic elements of capitalism, economic anthropologists risk imposing assumptions upon their analyses that may distort what they are trying to say. It is no better to impose a market-driven supply and demand system on egalitarian horticulturalists in the Amazon Basin than it is to assume that working-class people in the United States, many of whom live on the margins . . . and rely on a combination of extended family ties and the informal economy for their livelihoods, can be understood with the same non-market concepts that are appropriate for understanding stateless kin-based economies in tribes and chiefdoms.[84]

The solution is not one of free-form explanatory relativism (licensing one "domestic" theory of economy for every empirically observed economy), but the development of theoretical and methodological strategies that allow analysts purposefully to "cross and criss-cross between differently organized economic processes,"[85] both in situ and between places.

Engagements with the geography of heterogenous markets have begun to open up some of these issues.[86] Taking markets seriously—along with their social construction, institutionalization, and politics—clearly has to amount to more than a heterodox variant of marketcentricity. The Polanyian injunction here would be to take account of markets, but to take account of them among and in the context of their mutually constitutive others. This calls for economic-geographical research designs that span modes of integration (say, community economies and markets, or corporatized and informalized economies), rather than focusing on a single realm. It means theorizing across and with (economic) difference.

For Dialectics

The concept of the "double movement" represents one of Polanyi's most enduring legacies. Despite taking the rather cryptic form of a "colorless" euphemism, its function in his schema is essentially dialectical, in the sense that double movements are moments of socioinstitutional counteraction, brought on by the socially destructive overreach of commodification and marketization.[87] In *The Great Transformation*, capitalism is effectively saved from itself, its contradictory reproduction being secured only by way of the political vagaries and alternating currents of social protection, the irony being that while the pathway to laissez-faire capitalism in the nineteenth century was opened up by concerted state action, the subsequent responses of society were "spontaneous," diverse, and politically variable.[88] Here, what Burawoy relabels *active society* is held "in contradictory tension with the market," and more specifically with what Polanyi called the fictive commodities of land, labor, and money, invoking an always-more-than market economy capable of development "in multiple directions [and] assuming diverse configurations of state, society, and economy."[89]

On one side of this dialectical process, the forever-incomplete triple commodification of land, labor, and money sets the stage for, indeed inescapably provokes, *various* forms of "protective" socioinstitutional counteraction, which become entangled as contradictory externalities of the exchange process.[90] Forged in particular historical and geographical conjunctures, these counteractions are irreducibly political and therefore inherently unpredictable in terms of their precise form (where they run the gamut from fascism to socialism). This means that the umbrella terminology of double movements embraces everything from revolutionary class struggle to craven class compromise, and much that is not even found in between, though by the same token the concept's traction is that these politically variable responses are ultimately triggered by the (same) contradictory forces of marketization—necessitating precisely the kind of situational diagnosis, reaching across multiple modes of integration and straddling institutional domains, on which Polanyi insisted. They speak to some of the ways in which markets are prone to "overflow" into social spheres, leaching into other modes of integration, generating institutional frictions, and prompting new articulations between the exchange domain and its others. (Once again, the proper understanding of markets necessitates a more-than-markets approach.)

Just as the span of his own life ran from the dissolution of liberal capitalism through the long-run double movements of state socialism, authoritarianism, and Keynesian capitalism, Polanyi did not foresee, nor did he apparently believe, that the historical travesties of nineteenth-century laissez-faire would be repeated. Nevertheless, his conceptual schema has found posthumous relevance in the context of the deeply politicized mode of market rule that is neoliberal globalism. Since actually existing "market rule" can hardly be explained in the language of neoclassical textbooks to which its governing ideology formally defers, recourse to accounts of contemporary marketization that variously emphasize its *constitutively* cultural, political, sociological, and institutional form become necessary. Supplementing, rather than replacing, the Marxian emphasis on crisis tendencies in the accumulation process and on the workplace as a locus of social struggle, Polanyi's concern with the contradictions of the market nexus has proved to be remarkably prescient, in an era marked by compounding crises of deregulation and financialization, and by the accelerated commodification of natural and social worlds.[91] In Burawoy's hands, and married with a complementary rereading of Gramsci, this provides the spur for an ambitious methodological reconstruction, positioned purposively beyond classical Marxism. This reinvigorated form of sociological Marxism is purposefully molded for the contemporary circumstances of expansively variegated (but still less than total or universal) capitalism and globalizing (while still flawed and contradictory) market rule:

> [I]nstead of the tendency of capitalism to generate the conditions of its own demise, we have capitalism generating society that contains and absorbs crisis tendencies toward self-liquidation. Second, instead of the polarization and deepening of class struggle, we have the organization of struggle on the terrain of hegemony. [And in place of the] linear vision of history [we recognize] the independence of

economic and political developments so that rather than lining up for a singular future, advanced capitalism spreads out along different arteries, each with different possibilities. Political rather than economic crises are the switchmen that direct countries along different tracks. Moreover, the specific resolution of crises in one nation can redirect the trajectory of other nations. This is the final nail in the coffin of linear history—not only is there no single dimension of maturity along which nations can be arranged, not only is the engine of development made up of economic and political forces, but pressures and obstacles to development spring from other nations and from location in the global order itself.[92]

In place of the mechanical, linear histories, or teleological analysis of globalizing capitalism, this represents a (neoPolanyian) license for relational historical geographies of variegated economic transformation, animated by crisis and contradiction, as well as by a panoply of development models, strategies, and imaginaries. Once again, the analytical and methodological challenge is to theorize across—indeed, all the way across—spatially differentiated, heterogeneous economies. In a conjunctural context shaped by neoliberal globalism, this must problematize the manifold contradictions of the market nexus, but it must always do so within an analytic frame that exceeds this nexus—in the sense of a simultaneous embrace of extra-neoliberal politics and a more-than-capitalist vision of socioeconomic life.

The driving force of such dialectical processes—never striking equilibrium, never marching in linear progression, never trending to a teleological end point, but being subject to repeated disruption by notionally "disembedding" processes of marketization—might seem somewhat at odds with the well-known Polanyian metaphor of embeddedness. Indeed, if the social "bed" is conceived in literal and simplistically static terms, there is a real risk that embeddedness becomes a conservative methodological apology for institutional inertia, social drag, and political complacency. Double movements, however, must be seen as a restless and variable source of open-ended dynamism and political indeterminacy, the stakes and ends of which are never fixed.[93] While embeddedness represented a significant step in Polanyi's historical critique of the pathologies of laissez-faire capitalism and the complicity of free-market economics, standing as a corrective to the notion of a self-propelling market economy, its downsides include the inadvertent restoration of a different kind of market/non-market divide, along with the specious impression that economically dynamic and kinetic forces reside with markets (disembedding), while the social, ecological, and institutional "environment" is a space of friction and inertia, the source of reactive (or even defensive) responses.[94]

Raised to the status of a theoretical master concept, embeddedness threatens to "desocialize" the market once again,[95] albeit by more heterodox means, in effect by sequestering the socioinstitutional realm to the "bed," or to other modes of integration, rather than insisting on the socioinstitutional theorization *of* markets, as it were, all the way down. Contra Block, Burawoy also refuses to privilege the concept of embeddedness, on the grounds that to do so establishes little more than a weak rationale for a "static sociology" of cross-sectional economic difference, as opposed to a more dialectical understanding of relational and restlessly contradictory transformation.[96] Equally necessary, for this latter task, is the "uncommon sense" of the comparative method, since this can open up the potential for finding markets (plural) in variable geometries with other modes of integration, along with an array of double-movement-style social and political responses.

For Comparativism

A long-range objective of the Polanyian project was a postdisciplinary style of *comparative economy*, dedicated to the task of widening "areas of fruitful comparison."[97] Polanyi was a rigorous and restless critic of both economic determinism and economic solipsism. All economic formations and relations, he insisted, must be considered among their alternatives, far and near. Hence his programmatic concerns with "the shifting place [of] economy in society" and with the variable fashion in which "the economic process is instituted at different times and places."[98] This entailed not only critiques of the universal rationality and solipsistic reasoning associated with a singular "market mentality," but conceptually *and politically* generative accounts of alternative forms of economic coordination, like redistribution or reciprocity, conceived positively and in their own terms. Applying a Polanyian method, however, must entail more than the thick description of distinctive local economies, represented in commonsense categories, since the latter (and the empirical gaze they preconstitute) are always likely to be ethnocentric.[99] The knowing interrogation of always-revisable extra-local concepts and proto-theories must therefore play a central role in the methodology of comparative economy. And comparison can also be methodologically disruptive, in the sense that it should exceed the cataloguing of local economic conditions, in effect to position local socioeconomies within a reflexive spatial-relational frame and to place local economic practices, knowledges, and imaginaries in conversation with extra-local others. Comparison, in this context, performs the function of a methodological lever, opening up new ways of seeing the economic-familiar, while expanding the repertoire of alternative arrangements, achieved and imagined. It is also a tool for pattern recognition, and a prompt to explore contrasts and commonalities across cases.

It is here that the dangers of separating the "two Polanyis" (the reformist and the radical), or drawing inapt conclusions from his incomplete research program, once again loom large. And once more, there is a need for a more complete Polanyi than the one that history left behind. Polanyi's own project of pancultural comparative economy remained incomplete at the end of his life, partly as a result of the need that he apparently felt to work around, rather than engage directly with, the advanced capitalisms in his own backyard. As a result, variegated capitalism was not explicitly located within Polanyi's conceptual schema, for all its implicit presence. The subsequent ascendancy of neoliberalized capitalism, of course, means that this unfinished business must now be addressed, and explicitly rather than obliquely. Difference-finding and difference-*explaining* methodologies are therefore called for, which not only span but exceed the archipelagic and arterial formations of globalizing capitalism.

A "Polanyi-plus" approach to comparative socioeconomics must entail creative and border-crossing methodological explorations, which span capitalist *and* non-capitalist forms, the market *and* its others. Rather than some immodest extension of, or correction to, Polanyi's project, this can instead be seen as a contribution to its fulfillment. "Nothing could be more detrimental to a genuine comprehension of Polanyi's work," Gérald Berthoud has contended, than the separation of Polanyi the "theoretician of primitive and archaic societies" from Polanyi the "radical critic of our economic modernity," since this would belie what is a deeply and disruptively comparative approach. It is on this basis that Polanyi closes his case for an enriched form of substantivist economics and against the flattening, universalizing rationality of methodological individualism.[100] As Polanyi argued,

> To atomize society and make every individual atom behave according to the principles of economic rationalism would, in a sense, place the whole of human existence, with all its depth and wealth, in the frame of reference of the market. This, of course, would not really do—individuals have personalities and society has a history. Personality thrives on experience and education; action implies passion and risk; life demands faith and belief; history is struggle and defeat, victory and redemption.[101]

An alternative, non-orthodox methodological strategy is therefore required, one based on the principles of holism and institutionalism. This must critically engage with, while at the same time exceeding, the "market shape of things," moving on to attend to the many shapes that actually existing markets themselves take (in the context of a wide spectrum of cohabitative arrangements). Concrete research strategies that variously provincialize, contextualize, and institutionalize markets consequently assume particular significance here, alongside efforts to document, interrogate, and purposefully expand understandings of the role and reach (indeed repertoire) of non-market modes of integration (reciprocity, redistribution, householding, . . .), in order both to stretch the socioeconomic imaginary and to catalyze the search for what might be called "functional" alternatives, extending to what Erik Olin Wright read as "real utopias."[102]

It probably goes without saying that such efforts combine analytical pertinence with social urgency in a historical moment such as this, when market rationalities have once again acquired both political force and hegemonic purchase. In this context, relational comparisons are called for, above and beyond the static comparison of geographically distinct cases, to include research sites both connected and divided by common modes and processes of integration, and to prioritize research strategies that span or cross-cut modes of integration, highlighting their boundaries, conflicts, intersections, mutual tolerances, and overflows, both within spatially delimited research sites and between them.[103] At stake in such investigations must be "folk" as well as analytical models of economy,[104] interrogating heterogeneous socioeconomies through both comparative and historical means, and privileging neither dominant nor alternative visions in a preemptive or one-sided fashion, but holistically positioning each of these in relation to their others.

While checking market universalism is, in effect, an instinctive move in heterodox economics, it is no less important to guard against the analytical cocooning of alternative or community economies. The latter kind of secessionist maneuvering may be executed with the best of intentions, to preserve and indeed promote non-capitalist economies, but it does little to advance understandings of how such economies can be advanced and reproduced in late-neoliberal times, under competitive pressures, in the shadows of corporate power, or in the company of hostile or less-than-cooperative others.[105] While he would certainly have recognized the pervasive reach and diverse implications of neoliberal hegemony, Polanyi was no fatalist. After all, for Polanyi it is politics that ultimately shape economies, not the other way around.[106] The search for more humane and sustainable ways of living could be facilitated by the trenchant critique and denaturalization of current conditions, in tandem with creative explorations of the political economy of alternatives.

Theorizing with and across heterogeneity (socioeconomic, geographical, historical, ...) can therefore be considered to be integral to a Polanyian methodological sensibility. This must attend to institutionalized patternings of economic relations and their historical evolution; it must (especially in the context of neoliberalizing capitalism), problematize market rule, while positioning its actually existing expressions relative to their various others and alternatives; it must isolate but also span modes of integration, taking account of their interfaces, interactions, and interdependencies; and it must be constitutively comparative, exposing salient differences and relational connections across variegated economies, both in situ and between places. The approach need not be programmatically anti-market, but at a minimum would insist that actually existing markets come in "many variants" and that an adequate methodological reach must encompass what Polanyi called that "wider frame of reference to which the market itself is referable."[107] And, crucially, the historical conditions of neoliberal globalism demand that attention is paid to the marketization of relations between (local) economies; an enriched Polanyian methodology, supplemented with the world-system reach of sociological Marxism or complementary approaches to variegated capitalism, must provide for more than the "internal" deconstruction of heterogeneous economies; it must also attend to questions of uneven spatial development across these economies. Conventional methods of comparative research (such as the analysis, side by side, of contrasting and nominally separate cases) has but a limited role to play in this context, given the methodological importance attached to relational interdependence, mutual constitution, and part-whole relations. Instead, it provides a remit for new approaches to cross-case research design and theorizing with (sociospatial) difference, including the methodological innovations spurred by developments in conjunctural analysis and relational comparison.[108]

Conclusion: Substantive Differences?

Karl Polanyi is commonly regarded as an inspirational but somewhat idiosyncratic theorist. His analytical admonitions are invariably provocative and often generative, but they can also be cryptic and inconsistent. He may have walked the walk of substantivist economics, but this was a journey that he never got to complete. Polanyi made the case for enriching the repertoire of socioeconomic analysis by way of ambitious, category-stretching comparisons, both historically and geographically, but he is vulnerable to the charge that contemporary capitalist and market economies were neglected, at some cost, in his postwar research program. His critique of capitalism was largely historical, while postwar applications of substantivist economics favored "exotic" cases from the pre-capitalist world. The argument in this chapter has been that, while it is important to recognize these foibles and lapses, insofar as they speak to a wider program that for various reasons was frustrated, there is no reason that this should continue to hinder contemporary elaborations of that program: hence the approach adopted here of reading Polanyian legacy in a cooperative and creative spirit, not for iron-clad rules and finished formulations, but for its methodological potential.

There is much work still to be done in the service of the unfinished Polanyian programs of substantivist socioeconomics and comparative economy, which have been experiencing something of a revival.[109] Most productively, this would place a premium on reflexive theorizing in dialogue with an expansive array of concrete cases, rejecting both naïve inductivism and rigid deductivism. While hardly an empiricist, Polanyi never failed to learn from his cases, while at the same time working to locate them both in (geo)historical terms and within an evolving conceptual schema. In fact, he underlined the "need for circumspection before one attempts the task of mapping the changing place of concrete economies in actual societies."[110] This was the rationale for developing boundary-traversing research designs with the potential to reconstruct, rather than merely affirm, emergent concepts and theory claims.

The Polanyian approach is to engage substantively with actually existing economic formations, situating these both historically and geographically; it takes as axiomatic the variability, or variegation, of these real economies, deploying concrete research strategies to probe the registers, valences, drivers, and consequences of revealed difference; it duly acknowledges the irreducible heterogeneity of actually existing, hybrid economies, while striving to understand the mutually constitutive relations between the moving parts and the evolving whole; it is attentive to the dialectics of capitalist marketization, sustaining creative analytical tensions between understandings of its logics and limits; and it is skeptical of universalist claims, finding in difference and differentiation more than contingent noise or erroneous deviation, but the basis for branching points, conjunctural potentialities, and alternative pathways.

8
Arid Comparisons?
Economies of Difference

To say that this chapter follows the remit for a "spatialized" Polanyian methodology presented in the previous chapter may be literally true, but at the same time this is something of a misstatement. In fact, the two were conceived and produced together, as elements of what became an extended project, in response to an invitation from Matthew Tonts and Paul Plummer to spend a week in Western Australia, exploring the potential of geographical political economy approaches in the booming resource region of the Pilbara. Located in the northern part of the state, the Pilbara region is a two-day drive from Perth, and closer to the Indonesian capital of Jakarta than it is to Canberra. Conceived as a mobile seminar, the Pilbara expedition involved a mixed group of local experts and visiting interlocutors,[1] assembled with the shared objective of positioning the unique development experience of this extraordinary region in relational terms. It was an opportunity to think about *and in* the region, collaboratively and in conversation. Or, to put this in Polanyian language, we were variously engaged in the work of "placing" the Pilbara, historically, socially, and spatially, among its others, including the different ways it had become "tethered to the world."[2] One of the benefits of planning this trip several months in advance was that there was an opportunity to pose the question, with a reasonable amount of preparation time, what would Polanyi have made of the Pilbara? How might he have approached a regional economy such as this, methodologically?

This opportunity to take Polanyi to the Pilbara, methodologically speaking, was interdigitated with several months of work on the archives, on secondary materials, and on different approaches to Aboriginal economics. The weeklong visit itself would of course be insufficient for the purposes of primary research, although in other ways it was sufficiently vivid and informative to provoke a host of further questions and lines of inquiry. All of this was somewhat improvised, yet there was also a sense in which echoed some aspects of Polanyi's own method, which involved working with archives, contemporary

Variegated Economies. Jamie Peck, Oxford University Press. © Oxford University Press 2023.
DOI: 10.1093/oso/9780190076931.003.0008

reports, and secondary materials, rather than firsthand data production, not least during his later-career excursions into comparative economics.

This is not to suggest, of course, that a Polanyian exploration of the Pilbara somehow had to proceed without a compass. Among the notable examples, there was Bradon Ellem's well-established research program on the region's industrial-relations trajectory and culture, which would later culminate in a definitive monograph.[3] There was an extensive literature on Indigenous economic practices (and futures) in regional Australia, conducted by Jon Altman, Melinda Hinkson, and others, and significant contributions from Aboriginal scholars and activists such as Marcia Langton, Richie Ah Mat, and Noel Pearson.[4] And from an economic geography perspective, Richie Howitt's early work on resource development and Aboriginal communities had been framed in such a way as to practically anticipate a (neo)Polanyian reading:

> Elements of capital may be empowered in the restructuring process, but there is little that is inevitable or can be read off from a simplified caricature of either place or process. Articulation of international capital with diverse local and national interests during development of the export iron ore industry in the Pilbara region ... clearly demonstrates the complexity of the restructuring process [and] the importance of *dealing with restructuring in a holistic way*, rather than, for example, assuming the primacy of capital-labour relations. In the Pilbara, empowerment of international capital entailed not only trade-offs with labour, but also transformed the regional economy in ways which entrenched the powerlessness of local Aborigines.[5]

Analytical holism, practiced in this (proto)Polanyian fashion, means not just recognizing socioeconomic diversity but explicitly problematizing the complex relations between (entirely) different modes of socioeconomic organization, which are often contradictory but also mutually constitutive. It implies, furthermore, a skeptical treatment of those orthodox research practices that tend to operate "centrifugally"—beginning with and pivoting around a normatively defined center; working outward (or downward or backward) from that point to the supposed margins or to antecedent forms; and defining (or assuming) starting and end points according to the singular principle of market primacy. Instead, an alternative approach is implied which, at a minimum, would valorize different (not to say multiple) points of entry and different lines of sight. The Polanyian imperative in this context is to recognize and work across organizational forms and socioeconomic differences, in the service of a more substantively relational understanding, involving round trips between the constituent "parts" of the (weakly bounded) regional economy, as well as part-whole maneuvers.

In a starkly polarized region like the Pilbara, where both "under-development" and "over-development" have been periodically pushed to extremes and into crises, this calls for analyses of the Indigenous or "customary" economy that are positioned alongside (and in articulation with) the "mainstream," market or corporate economy, evaluating both on their own terms while holding a mirror to their habitual practices too. The corporate mining boom in the Pilbara has largely "[taken] place as if Aborigines did not exist," Paul Cleary has remarked,[6] yet the existence of Indigenous communities has certainly mattered, and continues to do so. Here, a substantivist analytic calls for relational and historicized investigation of internally heterogeneous and hybrid economies, for modes of inquiry that are socially, culturally, and institutionally expansive rather than essentialist or restrictive, and for interpretations that take account of, while at the same time exceeding, the dynamics of the contemporary marketized economy and the domain of transnational corporations. It also entails questions of "comparison" framed in different ways to the conventional, like-to-like comparison of discrete and contrasting cases. Here, the comparisons are intraregional and asymmetrical, and they involve extreme disparities in socioeconomic conditions and power relations.

If the previous chapter sought to develop a constructive and instructive reading of the Polanyian method, looking forward and outward with an eye to methodological potentialities (in the plural), the present chapter is self-consciously exploratory in a quite literal sense. It is concerned with a regional economy quite different from any of those that I have worked on before, one effect of which was an elevated sense of methodological reflexivity and intentionality (rather than taking things for granted), coupled with an awareness of the implications of different conceptual optics—understood as means to read, interpret, assemble, and narrate a highly distinctive regional economy. Taking Polanyi to the Pilbara, in this respect, served as a methodological experiment. Where this might go next, or elsewhere, is clearly a different matter, although it is hopefully indicative of productive paths still to be taken.

Taking Polanyi to the Pilbara

Polanyi himself never set foot in the Pilbara, or Australia for that matter, but what might he have made of this place if he had? Through what methodological maneuvers would he have sought to engage and make sense of its often-tortured history and just-as-often confounding present? How would he have accounted for the complex coevolution of its *longue-durée* Indigenous economy, sustainable for millennia but recently mired in intergenerational crisis, and the fickle but overwhelming attentions of extractive capitalism, a mode of development which of its own accord repeatedly tracks toward crisis? We can speculate that his answers to these questions would have been constructed not through stylized and monological models, but by recourse to the tangled and contradictory heterogeneity of the Pilbara's "real" economy, along with its deep and multilayered histories. Polanyi endeavored to denaturalize and problematize received understandings of market progress and socioeconomic marginality, persistently questioning the supposedly inevitable and the presumptively normative. There was always more than one story, more than one motor of change, and more than one pathway. And there were hidden pasts to be (re)discovered, as well as alternative futures to be imagined and grasped. Polanyi's "instituted" economy was polycentric and variegated, the product of continuing, historical processes of recombination. Perhaps, above all, economies were seen to be socially shaped and socially pliable.[7]

One thing that was cross-contextual about Polanyi's approach was his methodological framework, which was amenable to "applications" past and present, familiar and strange. Embeddedness—along with its corollaries, hybridity and contextual specificity—are in this sense "everywhere" conditions, certainly not serving as remits for monocausal analysis or methodological standardization, but for something quite different, as means to read local and situated formations, and their always evolving interactions. So the Polanyian framework can be mobilized and interrogated in the Pilbara (just as it might be in Pittsburgh or Phnom Penh) as a particular way to encounter and interpret this regionalized economy and its unique historical geographies. Furthermore, as a framework especially attuned to the recognition of socioeconomic difference and instituted inequalities, there can be no doubt that this is needed here. The Pilbara is home to an economy sharply bifurcated between explosive, unsustainable growth in monopoly-capitalist resource extraction and an acutely divergent form of unsustainability across the traumatized economy of the Traditional Owners, many of whom have been left in the "dust of the development," to borrow Noel Pearson's resonant phrase.[8] A vast and sparsely populated desert region, the Pilbara has recently been host to some of the most profitable and capital-intensive extractive activities on earth (based on the exploitation of iron ore, oil and gas, and manganese), an epicenter of the global resources boom. In this region, known as "China's quarry," the corporate sector relies on a large and amply remunerated workforce of "fly-in/fly-out" (FIFO) contractors, its transitory boom towns awkwardly coexisting with Indigenous communities at the cusp of social crisis. Booming and barren, this almost empty region is full of contradictions.

Presenting a Polanyian encounter with the Pilbara's diverse economy, the chapter next moves to synthesize a set of operative principles derived from substantivist methodology. This is followed by a contextual sketch of China's quarry, prior to an overview of this sharply segregated "economy of camps." The chapter then moves into a historical mode of analysis, tracing the often-destructive interaction between different modes, meanings, and manifestations of (economic and social) "development" in the Pilbara, from the initial moment of Aboriginal dispossession, through the rise and "normalization" of company towns, following the arrival of the corporate giants, the contested and episodic course of labor relations, to the open questions of Indigenous economic development. The chapter is concluded with reflections on the potential of substantivist economic geographies, in this and other (regional) contexts.

Mobilizing Polanyian Methods

Fred Block has speculated that the origins of the embeddedness metaphor can be traced to the mining industry, and to Polanyi's interwar explorations of British economic history, although the conceptual lineage also connects to the work of the classical anthropologist Richard Thurnwald, and indeed to an extended dialogue with Marxian historical materialism.[9] In practice, the embeddedness metaphor reflects Polanyi's conviction that actually existing economies must be understood in grounded terms, and in ways explicitly situated in their social, historical, and geographical contexts. Yet putting this approach to work, in practice, involves much more than invoking the metaphor of embeddedness, which in isolation may inadvertently resurrect the problematic binary between dynamic markets (as the source of progressive "movement") and an inert or slow-moving social base (the "bed").

Respecting the Aristotelian principle that the whole precedes the part, Polanyi maintained that "economic systems [can only be understood] in a social system context," and as Bernard Barber has put it, that such work on the "bits and pieces of the going economic system" must always be accompanied by a consideration of how these bits and pieces move and hang together, how they collide and (re)articulate, and how the heterogeneous, recombined whole is variously instituted.[10] This social-systemic approach was to be realized not by way of Parsonian abstractions or ideal types, but by situated, historical, comparative, and concrete research, complemented by dialogical forms of abstraction,[11] always engaging with the cultural and the material.

As the previous chapter argued, Polanyi's substantivist approach itself can be mined for methodological insights, four of which are especially relevant for the analysis that follows. First, and most basically, Polanyi took issue with orthodox economics for its deductive, rational-choice formalism, and its proclivity to impose a universalizing "market shape of things," indiscriminately, across behaviors, cultures, and situations.[12] His more qualitative and institutionalist alternative involved a close dissection of the organizational rationalities exhibited by a wide range of economic systems, past and present, with a view to their (relational) placement "back in the social whole."[13] In anticipation of the Pilbara case, this means situating market (and corporate-capitalist) forms both socioinstitutionally and among their "others," while observing the principle of parity of analytical esteem.

Second, Polanyi's extensive work with ethnographic and historical materials led him to distinguish three (and sometimes four) "modes of economic integration" or patterns of socioeconomic organization—reciprocity, redistribution, and market exchange (plus householding)—which were to be found in various permutations and combinations in actually existing economies. Skeptical of universalism and teleology, he conceived of all socioeconomies as heterogeneous and hybrid, tracing distinctive but often intersecting paths of development that were historically shaped but never preordained. The socioeconomic cocktail was, for Polanyi, always a volatile one, and it could be (re)mixed in a variety of ways. Marketization, in this context, is not a proxy for progress or a pointer to the highest stage of development, neither should markets be expected to exhibit a singular form. In the Pilbara, this perspective problematizes the manner in which distorted, socially dysfunctional, and overheated markets not only coexist with but are also *codependent on* other socioeconomic regimes, interpenetrating in complex ways with state-redistributionist and customary-reciprocal economies.

Third, the concept of the double movement captures the dialectical dynamism of economic systems always out of equilibrium, and perpetually disrupted by the alternating currents of commodification and marketization on the one hand, and various social responses and institutional maneuvers on the other. As Polanyi-Levitt cautions, however, the double movement "is not a self-correcting mechanism which moderates excesses of market fundamentalism but a contradiction in the Marxian sense of the word."[14] In the context of the Pilbara, this invites a critical analysis of the socially disruptive, always incomplete, and contradictory character of marketization and corporatization, together with their institutional preconditions and reverberations.

The amplitude of double-movement dynamics is perhaps best illustrated through historical analysis, but these dynamics also find ongoing expression in the diverse and daily failures of marketization, in unmanaged social and ecological externalities, and in the capricious politics of economic governance.

Finally, the Polanyian approach is restlessly comparative. In principle, it is applicable within as well as between spatially defined economies. For the Pilbara region, it means not only recognizing the "internal" dimensions of economic diversity, but also placing this diversity in social and historical context, and not simply theorizing "down" or "back" from what is presumed to be the most "advanced" or "modern" form of economic development. In a single-region setting like this one, it calls for an approach that connects (rather than sequesters) the spheres of an asymmetrically diverse economy, probing their mutually constitution. Furthermore, this kind of in situ comparison, turning attention to the unevenness of regional development on the "inside," is a further caution against analyses that are indexed to a presumed center, essential core, or evolutionary end point.

Of course, it would be quite antithetical to a Polanyian approach to stop here, at the stage of articulating bloodless methodological principles. The method was intended to be realized (and of course repeatedly revised) through application and adaptation. Hardly averse to abstraction, Polanyi nevertheless sought to deploy his conceptual formulations reflexively rather than dogmatically. Cangiani observes that Polanyi rationalized his historical-comparative methodology not by recourse to fixed, "theological" principles but by way of "an analysis of *facts*, in the Veblenian sense of an empirical study of the institutional features of the economy as a social process."[15] The chief concern of this chapter is the complementary objective of thinking "across" the facts of regional economic diversity, both historically and in the Pilbara's contradictory present, in a manner that is sensitive to the diversity of socioeconomic forms, institutions, and forces.

China's Quarry

Beyond its geographical coordinates, in the northern reaches of Western Australia, the desert economy of the Pilbara is a challenge to size up. Its population (at just over 50,000) is less than half that of Flint, Michigan, and smaller than that of the Pitcairn Islands, but its land area (of over 500,000 square kilometers) places it in the same very big league as California, Texas, Spain, or Thailand. Meanwhile, the region's outsized economic output, contributing as much as a third of the Australian total, means that its sparsely populated economy is comparable in size to that of Poland. Importantly, this is also a region with more (human) history than most, having been home to thriving socioeconomies for more than 30,000 years, only recently of the capitalist kind. Yet as Richie Howitt has pointed out, the model of corporate resource development has been such as to render "Aboriginal people a displaced minority in their own lands."[16] The Pilbara has been the anchor region for what the CEO of Rio Tinto once described as "the best iron ore business in the world," predicated on a corporate model designed to extract not only resources but super-profits of up to 70%.[17] This regional political economy has long been characterized by the "dominance of giants,"[18] including episodes of corporate enclosure that echo processes of colonial dispossession and violence practiced since the nineteenth century.

As the "engine room" of the Australian economy, the Pilbara would become a key driver of macroeconomic variables like trade balances and GDP, not to mention interest, inflation, and investment rates, during the country's long commodity boom.[19] "For global corporations," Ellem has explained, "the Pilbara has become an astonishingly important and profitable site," successive resource booms having integrated the region into the transnational "flows of capital and product markets which make up the global trade in ores and steel."[20] The corporate mining sector relies on massive amounts of fixed capital investment, but this has never translated into stability. Instead, the sector has veered periodically into crises of its own (making), especially in its employment relations and in the fraught spaces of social reproduction. Notoriously, mining companies have been known to fly in sandwiches from Perth, more than two thousand kilometers away, to corporate events in the Pilbara, sending dirty laundry in the opposite direction.[21] The FIFO labor supply is mobilized on a similar basis, spawning what the *Wall Street Journal* has called "a class of nouveau riche . . . living for weeks in dusty small towns" known as "donga" camps, often on spectacularly high wages.[22] These are some of the principal sites of what the Australians call "bogan culture," monied but rough-and-ready. Nevertheless, the heavily tattooed high-school dropout who was profiled by the *Journal*, James Dennison, was portrayed as "[a] precious commodity himself."

The original inhabitants of this rugged landscape have been largely excluded from the corporate mining boom, which has been driven by successive waves of growth since the 1960s, first from Japan and subsequently from China.[23] In fact, the industrialization of the Pilbara actually "erected new barriers" to Aboriginal economic participation.[24] On many measures, the traditional or customary economy of the region has continued to decline,[25] despite blistering growth in the adjacent, corporate economy, while many of its communities exist in parlous states of social debilitation and economic detachment. Yet to consign the Pilbara's customary economy to the status of a historical anachronism or late-welfare basket case would be to commit an analytical error as well as an ethical lapse. It warrants understanding on its own terms, with reference to its own consequential history and emergent futures.

The Pilbara's Indigenous communities and their long-lasting customary economies have been repeatedly pushed to the point of crisis, through damaging and sometimes deadly interactions with corporations, markets, and the state.[26] Initially, this took the form of a violent but incomplete subjection to pastoral capitalism, to be superseded by the imposition of serial states of contingency, marginalization, and exclusion, not least as outcomes of the ongoing restructuring of the adjacent economies of corporate extraction and state welfare. More recently, the inherent fragility of the mining corporations' "social license" has enabled Aboriginal communities to gain some limited toeholds in the market economy, courtesy of targeted employment schemes and land-rights concessions.[27] Corporations like Rio Tinto have found it expedient (and politically necessary) to acknowledge the "economic independence" of Indigenous communities, committing to "mutually advantageous" forms of development, sufficient to enable not just participation but integration. There are markers of this, for example, in the displays of Indigenous art that adorn corporate brochures and visitor centers, while there is also a modest amount of subcontracting to Aboriginal-owned suppliers. But with very few exceptions, corporate policies are unilaterally made and imposed. There is no place for other "cultures" here; it is expected that they are left at home. As representatives of Rio Tinto have written:

> A mine site is an industrial site and an industrial ethos must prevail in order for the health and safety of all employees to be protected and in order for world-class management of resources to occur. This concept of the site being a "bubble" of industrial culture is well understood and accepted as necessary by most Aboriginal people. Whatever rich cultural life Aboriginal employees may lead off site, they are industrial employees whilst on site.[28]

The "bubble economy" of the corporate resource sector, however, must also be seen as a culture, with its own norms and "rules." It is but one part of an intricately fissured socioeconomic landscape. And just as "mainstream" market capitalism exists within a cultural integument, Aboriginal economies exhibit their own forms of competition, innovation, and entrepreneurship.[29] This raises the question of how normality itself has been constructed.

So even if the corporate mining business developed, for the most part, "as if Aborigines did not exist,"[30] this does not mean that the story of the Pilbara's regional economy has to be narrated in these same terms. Neither should it be assumed, a priori, that the Indigenous socioeconomy is inert and remnant, whereas the corporatized, market economy is dynamic and progressive, or that the two are entirely independent, separate spheres. In fact, the mutual articulation between the customary and market economies of the Pilbara has a long and tangled history. As a matter of principle, the actually existing market economy of the Pilbara, in all its mutations, is no "more economic" than that of the Traditional Owners; it is *differently* economic. By the same token, there is no reason for Indigenous, customary economies to be understood in cultural(ist) terms, or represented as somehow "more cultural" than what is conventionally known as the "mainstream," "real," or market economy.[31] Yet this is a common—not to say normal—form of (mis)representation: the alleged failures of Aboriginal society are routinely pegged not only to cultural causes but to the purported absence of those "economic" rationalities, values, and incentives that are associated, as if naturally, with mainstream Australian society.[32] In conventional interpretations, the customary economy is duly over-socialized (overdetermined by culture), while the market economy is under-socialized (overdetermined by economics). Not only does this naturalize the market economy, deflecting attention from its own cultures, institutions, and social pathologies, it can render Aboriginal economies practically invisible, as if residues of some distant and receding past, while apparently justifying all manner of heavy-handed "interventions." Working against these distortions is not simply an outback form of political correctness; in Polanyian terms it is a methodological axiom.

An Economy of Camps

Successive attempts to "normalize" the market economy of the Pilbara, while sustained, have been repeatedly frustrated. In the 1960s, when mining corporations first moved in, the preferred strategy for securing a (white) labor supply involved the costly and complicated business of building company towns. Initially conceived as "model" settlements—modern suburbs in the desert—these new towns would prove to be anything but, later being transferred to public jurisdiction through a process actually known as "normalization." The former company towns, however, have continued to face severe challenges of social development. Having unloaded the fixed costs of social reproduction, the corporate mining sector would engineer a quite different spatial fix, this time based on the rotating deployment of FIFO workers, housed in temporary donga camps, some of which have grown to the size of small towns in their own right. These camps can be seen as symbols both of the socially truncated existence of the mining industry's transient workforce and of a fickle commitment to social reproduction on the part of the mining corporations.

FIFO workers will typically transit into the region on two- to six-week rosters. They live in air-conditioned semi-detachment from local residents (not to mention from their own families) in utilitarian camps, prompting some regional observers to talk of the emergence of "quasi-gated communities," and to complaints that FIFO workers only "take" from the Pilbara's communities without making meaningful contributions in return.[33] Some FIFO workers save and remit scrupulously, while the culturally maligned "cashed up bogans" are known for consuming vigorously and conspicuously.[34] Together, they have driven regional housing and living costs to unsustainable levels, leading corporate managers to grumble about wage inflation (as if they were mere bystanders), while long-time local residents protest that they have been priced out of their own communities.[35] FIFO has enabled companies like Rio Tinto and BHP to "overcome the one big weakness they have in relations to labour—that of being stuck in one place."[36] In effect, FIFO outsources, individualizes, and marketizes processes of social reproduction at a price lower (and more "manageable") than the deeply sunk costs of maintaining company towns. In a broader sense, the fact that such arrangements (with their six-figure salaries, plus expenses) are deemed "economical" at all is entirely contingent on the international commodity prices, and therefore on the current configuration of global markets, trading regimes, currencies, and so forth.[37] The social costs, mostly uncalculated, are widely seen to be unacceptably high.

Such are the disjunctive conditions in the supposedly "advanced" sphere of the Pilbara economy. The geographical fixity of ore and gas deposits, and the capital-intensive character of mining operations, may give the impression of permanence, indeed embeddedness, but in other respects the corporate presence in the Pilbara is transitory: the life of major mining operations may be no more than three or four decades, while their viability is always vulnerable to the movements of offshore commodity markets. The corporate labor-contracting regime, too, has been constructed in such a way that the preferred workforce is effectively contingent, the FIFO faucet being adjusted on a continuous basis, its on-call workers understanding this anti-social contract to be a temporary one.

The predominantly white market economy has for years been overheating to the point of dysfunction. The somewhat bedraggled mining town of Tom Price for a while registered the highest incomes in non-metropolitan Australia,[38] but struggles to sustain basic community institutions and facilities, or to maintain adequate educational, social, and medical services. Rolling crises of social reproduction span this diverse economy; they are not the preserve of just one of its communities. The Pilbara has some of the highest wages and rents in Western Australia, and one of the lowest unemployment rates; yet the Indigenous unemployment rate, much higher across the board, has been higher in the Pilbara than elsewhere, while median incomes for Aboriginal residents are less than half those of the non-Indigenous population.[39] The life expectancy of Indigenous men, at less than fifty-five years, is comparable with rates found in the least developed regions of Africa.[40] There are but a few hundred Aboriginal people employed in the mining industry, more than half of whom are employed by a single Indigenous-owned contracting company.[41] Meanwhile, the mining sector directly employs one-third of the region's non-Indigenous residents, indirectly supporting most of the rest.

A program of "Indigenous dialogues" conducted in the region arrived at the following conclusion: that while "the Pilbara generates most of the country's wealth through mining companies [its] Aboriginal communities are still experiencing poverty and third world living conditions."[42] Indigenous employment in the resource sector barely exceeds the tokenistic minima called for by the governing ideology of corporate social responsibility and quasi-contractual offshoot, the Australian Employment Covenant (AEC). Brainchild of Andrew "Twiggy" Forrest, Pilbara-born billionaire, mining magnate, and one of Australia's richest men, the AEC was launched in 2009 as an industry-led initiative with the intention of "closing the gap" between non-Indigenous and Indigenous employment rates, by way of (voluntary) "commitments" to employ Aboriginal workers. The corporate imperative here has little to do with the resource industry's endemic skill shortages (currently being "managed" by the FIFO regime), and much more to do with the challenge of maintaining political legitimacy, the "social license" to mine. The president of BHP Billiton Iron Ore puts it this way:

> Land access and reconciliation issues [are] the backbone of [the company's] commitment. Simply, BHP Billiton has embedded the core values of reconciliation ([based on] relationships, respect and opportunity) into the way we do business with indigenous communities.... By making a real and true commitment to indigenous employment, we will leave a bigger, more enduring footprint. And it will be a human one.[43]

BHP Billiton, where the rate of Aboriginal employment was under 7%, launched the Purarrka Indigenous Mining Academy in 2009, in partnership with Ngarda Civil and Mining Pty, an Indigenous-owned contracting company. About twenty trainees per year were recruited into a "comprehensive lifestyle development and mentoring program," designed to allow participants to "learn how to conduct themselves, mix with others, understand the workplace culture and the discipline required to be fit for work (early nights and mornings, etc.), and how to balance work and family responsibilities."[44] Behaviors that are "taken for granted by people who have participated in a work culture," the program's guidelines state, are nevertheless seen to represent "learned qualities" which for some trainees "can pose a real challenge."

Despite their modest scope, AEC agreements have acquired a significant degree of symbolic resonance in the corporate and governmental spheres, where they are the subject of continuing public-relations efforts. Aboriginal workers now account for around one-tenth of the employment roster at the major resource operations in the Pilbara; these corporate "integration" initiatives have tended to target *already* employed Aboriginal workers, many of whom are "flown in from major towns and cities" around Australia, rather than being recruited locally.[45] Accusations of tokenism, not surprisingly, are commonplace.[46]

Corporate and governmental employability initiatives invoke, and seek to work upon, deficient subjects of the market economy, on the basis of a semi-official diagnosis that "Aborigines do no behave like other Australians."[47] In its most toxic formulations, this extends to a comprehensive indictment of "workless" elements in Aboriginal society, which are seen to be racked by welfare-dependent lifestyles and rent-seeking behaviors, and rendered responsible for their own poverty and unemployment by virtue of deficits in education and socialization. Allegedly debilitated by the ready availability of what is colloquially known as "sit-down money," and larded by "Remote Area Exceptions" to work requirements, these communities are scolded for their inability to take advantage of the AEC's corporate largesse: "Aborigines . . . in remote areas do not have sufficient literacy to read and sign [a] simple employment covenant."[48] The Pilbara's actual Aboriginal history, however, hardly aligns with narratives of immobilized, unproductive, and dysfunctional subjects.

Aboriginal Dispossession and Colonial Capitalism

The Pilbara has long been home to one of the world's original "affluent societies," to borrow Marshall Sahlins's ironically turned phrase.[49] At the beginning of the nineteenth century, the standard of living of the average Aboriginal person was comparable to that found in Europe, albeit one far more equitably distributed than in the class-structured economies of the nominally civilized world.[50] Meanwhile, the market value of the Pilbara's underground resources was effectively zero, by virtue of its position on the far periphery of the colonial economy. British government geologists had calculated in the 1880s that the region contained "enough [iron ore] to supply the whole world," but decades later this resource was still regarded as "practically worthless."[51] This situation did not significantly change until the 1960s, when the granting of mining rights in the context of surging industrial demand from Japan effectively instituted a new, corporatized economy in the Pilbara.

"When a group of Aborigines hunt, gather, cook and consume goods such as lizards, grubs and ants, they are certainly engaging in economic activity," Ernest Fisk maintained, albeit a form of economic activity barely legible and hardly "quantifiable in monetary terms [since it] cannot readily be observed through the market-type operations that are the source of most economic statistics."[52] By the same token, the capitalist market economy was practically irreconcilable with the principles that had long governed the Aboriginal economy, those of reciprocity, kin-based redistribution, and socially sanctioned need. In the words of the Pilbara's Don McLeod, a passionate defender of Aboriginal rights and a practical advocate for Aboriginal socioeconomics, capitalism represented an "economy of greed."[53] It involved not only the accumulation of money, evidently for its own sake, but also the unnecessary hoarding of resources like livestock, alcohol, and tobacco. While the social relations of capitalism are predicated on the tendential commodification of land and labor, in Aboriginal societies these are both spiritually inseparable and economically inalienable: "It would be as correct," in the latter culture, "to speak of the land possessing men as of men possessing land."[54] Governed by what McLeod called the "Law of the Blackfellows," Aboriginal socioeconomies were effectively self-sufficient and self-regulating, relying as they did on "cooperation rather than coercion."[55] If circumstances led to a local surplus of food, for example, this would be shared with neighboring groups, usually in the context of ceremonial events, organized according to Tribal Law.

Buckley and Wheelwright drew the conclusion that "the basic difference" between Australia's Aboriginal people and the settler populations "of the last two hundred years [is to be found] not in skin pigmentation but in social organization."[56] Even if it fell short of the romanticized "bush paradise," the Indigenous economy at the time of European settlement was nevertheless sustainably organized around the principles of sufficiency and sharing, the requirements of subsistence being met in the context of a relatively short working day. Distinctive definitions of work, responsibility, and surplus allocation prevailed, extending to a wide range of reciprocal and redistributive practices, disseminated through traditional knowledge.[57] The blending of kinship, socioecological, and "economic" relations, enshrined in practices like demand-sharing and communal property, formed the basis of a distinctive "Aboriginal ontology."[58]

This largely peaceful and self-sufficient society was, however, on a collision course with colonial capitalism. This began as a "fight for land," albeit one waged on unequal terms, subject to "complete incompatibility between the two systems of land use."[59] It would also entail repeated attempts to subjugate and commodify Aboriginal labor, at the behest of the colonial state, policing authorities, and frontier pastoralists—a process that remains incomplete to this day. The rhetorical turns of Marx and Polanyi are not out of place here. To part-paraphrase them both, this was clearly an instance in which the road to primitive accumulation and capitalist exchange "was opened and kept open by an enormous increase in continuous, centrally organized and controlled interventionism," exercised in this case over intercontinental distances, as communities were "suddenly and forcibly torn from their means of subsistence" by way of colonial-state expropriation.[60]

Even though the "impact of European capitalism upon the Aboriginal subsistence economy [would be] catastrophic,"[61] none of this was achieved without friction, contradiction, or indeed a certain degree of mutual adjustment. The model for the development of what was known as the Swan River colony of Western Australia had been established by the English landowner, Thomas Peel. In the 1830s, Peel formulated a scheme to take advantage of the colonial state's offer unilaterally to grant the title to large tracts of land to those capable of mobilizing a suitable labor force. (As a cost-control measure, the forced labor of convicts would not be furnished to this regional class of primitive accumulators, as had been typical in Australia's eastern colonies). Peel's plan for the Swan River colony was based on the ruse of exchanging the price of passage from Britain for a contract of indentured servitude to a local employer, usually for a period of five years. As Buckley and Wheelwright recount, the scheme was immediately mired in crisis, as rates of settler immigration were unexpectedly low, and much of the land proved to be unproductive; soon, the resources of the local capitalist class were almost entirely absorbed by the wage and subsistence costs of their indentured workforces.[62] This hapless outcome was ridiculed by Marx himself, after reading accounts in the London newspapers, who wrote of "[u]nhappy Mr. Peel, who provided for everything except the export of English modes of production to Swan River!"[63]

What passed as Aboriginal policy in the region was being shaped by the often confounding and contradictory exigencies of British colonial rule. This aspired to extend, albeit in principle, an attenuated version the rights of the liberal subject and the status of "protection" to Aboriginal people, albeit within the prevailing ethos of social Darwinism. These aspirations were occasionally animated by humanitarian concerns, for example from anti-slavery campaigners, when reports of social conditions reached metropolitan audiences in Perth and London. The distant pulse of these "civilizing" interventions, however, repeatedly contradicted with, and was overridden by, the blunt imperatives of frontier pastoralism and the harsh practicalities of bush governance. Even though, formally, a state of war could not exist with what were de jure colonial subjects, the violent expropriation of both land and labor proceeded almost unchecked. It would eventually be met, rather unevenly, by Aboriginal resistance, in the form of localized burnings of grass or destruction of stock, but this too was soon repressed. "By the 1860s, the Aboriginal labor camp had become an essential adjunct to the station economy" of Western Australia, but this had been fashioned through a state of regulatory exception, in which Aboriginal workers were denied rudimentary human rights, let alone effective employment rights.[64] As Rose concluded from her oral histories of Aboriginal station workers, "while Aboriginal labour was required, Aboriginal people were treated as if they were expendable."[65]

Across the pastoral stations of the Pilbara, where Aboriginal workers were widely employed as stock hands and shepherds, the provisions of the Aboriginal Protection Act of 1886 included an absurdly one-sided labor contract. Employers of Aboriginal labor were required to provide basic rations, medical care ("when practicable"), a blanket, and one pair of trousers, but stipulated no payment of cash wages. Even these obligations, as the Royal Commission of 1905 discovered, were barely observed either in letter or in spirit. Recruitment and retention would routinely occur with the assistance of the police and the inhumane (but widespread) use of neck chains, periodically degenerating into yet more brutal forms of frontier justice. Aboriginal men from the age of fourteen were effectively indentured, for life and without pay, to white station-owners. It was, de facto, a slave regime.[66] Recognizing that Western Australian Aborigines had been denied even the minimal rights of liberal political subjects, the Royal Commission held out the faint hope that they might at least be recognized as valid, if marginal, subjects of the liberal economy. The status of a "unit of labor" was deemed to warrant a cash wage of five shillings per month—equivalent to the lowest wage paid at the time, across the Pacific colonies, by the German administration of New Guinea.[67]

But again, such was the remove from official surveillance, compliance with this international "going rate" was sporadic at best.

Subsequent legislation, through to the 1930s, "left Aborigines with a legal status that had more in common with that of a born idiot than with any other class of British subject."[68] Some station owners in the Pilbara were known to treat their Aboriginal employees with a modicum of paternalist consideration, but the more general pattern was considerably more wretched. It was not uncommon for station owners deliberately to undermine the option of return to Aboriginal communities (and land-based livelihood strategies) by killing hunting dogs, destroying game, and monopolizing water supplies. Should these measures fail to suffice, forced re-employment through the application of neck chains was a practice that persisted into the 1940s. This brutal program of racial subjection was justified by a "bastard mélange of pseudo-Darwinism and the assumptions of the stock breeder."[69] This truly primitive (but in its own way hybrid) form of frontier accumulation had developed in advance even of the pretense of establishing a rudimentary Aboriginal labor market; "Aborigines felt no desire or compulsion to adapt to capitalist society," Buckley and Wheelwright observe, "while prospective employers provided no incentive for them to do so."[70]

This is not to say, however, that there was no mutual adjustment between these apparently irreconcilable modes of economic organization. A range of "accommodative" practices gradually evolved in the Pilbara. These effectively sought to exploit positive-sum "interdependences" between the economies of Aboriginal subsistence and pastoral capitalism, albeit almost entirely on the terms of the latter.[71] For example, as the intensity of work on the stations slackened during the summer, Aboriginal laborers could be released on "holiday rations," allowing some opportunity for the resumption of traditional social and subsistence practices, kinship ceremonies, and "walkabout." Pastoralists also fought to keep Christian missions out of the Pilbara (quite successfully, until the Second World War), on the grounds that this might re-socialize the Aboriginal labor supply, making for "lazy and cheeky" workers with aspirations beyond station work, or (worse still) disruptive notions of social rights.[72] The culture of walkabout, and the presence of an alternative, subsistence economy, also enabled the coding of Aboriginal labor as secondary and seasonal,[73] and thereby institutionalizing a contingent relationship with this rudimentary wage-labor market.[74]

Alongside the processes that, over the course of more than a century, had been driving the real subsumption of Aboriginal labor within the pastoral economy, the indigenous subsistence economy was dragged out of socioecological equilibrium and into intergenerational crisis. Successive waves of epidemics, imported with the European settlers, ravaged the Aboriginal population. Lives increasingly lived on the stations disrupted kinship networks, communal obligations, and the transmission of traditional knowledge. Young Aboriginal men socialized into the pastoral economy were deemed ill-suited for progression through the various stages of ritual initiation and acculturation, limiting progression into the higher echelons of the system of Tribal Law, and eroding community leadership capacities. But notwithstanding these existential pressures, this was far from a moribund, residualized socioeconomy. Some Aboriginal communities were able to keep their distance; others fashioned new, small-scale economies of their own, including pearl diving and tin mining. Aboriginal women, in particular, were significantly involved in the latter activities, notably via the so-called yandy system of panning for tin deposits, which was labor intensive yet relatively productive.[75]

Yandy was the title of an acclaimed documentary novel, published in 1959 by Donald Stuart, which was set against the backdrop of arguably the most momentous event in the social history of the Pilbara, the Aboriginal pastoral workers' strike.[76] Beginning in 1946, not only does this remain Australia's longest strike, at more than three years in duration, it retains the distinction of being "one of the few which has involved both a fundamental challenge to management control and an alternative vision of freedom from that control."[77] Aboriginal workers, even after they had gained a tenuous form of access to the wage-labor economy, had been excluded from the formal awards system, which set minimum wages and conditions for many industries, including the pastoral sector. Acute shortages of white male workers during the Second World War, which brought Japanese bombing raids on the Pilbara towns of Port Hedland and Exmouth, had opened up new opportunities for Aboriginal employment in waged occupations from which they had been traditionally excluded. But the resulting move to establish an "Aboriginal award" (pegging wages to a fraction of "normal" rates) merely reaffirmed racist employment norms.[78] The issue of (continued) wage suppression was much more than a matter of material or instrumental interests, however, since it spoke to received cultural understandings of the meaning of employment relationships, which on the other side were never read as merely contractual in nature: "As in traditional Aboriginal life, a social obligation was implied," so the resistance to wage increases on the part of station managers "called very much into question this implicit assumption."[79]

The proposal for a strike was germinated during a six-week meeting of senior Lawmen at Skull Springs in 1942, "an event of great significance, the sort of Law meeting that took place traditionally perhaps once every fifty years."[80] Meticulous preparations, coordinated across the far-flung network of pastoral stations, separated by hundreds of kilometers, were in their own right significant feats of political networking and social organization. Strike plans were communicated by way of coded messages, inscribed on the labels of food tins delivered to the stations, marking the countdown to the walkout in May 1946.

The protracted labor dispute was the occasion of multiple transgressions, on the part of employers and the authorities, both of ethical principle and "white fella law." The strike's leaders—Clancy McKenna, Dooley Bin Bin, and Don McLeod,[3] the only European involved—were incarcerated multiple times on trumped-up charges, later to be reluctantly released, while station food rations were also (illegally) denied. Working in concert with the pastoral capitalists, the authorities formally excluded station Aborigines from a six-kilometer zone around the town of Port Hedland, an initiative later countered by the establishment of a protest camp three kilometers from the town. As Hess recounts:

> The central issue of the strike was the workers' right to organize, or more precisely to select representatives to negotiate on their behalf. [More than] an industrial demand [this] was also a political demand, which went to the heart of the system of "protection" by asserting that the owners of the means of production and the agents of the state, which acted as their handmaiden, did not have the right to act on behalf of the people. Subsequently the strike led to the establishment of self-managing communities as some strikers sought to achieve control of their social and economic situations. Some of these communities maintained that they were still on strike, decades later.[81]

The dispute was never formally resolved. Descending into a multi-year war of attrition, it was characterized by an escalating program of interventions designed to undermine Aboriginal organization, leadership, and the strike's support in the community; each and every concession from the employer side had to be won, either by social action or by legal appeals. The long-run response on the part of the authorities was not to grant rights of bargaining, self-determination, or workplace organization, and certainly not rights to land, but rather to intensify programs of paternalist social management modeled on measures imported from the Territory of Papua New Guinea.[82] For example, government support was provided for the establishment of Christian mission schools, even though self-organized schools were already in existence at two of the strike camps.

The Pilbara strike may have attenuated the "worst abuses of Aboriginal labour, but [it] did not bring equal pay."[83] However, it did establish the basis for a new kind of socioeconomic movement on the Pilbara, spawning Indigenous organizations with remits in health, education, and social programming, as well as economic interests in mineral prospecting, including formal company structures, which in aggregate would soon be employing more than the (declining) pastoral industry.[84] It is therefore appropriate to conclude, as Holcombe does, that the strike was more than a "reaction to development, but *created* development opportunities," extending, as Howitt points out, to "alternative models of Aboriginal participation in the economy."[85]

Far-off developments in the Fordist manufacturing economies, however, would set the scene for a yet more asymmetrical war of attrition that the Aboriginal people of the Pilbara would effectively lose. As the mass-production economies of North America and Western Europe surged during the 1950s, soon to be joined by Japan, the resulting industrial boom prompted transnational mining companies to embark on a "world-wide hunt for cheap, easily available, mineral deposits," a search that targeted "unprotected" sites under de facto colonial administration.[86] The (market) value of the Pilbara's iron ore deposits was no longer zero, as it had been on the first encounter with colonial geologists. Even though, at the level of economic practice, "it was the Blackfellows who opened up the Pilbara for mineral exploitation,"[87] profits from this radically revalued resource economy would be monopolized by the state and by industrial capital.

New histories of the Pilbara were soon being made. In 1952, the world's largest deposits of iron ore were once again "discovered" by Perth landowner Lang Hancock. The so-called King of the Pilbara then spent years lobbying the federal government to lift its embargo on iron-ore exports.[88] When this was removed, in 1960, and the Western Australian government began to grant exploration permits, Hancock promptly sold his rights to Rio Tinto, duly becoming one of Australia's richest men. His blasé obviation of Aboriginal land rights, that "[n]othing should be sacred from mining,"[89] contained a bitter truth: even after the Traditional Owners were belatedly granted native title and land rights, this did not extend to mineral resources.[90] In the Pilbara, though, there were more immediate concerns. As the mining corporations moved in during the 1960s, the incremental gains that had been secured by Aboriginal communities in struggles against pastoral-capitalist exploitation were promptly reversed, such that the "whole movement [was] scattered and engulfed in the great new developments in this area."[91]

Corporate Enclosure and the Limits of "Normalization"

By the early 1960s, on the heels of the federal deregulation of the iron-ore trade, a full-scale corporate mining boom was underway in the Pilbara. Soon, 90% of Australian iron-ore production was coming out of the region, its population ballooning by tenfold between 1961 and 1976.[92] An American geologist, Tom Price, had discovered another massive deposit in the Hamersley Range, the site of what would become his eponymous company town, founded by Rio Tinto in 1965. White labor was imported for the new mining operations, along with the materials necessary for the construction of a new "macro-landscape" of roads, railways, power lines, ports, and brand-new company towns.[93] In a compact brokered by the Western Australia Country Party, mining employers agreed to import labor from Australia's capital cities, rather than compete for local workers with the struggling pastoral sector, with the result that "the poverty and powerlessness of most Aborigines was reinforced" by the mining boom.[94] Few Aboriginal people were able to access the strictly balkanized housing and labor markets of the company towns, or their services.

In the BHP town of Newman, developed in the late 1960s, the company was known to have made concerted but "quiet efforts to get rid of both Aboriginal employees and the small group of local Aborigines who were living on the edge of the town."[95] With a workforce of around 4,000, it had employed no more than 15 Aboriginal workers by the early 1980s.[96] The Pilbara's nine company towns, which were literally "closed" to outsiders during their formative years, vividly symbolized "the extent to which control over social as well as economic development [had been] ceded by the State government to the mining companies in the interests of rapid and large-scale resource exploitation."[97] While ethnically and economically almost monocultural, these towns were from the outset affluent, at least in monetary terms, given the high wages paid in the corporate mining sector and the "compensations" necessary to lure white families out to what was typically described as an "inhospitable" region.

The Pilbara's company towns soon developed distinct cultures of their own. Notwithstanding their functionalist design, the new towns were barely functional in social terms. "[D]esigned to convey an air of permanency," in a form reminiscent of "southern Australian suburbia,"[98] the company towns owed their existence to the singular purpose of mineral extraction, with an expected life span equivalent to the productive life of the mines. Normatively white, they were planned, built, and occupied with no reference to the surrounding Aboriginal populations. A culture of corporate paternalism prevailed, indexed to a preferred workforce. As Hamersley Holdings wrote of its company towns, "the role of the family is pivotal," these being designed as places where a "happy and contented workforce" could enjoy

> a standard of living that is congenial as is possible in the arduous and challenging environment of the Pilbara. . . . Bowling greens, golf courses, boat clubs, swimming pools, sports ovals, kindergartens and the like can be justified only within the guidelines of . . . Hamersley's philosophy. . . . "A company is a matter of men, relationships and economics. Of these, the most important is men."[99]

The employment and accommodation policies of the mining companies were organized around the perceived needs of married men, "[o]veraward wages, high levels of overtime, and cheap housing attract[ing a migrant] workforce that was predominantly motivated by money."[100] Within this heteronormative environment, single (white) men were not only regarded as a turnover risk by personnel managers, but in a premonition of bogan culture they were "stereotyped . . . as rowdy, uncouth, undisciplined, given to hard drinking, foul language, and brawling. Interaction between them and [families was] minimized and every effort is made to prevent their having contact with female residents (mostly wives and daughters of married workers)."[101]

The Pilbara was widely perceived at the time to be an environmentally *and socially* hostile environment for the incoming corporate workforce, but particularly for the mine workers' trailing families, who were enrolled in a costly, natural experiment in desert suburbanization. There were particular concerns, according to the architect of the new town of Shay Gap, that this start-up community would be "frightening for women-folk," who were often isolated at home, with truncated social networks and access to few, if any, waged-employment opportunities; while the men were found to be prone to overwork and alcoholism, the town's women were susceptible to anxiety, depression, and neurosis.[102] The town's planning philosophy internalized this gender order. As its architect explained:

> The single man is not part of the community. He forms his own associations with his fellow "single man," establishes a pattern of life within the restrictions of the facilities provided and develops a work pattern designed to take maximum advantage of overtime. He has few outlets for his emotions, the marriage market and sexual opportunities are practically non-existent.[103]

The single men's quarters in Shay Gap were duly segregated from the family areas, and designed, as a project engineer recalled, to "provide a motel like ambiance."[104]

Following the discovery of large-scale natural gas reserves in the early 1970s, the expectation of new rounds of investment and job growth in the region prompted the federal and state governments to develop a "Pilbara concept." The social component of the plan involved further attempts to normalize suburban lifestyles, including the principle of home ownership, again with particular attention to a preferred gender order. In fact, 1973 saw no fewer than three major conferences, in Port Hedland alone, concerned with the "plight of women in the Pilbara." The federal government's *Pilbara study* fretted that the company towns had become sites of aggravated social pathology:

> The typical housewife is seen as trapped inside her air-conditioned house by the extreme heat outside, she is subject to the gossip and "bitchiness" of her neighbours and she is powerless to alter the situation. Inactivity, frustration and lack of involvement leads [sic] eventually to self-pity, introvertedness and apathy which is evidenced in the higher than normal evidence of psychosomatic disorders.[105]

Long overtime hours and "time spent at the pub," on the other hand, were associated with elevated rates of alcoholism among men, although the government researchers seemed to be reassured by the fact that, ultimately, the "nature of a man's social interactions are determined by the quality of supervision, the structure of immediate work group, the union regulations and the climate of industrial activity (rest/unrest)."[106]

Residents had been subjected to "intense scrutiny by sociologists, anthropologists and architects to determine the viability of [various] social engineering techniques," Shay Gap's master planner reported, but for all the concern with "stress-relieving" design features, the "climate, the isolation, [and] the paternalism of company towns [continued to] generate conditions conducive to the growth of sociological crises."[107] For its part, the *Pilbara study* concluded that the "breakdown in family life in the Pilbara can probably be attributed . . . to the wide separation between the man's world and the housewife's world" in the company towns.[108] Scarcely acknowledged, however, was the even wider gulf between the "over consumerism [of] the new towns and dire poverty in the Aboriginal population."[109] Parenthetically, the *Study* remarked that "the plight" of the new towns' Aboriginal neighbors will be worsened unless they are provided with the means and the confidence to take advantage of the coming opportunities. . . . The companies have made offers of training and employment on basically the same terms as for white employees, but . . . it is understandable that few have achieved the standard demanded."[110]

Notwithstanding the company towns' internal propensity for social pathology, the male pioneers of desert suburbia also inhabited a purified form of "company space,"[111] the new mining workforce displaying relatively conformist lifestyles and attitudes. There was some resentment of the "penetration of company influences into the social fabric of the company towns,"[112] but in general these were aspirational communities, existentially centered on the corporate mines. Even though nearly all training was acquired (within a few weeks) on a job that often involved long hours operating heavy machinery, the majority of company-town residents regarded themselves as "middle class," reporting generally favorable attitudes toward their monopoly employers, but limited engagement with (or sympathy for) public services and their underlying ethos, which were seen to be remote to the point of practical irrelevance,[113] and which in turn left barely a mark on this privatized suburban landscape.

It was not local sentiment, then, but corporate economics that led the company towns to be gradually "normalized"—that is, transferred to local government administration or "opened"—from the late 1970s. Normalization occurred in the context of a series of "secretive deal[s] between the companies and the state government."[114] Having secured reduced royalty rates in exchange for building the towns in the 1960s, the mining corporations were now facing a profit squeeze, weakening international markets, and new tax rules—prompting this move to offload the costs of social reproduction to the state and to the workforce. These pressures coincided with the development of an increasingly militant workplace culture, together with frequent strikes and job stoppages, not only over employment conditions, but also over town amenities and services.[115] Having evolved from a unilaterally managed space of corporate enclosures in the 1960s to a site of (white) labor organization—a "union place"—by the late 1970s, the Pilbara would become a byword for industrial strife and "restrictive practices" by the 1980s.[116]

Having become a different kind of hotbed for innovative labor-union activity, the Pilbara would foment another of Australia's signature disputes, albeit in a context of a discontinuous industrial relations history, substantially disconnected from earlier episodes of Aboriginal militancy. A strike at the Robe River iron-ore operations saw the company sidestepping the conciliation arbitration system in favor of an unprecedented, litigation-based strategy. The mine owners sued the unions for damages, taking the dispute (expensively) through the courts, marking the beginning of an employer offensive that would eventually cause organized labor to "lose" the Pilbara.[117] This radical departure from previous practice "drastically chang[ed] the field of conflict between capital and labor in Australia."[118] As Bradon Ellem has explained, the right to manage was boldly reclaimed by the region's largest corporate players, with the connivance of governments at the state and federal levels, effectively breaking the local unions.[119] The suburban paternalism of the company towns had first given way to a period of regulatory reform and increased militancy—the Pilbara's own double movement, perhaps—promptly followed by a yet more profound countermovement, in the form of the restoration of barely diluted corporate rule. By the end of the 1990s, the ground had been prepared for a new regime of individualized contracts, which would eventually become the region's (proto)typical employment form.

A minority practice through to the early 1990s, FIFO soon evolved into the "preferred system" for the mine operators.[120] Having tried (and failed) to internalize social reproduction in the company towns, corporate Pilbara's original sociospatial fix, this function would now be externalized and individualized. Employers account for this shift by reference to intensifying competitive pressures, localized skill shortages, and the "prohibitive" costs involved in the construction and maintenance of company towns.[121] It was estimated that 15%–20% of mining and related employment in the Pilbara was accounted for by FIFO by 2000, rising to 49% in 2010, and around 60% of the 55,000-strong workforce by 2020. A dedicated "regional terminal" at Perth airport, designed to accommodate FIFO traffic, was opened in 2012.

The imposition of individualized contracts and FIFO employment arrangements represents more than a recalibration of the balance of power in the workplace; it signifies a much deeper social transformation. FIFO practices outsource social-reproduction costs while subverting the threat of workplace militancy, indeed of labor organization itself. They have individualized not only work but living conditions for the mining workforce. No longer company (town) men, mine workers would become contractualized "entrepreneurs of the self," semi-detached from enduring sources of sociality both at work and at home, and existing in a state of extended contingency. The space of social reproduction is duly relocated from the faux suburbia of the company towns to the actual suburbia of Perth and Australia's other major cities. Meanwhile, as an outsized appendage to a characteristically brusque local culture, openly scornful of big-city niceties, the donga camps have become associated with their own styles of self-reliant knuckling under (see Figure 8.1).

For some time, it has been clear that the sustained expansion of FIFO, along with individualized contract and subcontracting arrangements, was cutting "a swathe through the towns and demoral[izing] locals."[122] The practice has

Figure 8.1 A Pilbara welcome
Source: abloveridge.com, reproduced with permission of Anthony B. Loveridge

been widely criticized for its social costs, both for workers' detached families and across those Pilbara towns that have witnessed a hollowing out of some of the best-paid jobs in their local labor markets, along with fracturing social networks and deteriorating community amenities. A report commissioned in 2004 by the Pilbara Regional Council, which was understandably circumspect in its criticisms of the mining industry, deployed focus groups to document the upside of FIFO (which included "personal independence and freedom . . . financial satisfaction . . . bonding and mateship [and the] strengthening of coping skills"), while also documenting a series of "negative experiences," including:

Poor communication;
Loneliness and isolation;
Abandonment of responsibilities;
Marital dysfunction;
Family dysfunction;
Grief and loss;
Depression;
Possible substance abuse;
Personal devaluing within the family unit;
Guilt at leaving the family.[123]

While the Pilbara's mining corporations rode the global commodity boom, which barely stuttered during the international financial crisis of 2008–2009, the region itself was sliding (back) into social crisis. FIFO has been described by one local politician as the "cancer of the bush."[124] In 2008, the region's major development agencies, along with the Regional Council, issued "an urgent call to action to rescue Pilbara communities," citing spiraling costs of living and deteriorating social sustainability, while others denounced the "project mentality" that had accompanied the region's extractive and balkanized mode of development, advocating a shift in corporate and governmental thinking "from projects to places."[125]

A response to these pressures came in the form of the state government's Royalties for the Regions (R4R) program, intended to redirect one-fourth of mining royalty revenues into regional-development initiatives. This turn in regional-development discourse has been associated with the technocratic embrace of strategic planning frameworks, fueled by redistributive largesse, and the kind of community-based investments initiatives beloved of locally elected officials.[126] R4R was also welcomed by the region's mining corporations, who have rediscovered a commitment to developing the "social infrastructure [of the Pilbara to] a standard commensurate with suburban Perth," as long as the fiscal responsibility remains a governmental one.[127] New motifs in resource-industry discourse include the licensing of culturally legible but always voluntary contributions to "community capacity building," predicted on the condition that the FIFO regime has become "a permanent feature" of the landscape, providing, as it reportedly does, "flexibility for the industry and choice for workers."[128]

A moment that crystalized the tensions and limitations of the FIFO paradigm was the donga dispute of 2009–2010, triggered when 1,500 workers at the Woodside gas project walked off the job in protest against a management decision to restructure accommodation arrangements. No longer would FIFO employees get to return to the same dongas, as they cycled back for their regular rosters. Instead, management sought to increase utilization rates and reduce costs by adopting a "moteling" model, rotating workers into available units. As utilitarian aluminum boxes, dongas are rendered habitable by air conditioning and the right to humanize the space with personal items, family photographs, and other homely comforts. "We're isolated from our families, we live in the desert and we live in little tin boxes," one striker reported; some measure of stability and sociability having been provided by the opportunity to get to know neighbors and to personalize living circumstances otherwise prone to sterility and anomie.[129] Like the company towns before them, the donga camps had become a focus for concerns around mental health, following reports of elevated rates of depression and suicide.[130]

For its part, Woodside's management intransigently maintained that the new moteling scheme was "non-negotiable," with workers facing fines of up to A$28,000 if they failed to return immediately to work, under a new strike notice law that rendered the walkout technically illegal. Political leaders sided with the company: Western Australia's premier lambasted the strikers for what he branded as "greedy" and "un-Australian" behavior, insisting the strike had to end before it undermined the nation's productivity.[131] The president of the local chamber of commerce ridiculed the strikers' complaints about domestic comforts, accusing the unions of planning to "cripple our town," and portraying the dispute as "an insult to the rest of the community when you have up to 10 people sharing a four-bedroom house [in Karratha] to pay the rent."[132]

Ironically, while the much-weakened unions were not directly involved in the original walkout, they were drawn into negotiations to resolve the dispute. Despite this constructive engagement, management complained that it was illegitimate for the unions to have worked to build community support for the strike action, no doubt fearing a resurgence of earlier local experiments in community unionism, which had issued a creative challenge to managerial unilateralism.[133] In the spirit of the individualized contracting regime that Pilbara employers had successfully imposed, the dispute was portrayed as a matter of "individual responsibility" by managers, backed by the legal threat of significant personal fines. Even though the donga dispute was eventually settled, largely in the employers' favor, after the battle (once again) was taken to the courts, the tide was beginning to turn. A court ruling of July 2011 voided the non-union collective agreements fashioned by Rio Tinto, opening opportunities for the unions to re-establish a foothold in the mining industry and in the region.

While this modest correction to the severely unbalanced industrial-relations regime may slow the transition toward individualized and commodified employment relationships in the distended core labor markets of the Pilbara, its effects on "fly-over" communities seem unlikely to be significant. The regional multiplier effects of the FIFO system barely exceed the trickle of expenditures on alcohol, cigarettes, and daily groceries.[134] Across the region's high-wage economy, the extractive logic of corporatized mining—"dig-it-up and ship-it-out [and] when the mineral deposit [is] exhausted, leave"—has been married to a reconstituted core-worker rationality based on the tenet of "save and leave."[135] On the face of it, iron-ore mining and natural-gas extraction are among the most geographically embedded of activities, yet with workers commuting by airplane and resources leaving by train and tanker, their regional externalities and multiplier effects seem almost perverse, inflating as they do the costs of living for permanent residents while free-riding on frail community infrastructures.

In a context in which the Pilabra's remaining iron-ore deposits might take another 10–25 years to work out,[136] the R4R program redirected substantial investment funds into community-infrastructure projects, health, education, and training schemes, and initiatives intended to diversify the regional economy through tourism and agriculture. R4R included an ambitious plan to build "modern, vibrant cities" in the Pilbara. This can be seen as the latest attempt to engineer a kind of "normalization," echoing earlier efforts to fold the company towns into governmental jurisdiction:

> The new buzzword in Karratha is "normalization"—the process by which this dusty boom town, with its high rents, fly-in-fly-out swagger and lack of amenity will again be the sort of place where a family can afford to live in a decent house, whether they work in mining or not.... [W]ork is underway on a host of new community assets—a youth centre, recreation centre, family centre, and more housing [along with a] luxury apartment development, that will have pools and other "resort-style" accoutrements.... [But today, what] will be a developed waterfront is just red dirt and mangroves. There is no cinema, and few places to lunch. Vibrancy seems some way off.[137]

The so-called Pilbara Cities Initiative is also another attempt to resolve rolling crises of social reproduction around the region's corporate mining sector, which built company towns in exchange for reduced royalties in the 1960s and which now syphons a share of royalty revenues back into social-infrastructure spending—all along, with state and federal governments as dependable allies.

Indigenous Exclusions

In the 1960s, when the ore fields were being opening up and the newly built company towns (designed as "closed" developments) were variously ignoring and excluding Indigenous communities, Aboriginal families were migrating toward coastal towns such as Roebourne and Port Hedland in order to gain access—for the first time—to opportunities for formal schooling.[138] Despite a long history of engagement with mining activities, Aboriginal workers and Indigenous mining groups were denied access to the commoditized resource economy during this period, the Pilbara being "opened up" by a developmental accord struck between the Western Australian state government and international capital.[139] As McLeod recounts: "the Blackfellows ... were pushed aside to make way for the multinational mining companies."[140]

During this time, Aboriginal people were belatedly granted access to the Australian welfare state, subject to reclassification as "unemployed" subjects of a liberal market economy. One of the more developmentalist initiatives associated with the moment of liberal-welfarist expansion was the Community

Development Employment Program (CDEP), a community-based job-creation program intended to improve work readiness and employability in remote regions. Some of the programming flexibilities associated with this new scheme facilitated a measure of complementarity with the Aboriginal socioeconomy, mixing cash payments with reciprocal livelihood strategies and providing "participants [with] the opportunity to pursue cultural and non-market prerogatives alongside waged work."[141] This moment of progressive program development, however, proved to be short lived. CDEP soon become a target for conservative critics, who railed against its alleged permissiveness (since participants were not "chased to find work"), its recognition of community needs and social-economy objectives ("pretend jobs"), and the practices of blending projects and redistributing funds at the local level (rent-seeking, "double-dipping," "big-man" politics), ostensibly on the grounds that "[p]retend jobs are destructive of the self-esteem and confidence essential to entry into the labour force."[142] Over time, such culture-of-welfare critiques have gained increased traction, including in some parts of the Aboriginal community itself, in lockstep with the advocacy of new policy models, grounded in the principles of waged-work activation and individual responsibility, trends that have been punctuated by an escalating series of moral panics.[143] This reached its nadir with the Howard government's notorious "Intervention" of 2007, which targeted Aboriginal communities in the Northern Territory as "greenfield sites" for experiments in invasive neo-paternalism.[144]

This trajectory was interrupted by the National Apology in 2008, but the subsequent policy framework, known as "Closing the gap," effectively re-legitimated a remediative or corrective approach,[145] designed to attach Aboriginal workers to the market economy under the signs of individualism, incentives, and (self-)improvement.[146] CDEP projects, in their traditional form, were phased out by 2012, being replaced by a new regime of "soft" federal targets, corporate covenants, and a more direct coupling of employability schemes and individualized welfare. Under the cloak of (neo)liberal good intentions, this can be seen as another iteration of the extended historical process of folding the Indigenous economy, and its subjects, into the modernizing embrace of cultural homogeneity and economic sameness. Altman and Hinkson maintain that such measures seek to impose on Aboriginal communities a market rapprochement, fostering a "new kind of disciplined Aboriginal subject," embracing both the risks and the "individualised aspirations of neo-liberalism."[147]

Some of these arguments now find echoes in policy debates within the Aboriginal community. For example, Noel Pearson has argued:

> We have to get rid of the passive welfare mentality that has taken over our people. The right to self-determination is ultimately the right to take responsibility. Our traditional economy was a real economy and demanded responsibility (you don't work, you starve). The whitefella market economy is real (you don't work, you don't get paid). After we became citizens with equal rights, we lost our place in the real economy. What is the exception among whitefellas—almost complete dependence on cash handouts from the government—is the rule for us. There is no responsibility and reciprocity built into our present artificial economy, which is based on passive welfare (money for nothing).[148]

Others, like Richie Ah Mat, contend that there is no "fatal contradiction between our culture and identity as an indigenous people and the development of a real economy," rejecting the proposition that "the cultural challenges facing our people's participation in market society represent cultural contradictions that are insurmountable."[149] Ah Mat also spurns, as a welfare-statist bromide, the notion that "[i]mproved service delivery with indigenous participation will ... be enough," insisting that Aboriginal communities need to foster new forms of enterprise development and wealth creation: "the existence of capitalism is something we can do nothing about," he argues; "What we have to do is face up to the reality that we live in a market society and economy, and we are located at the most miserable bottom end of it."[150]

In the context of generalized subjection to the disciplines and exclusions of the contemporary market economy, the negotiation of mining rights and employment covenants can be seen to provide, for Aboriginal communities, a rare moment of leverage. Acknowledging what continue to be profoundly asymmetrical and racialized power relations, corporate and governmental actors now find it necessary to recognize and (to some degree) "accommodate" the interests of the Traditional Owners, by way of ameliorative actions, selective concessions, and redistributive spending. These maneuvers have proved to be (politically) necessary, even as they remain manifestly inadequate from an Indigenous perspective.[151] On the other hand, even as the customary socioeconomy has been distorted and suppressed through a long history of asymmetrical struggles with capitalist and state interests, this nominally "alternative" socioeconomy should not *only* be understood in these terms, in the shadow of supposedly more "advanced" economies—and as a vestigial, inert, or archaic economy, lacking dynamism, capacity, or indeed its own logic.

The Pilbara's Indigenous communities have learned to survive, although hardly thrive, by forging flexible connections with the state and market economies, assembling (admittedly precarious) livelihood strategies through income packaging, risk sharing, networked redistribution, and culturally mediated reciprocity. They have made what they can of relations with the mainstream economy, oscillating less than voluntarily between racialized exclusion and contingent attachment, while finding ways to live with state strategies that have lurched between repression, abandonment, paternalism, exclusion, and assimilation. The Indigenous, customary economy has existed, for generations, in a state of complex interdependence with this "mainstream" economy. As Sercombe puts it:

> In the customary economy, the primary focus of the moral economy is on the process of *distribution and exchange*. Aboriginal persons are not so concerned about how one makes an income, but more interested in what one does with it.... At the point at which the mainstream economy is insistent (that is, production), the customary economy is flexible. Where the customary economy is insistent (that is, distribution and exchange) the mainstream economy is flexible. This allows a sustainable, if not always comfortable, co-existence [and it] explains why the customary economy has not been, and probably will not be, extinguished by the dominant capitalist economic system.[152]

This kind of lateral (but still critical) comparative reading of the customary and mainstream economies responds to the Polanyian intuition to seek to understand distinctive modes of economic organization in their own terms as well as relationally—and without subjugating one, a priori, to the other. What Altman tellingly portrays as a "hybrid economy" is therefore composed of three relatively autonomous spheres (customary, market, and state). Distinctive (and "positive") features of the customary economy, in this hybrid context, include an ethic of generosity rooted in demand-sharing as a form of social pragmatism and risk management; a reliance on reciprocal relations, embedded in kinship networks, in which flows of goods, services, caring, and cash enable and reproduce social relationships; and socioeconomic subjectivities that honor a combination of egalitarian principles and kinship hierarchies, managed through studied forms of indirectness and obliqueness, as means of meeting socially differentiated obligations while avoiding direct refusals to "borrow," say, money or living space.[153]

With so many opportunities to develop alternative economic strategies based on the recognition of cultural difference and socioeconomic diversity, "why," Altman rhetorically asks, "would government policy seek to force these people into the alien mainstream?"[154] Yet the phase-out of CDEP after 2007 and the subsequent tightening of welfare rules seemed to promise precisely that. In this context, Altman's notion of the hybrid economy stands not only as an analytical corrective, intended to "properly complexify" Aboriginal economies, since "[t]he hybrid economy is different everywhere."[155]

The stakes in this discussion could hardly be higher. Notable figures such as Noel Pearson, Marcia Langton, and Richard Ah Mat have been pressing a different line, arguing that, possibly in the interest of its very survival, Aboriginal society must forge more viable connections with the corporatized, market economy. Ah Mat refuses to jump to the terminal conclusion that "capitalism and black fellas are mutually exclusive to each other," asking how it might be possible for Indigenous entrepreneurs to "make wealth like white fellas, but ... distribute wealth like blackfellas."[156] Pearson maintains that the rejection of passive welfare and the embrace of the "real" economy are necessary for the social survival of the Aboriginal community, although among other things this will require the root-and-branch reform of the land-rights and Native Title regime, which effectively internalizes corporate advantage: "no place is this [corporate advantage] as egregious as the Pilbara, where two of the world's largest companies—BHP Billiton and Rio Tinto—are digging out ribs of gold, and the blackfellas live in the miserable shadow of the rapacious wounds."[157] As Pilbara-based activist Veronica Rodenburg has observed, "We arguably work in the richest place on the planet, but we work amongst the most incredible levels of poverty and dysfunction."[158] In the construction of alternative futures, there is no need, Marcia Langton insists, to fall back on romanticized visions of a "world [that for Indigenous people] no longer exists in much of Australia," since this runs the risk of normalizing the very disadvantage it seeks to counter.[159] Thinking socioeconomics in hybrid terms, however, is not simply an appeal to political-economic nostalgia, or a matter of promoting idealistic "alternatives" to those mainstream economies under the direct management of corporations and the state; it is also a question of imagining *and then constructing* new forms and practices of hybrid socioeconomic development. Maybe it will ultimately prove possible, as Richard Ah Mat puts it, to "make wealth like white fellas, but ... distribute wealth like blackfellas."

Conclusion: For Substantive Economic Geographies

This chapter has sought to operationalize not only a reading but a writing of a substantivist, Polanyian economic geography in a fashion that might be methodologically suggestive. This has meant thinking across a racially and organizationally divided regional socioeconomy, in a manner that is attentive to the distinctive rationalities (instituted modes of integration, in the Polanyian lingo) of its various "moving parts." The Polanyian presumption here has been that the customary/Indigenous and corporate/market economies—considered in transversal, relational terms—are *both* dynamic and continuously evolving, not that one is practically inert while the other (naturally) epitomizes forward progress. Abject failures of social reproduction have been features of *both* economies, albeit in very different forms, and they have impacted not only those communities banished to the margins of market society.

Polanyi's substantivist methodology provides a license to explore "real" economic forms across diverse economies (with an obligation to consider the full "social span" of those economies), rather than theorizing from a presumptive "center." This entails the unhiding of subjugated and "alternative" economies, but also subjecting these to the kind of transversal-relational analysis that explicitly problematizes their complex articulations and respective positionalities. The analysis must make room for the recognition of the various cultures, components, and moving parts of the economy, recognizing both their distinctiveness and their mutual interactions; it can be seen as an antidote to the orthodox practice of imposing an economistic "market shape of things," while also cautioning against a commonplace habit in more critical circles of analyzing alternative economies as if they are somehow separate or autonomous.[160] This is an approach, then, that validates and recognizes socioeconomic difference (the deconstructive moment, methodologically speaking), but which also calls for a holistic analysis of the often contradictory ways in which the resulting hybrid forms are recombined and instituted (the reconstructive moment).

The Pilbara may be a region of sharp divides and discordant histories, but the "camps" that are to be found in both its corporate and its customary economies have long existed in relation to one another. These uneasily cohabiting socioeconomies can be seen to be mutually articulated, but they also have their own logics, laws, and lores. This is true even of historically dominant processes, such as those of capitalist accumulation and market socialization. After all, the initially fragile economy of pastoral capitalism in the Pilbara, constructed during the period of white settlement, was fundamentally dependent on Aboriginal labor, and it would later be episodically reshaped by Aboriginal politics. The corporatized, extractive economy also has an Indigenous precursor, albeit one suppressed by the state-facilitated, monopoly-corporate model that has been dominant since the 1960s. This "dominance of giants" is never complete, however: the legitimacy of the latest rounds of multibillion-dollar investment continue to be predicated on a contestable and in some respects tenuous social license to mine, exposing the fraught political interface between Aboriginal rights, federal oversight, and corporate action. The politics of this dispossessive economy are being managed, far from sustainably or equitably, through the selective governmental redistribution of mining royalties on the one hand and through the voluntaristic rubric of corporate social responsibility on the other. From an Indigenous perspective, these are economies of consolation. They mark the contemporary limits of Aboriginal economic citizenship in the Pilbara.

This said, there is no justification for consigning the customary economy of the Traditional Owners to pre-capitalist irrelevance, or passing it off as some cultural artifact. Even as it has been repeatedly, and often violently, subjugated, the Aboriginal economy of the Pilbara has itself evolved, both independently and in dynamic articulation with the region's market economy. Repeated attempts to marginalize, silence, and erase Aboriginal livelihoods and indeed economics, cumulatively to the point of their near obliteration, should not be mistaken for a natural order of economic things. Yet neither a nostalgic nor a static conception of the Indigenous, customary economy will suffice. This is one reason why a loosely metaphorical reading of social embeddedness (Polanyi "lite") cannot be, on its own, enough. The responsibility of substantivist inquiries, in this context, is not artificially to reflate the Indigenous economy, but to find and "place" this economy among its others. This not only means unhiding the economic in overly "culturalized" readings of Aboriginal society, but also entails digging into the sociocultural bases and preconditions of "mainstream" economies, which are rarely as functional and rational as conventional representations imply.

Read for their open-ended methodological potential, substantivist economic geographies should seek proactively to sample on, *and across*, socioeconomic difference, rather than to assume, a priori, conventional understandings of equilibrium, hegemony, normativity, centricity, convergence, or trajectory. They should embrace methodological holism, probing the distinctive rationalities and instituted forms exhibited by different socioeconomic formations and modes of integration, but exploring their articulations, interdependencies, and relational connections, rather than falling back on analytical separatism. They must aspire to socioinstitutional holism too, taking account of reproductive and redistributive circuits, rather than "reading off" from privileged sites of production, or "reading back" from the supposedly advanced corporate-market economy to some remnant other. And while they should be deeply skeptical of claims to the self-acting capacity, long-run competitive advantage, or normative-historical superiority of market systems, critical interrogations of actually existing markets, in all their mutating and variable forms, have their place too.

9
After Variety

Unevenly Developing Capitalism(s)

The shared remit of this and the following chapter is an epistemological one. This chapter begins by re-engaging with some of the generative themes of the book—the distinctive analytical perspective of geographical political economy, critiques of varieties-of-capitalism (VoC) orthodoxies and ideal-typical reasoning, the challenge of working with and through sociospatial difference—in order to build a case for theorizing capitalist diversity through the lens of uneven and combined development (UCD). The concept of uneven development, as the typical shorthand in economic geography often has it, has a checkered history all of its own. Often deemed to be a source of unnecessary complications in the "non-spatial" social sciences, even the critical ones, uneven geographical development became a focus of active theoretical concern for prominent geographers like David Harvey, Doreen Massey, and Neil Smith during the 1980s—a period when the sociospatial ordering of capitalism itself was undergoing a phase of accelerated transformation. The recognition of uneven development would subsequently become baked in, as an ontological premise, for geographical political economists.[1] But during the "long 1990s"—dominated as it was by the ideological common sense of globalization, but dragging on until the global financial crisis of 2008—active engagement with questions of uneven development tended to take a back seat to concerns focused on the (internal) dynamics of growth regions, the productive power of clustering, and the capacities of corporate networks. Among geographical political economists, uneven development was never really repudiated, but it receded to the background, to be taken almost for granted, while attention to its active theorization waned. There has been something of a sea-change, however, in the long decade-cum-interregnum that has followed the global financial crisis of 2008, when questions of uneven development have been opened up again, albeit in different ways, for what are manifestly different times.

It is no coincidence, surely, that this has once again been a period in which the gestalt of capitalism, as an unevenly globalized spatial order, has itself been palpably changing, often in unprecedented and disruptive ways. The ascendancy of China, the emergence of reactionary populisms, the (re)turn to authoritarian governance, long-run crises associated with social care and climate change, the arrival of platform modes of capitalism and new waves of automation, historic shifts in financialization and monopolization... the list goes on. Accompanying these disorientating and transformative developments, and seeking to make sense of them, have been new waves of creative theorizing around uneven development itself, and this time not only among geographers, but also in anthropology, historical sociology, international relations, postcolonial economics, economic history, and more.[2] New approaches to capitalist and more-than-capitalist diversity have been proliferating too, many of which have been outrunning the short-lived orthodoxy of VoC theorizing. Not only have the real-world dynamics of capitalist transformation been overflowing the restrictive register of VoC analysis, it has become increasingly evident that the varieties approach itself was very much a product of its time—the long 1990s—when it served as a perhaps necessary but ultimately insufficient response to narratives of global convergence and unchecked (neo)liberalization. For a time, the parsimonious heuristics and crisp typologies of the VoC approach had catalyzed "an unprecedented outpouring of high-quality research and debate,"[3] elevating the approach and its stylized facts to the status of a standard position in teaching and texts.[4] The heyday of VoC research turned out to be quite brief, however, as a growing band of critics and skeptics took objection to its methodological nationalism, its reliance on static, case-by-case comparisons and taxonomic simplifications, its implicit functionalism,[5] and not least, the real-world uncertainties that now surround the very idea of "advanced" capitalism.[6] A normative undercurrent in VoC theorizing had long informed what had been, at least in part, a tacit defense of European-style CMEs against an LME model that, notwithstanding its own limitations, always had Gresham's Law if not history on its side, the bad demonstrating the short-term capacity to undermine the good. Yet the global financial crisis and its extended aftermath had also eroded the LME model itself.[7] Insofar as the twin-peaks image of capitalism was ever accurate or sufficient, the world after 2008 certainly began to look very different. Comparativists were duly altered to "the probability of substantially *messier outcomes* as far as capitalism's future is concerned," Bohle and Greskovits observed, "Occam's razor no longer favor[ing] the neat division of contemporary capitalism into compact varieties."[8] Some have drawn more radical conclusions in this apparent "age of entropy," asking whether capitalism itself, of whatever stripe, has much of a future.[9]

The provisional label of "post-VoC" has been applied to the various lines of comparative-capitalisms research that have proliferated over the past decade, motivated by more or less forgiving critiques of the VoC approach, and prompted to varying degrees by the challenge of accounting for post-2008 patterns of political-economic restructuring, realignment, and recombination.[10] Instrumental here has been a belated recognition of a radical "underestimation of the really existing diversity of contemporary capitalism" in the VoC orthodoxy, responses to and reactions against which have involved "an expansion of the geographical scope of [comparative capitalisms] research," marking an "incipient 'globalization' of the field," most actively at the "interface between left institutionalism and neo-Marxism."[11] In the process, some of the old boundaries between development studies, international political economy, heterodox and institutional economics, economic anthropology, historical sociology, and economic geography have been dissolving, as new lines of dialogue and debate have been opened up. In some strands of this work, what Ian Bruff and colleagues call "the gravitational pull" of the VoC methodology remains in evidence, as the original framework has been variously extended and recalibrated.[12] Elsewhere, the break has been more fundamental—sometimes invoking the VoC paradigm as a foil, on other occasions building from quite different conceptual premises.

In the field of geographical political economy, the rubric of variegated capitalism may have sufficed for a time as a holding position, but it is surely true to say that what may have been a theoretically necessary critique remains, at this point, methodologically insufficient. It may have suggested some alternative points of theoretical departure, but when it came to the matter of an alternative conceptual framework, coupled with an alternative methodological rubric, there was work still to be done. In this context, the "rediscovery" and then reanimation of the concept of UCD has been proving to be generative,[13] as has the renewed interest in codifying and elaborating various forms of "conjunctural" analysis, the methodological implications of which will be further explored in Chapter 10. As David Harvey once observed, when reflecting on the limitations of his own *Limits to Capital*, more than two decades after the book's 1982 publication, "a decent theoretical understanding of uneven geographical development still remains to be written," which he put down to the uniquely "disruptive" consequences of dealing with questions of spatiotemporality in theory-building efforts, since these really needed to be accounted for "at the very start rather than at the end of the analysis."[14] Stuart Hall had also long been of the view that "uneven development [was a] concept in the old Marxist literature than needs to be rethought."[15] This is arguably not a once-and-for-all task; as if UCD presents as an intractable problem awaiting a definitive solution. Rather, it is a problem of (and for) the ongoing work of conjunctural theorizing.

The task of this chapter, accordingly, is to begin to marshal the resources necessary to engage this demanding problem, prelude to the methodologically focused discussion in Chapter 10. First, however, there is some preparatory work to do. As Bob Jessop has observed, "No consensus exists on schemes for exploring the unity *and* heterogeneity of capitalism," for making sense of the complex existence of capitalism as an unevenly developed and multiform world system at once deeply integrated and pervasive but at the same time neither singular nor homogeneous.[16] Working away at this puzzle of the (re)production of difference in and through capitalism's contradictory development cannot be reduced to a matter of replacing one framework with another, or building a better classificatory mousetrap; it entails ongoing processes (and practices) of reflexive theorizing and methodological development. As Stuart Hall once said, this inescapably involves "constantly losing and regaining concepts," the breaking and remaking of which is the continuing work of theoretical practice, involving necessary "detour[s] on the way to something more important."[17]

In search of some of the more promising of such detours, the chapter begins by picking up a number of currents in post-VoC theorizing, which have been opening up new avenues for the conceptualization and mapping of capitalist diversity. Beyond the ritual flogging of a dead heuristic, these post-VoC lines of inquiry have yielded transformative critiques of the rise and fall of this distinctive epistemological framework, accounting for its (passing) appeal as well as its limits, while consolidating what amount to alternatives. Historicizing the VoC moment, with which the chapter begins, can also inform the necessary work of historicizing UCD, the generative potential of which is explored through the remainder of the chapter. The overarching task here is to elaborate a framework for the critical study of capitalism's spatiotemporality, its character as a variegated, conjunctural, and "terraforming" phenomenon, by effectively internalizing the problematic of UCD from the get-go.[18] As Neil Brenner has emphasized, this cannot simply be a matter of "adding in" space as a (single) dimension of the capitalist restructuring process, let alone some merely empirical refinement; to engage with UCD is to provoke far-reaching questions of conceptualization and methodology.[19] "Uneven development" is more than an untidy fact of life, more also than a background condition. In its confrontation with the immanent and multidimensional character of UCD, the chapter proposes three "cuts" at the question: place and positionality, hybridity and holism, and temporality and transformation. These are intended

Old and New Capitalist Futures

The future of capitalism is not what it used to be. What is more, the future of capitalism does not appear to be *where* it used to be. Back in the early 1990s, it was not uncommon to hear versions of the *Economist*'s triumphant declaration that "[t]he collapse of communism brought universal agreement that there [is] no serious alternative to free-market capitalism,"[20] this also being the time of Deng Xiaoping's fateful and now storied "Southern Tour," ostensibly to secure a unidirectional and irreversible path to capitalism in China by way of "reform and opening up." As Thomas Friedman would later put it, in a crowning statement for that globalization decade, "the free market is the only ideological alternative left," the choices having been reduced to "free-market vanilla [or] North Korea."[21] A decade later, things looked very different indeed. In the aftermath of a global financial crisis incubated in the supposed heartlands of neoliberal capitalism, the *Economist* declared that "[t]he era of free-market capitalism has come to a juddering halt," and possibly worse still, that this "crisis of liberal capitalism has been rendered more serious by the rise of a potent alternative: state capitalism."[22] As the would-be capital of an apparently Eastward-tilting world order, China had achieved the most spectacular economic transformation in recorded history, with the assistance of an ostensibly sui generis strategy variously named as "perestroika without glasnost," neoliberal authoritarianism, market socialism, state capitalism, or some other neologistic formulation.[23] Meanwhile, the economic and political fortunes of the remaining BRICS (Brazil, Russia, India, and South Africa) were beginning to diverge quite dramatically, Japan remained in the slow-growth doldrums, and first the Brexit referendum and then the Trump election would augur a phase of radical uncertainty and reaction in the debased capitals of the neoliberal revolution.[24]

Surveying this shifting terrain, Sandro Mezzadra and Brett Neilson conclude that a fundamental spatiotemporal reconstitution of capitalism has been underway, with no guarantee that the accompanying contradictions, which if anything seem to have intensified during the COVID pandemic, can be managed within the extant order:

> There is a growing sense that capitalism now, more than any other time since the end of World War II, has entered a critical condition. The crisis of 2007–2008 has

cemented a historic downturn that began with the end of postwar prosperity in the 1970s and, punctuated by spikes and troughs, acquired intensity as the world economy became more interconnected and globalized. Declining growth rates, deflation, rising levels of indebtedness, bailouts, labor precarity, and ever widening gaps in social and economic inequality are only the most obvious symptoms of this change. A peculiar temporal scrambling of crisis and recovery characterizes the current economic condition, such that a cyclical logic of boom and bust no longer seems to apply, deep-lying structural factors guide the transformations at hand. Yet more is at stake than economic turmoil. A social and spatial disruption has crossed the processes of capitalist globalization, shattering geographical hierarchies. The faltering of US hegemony in the face of the rising BRICS [along with] "currency wars" and turmoil around the persistent global hegemony of the dollar, the reshuffling of geographies of development, novel articulations of nationalism and neoliberalism, and the emergence of new regionalisms and patterns of multilateralism are some of the features of the reorganization of the contemporary world.[25]

For Mezzadra and Neilson, it follows that "the need for a spatial perspective on current capitalist crisis is manifest," not least because "[n]ew and emerging centers of accumulation have become sites of intense social struggle, while it has apparently become increasingly difficult even to "*locate* the 'most advanced' tendencies of capitalist development."[26]

Of course, questions concerning the relative performance, future prospects, and comparative character of capitalism are as old as capitalism itself. In *Capital*, Marx famously took England's factory model as "the classic form," and by implication its most advanced manifestation,[27] although he also made frequent reference to the comparative (under)performance of other national economies, while the methodological notes in the *Grundrisse*, in particular, spoke to a much more elaborate conception of "multiple determinations," complex interdependencies, modes of articulation, and conjunctural formations.[28] The idea of "development," too, is freighted with fundamentally stadial conceptions of modernist progress and, for laggards especially, fundamentally Eurocentric prescriptions for catching up, or climbing the ladder, while even the supposedly "advanced" capitalisms of the postwar period would be routinely exhorted to examine themselves in the mirror of the American way.[29] During the Cold War, the ultimate other that was communism occupied a space ostensibly exterior to capitalism, of course, the source of ideological taint for more interventionist, socialist, or welfare-statist modes of development both in the decolonializing "Third World" and in the West, including some varieties of Keynesianism and developmentalism.[30]

As Streeck and others have argued, models of convergent capitalist development, invariably sutured to idealized depictions of "advanced" capitalism, generally held sway until the last three decades of the twentieth century.[31] The widespread (if profoundly uneven) onset, during the 1970s, of industrial-relations strife, macroeconomic instability, deindustrialization, stagflation, and a series of fiscal and oil crises, coinciding with the rise of Japan and other rapidly industrializing economies across Asia, prompted formulations like the "new" international division of labor, which began to unsettle assumptions of an orderly progression toward a Westernized economic future. Questions of comparative economic and institutional performance accordingly began to assume a new (and different) salience, not to say urgency, focused initially on (the promise of) new configurations of corporatist governance and employment regimes, and subsequently on alternative models of enterprise organization and innovation-intensive growth. Entering the 1980s, in the face of slow growth and deepening political divides, the United States and the United Kingdom doubled down on their (neo)liberal modes of development, in parallel with the rise of modestly "alternative" economic imaginaries, including Japanese systems of quality control and just-in-time inventory management, the neoMarshallian industrial districts of the Third Italy, developmental-statism in the Asian tiger economies, Scandinavian innovation cultures, and more.[32] Then, the collapse of the Soviet bloc breathed new life into the idea, for a while, that the arc of history was bending toward free-market capitalism, now in the shape of a borderless world powered by a new generation of information and communications technologies and guided by benign combinations of light-touch regulation and third-way politics. Once again, the one best way and the ultimate stage of capitalism closely resembled the American way.

The globalization decade of the 1990s—as a cultural Zeitgeist, as a geopolitical moment, and as a distinctive episode in social theory—can be seen in retrospect as the complex outcome of the quite particular world-historical "vacuum" created by the fall of state socialism to Europe's East, by a seemingly terminal unraveling of the postwar social settlement in the post-Keynesian world, and by the (resulting) opportunity to generalize, if not universalize, an Anglo-American model of expansive neoliberalism.[33] In other words, this was a conjunctural geohistorical moment of a quite specific kind, (mis)representing itself in discourses of globalization with their tropes of deterritorialization and deregulation, seamless market integration, progressive corporate rule, disappearing borders and nation-states, and so on. Free-market capitalism was declared triumphant. "One world, ready or not," became the new exhortation.[34]

This was the context in which the VoC approach was incubated, and where its measured and in some ways modest distinctions between liberal and coordinated modes of governance, and the CME versus LME model of capitalism, gained traction.[35] In this treatment, enduring sources of capitalist divergence—readily associated with received distinctions between *Gemeinschaft* and *Gesellschaft*, and between American individualism and the European social model—were rendered as alternative poles of institutional equilibrium. The VoC approach neatly split the difference on the questions of advanced-capitalist diversity, viability, and performance, positioning LMEs and CMEs as symmetrical ideal types, while maintaining that neither should be considered inherently "superior" to the other.[36] Moreover, it catalogued the kind of mainstream institutions with which the very best of capitalisms could not only live but actually thrive. In this sense, it was a reformist theory, built in and for the globalizing times.

Rapidly canonized, the VoC approach made itself readily available for game-theoretical applications, for "lateral" extensions across other national cases and (sub)types, and for all manner of affirmative and adaptive uses in conjunction with country-level data sets, having been fashioned to sit alongside, and more ambitiously to engage with, orthodox economics, from a position at least adjacent to its own territory.[37] This said, the VoC intervention was designed to be at least moderately disruptive of neoliberal and neoclassical orthodoxies, attempting the balancing act of deferring to the purity of the LME model, by way of a somewhat indulgent reading of its American form, as the free-market, small-state ideal rendered as (if) institutionally real, while demanding equal air time (and analytical respect) for its European cousin. In contrast to Albert's more pejorative treatment of transatlantic differences, which had sounded a warning at the beginning of the globalization decade that the "Rhinish" model was about to fall prey to Anglo-American neoliberalism, the Hall and Soskice project sought to represent the two capitalisms as functionally coequal models, offering an apparently even-handed counter to the Americanizing-cum-globalizing mainstream by smuggling in, under the cover of economic scientism, a "more or less explicit normative bias in favor of some sort of social-democratic or communitarian, welfare state-supported, or otherwise solidaristic 'embedding' of the capitalist economy."[38]

As David Coates has argued, for all its studied centrism, the VoC approach was "at best a 'Third Way' defence of managed capitalism, one heavily imbued with an orthodox understanding of basic market rationalities, and one that conceded the appropriateness of neoclassical economics as a guide to the inner workings of LMEs, if not to that of CMEs";[39] echoing the third-way conceit of equidistance between (reformed) welfare-statism and (moderated) neoliberalism, the philosophical affinities and practical slippages of which were clearly on a slope tending in the direction of the latter, not the former. This was, after all, an analytic grounded in rational-choice micro-foundations rather than social struggle and asymmetrical power relations; it favored a correspondingly weak variant of institutionalism, based on the formal domains of economic governance at the national scale; and it read the world mostly through the eyes of firms, positing a level playing field of competition between a favored cluster of national economies, while noting in passing certain strategic advantages of the LME model in game-changing innovation, short-term adaptability, and in financialized development.

While superficially balanced, the maneuver of placing LMEs and CMEs side by side, on the (same) level, and for all intents and purposes in "pacific" competition, had the effect of privileging benign institutional differences over the disruptive commonalities, connections, and contradictions of capitalism. What might be said in the defense of the VoC intervention was that it held open, or reopened, the question of capitalist diversity in the face of convergence arguments embedded in neoliberal politics, neoclassical monism, and orthodox globalization discourse, albeit in ways that misconstrued not only diversity but capitalism itself. As Hodgson has observed, in relation to another difference-splitting feature of the VoC literature, this work can also be read as a counter to

> the traditional Marxist and market-fundamentalist notions that only one type of capitalism (or one developmental track for capitalism) is feasible, normal, or desirable. Those counterarguments are important. But variety does not imply that it is impossible to define capitalism; this would be a misunderstanding of what *definition* means. As in biology, variation across a population does not preclude a common essence for a genus or a species. In fact, the understanding of that common essence helps us appreciate the nature and scope of the variation or change.[40]

The challenge here, and surely one of the reasons why critics have repeatedly taken the VoC project to task for losing sight of (historical) capitalism itself,[41] is to think of difference and commonality, the parts and the constitutive whole, "national" and "global" capitalisms, and so on, *together* and dialectically, rather than separately or sequentially. In putting institutional variety first, by theorizing stable varieties *of* capitalism rather than disruptive variety *in* capitalism, by privileging a static understanding of (national) diversity over simplistic notions of (global) convergence, the VoC project may have exploited an opening in millennial narratives of globalization theory, but in doing so it constructed a trap of its own making. Effectively freezing the process of historical change itself, it read off, from a particular historical moment, a single axis of revealed difference within the privileged world of advanced capitalism, sanctifying "safe" differences as theoretical types.[42] The two varieties existed in mutual isolation, their "coherence" being displayed on the inside, within domestic institutional spaces. LMEs and CMEs were therefore both cocooned and placed at a reassuring distance from one another, separated by the North Atlantic but coexisting in pacific competition. Not only does this approach take insufficient account of the rivalrous relations and intricate interdependences *between* a select club of national capitalisms, it also blurs out much of the actual world, while depriving the *inter*national (or global) scale of its requisite political-economic and institutional complexity, not to say its geography.

Contrary to the impression left by the hyperglobalist moment of the 1990s, the global sphere is not a barely occupied space of free and fluid markets. Nevertheless, it was in part "by grossly oversimplifying the globalization debate," Bohle and Greskovitz have argued, that VoC scholars "missed an important dimension of contemporary capitalism ... an emergent institutional and social reality beyond the *confines of the nation state.*"[43] More than an ocean of white space separating institutionally distinctive islands of capitalism, the global is in its own way a densely structured and sociologically complex sphere; "internationality" has its own character, qualities, and granularity; the global is not some rarified, abstract space, hovering above the supposedly "more concrete" terrain of institutions and grounded practices.[44] To return to Stuart Hall's cautions, issued at the start of the globalization decade: "I am asking that we do not think of globalization as a pacific and pacified process," nor in "too unitary a way," and yet, he insisted, we *do* need to think about it, about its polymorphic but planetary constitution, about its complex and ongoing construction through dominant and subordinate particularisms.[45] He went on to explain that

> what we usually call the global, far from being something which, in a systematic fashion, rolls over everything, creating similarity, in fact works through particularity, negotiates particular spaces, particular identities and so on. So there is always a dialectic, a continuous dialectic, between the local and the global.... What we call "the global" is always composed of varieties of articulated particularities.[46]

The VoC literature hardly ignored the global domain, which was often read through the lenses of regime competition and liberalization, but its analytic gaze remained insistently focused on national economic spaces and domestic institutional domains. It was not always that way, however. Earlier iterations of VoC research had traced similar kinds of "dual convergence" tendencies, polarizing around LMEs and CMEs, to macro-scale shifts in the global economy, and then to a wider array of meso-scale institutions (including unions and central banks, as well as firms) as mediators of the resulting pressures and opportunities, but it was the firm-centered, micro-foundations approach of Hall and Soskice that caught and made the wave, "revolutionizing" (or rather, reforming) the field of comparative political economy.[47] That it did so, however, is a matter of both content and context. With its "firm-centeredness, parsimony, and reliance on conceptual tools borrowed from economics," the VoC approach "entered the field in the right historical moment," Bohle and Greskovits have reflected, combining calculated scientific appeal and recalibrated normative concern in a fashion that "fit this *Zeitgeist* better than other approaches."[48]

It was in this context, on the heels of a robust period of American growth, achieved alongside European resilience, that the VoC articulated not one but two "best cases" for advanced capitalism. And it was by refining ideal-typical models on the basis of the revealed properties (and received understandings) of this pair of "exemplary" cases that the VoC literature made its own case *both* for the American version of classically free(r) market capitalism and the (ostensibly) "more" socially embedded solidaristic, and egalitarian German model. As Crouch explains, Hall and Soskice were "not building out their theory deductively, but [were] reading back empirical detail from what they want[ed] to be their paradigm case of an LME—the USA—into their formulation of the type," stylizing this as a free-market model; this was to elide the empirical comparison of cases with the construction of conceptual categories, even though "it is logically impossible to derive the characteristics of a theoretical category from the characteristics of an example of it," given that understandings of the former precede observations of the latter.[49] The result, in the case of the LME, is a curious amalgam of neoclassical idealization, circular reasoning, and what Andrew Sayer, after Marx, called "chaotic conception." A chaotic concept "arbitrarily divides the invisible and/or lumps together the unrelated and the inessential, thereby carving up the object of study with little or no regard for its structure and form."[50] Even while holding in abeyance the matter of the "external" conditions of existence for the US model of the LME (such as its reliance on pools of migrant labor deprived of social and employment rights, the availability of cheap inputs to household consumption, or its complex interdependencies with "Chinese" capitalism), the "internal" integrity of this case-turned-type must be questioned in light of the fact that its circumscribed institutionalism conveniently excludes large-scale features of constitutive significance, like the military economy, privatized care, the Mexican border, and the prison system.[51] This less-than-innocent act of bracketing evidently has a role in maintaining the illusion of an approximation between the actually existing form of US capitalism and the small-state/free-market ideal of neoclassical economics and neoliberal ideology. It is difficult to escape the conclusion that the bundle of institutional forms that are rendered "coherent" in the LME model, to the point that they resemble a game-theoretic operating environment, is the outcome of a selective and somewhat stereotypical reinterpretation of the American case, in the fashion of a stand-in and stand-alone ideal type.[52]

A parallel set of arguments can be marshaled in relation to the CME model, as a stylized and generalized reading of the German case, plus complementary features of several of its OECD-world "relatives"; suffice it to say that the recurrent concern in the VoC literature that this somewhat more earthly model might be vulnerable to regulatory undercutting, in a world tendentially structured in favor of LME-style financial liberalization, has yet to play out in the expected fashion. Ironically, the 2008 financial crisis, incubated within the LME model itself and its de facto heartlands, would take a particularly heavy, self-inflicted toll on the economies of the United States and the United Kingdom, tarnishing claims to model status and sending shockwaves across the pacific waters of VoC world. As David Coates put it, the reverberations of what appeared to be an open-ended and global financial crisis meant that

> where the deckchairs stood on the deck of the *Titanic* suddenly mattered less than the fact that they were all going down on the same doomed ship. In calm waters, the difference between ships is fascinating. In storms, the only thing that matters is the weather. What had been ignored in the VoC debate (underlying capitalist contradictions), and what had been marginalized (cross-national linkages between economies), suddenly in late 2008 moved centre-stage again, and a conceptual universe preoccupied by minute institutional variation could suffice no more.[53]

While the outfall of the global financial crisis was anything but uniform, in geographical, social, or institutional terms, it would be apparent that the VoC moment, with its reductionist reading of capitalism at its hypothetical best, seemed well and truly to have passed, in both a political and analytical sense. As Matthias Ebenau read the situation, its "typological simplification, microeconomic bias, overemphasis on institutional stasis, and theoretical nationalism" rendered the VoC framework "fundamentally unsuited for grasping the variegation of capitalism on a global scale."[54] Likewise, Wolfgang Streeck observed that the "sudden outbreak of crisis" underscored the need to focus on "what different national capitalisms have in common and how they hang together, as opposed to where they differ," calling for a "paradigm shift" away from VoC-style static institutionalism in favor of a renewed emphasis on "dynamic commonalities," within an *internally diversified capitalist world system* [in such a way as] not to deny differences, but place them in a context of strong economic and political interdependence."[55] The VoC paradigm, Coates concludes, was "very much a product of its time," mutating after the global financial crisis of 2008 into more of a "touchstone ... rather than a starting gun" for the reanimated field of comparative political economy.[56]

Would-be successors to the VoC approach are no less conjuncturally situated, of course, no less products of their time and circumstances. The rise to truly global significance of China, in fact, has spawned new rounds of two-solitudes theorizing, with the United States retaining its familiar role of the paragon of liberalized, free-market capitalism, while China becomes the proxy for statist development, albeit as a model unto itself.[57] This said, the sense of cartographic certainty—founded on a well-documented map of bordered national capitalisms, enduringly clustered around two magnetic poles—does seem to have eroded. As an editorial in the *Socio-Economic Review* put it: there is now an increasing awareness that too many ostensibly "universal" vocabularies draw "implicitly from the US context" as a proxy for capitalism in its ideal or most advanced form, that the "understanding of institutional diversity and political economic dependencies from a truly worldwide perspective remains glaringly underdeveloped," and that the work of building "new and better theories" of economic diversity is very much a work in progress, requiring "more field work, more fresh and original data, and more ethnography."[58]

While some of its stylized facts persist, there is sense that the VoC project has stalled, if not run its course, but also that new trajectories in comparative capitalism research have yet to be fully consolidated. Not coincidentally, the focus of critical attention has shifted to (some of) the regions that were previously marginal to the VoC imaginary, if not off the map altogether, such as Central and Eastern Europe,[59] Latin America,[60] and China.[61] A series of more inductive and exploratory mapping exercises, furthermore, have called attention to a world of largely unexplained differences, unnamed hybrids, and codependent formations.[62] The moment of "peak" VoC theorizing having passed, along with its misplaced certainties, the paradigm is now more often invoked as a foil or convenient heuristic than as a go-to framework, with various lines of contention generating a handful revisionist projects, but more often than not triggering a search for more radical alternatives. In this respect, the principal lines of critique that were summarized by Bob Hancké, Martin

Rhodes, and Mark Thatcher on the cusp of the global financial crisis seem to have ossified, marking in retrospect the outer limits of the project rather than an occasion for its reconstitution:

> A salvo of critique provoked by the Hall-Soskice approach to VoC theory has raised many points of contention: that it is too static and focused on permanency and path dependence, missing important elements of economic change . . . ; that it is functionalist . . . ; that it ignores the endogenous sources of national system transformation and "within-system" diversity . . . ; that [it] has a propensity to "institutional determinism" in its mechanistic conception of institutional complementarities and neglect of underlying power structures . . . ; that it has a truncated conception of the firm as an "institution-taker" rather than an autonomous, creative, or disruptive actor and neglects variation among firms within national models . . . ; that it divides the world into reified notions of LME and CME archetypes and lacks the tools for moving beyond this bifurcation . . . ; that VoC theory is not built deductively to create Weberian "ideal types" that could be used for the construction of hypotheses, but rather creates "types" by reading back empirical information from the countries it seeks to make paradigm cases . . . ; that it has a manufacturing bias . . . ; that it treats nation states as "hermetically sealed" and neglects the linkages between them and the forces of convergence and globalization . . . ; that it is "apolitical," equilibrium-biased and downplays conflict . . . ; that it is sex blind" . . . ; and that it neglects the role of the state.[63]

For present purposes, two conclusions can be drawn. First, the VoC moment stands as a reminder that accounts of the present form and future trajectories of capitalism, especially those that resonate politically or capture some mood of the times, are *themselves* creatures of context; these imaginaries of capitalism are coproduced with the historical geographies of capitalism that they purport to describe, analyze, diagnose, and anticipate.[64] This is something that can be certainly be said of the interrelated moments of universalist globalism in the 1990s and the rediscovery of (minimalist) variety that immediately followed, just as it seems to apply to earlier theories à la mode too, such as those focused on visions of incipient Japanization or flexible specialization, Italian-style. Second, there is much (still) to learn from these experiences, and the parallel historical geographies of model-building and theory-making. In light of the proto-methodological goals of the present chapter, while there are easy critiques to be made of parsimonious formulations like the VoC approach, with its static and geographically stylized ideal types, weak counterclaims that the world is more complex will not suffice as ends in themselves. No doubt Occam's razor will keep swinging, tending to favor sparsely formulated and tightly rationalized rubrics over those that variously accommodate, wrestle with, live with, and work with diversity, divergence, difference, complexity, contradiction, and conjunctural specificity, but as Crouch points out, "parsimony must not become an excuse for inaccuracy and ignoring important diversity,"[65] or an alibi for misrepresentation and misdirection. The challenge of how to recognize and account for "important diversity" cannot be adequately answered simply by adding more varieties of capitalism, or by issuing trite, plenary claims about the extra-theoretical complexity of the actually existing world. However, according to what alternative methodological coordinates, grounded in what "alternative" epistemological principles, might this world be understood?

The stubborn problem at the heart of the VoC debate is not that it fails to allow for "enough" variety, or even that it only captures that variety in a limited way. More serious is its tendency to reproduce the habit of mind that is theorizing around, or against, a geographically indexed and putatively normative model of "standard," free-market capitalism. There is a defense of the VoC program that, if nothing else, it represents a marked improvement on the singular worldviews of neoclassical economics and neoliberal politics. But if supposed exceptions to the norm of standard-issue capitalism are gathered together in the form of a single counterpole and under the sign of a more social "elsewhere," the problem of (free) marketcentricity has been merely repositioned and then reinscribed, not overcome. As an almost uniquely unreflexive science, orthodox economics cannot see this problem, since exceptions to its eternal rules are typically coded in terms of obstacles, interferences, and impurities. Mainstream institutionalism, working more deliberatively, has demonstrated a capacity to find and classify differences, but VoC studies have been content to work with pregiven categories and containers, as well as in the shadow (or mirror) of economic orthodoxy. Geographical political economy, on the other hand, takes it as axiomatic that capitalist transformation and restructuring—which is continuous, contradictory, and crisis-prone, trending toward neither long-run equilibrium nor stadial evolution—*constantly (re)produce economic difference,* rejecting as radically insufficient both cross-sectional mappings of national capitalisms and hierarchical readings of the world system, but generally demurring from anything approaching an explicitly articulated and broadly shared alternative. With Stuart Hall, many would likely accept the proposition that "one of the most profound insights of Marx's *Capital* . . . is that capitalism only advances, as it were, on contradictory terrain," in the process having no alternative but "to incorporate and partly reflect the differences it was trying to overcome,"[66] subsequently to remake and refract economic difference both in its own image and through complex coevolution with always more-than-capitalist worlds. Related to this, along with geographical political economy comes a broad acceptance of what might be called relational methodologies, which variously presuppose and problematize sociospatial difference, allied to a battery of mostly close-focus methods, applied across a range of local and network contexts. If this represents a different point of departure, maybe even a different economic ontology, to what extent is it possible to articulate corresponding principles of analytical pertinence?

Theorizing through Difference

In seeking to build answers to this question, the remainder of the chapter works with principles alternately drawn from a variegated capitalism perspective and from renewed conceptions of UCD. While these might be considered to be two sides of the same coin, their respective genealogies are really quite different. The notion of variegated capitalism can be considered to be a post-VoC formulation in the sense that it was developed through a critique of that earlier paradigm, and was therefore partly predicated on a series of contrastive analytical maneuvers (see Table 5.1 in Chapter 5). Skeptical both of static institutional comparativism and of universalizing essentialism, this intermediate maneuver of a different kind problematizes the unevenly integrated, polymorphic, and "fractal" character of capitalism, its heterogeneous mutations and terraforming dynamics, and its contradictory "unity in difference." There is a rejection, in other words, of the false choice that had been presented between, on the one hand, singular, essential, and "global" theories of capitalism, and on the other, a reductionist reading of "variety" based on a twin-peaks condition of "advanced" capitalism. Certainly, the moniker of "variegation" signals more than a semantic distinction. While "variety" carries connotations of taxonomic classification and static differentiation, to variegate is, according to the *Oxford English Dictionary*, "to diversify; to invest with variety; to enliven with differences or changes," in the sense of a complex, polymorphic whole constituted through dynamic differences that are integral to itself.

Bob Jessop has acknowledged the origins of variegated capitalism in critique while also pointing to its generative, if disruptive, potential:

> Variegation is an important concept for thinking about capital accumulation, political domination, and neoliberalization. It was introduced as a considered response to the risks involved in treating varieties of capitalism in mutual isolation or

assuming that there is a single world system with its own master logic that governs the place and mobility of different economic spaces therein. . . . It further posits that . . . different economic spaces and their associated political regimes have unequal capacities to shape the world market and to exploit, displace and/or defer their respective problems, conflicts, and crisis-tendencies. . . . [An] emerging *single, but fractally organized, variegated capitalism* [is seen as] the product of structural coupling, co-evolution, complementarities, rivalries, tensions, and antagonisms among varieties of capitalism [which] are coupled not only through their territorial instantiation . . . but also through entanglements at different scales and through networks.[67]

There is here an at least germinal alternative conception of capitalist spatiality, even if it is hardly a recipe for sparing, parsimonious analysis, or for stylized abstractions light on substantive content and contextual specificity. Rather, it is suggestive of a relational grid, or matrix, of differences in connection, pursuant to a conception of capitalism as constitutively polymorphic as *read through* the prismatic lens of uneven spatial development, not as some frozen map of difference, but as an evolving and multipolar complex of conjunctural formations, contradictory dynamics, and moving articulations.

The extended lineage of UCD, uneven in itself, tells a somewhat different story, even as there are points of overlap and complementarity. More than a century old, concepts of UCD have been lost and found repeatedly over the years, falling into disrepair and disrepute in some quarters while languishing in others. In geographical political economy, the more or less uncontested status of a (generic, received) understanding of UCD has been associated with a curious form of neglect in the past three decades. The period of active problematization and creative renewal, in the 1970s and 1980s, was followed by something of an impasse. Behind this impasse lay not one but *two* compelling approaches to the problematic of uneven geographical development. The first, after David Harvey and Neil Smith, has traced UCD to (or perhaps more accurately *from*) the dynamics of capital accumulation, and countervailing tendencies for equalization and differentiation, concentration, and dispersal, in a fashion largely abstracted from the concrete consideration of particular social, historical, or geographical configurations.[68] The second approach, after Doreen Massey, has tended to encounter unevenness through the particularly of those concrete and "local" forms, and their layered complexities, interrelations, and articulations, favoring more grounded treatments of the (re)formation of spatial divisions of labor and emergent modalities of governance.[69] If the former is associated with abstractions often rich in metaphorical imagery but typically light on substantive social content, several steps removed from historical and geographical specificity, the effort to grapple frontally with complexity and contingency in the latter is liable instead to generate contingently freighted and content-laden abstractions. Or to put it more directly: while David Harvey and Neil Smith developed their arguments around UCD principally in relation to the contradictory dynamics of capital accumulation, with actual places, cases, and sources of specific social agency invoked only in generic terms, or for the purposes of exemplification, Doreen Massey's approach was to advance a parallel (if somewhat complementary) set of arguments *through* the specificities of place, positionality, and social experience, via the medium of more situated (and one might say, empirical) treatments of specific and intersecting social relations.

There is no wave of the magic wand that can unify these approaches to UCD, one of which begins with abstract dynamics and laws of motion, the other with concrete conditions and mediating forces, even as there is surely no reason for them to be engaged as if irreconcilable opposites. Instead, the remainder of this chapter seeks to pursue not a third way but an intermediating path, asking what principles of analytical pertinence and guidance might be considered consistent with the precepts of *both* of these conceptions of UCD, and with the accompanying notion of variegated capitalism more generally. What, in such a context, might critical or symptomatic case studies look like? Where to begin, how to "cut in," and how to frame the scope and scale of inquiry? How to theorize with "test" cases (and test*ing* cases), rather than downward or backward from (presumed) best cases? How to read the general and the particular, the global and the local, the generic and the granular, in conjunction rather than in opposition?

As a means to clear the ground prior to addressing these demanding questions, a couple of "negative" methodological injunctions, or places *not* to start, warrant a mention. First, there is a need both to acknowledge, and to take active steps to transcend, Eurocentric and metrocentric formulations, some of which are deeply inscribed into the methodological architecture of, and rationale for, the comparison of "advanced" national economies, especially where these privilege the primacy of internal causes, selectively identified, and where certain economic formations or institutional sites are privileged, a priori, over others, as premonitions of more generalized trends or templates for development. Second, it is necessary to be wary of approaches that reproduce or otherwise defer to certain "standard" or normative readings of capitalism, either by way of implicit forms of stagism (indexed to supposedly "advanced" or leading-edge versions of capitalism), or through the mobilization of dubious abstractions (such as free-market or small-state capitalism). Both of these can be seen as injunctions against unreflexive modes of normative or "centric" theorizing, the precepts of which are sometimes baked into research designs and questions, either implicitly or explicitly.

In respect of these methodological cautions, alternative cues might usefully be taken from recent lines of work in critical development studies, historical sociology, Indigenous studies, international political economy, and postcolonial studies, which have their own critiques of Eurocentric theorizing and stage models of unilinear development, and where there has also been a productive reengagement with of the concept of UCD. For example, in *How the West Came to Rule*, Anievas and Nisancioglu operationalize a relational-processual approach in which "capitalism is best understood as a set of configurations, assemblages, or bundles of social relations and processes oriented around the *systematic reproduction of the capital relation*, but not reducible—either historically or logically—to that relation alone," insisting on the rejection of analytical (and political) positions premised on the claim that "a certain phase (or place) in capitalism's history or geography as 'pure,' 'ideal-typical,' 'unchanging' or its 'highest stage.'"[70] One of the striking things about the sweeping historical reach and panoramic scope of Anievas and Nisancioglu's work is the dexterity that is displayed while working, in a relational fashion, "across" conjunctural moments and contexts, rather than being consumed by them. Building from different foundations altogether, Jessop also recognizes the deep-seated differentiation of capitalism in his rigorous conception of the constitution of the world market, as the "ultimate horizon of capital accumulation."[71] These quite distinctive approaches share some degree of common ground with the handling of endemic sources of uneven geographical development in the work of David Harvey or Neil Smith. There are some contrasts, on the other hand, with the methodological center of gravity in the field of geographical political economy today, with Doreen Massey's more intricate style of relational political economy, and with approaches that work through and then quite carefully "outward" from more localized conjunctural contexts. Here, the global is more often read through the prism of the relationally constituted and closely observed local, on terrains defined by social specificity, more granular and intimate registers of difference, and "necessary complexity."[72] Here, UCD is read not on the wide screen of global panorama but through more situated and closely focused optics.

Along with this characteristically more grounded orientation comes a predisposition toward the disaggregation (or disputation) of expansive, comprehensive, or "jumbo" concepts, especially where these reproduce traits of masculinism or structuralism. Summarizing incautiously, it is probably fair to say that geographical political economy finds its methodological comfort zone, and maybe also its comparative advantage in the intellectual division of labor, in the realm of the complex and the contextual, working with specificity and particularity, and with the aid of quite finely calibrated and flexible concepts, theories, and frames. The focus is not only on the "restructuring present," but also on the "restructuring proximate." This is consistent with a preference for firsthand and "dirty hands" modes of inquiry over the building and refinement of clean models, and for methodological craft and creativity over deductive scientism.[73] There is an ongoing dialogue between relatively plastic and revisable theory claims and the firsthand practices of sifting of "facts on the ground," together with an eclectic disposition and a facility for the creative development of midlevel concepts.

These methodological orientations have been undeniably productive, but they also carry with them two recurring challenges with relevance to the objectives of this chapter: first, they amount to a standing invitation to play the complexity card, and to call empirical exceptions, both of which can in principle open paths to explanatory enrichment but which can also sap or undermine nascent concepts; second, the reflexive skepticism concerning "outsized" (or global) theory claims, along with the preference for more grounded and close-focus investigations, has arguably yielded distorted, truncated, or dismissive conceptions of the more-than-local, reducing this (only) to network relations or pejorative references to structurally overbearing or naively flat versions of globality. This can be seen, in methodological terms, as a default to the local, with explorations that venture beyond this comfort scale being met, not uncommonly, with an almost instinctive skepticism, being prone to portrayal (or dismissal) as sweeping, structuralist, or totalizing. Although Massey's widely accepted injunctions in favor of relational and positional theorizing mitigate against easy slippage into introspective localism, they do not seem to have prevented the development of ingrained habits of reading local cases as self-evidently distinctive, or as exceptions to some wider order or pattern, the coordinates and dynamics of which are left un(der)specified, or portrayed in primarily negative terms. In practice, the extralocal, the interlocal, the international, the planetary, and the global are often conceived, handled, and engaged quite differently from the ostensibly more concrete and immediate "local," being reduced to secondary or backstage status. In this methodological condition of nearsightedness, what lies beyond tends to remain out of focus.

In this vein, Jason Moore has called attention an aversion to world-historical thinking in contemporary economic geography, which tends to leave largely vacant considerations of the *place* that is global capitalism:

> [C]ritical geography continues to privilege the region (and smaller scales like the city and the body) over systematic processes that are no less real, no less historical, and no less geographical than the region, city, or body. This means that geographers have been adept at richly detailed regional studies and at social theory abstracted from analytical history. This has favored the proliferation of empirically rich, and theoretically imaginative "case studies"—but at a cost. We still lack a field of inquiry that engages with capitalism as a historical-geographical place with its specific forms of power, re/production, and culture. That's a problem because regional change in capitalism contains an irreducibly geographical dimension that is world-historical.[74]

These circumstances perhaps go some of the way toward explaining why the configuration of the world system with its historically embedded geographies of uneven development can be quite readily but also rather passively acknowledged; safely relegated to the back stage, they exert little more than an impressionistic or distant influence on what is deemed to be the "real" action, front-of-stage. They are, once again, out of focus. It is certainly not to imply that locally grounded investigations and close-up methods have been somehow unproductive or misconceived to suggest that side effects of their (favored) use include inattention to "bigger" geographies, to the social worlds of "internationality," to the macro as a site, scale, *and place* of distinctive social and institutional practices (and not just a playground for ideological mystification and bad abstraction), and to the global, the international, the geopolitical, and the more-than-local as, in their own ways, "thick spaces."[75] And for all the injunctions to relational thinking, if there are explanatory and methodological deficits in contemporary economic geography, they arguably concern the spaces and scales of the extra-local, the spaces (and relations) *between* sites, places, and networks, and the emergent, more-than-the-sum-of-the-parts properties of certain *inter*regional and *inter*national orders, regimes, and formations.

Working in this broad direction, the remainder of the chapter seeks to specify three relational methodological maneuvers with potentially constructive roles to play in the conjunctural analysis of unevenly developed, variegated capitalism. While the rationale for relational methodologies is not a prescriptive one, neither is it neutral or ambivalent. Just because there is no one best way, this does not mean that anything goes. If there is really no such thing as a pre-theoretical methodology, no such thing as a theory-neutral research design or mode of inquiry, then methodological choices are inescapably tangled up with theoretical commitments and (pro)positions. It follows that the concepts of UCD and variegated capitalism are not methodologically neutral, even if their methodological implications may have been, to this point, less than fully explicated.

A useful provocation here is Jessop's identification of the need to develop, in the context of capitalist variegation, conceptual and methodological vocabularies sufficient for the "stepwise discovery of the overdetermined complexity of cases."[76] His own dialectical responses to this charge, paralleling those of Wolfgang Streeck,[77] tend to involve working "inward" from the macro-level problematic of capitalist integration at the scale of the world market, through the patterned contours of variegation, to the embedding (or integration) of different varieties, with their local complexities, encountered as it were from the outside. The complementary and supplementary move that is proposed here, which begins on what for economic geographers is rather more familiar territory, is to move "outward" from the local, the urban, and the regional. The three steps to be taken in the remainder of this chapter begin with questions of place and positionality; next, the discussion turns to the problematics of hybridity, interdependency, and holism; and finally, this complex and heterogenous terrain is imagined in motion, as attention is turned to temporality and transformation. As dimensions of a relational methodology in the making, each of these steps is associated with a different bundle of conceptual resources and methodological injunctions.

Place and Positionality

It was with an ordinary walk down Kilburn High Street that Doreen Massey famously chose to illustrate her catalytic conception of the "global sense of place," evocative as it would be of an open-ended and processual understanding of the local, an always emergent site of "throwntogetherness," intersecting trajectories, and unplanned encounters.[78] At its heart, this can be seen as a conjunctural understanding, signifying a prismatic perspective on *and from* place, one that really has nothing to do with the introspective, the parochial, or with bounded and delimited spaces on a map; rather, it is a *meeting* place, a constellation of ongoing journeys, a space of (politically and causally) indeterminate intersections, a site of tangled relations, conflicts, and reconciliations, where there is always the potential to assemble distinctive combinations, to make something new, to cut new pathways, and therefore where politics always matters. This is also an understanding of place as a kaleidoscopic vantage point on the world, as the locus of always moving relations, as a situated perspective on what is a moving terrain and open horizon. It follows that place is not static and unchanging, the other of time, and neither is it some container of fixed attributes and identities. In other words, this is an "extroverted" and non-essentialist conception of place, one that is not reducible to the making of "ritualistic connections to 'the wider system' [of] international capitalism," but instead:

> what gives a place its specificity is not some long internalized history but the fact that it is constructed out of a particular constellation of relations, articulated together at a particular locus, meeting and weaving together at a particular locus.... [Rather than] thinking of places as areas with boundaries around, they can be imagined as articulated moments in networks of social relations and understandings, but where a large proportion of those relations, experiences and understandings are constructed on a far larger scale.[79]

Rather than seeing place as a territorial repository of provincial details and exclusively homegrown capacities, this is an understanding of place as a specific nexus of intersectional relations and constitutive articulations, where things come together, clash, and combine, in an occasionally coherent but never contraction-free fashion. Places are also understood to be sites for the refraction of ostensibly "larger-scale" processes, relations, and understandings, often in ways that belie crudely hierarchical conceptions.[80] This implies an approach to the issue of particularity and specificity of place that is not an invitation to pre-theoretical inductivism, nor is it merely a "question of taxonomic disaggregation," but instead concerns "the articulation in any one instance of criss-crossing axes of causality and influence."[81] It entails a conjunctural understanding of place as the arena for the collision and combination of multiple lines of determination.

This elevates place from a site of contingency and minor happenings to one of casual significance and political potential. And crucially, it conjures an imaginary of place in a constitutively significant world composed of other places, highlighting the dimensions of *relative* location, situation, and positionality.[82] This is a relational conception of place that invokes more than two-dimensional differences, but a complex cartography of constitutive relations and mutual interdepenencies. "Connection, as well as differentiation, is what it is all about," Massey maintained.[83] Her relational conception of place implies a necessary concern with positionality, coupled with an understanding of the global as a world of places. In principle, these arguments ought to inoculate economic geographers from any temptation to invoke "domestic analogies," where single (local or national) entities are taken as indicative of a type or category or system, the internal (and supposedly endogenous, independent) characteristics of those entities then being projected onto that system, for instance with the United States standing for advanced capitalism, or Silicon Valley as a template model for innovation economies.[84] Instead, what Eric Sheppard aptly calls "thinking through place" involves similar kinds of connections between the ostensibly out-there, up-there, or elsewhere and the in-here of localized places and spaces: "Rather than beginning with 'facts on the ground,' theorization should start with the broader conjunctural context that is constitutive of such empirical differences—but to do so geographically," an approach that Sheppard characterizes as a *"positional* conjunctural analysis."[85]

The methodological implications of this orientation are far-reaching, even if they remain no more than sparsely codified and sporadically realized in the field of geographical political economy. Recognizing as it does, at an ontological level, that places-in-connection are constitutively interrelated, in contrast to bounded places as discrete and independent entities with fixed (internal) attributes, this position is fundamentally incompatible with "methodological internalism," where causal explanations and analytical narratives are sought and found principally on the "inside." Instead, it is a conception of place congruent with those relational methodologies that seek as their main objective, Go and Lawson observe, "to unsettle taken-for-granted boundaries, static entities, and presumed substances," refusing to take as pregiven or natural categories and units of analysis (or indeed "cases").[86] This means that the definition and delimitation of cases, categories, and research sites can never be an innocent or routine question; it is tangled up in ontological assumptions and questions of conceptualization.[87]

Many of these arguments have been rehearsed through what are by now well-established critiques of methodological nationalism—and the practice of endowing received territorial entities with properties like internal coherence, bounded features, functional integrity, comparative equivalence, intrinsic logics, and explanatory salience—although the implications of a somewhat analogous inclination toward methodological localism have not been explored with the same degree of critical intensity. Conventional, side-by-side comparisons of "national" (or for that matter "local") capitalisms often reproduce these problems of methodological territorialism and internalism, since their concern is with ostensibly integral and "interior" qualities, rather than with relations. These problems are compounded when one or other of these models (implicitly or otherwise) is associated with purer or less corrupted capitalisms, or with "frontal" qualities that are held to indicate, at the same time, world-remaking propensities and the deficits of a lagging hinterland. As Anievas and Nisancioglu have pointed out, such internalist stories, which emphasize autonomous and endogenous capacities, are among the "founding myths of Eurocentrism,"[88] alongside the sequentialism implicit in assertions of first-mover or advanced status, and the underlying methodological principle that societies are "self-contained, self-constituting entities [following] a unilinear modernization path," as opposed to "polymorphous 'hybrid amalgams,'" shaped through transnational relations.[89]

The VoC paradigm was predicated on just such an approach, reducing multidimensional variegation to an austere reading of two-tone variety, paying virtually no attention to the relative locations, within the world system, of its favored (national) cases, and constructing its accounts of causal determination largely from the "inside," as matters of domestic institutional capacity and embedded behaviors, cohering at the national scale. Furthermore, after stylizing and stereotyping a far-from-innocently-chosen cluster of national economies, these are then placed on a dehistoricized, imaginary plane, as ideal types or best-case models, rather than in the actually existing world system. The problem with this kind of deployment of ideal types, Sayer explains, is not that objects of analysis are read selectively, privileging certain relations or processes, or abstracting one-sidedly from these, since most concrete research strategies and modes of theorization (must) do this, in some fashion or another. The problem is that ideal-typical reasoning "pays no attention to the structure of the world and hence is unable to recognize that some selections are better than others according to their relationships with this structure."[90] Ideal-typical models of capitalism are theorized as if they were operationally discrete and functionally independent "isolates," a maneuver that arbitrarily breaks chains of causation and connection, as it were, at the border. Furthermore, there is a recurrent tendency to invoke *Western* ideal types as yardsticks for rationality, modernity, and normality, against which difference is gathered, often in the shape of a singular Other, or counter-type.[91] In contrast, the goal of relational methodologies is to call attention to the constitutive connectivities between such entities, along with their reciprocal embeddedness in "the structure of the world" (which itself is emergent, not preemptively given). These maneuvers are unlikely to yield discrete and tidy categories, although at a minimum they underscore the distorting and misleading effects of the imposition of such categories.

The heterogeneity and diversity of contemporary capitalism(s) plainly exceed the VoC school's reductionism, but there is nothing to be gained from infinite regress into empirical specificity and categorical disaggregation. Lacking robust criteria for determining how many varieties there are, or could be, the VoC-inspired literature tends to opt for between two and six, with a combination of presentational aesthetics and a preference for aggressive parsimony tending to favor "tougher" and more uncompromising approaches to categorical discrimination.[92] Pivoting around its own minimal vision of difference ($n = 2$), the VoC approach usually opts to "stretch" (or relax) its taxonomic categories laterally, by adding national cases where these cannot be reconciled with, or positioned between, one of the polar alternatives.[93]

Finding difference within capitalism differently cannot simply be a matter of reconciling to some jigsaw-puzzle version of capitalist multiplicity, comprising a random number of local pieces, each with its own separate and internal logic. Rather, it can usefully build from an understanding of capitalism as a constructed, polymorphous, and variably institutionalized system. This recalls Anievas and Nisancioglu's take on capitalism as "a set of configurations, assemblages, or bundles of social relations and processes oriented around [but not reducible to] the systematic reproduction of the capital relation."[94] Or as David Harvey has succinctly put it, Marx "viewed capital as a loosely coupled ecosystem of diverse parts powered by the search for profit or surplus value."[95] Adequate conceptions of capital*ism* too must account for the (array of) socioinstitutionally stabilized ways in which the attendant ecosystem is organized, which might involve mapping the contours of capitalism, as Nancy Fraser has it, as an "institutionalized social order," or in Geoffrey Hodgson's terms, as a "[c]omplex constellation of different institutions," realized in variable geometries, which do not oscillate around some pregiven standard, universal or essential model.[96] Definitions must likewise attend to variegation and UCD as conditions of capitalism's existence, not as inconvenient distractions from (or obstacles to) some hard-core definition, or as mere variations on a general theme safely left to the latter stages of the analysis. The *placing* of capitalism, in this sense, is a front-end problem of conceptualization.

In a parallel fashion, Anievas and Nisancioglu also resist attempts to reduce capitalism, in singular terms, to market dependence, to class-based exploitation, or the generalized commodity form, since its necessarily configurative character is imbricated in "a wider complex web of social relations that stretch our understanding of capitalism far beyond what is captured in any of these phrases," such that:

> To say what capitalism "is" runs the risk of reducing capitalism to a thing, which tends to obscure the multivalent connections in society that facilitate, structure and ultimately limit its reproduction. More specifically, it carries the implication that any given social factor contains an essence that is logically independent of other factors to which it is related.... [Instead, capitalism must be seen to encompass] historically specific configurations of social relations and processes. Such a relational-processual approach helps us move away from "abstract one-sided" self-representations of capitalism [in order to see] capitalism not as a fixed entity,

but as one that morphs and reconfigures social relations according to certain historical problems, challenges, struggles, contradictions, limits and opportunities.[97]

It follows that as a necessarily variegated phenomenon, capitalism should be explored, mapped, and theorized across historical *and geographical* configurations, rather than pivoting around an Archimedean point fixed in either time or space. Capitalist configurations are assembled in places as well as over time, through relations of interconnectedness that reflect and bear upon the configurations realized (and realizable) in other places.

Equally skeptical of unilinear narratives, theoretical reductionism, and stage models, Doreen Massey made a parallel case for rigorous conceptualization across and in dialogue with concrete cases, while eschewing any self-imposed "restriction to what is sometimes called 'local' theory."[98] Hers was a method of articulation that worked through the prism of the local and the particular while refusing to tune out, or lose sight of, what she called the "broad structures" of capitalism, an approach to theory building that was keyed into (social and geographical) difference while working across a plurality of conjunctures. Local difference, variations, and exceptions were not invoked in order to invalidate or incapacitate cross-contextual categories of analysis, but as means to (re)build such categories, and to develop more effective modes of conceptualization, explanation, and intervention with sociospatial difference confronted on the "inside." The architecture of the spatial division of labor approach was exemplary in this regard. Massey "recogniz[ed] from the start the existence of and importance of variety . . . building that into the manner of initial conceptualization," while never confining the subsequent analysis to "local structures" or some allegedly irreducible quality of uniqueness:

> *Spatial Divisions of Labour* rejects metanarratives [yet] broad structures . . . which are assumed to be multiple, non-totalising and without pre-given narratives are . . . necessary to the approach. . . . [O]utcomes are uncertain, history—and geography—have to be made. [There is] a lesser commitment on my part to tying everything down, hammering it into place, so that there is an overarching "order" in which I know where everything is (for I don't and never can). . . . For me [theory] most usefully relates to a process of rigorous conceptualisation, itself drawing on previously-achieved understandings of the phenomena in question, and which in turn will involve the identification of potential causal structures. It does not imply propositions about necessary empirical outcomes.[99]

Massey's version of the method of articulation, or "thinking in terms of relations," was grounded in the recognition of "the *interdependence* of phenomena

[like] regions within an economy," after which it is (only) through a combination of "theoretical scepticism [and] empirical evaluation," not least in the "laboratories" that are concrete cases that there can, in principle, be "access to causality."[100] Relational methodologies consequently demand that theoretical development and empirical investigation proceed in tandem, or dialogue, and that their combination should take account of concrete conjunctures that are geographically as well as historically situated.[101]

There is a double injunction here, against "contentless" and unsituated abstractions, detached from spatial context, and also against the kind of methodological internalism that privileges autonomous or essential capacities and dynamics over the interdependent, the intersocietal, and the interlocal. It can be read as a further caution against the a priori isolation or separation of cases, and against conventional modes of side-by-side comparison based on pregiven and discrete entities, favoring instead relational methodologies. An intriguing way to realize this is through what Philip McMichael calls "incorporated comparison," in which the units and objects of analysis, their constitutions and contexts, are themselves necessarily subject to theorization, while comparative maneuvers are integrated into the process of conjunctural inquiry itself, "process-instances [being] compared because they are historically [and geographically] connected and mutually conditioned."[102] In contrast to the formal comparison of reified entities that, in the process, are detached, isolated, or abstracted from their time-space location, constitution, and relative positionality (as if questions of interconnection and interdependence were of secondary consequence, could be frozen, or easily controlled for), this relational methodology demands that the (always provisional) positioning of cases should be integral to the substantive analysis of social processes (whether this be a financialized mode of governance, a production-consumption network, or a regime of social reproduction), while it neither requires nor assumes the prior existence of a complete "mental map" of the wider world system, since the latter should be considered immanent in what is an emergent process of conceptual mapping.[103]

Incorporated comparisons can be developed over time (comparing temporally defined episodes or moments, not as discrete periods, but in relation to ongoing, if discontinuous, historical processes), cross-sectionally (between spatially defined locations similarly positioned within an extralocal web of relations), or in combinations of the two. From the perspective of geographical political economy, this approach to comparison facilitates (a range of) analytical cuts into relationally connected and constituted social phenomena not necessarily at "system scale," but at the level of (concrete) conjunctures, working substantively with what Massey once called "symptomatic" cases, or what Stuart Hall referred to as "vital signs," on moving terrains of social transformation.[104] Rather than working inward from the variegated ordering the world (market) system, and then reading relations in terms of differentiated modes of insertion,[105] incorporated comparisons tend instead to work outward from critical or symptomatic cases (not ideal-typical or prototypical cases), reading relations in terms of emergent forms of articulation within what must be more open and movable horizons of analysis.

The latter was characteristic of Massey's approach, theorizing through (and out of) what she once called the "laboratories" of local cases.[106] The scare quotes are necessary here, since these were never seen as separate or insulated sites, the location of contained and closed systems. Instead, her prismatic methodological perspective, reading as it did the global both within and through the local, while connecting a dynamic and open sense of place to questions of positionality, at all scales from the intralocal to the interlocal. Yet just as it established a mandate for theorizing through place, Massey's approach came with a caution against theorizing "down" from supposedly paradigmatic places or sites to which "advanced" features are implicitly or explicitly ascribed. Instead, the exacting methodological injunction was to theorize across places, in the plural, in order to capture the variegated nature of capitalist restructuring and its mediated outcomes. (Invoking as this does a landscape ontology structured by diverse interconnections and mutual relations, it is antithetical to epistemological strategies predicated on views from presumed "centers" or indeed "futures.") Methodologically speaking, this opens a different kind of space for local investigations, not just as cases chipped off some larger whole ("global capitalism"), on the basis of already known (or assumed) relations, but as theoretically salient, conjunctural formations, within which matters of positionality are not "external" but always immanent.

Massey's global sense of place involved not only holding on to but also taking down the global, as an all-encompassing force-field dictating events from above, deflating an extraterrestrial worldview that itself was conjuncturally as well as ideologically produced. Massey also critiqued the false equivalences that were often made between the global-and-the-abstract and the local-and-the-concrete, and between global space as a zone of unmoored forces and local places as the sites of (defensive or offensive) responses. She argued that "[i]f space is to be really thought relationally ... then 'global space' is no more than the sum of relations, connections, embodiments and practices. ... Space is not the outside of place; it is not abstract, it is not somehow 'up there' or disembodied."[107] Yet while the global may also be a place, it does not necessarily follow that it is either the same place, or the same *kind* of place, as the local. As such, the global *is* arguably more than the sum of its constitutive parts, and certainly different from the sum of those parts. Following Rosenberg, the intersocietal and the international are domains of ramifying effects that are not necessarily reducible to the sum of their parts, by virtue of what he conceives as the interactive, "strategic dimension of combined development" and its associated "causal scatter effect[s]."[108] The methodological resolution to the transversality implied by place-to-place interaction effects, and their ramification into "global" conditions that are emergent rather than pregiven, cannot be to privilege the global over the local or vice versa. Rather, it calls for dialectical analysis across these scales, domains, and dimensions, and through the medium of UCD.[109] By the same token, capitalism is not to be conceived in essentialized terms, as if unfolding through space and time according to its own (internal) motor of reproduction-cum-replication; capitalist formations may be assembled in place, but they are assembled in a fashion conditioned by *other* places, other social orders, and other capitalist formations. As Makki explains, reading UCD in this manner is not simply a matter of pluralization:

> It is not that the same "logic of capital" operates differently from one place to another, but rather that [capitalism] is itself differently configured, with correspondingly distinct effects, across the socially uneven political multiplicity of the world.... [T]he idea of uneven and combined development suggests a relational and differentiated conception of capitalist development. And rather than abstracting from historical [and geographical] specificities, it brings these ever more sharply into focus. As an explanatory procedure, this requires a back and forth movement from epochal analysis towards greater historicity and the grounding of variant patterns of social change in the inter-societal constellation of power relations. This is an approach that is inimical to schematic formulas that can be mechanically applied everywhere against recalcitrant historical realities, or turned into fetishized abstractions that substitute the simplicity of an idea for the complexity of the world.[110]

For Massey, too, adequate responses to globalization were never reducible to a localizing countermove; her intention was not to conjure some mirror-image "view from below." Instead, the local is conceived in a more orthogonal fashion, as a space of constitutive articulations and generative intersections.[111] Place and positionality, differentiation and connection, are what it is all about.

Hybridity and Holism

In a letter to Engels in 1871, Jenny Marx complained that her ailing husband taken to the self-imposed task of teaching himself Russian with an intensity such as to suggest "a matter of life and death."[112] Engels subsequently counseled Marx that he might need to change his "way of living," if only in the interest of making progress with volume two of *Capital*. But Marx had been thinking further ahead. Although his deteriorating health would frustrate these plans, his ambition had been to place Russia at the center of volume three, in a role analogous to that played by England in volume one, necessitating intensive research on Russian economic and social history, in addition to assessments of its contemporary politics. (The rigors of volume three would also demand advanced skills in algebra and higher mathematics, for which Marx was training himself too.) What fascinated Marx about the Russian case was its complex *combination* of "archaic" forms, revolutionary pressures, and emergent capitalist dynamics—the latter a premonition of what would later come to be known as the challenges of "development," tempered in this case by a belief that these intensified conditions of "economic, moral and intellectual decomposition" might be harbingers of the fact that "[t]his time the revolution is going to start in the East."[113] Hardly reducible to the question of catch-up, or transition, as the modernization paradigm would later have it, Teodore Shanin argues that the import of these volatile circumstances, for Marx, was that they called attention to "the newly perceived notion of 'uneven development,' interpreted not quantitatively (i.e. that 'some societies move faster than others') but as *global interdependence of societal transformations*."[114]

Sometime later, Trotsky would develop his more elaborate notion of UCD—not coincidentally, with the Russian question also at its fulcrum. The (relative) status of these germinal ideas, which were never to be fully addressed in the posthumously assembled version of volume three, has been a matter of some debate among Marxologists ever since, with some reading the embrace of UCD and conjunctural complexity as a vital clue to the evolution of the "late Marx," and others insisting on the presence of much stronger continuities with the Marx of volume one. Invariably at issue in these debates, the preface to the first (German) edition of volume one had included what has since become a notorious statement, to the effect that its theoretical scheme had been worked out on the "classic ground" of the English case. This statement seemed to indicate that the "advanced" case of the English factory system foretold the future of the capitalist world, but a far more prosaic interpretation is also plausible, that this was little more than a prefatory hook aimed at continental readers of a book freighted with English examples and illustrations: "*De te fabula narratur!*" or "The tale is told of you!"

> England is used as the chief illustration in the development of my theoretical ideas.... Intrinsically, it is not a question of the higher or lower degree of development of the social antagonisms that result from the natural laws of capitalist production. It is a question of these laws themselves, of these tendencies working with iron necessity towards inevitable results. The country that is more developed industrially only shows, to the less developed, the image of its own future.[115]

These remarks have been taken by some as a self-incriminating revelation of the essential(ist) Marx—the teleological stage theorist, reading off iron laws, as if for universal application, from a pivotal case—but more charitably by others, as clues to the evolution of Marx's own thinking. In light of the (ongoing) potential of the concept of UCD, the charitable interpretation seems more constructive, not least given the accumulation of ample evidence that Marx's attention in his final years had, indeed, turned decisively in the direction of interdependent development, the complex roots of political mobilization in different countries, and the rise of contending "pivots of history." Seeking some final arbitration of Marx's position on this question may be somewhat beside the (methodological) point, but it is fair to say that, in his later-in-life thinking around the Russian case, Marx was grappling with the fundamental questions of UCD.[116] On this basis, Sayer, Corrigan, and others have comprehensively rejected the assertion that an evolutionary, stage model of capitalism should be seen to represent an "essential kernel" of Marx's thinking, or for that matter all subsequent varieties of Marxian analysis.[117]

Teodor Shanin acknowledges that while Marx's investigations of the "peripheries of capitalism" may have been truncated, and that while his knowledge of India and China, like others of his "generation of Europeans was remote, abstract and often misconceived," his incomplete explorations of the Russian case spoke to a determination to "*consider 'uneven development' in all its complexity*," rather than to continue to defer, more singularly, to the "classic case" of English capitalism:

> Marx had ... come to accept the multiplicity of roads [even] within a world in which capitalism existed and became a dominant force. It meant (a) an anticipation of future societal histories as necessarily uneven, interdependent and multilinear in the "structural" sense; (b) the consequent inadequacy of the unilinear "progressive" model for historical analysis [and] (c) first steps toward the consideration of the specificity of societies which we call today "developing societies."[118]

This was not, notably, a perspective that Engels fully shared, and it would be downplayed in the posthumous (re)construction of volumes two and three: "the very heterogeneity of structure and motion [of capitalism] around the globe were to Engels less of a problem," than they were for Marx, Shanin notes, and not only "less of a bother [but] less of a trigger to new analysis."[119] Nevertheless, the published version of volume three did include an acknowledgment that actually existing capitalism would be marked by "infinite variations and gradations in appearance," reflections of "innumerable different empirical circumstances, natural environment, racial relations, external historical influences, etc.," the shape of which "can be ascertained only by analysis of the empirically given circumstances."[120]

The implications of this perspective, and the methodological optic of UCD that it invokes, are far-reaching. First, the analytical procedure of synecdoche, in which one part is taken to be representative of the whole (as in English factory capitalism ≈ capitalism), is effectively precluded, along with any notion of sampling from a presumed *locus classicus*, or privileging central tendencies. Synecdoche can be seen as a variant of the domestic analogy, where a single entity (e.g., a regional or national economy) is taken to be prototypical, and then projected onto the wider system. Second, the existence of unevenness, variegation, diversity, and variety are more than nagging questions of empirical complexity; fundamentally, they reflect an "ontological premise of 'more-than-one' [which] stretches the referent of the term 'development' across the conceptual space of multiple instances," indeed multiple sites and pivot points.[121] Beyond the simple pluralization of development trajectories, this recalls the problematic of interdependence, undermining the basis of not only concepts of societally independent development but also sequential stage models. Third, this conception amounts to a tacit recognition of relationality, since the development process itself becomes the complex outcome of interactions and interdependencies, infused with questions of politics and political strategy. Fourth, this condition of interdependency means that processes and categories are rarely, if ever, synonymous with sites, or sequestered to places (with "advanced" capitalism living here, say, and "developing" capitalism residing over there), but span across and coexist within these locations. And fifth, heterogeneous economies, contradictory combinations, the formation of amalgams, hybrids, and alloys—all of these are (necessary) conditions both of the parts and the emergent whole, as characteristics both of "local" capitalisms and the evolving world system.

If these represent some of the minimal methodological accompaniments of a UCD perspective, it must be said that they position orthodox VoC scholarship less as a (limited) step in the right direction, more as a cul-de-sac.

Obfuscating relations of interconnection, the VoC approach also tends to seek (or to assume) institutional coherence and super-modular effects in the context of a prevailing methodological nationalism, glossing over intranational diversity and underestimating international interdependence, its depictions of national systems being assembled in the form of a "holistic image, which gives the impression of extreme coherence" at the national scale.[122] Here, the two worlds of capitalism are not only presented as functionally discrete, they are also said to display a high degree of internal coherence—as (if) fish or foul, each with its own organic structure. Relational methodologies call attention, in contrast, to the connectivity of places, locations, and models, problematizing coexistence, combination, and contradiction.

As a practical matter, alternatives to VoC minimalism (must) carry the burden of complexity, but there is no reason for them to do so in a methodologically unprincipled or theoretically defeatist manner.[123] In this respect, there are two necessary—but also generative—points of analytical departure that warrant closer attention: hybridity and holism. To begin with the issue of hybridity, as Massey always emphasized, places are never internally homogeneous. Heterogeneity implies more than random noise, however, more than an accumulation of contingent details.[124] The inescapable multiplicity of local economies might be approached in terms of Hodgson's "impurity principle," the provocative premise of which is that "every socioeconomic system must rely on at least one partially integrated and structurally dissimilar system to function."[125] This formulation underscores the necessity of ("internal") economic diversity without prescribing its form or indeed its consequences. Furthermore, there is no presumption of functional coherence, but an invitation to explore the variable configuration of socioeconomic formations. (This might extend to the recouperation, and theoretical repurposing, of the rather forlorn idea of the "mixed economy.") Hodgson's proposition—which holds for all economic systems, he argues, and not just capitalism—implies that the "theoretical analysis of a specific economic system cannot rely entirely on concepts drawn exclusively from that system," be these concepts relating to profit-centered accumulation, reciprocity, or market primacy, with the implication that "[a]ll acts [of] categorization and abstraction must, therefore, be provisional."[126] This recognition of the necessary heterogeneity of (all) economic systems is compatible with Polanyian socioeconomics, with some postcolonial theories of capitalism, with Gramscian interpretations of complex hegemony, and with the proposition advanced by Vinay Gidwani and Joel Wainwright that the reproduction of capitalist development internalizes, as a condition of its own existence, "heterogeneity as part and parcel of what we name 'capitalism.'"[127] Yet it also raises, without necessarily resolving, the methodological challenge of accounting for the complex and often contradictory *coexistence* of economic forms and formations—the ontological condition of more-than-one, which holds for the internal heterogeneity of regional economies (as more-than-capitalist formations, as embedded market orders, as productive regimes coproduced with institutions of social reproduction, etc.), as well as the complex coexistence and relative positionality of these economies in more-than-local worlds. To borrow a late-Marxian formulation, the impurity principle presents as an analytical priority the non-reductive interrogation of concrete conjunctures as the synthesis (or articulation) of multiple determinations, along with parallel efforts to map "diversity within unity" across multiple sites and situations, across borders and social divisions, and so forth. There is no justification for relegating these questions—relating to local heterogeneity—to secondary status in relation to the elaboration of (one-sided) abstractions or nominally "pure" models, even if the latter is more often represented as the royal road to science.

This underscores the need for genres of conjunctural analysis, such as those advocated by John Clarke, which emphasize "multiplicity, heterogeneity and the condensed dynamics of over-determination," while seeking to avoid "the short-circuiting tendencies of reductionism by demanding attention to the multiple tendencies, forces and contradictions that [comprise] the present moment."[128] And there are strong resonances, too, with the Polanyian maneuver of "placing" heterogeneous socioeconomies, also conjuncturally, by means of the substantivist "study of the manner in which the economic process is instituted at different times and places,"[129] the metaphor of embeddedness focusing attention on always incomplete processes of social regulation, working as they do across divisions of class, gender, and race, contending social interests, dominant and subordinate ideologies, and contradictory dynamics. A key insight of the late Polanyi was the need *simultaneously* to theorize coexistence (incidentally, the name of a short-lived journal that he founded toward the end of his life) in the context of an interdisciplinary project styled as comparative economy.[130] Within a regional economy, say, this would call for transects across socioeconomic diversity sans any a priori determination of dominant "centers" or preordained futures. It therefore implies a rejection of those developmentalist and diffusionist imaginaries that read backward from "advanced" capitalism, or which project a future of market-assisted convergence.[131] And it demands attention to localized configurations of socioeconomic difference and their contradictory governance in a manner attentive to both their proximate and more distant articulations.

This is not a remit for theorizing exclusively from dominant centers, for disaggregating economies into smaller and smaller pieces,[132] or for the kind of empirical deconstruction that merely unravels extant conceptual categories, but it does mean recognizing and theorizing *across* real sources of socioeconomic heterogeneity, figuring out how those "bits and pieces of the going economic system" move and hang together, how they variously articulate with one another, and how the resulting, heterogeneous whole is "instituted."[133] Certain kinds of "pattern recognition" across cases and contexts have a role here, too, not for drawing inferences directly from observed regularities, but as prompts for causal and contextual exploration. This is a rationale, again, for working across difference and diversity, rather than narrowing the optic to a putatively "singular" form, or favoring "smaller" and more homogenous cases over "larger" and more sprawling domains of analysis. The reflexive interrogation of "bridging" concepts, those with potential (and adaptive) applications across cases and contexts, has a particularly important role to play here, notably through their ongoing reconstruction in dialogue with a diversity of empirical inquiries. None of this is to gainsay in any way the role (and indeed advantages) of closer-focus and more ethnographic inquiries. But it is to make the argument these should not be limited to the study of phenomena that are ostensibly "small," local, or intimate, that they should not be cast in opposition to inquiries, or concepts, associated with a more expansive remit. Examples like C. K. Lee's work on "Chinese" modes of investment in Africa demonstrate how it is possible to deploy such close-focus methods while at the same time working across expansive and causally rugged terrains, uncovering and documenting patterns rather than reading these off from abstract formulations, and "seeing" multiple configurations of capitalism, rather than extrapolating only from one.[134] Anthropological engagements with UCD, such as those advocated by Sharryn Kasmir and Lesley Gill, are also indicative of how the resulting methodological questions can be opened up in new ways, including by finding uneven development on the constitutive inside of locally grounded investigations.[135]

The value of these methodological maneuvers is that they tackle the issue of dominant (or hegemonic) forms as a question, rather than presupposing a deductively imposed answer; they foreground conjunctural heterogeneity, rather than theorizing contingency in the shadow of the dominant; they allow even the (local) familiar to appear newly strange, when approached from different (or "residual," "subordinate," "alternative") vantage points; and they call attention to articulations between localized forms of difference and their more-than-local fields of constitution and configuration. If analytical entities (or case-study sites) are not presumed to be self-contained and internally coherent, but heterogeneous combinations shaped by relations near and far, then there is a basic methodological injunction to acknowledge and problematize "internal" diversity in the context of moving terrains of geographical unevenness.

Where the concept of UCD has some utility here is that not only does it imply a multipolar worldview, an ontology of "more than one" in Rosenberg's terms, but that it also requires the kind of dialectical analysis that toggles back and forth between the moving regional parts and the also-moving transregional whole.[136] This is to raise questions *both* about the kind of top-down inquiries that begin with, and largely stay with, the world system, *and* those approaches to bottom-up analysis that privilege and remain with the local. Neither can suffice as a stand-alone strategy, since the imperative must be to work between these scales of analysis. Trotsky's own conception of UCD may have been in itself methodologically somewhat incomplete, but there was radical potential in its juxtaposition of unevenness (as an elemental condition) and combination (as a fundamentally relational formulation).[137] This perspective placed Trotsky's reading of UCD closer to the later Marx than to the author of the first volume of *Capital*. In his discussion of socialism in one country, for example, Trotsky took issue with the implications of the prefatory warning, *De te fabula narratur!*

> This statement of Marx which takes its departure methodologically not from world economy as a whole but from the single capitalist country as a type, has become less applicable in proportion as capitalist evolution has embraced all countries regardless of their previous fate and industrial level. England in her day revealed the future of France, considerably less of Germany, but not in the least of Russia and not of India. The Russian Mensheviks, however, took this conditional statement of Marx unconditionally. Backward Russia, they said, ought not to rush ahead, but humbly to follow the prepared models. To this kind of "Marxism" the liberals also agreed.[138]

If the alternative analytical entry point is "the world economy as a whole," however, an objection might be that this would be to presume prior knowledge of that global system *qua* system, or some predetermined mental map of the world. It would be, as John Clarke has pointed out, to substitute a methodological globalism for a methodological nationalism, and therefore to achieve little more than a "shifting [of] scales while avoiding the challenge of rethinking place and space," his cautiously suggested alternative being to draw upon "Massey's work [on] the relational production of place in ways that make conjunctural analysis simultaneously richer—and more difficult."[139] This is difficult because it necessarily involves theorizing in some fashion with UCD, and across the matrix of spatial difference itself, as opposed to adopting one or another of the two more conventional alternatives: that of theorizing *centrifugally*, and out from a presumed center in a radial or diffusionist manner, or *centripetally*, inward from a system-wide perspective in accordance with a logic of integration, slotting the parts into a known whole.

The logic of centrifugal theorizing is to project the known part onto the lesser-known whole. Domestic analogies of one kind or another are an occupational hazard here, as is the risk of reproducing Eurocentric and metrocentric modes of analysis. These mobilize what have been called "arch-models," models that express in allegedly "pure" form the logic of a dominant paradigm.[140] A countermove in this context, albeit in the form of a negative methodological injunction, is to resist starting from here, and furthermore, to "avoid core definitions that posit the normativity or normative force of European or other 'Northern' cases."[141] A more positive maneuver is the methodological jujitsu move in which the weight of dominant or hegemonic models are (knowingly) used against those self-same models, identifying alternatives, counter-models, and exceptions not in the service of some simple act of denial, distancing, or refutation, but in order explicitly to position these in states of relational tension.

Temporality and Transformation

Eric Wolf began the monumental endeavor that was *Europe and the People without History* by assuming the perspective of an "imaginary traveler roam[ing] among the populations of the four continents" in the year 1400, a journey that would reveal a world not of isolated peoples and settlements, but one "already burgeoning with regional linkages and connections," connections that the "subsequent spread of Europeans across the oceans" may have *re*made but certainly did not unilaterally make, even if they brought "regional networks into worldwide orchestration . . . subject[ing] them to a rhythm of global scope."[142] Working in the idiom of the anthropologist, but refusing to be constrained by the field's ingrained methodological habit of treating communities as "self-contained, self-reproducing and . . . self-stabilizing systems," Wolf sought to trace this "global tapestry" of interactions and connections while continuing to favor the "insider's view and the significance of the small scale for the large scale."[143] Writing against the pervasive tendency to naturalize and to reify entities like "nation" and "culture" as if they were functionally independent, thing-like structures, Wolf had set out to explore the social world as a "manifold, a totality of interconnected processes," committed to the view that "inquiries that disassemble this totality into bits and pieces and then fail to reassemble it falsify reality," by abstracting those bits and pieces, countries and communities, from the social fields and constitutive relations within which they were mutually constituted, by treating them as if they were islands populated by so many Robinson Crusoes.[144] The book invoked an understanding of the "world as shaped by a vast set of cosmopolitan linkages, conjunctures and force fields mediated and transformed by local cultures, politics and places,"[145] Eric Hobsbawm praising its novel "concentration on interaction, intermingling and mutual modification," indeed its "unique sense of human geography," even as he found it to be ultimately more concerned with "connections than causes."[146]

While Wolf had insisted that, in order to understand the world of 1400 and the centuries of polycentric transformation that followed, "we must begin with geography," he would eventually end with history, concluding that it was, above all, variable deployments of "social labor, mobilized to engage the world of nature" that shaped the fates, fortunes, and forking pathways confronted by people, places, and economies, and which in the final analysis set "the terms of history."[147] This was a pre-capitalist world, of course, largely defined by unevenness, and populated by a diverse array of socioeconomies coexisting in a state of "asynchronous simultaneity," to borrow Justin Rosenberg's phrase, the connections and interrelations between which were also marked by unevenness. As Rosenberg has said of this conception of UCD:

> Its causal weft appears at first to be quilt-like, linking together a number of regional constellations of uneven development. [Such a] vantage point (with the "patches" thus viewed as both distinct from and yet interconnected with others) enables us to see something often emphasized by world historians. Knock-on effects reverberate serially across two or more constellations, gathering force or dispersing, often changing their form as they go, and impacting indirectly on remote social settings whose members played no role in the genesis of the causal process.... The quilt metaphor [also] helps us to imagine an uneven but continuous causal "pattern" without a visual centre. . . . Soon, however, the metaphor starts to break down. For if the causal centre of combined development as a whole is nowhere, it is also everywhere. Every member of every constellation thus imagined is itself the centre of its own unique constellation of entities, even while it simultaneously occupies a range of different positions in the different constellations of each of its neighbours. Not only, therefore, does the "quilt" have no centre: its pattern cannot even be imagined from a single point of view. And this causal scatter-effect is further compounded if we add the dimension of time, in which different "patches" of differing sizes are continually emerging, reconfiguring, changing their coordinates and redissolving, in line with the (spatio-temporally uneven) rise and fall of "powers" in different parts of the world.[148]

Metaphors like quilt, tapestry, and patchwork, which when extended into a third dimension can be seen as landscape or terrain metaphors, may in this sense be necessary yet insufficient. They invoke a transversal vision, across jigsaw-like patterns of difference, but in their denial of a focal center could be criticized for substituting normative centricity for little more than a methodologically unfocused blur. What is to be made of this "lateral field of causality over and above [local] determinations?"[149] If there are no islands of endogenous, free-standing causality, but instead only an unruly state of promiscuously distributed causality, is there no alternative but to sink into the swamp of haphazard indeterminacy? How to envisage, navigate, and engage this multipolar world, with its abundance of "causal scatter-effects," somehow determining (more) meaningful points of entry and lineages of connection, if the very idea of a singular "location," or locus point, is deemed to be inherently problematic? These are perhaps among the reasons why Neil Smith, in his retrospective on the troubled history of UCD, variously characterized the concept as enigmatic, arcane, and degenerative.[150]

Following what we might now consider to be the first "rediscovery" of UCD, in the 1970s, commonplace usage of the contracted form "uneven development" rendered the notion of combination, quite literally, the poor relation, barely warranting even a mention.[151] The (spatial) unevenness in all social systems, including capitalism, may have been recognized as an intractable transhistorical condition, but more recent work has been making the argument that the notion of combination may prove to be the "*real* theoretical innovation,"[152] elaborating Trotsky's original formulations in order to reposition UCD within a more comprehensively relational understanding of socioeconomic transformation.[153] Trotsky's distinctive take on the "advantages" of late development was to suggest that "backward" regions possessed the unique opportunity of combining "the latest conquests of capitalist technique" with inherited social forms, thereby "skipping a whole series of intermediate stages" and forging in the process an "amalgam of archaic with more contemporary forms." There is, it has to be said, a measure of latent stadialism in this formulation, since developmental stages effectively precede both the act of "skipping" and the moment of recombination in lagging regions, while Trotsky likewise envisioned what Makki portrays as a "parabolic" arc through an integrated world economy ("not as a sum of national parts but as a mighty and independent reality"), the imperious dominance of which nevertheless foretold its own ultimate demise.[154] None of this, however, need detract from the epistemological potential of the concept of (uneven and) combined development, and as a receipt for the critical investigation of the "interlacing and fusion" of modes, models, processes, and practices of development, together with the "causal intermingling" of these multiple determinations in all manner of hybrid and recombinant formations.[155]

Geographical unevenness may be a prerequisite and precondition for spatial (re)combination, but the latter presents as a potentially fecund source of "multiplier" effects in both social and explanatory terms. In static or cross-sectional sense, the idea of combination implies that national or regional economies are "amalgams," admixtures of inherently "local" or sui generis features and those born of the multiplicity of constitutive relations with wider social fields, from trade regimes to colonial domination, from corporate supply chains to diasporic networks. (There is an affinity here with Massey's relational conception of place.) In dynamic and historical terms, however, this idea not only implies but necessitates an ontological condition of interdependence, interactivity, multiplicity: conjuncturalism, in other words, all the way down (or across), with the international, or interlocal, not being dismissed as some abstract, asocial, or "out there" realm, but as a conjuncture of conjunctures, a "super-conjunctural" space, that exceeds the sum of its diverse parts in the sense of being reciprocally constituted through their *inter*relations. This super-conjunctural, or intersocietal, realm does not exist simply "above" or even in "between" regions and nations, since it is both a "dimension of their being" and, in its own terms, a site of emergent, irreducible causal capacities.[156] To take some concrete examples, trading blocs like the European Union, Mercosur, and the United States–Mexico–Canada Agreement can be seen as institutional life-worlds that are shaped in a super-additive fashion by (while not being entirely reducible to) the powers and interests of their respective member states, just as those member states operate with capacities (and under constraints) coproduced in part through those nominally "external" relations. Regimes of financial austerity operate in similarly "inside/out" manner, in part by applying the whip of external necessity, and "disciplining down" in social and scalar terms, but by simultaneously enabling and constraining "local" capacities too.[157]

If this is, as it should be, a further caution against methodological internalism, it is also suggestive of a suite of alternative methodological strategies that might be gathered under the umbrella term "transversalism," which embrace the ontological principle of more-than-one, which reach into mutually constitutive fields that take account of but also exceed the local, and which seek to work across the sociospatial cleavages and asymmetries. This does not necessarily mean "going big," methodologically speaking, or cutting into the system at the level of the system "as a whole," although it does call into question those preemptive methodological strategies that purport to address the nominally large by rendering it notionally small.[158] "Reducing" to the local scale cannot fully account for such supralocal effects and forces, even as local inquiries have (other) important roles to play. Similarly, cross-contextual "covering" concepts, while always subject to critical scrutiny and potential reconstruction, should not be seen as inherently problematic acts of violent abstraction, at least where they are formulated in such a way as to seriously engage with (internal) difference and constitutive relationality.

None of this is static, of course. The very idea of development in the UCD formulation signals moving forces, capacities, and contradictions, even if it does not necessarily imply a modernist march, onward and upward. To place the concept of UCD in motion means rejecting not only stagism, but singular understandings of trajectory too. Notwithstanding the limits of his own empirical investigations, what Marx came to appreciate later in life was that uneven geographical development meant more than cross-sectional difference, like the patchwork quilt in Rosenberg's metaphor, more even than the coexistence of multiple evolutionary dynamics, but as Shanin points out, an ontological state of heterogeneous transformation, or "multidirectionality... within a capitalist-dominated (and socialism-impregnated?) world of mutual dependence," on top of which were piled additional layers of proliferating heterogeneity "resulting from that very interdependence."[159]

Now, this seems like an appropriate place to respond to the charge that such difference-finding maneuvers "within" the spaces of capitalism are liable to end up, albeit by way of a circuitous journey, in a predictable place, endorsing once again some new version of universality, albeit with more sophisticated trappings. Some of the most telling articulations of this charge have come in the wake of Chakrabatty's critique of historicism, and the tendency to portray capitalism as a "force that encounters historical difference," in a manner effectively external to itself, ultimately to subsume that difference into "diverse vehicles for the spread of its own logic."[160] Even though this tendency was hardly absent from Trotsky's original formulations, the concept of UCD need not be mobilized in such a circular and self-defeating manner. First and most fundamentally, if capitalism is understood as a polymorphous, conjunctural, and heterogeneous formation, rather than as a fixed socioeconomic order bolted down to an essential(ist) and invariant core, then questions relating to its inherently variable "constructions," as well as to its multipolar and interactive "reconstructions," cannot be matters of airtight theoretical predetermination or indeed political foreclosure. Definitions of capitalism that variously call attention, not singularly but *together*, and in different configurations, to the generalization of the commodity form, the centrality of wage-labor and its attendant class relations, the compulsion of competition and the spur of profit, the sanctification of private property rights, and the spread of commodification and marketization, not in isolation but in an array of contradictory combinations, explicitly acknowledge this conjunctural character.[161] Second, recognition of such an unstable *and variant* core mitigates not only against the use of artificially "frozen" ideal types or standard operating models, but also against recourse to "contentless" abstractions, since as a dynamic and polymorphous system capitalism is, and can only be, "multi-configurational." This condition of multiplicity means that the spatiotemporal constitution of capitalism, and indeed the ontological precepts of UCD, cannot be reduced to auxiliary considerations or downstream matters of empirical elaboration.[162] Variegation, in this sense, signals more than some scattering of empirical facts on the ground; it is an ontological condition. Third, just as this approach precludes linear or diffusionist conceptions of capitalism, entrained on an imagined place (or period) taken as a proxy for its highest or most advanced form, the inverse is also true: there really is no such thing as an aberrant, exceptional, or deviant form. From a methodological perspective, such (apparent) outliers can be especially generative sites of inquiry, as places to stress-test and reconstruct categories and concepts, as the locations of newly built configurations, real-world experiments, counter-models, and so on.[163]

Fourth, the contradictory incompleteness of the capitalist accumulation process, its dependency on structures of (social) reproduction beyond its own ambit, Hodgson's impurity principle, and the Polanyian understanding of coexistent modes of integration, all of these underscore the point that capitalism combines not only with other versions of itself, but with its actual others. Another rationale for conjunctural methodologies, then, is that the register of capitalist hybridity is both an elastic and a crisis-prone one, the roiling scope of which is not especially well captured by passive metaphors like embeddedness.[164] Just as there are no guarantees, there are no guardrails either. Fifth and not least, the very fact that conjunctural, recombinant formations are not functionally pregiven or tendentially coherent ascribes both significant status and relative indeterminacy to proto-hegemonic projects, economic imaginaries, programs of institutionalization, counter-movements, and acts of resistance and protest; all are spaces of ongoing struggle, contestation, and (fragile) normalization. Against the accusations of abstract structuralism that are sometimes leveled against the concept of UCD, this speaks to the "necessity of an agential analysis," together with a recognition that conjunctural positions are never stable or fixed, the maintenance of consent and common sense (also) taking political work, no less so than the unpredictably distributed work of dissent and contestation.[165]

Once again, while the methodological implications of this approach may appear to favor panoramic or system-level analyses, encompassing the scale of the intersocietal, they are also compatible with more granular, closer-focused investigations, particularly where these are positioned on fault lines and in friction zones, in spaces of crisis and contestation, contradictory transformation, bold experimentation, and so forth. In this spirit, Pickles and Smith make a case for modes of conjunctural analysis that are "politically committed to constantly interrupting the totalizing thrusts of modernist and historically developmental accounts of economic change by focusing on those many ways in which economic transitions are always transformations [and] always embedded in diverse social relations."[166] The methodological injunctions, in fact, cut both ways. In the case of analyses that take as their entry point (and overriding concern) the macro and the interlocal, they demand recognition of the fact that this is no unmoored and extraterrestrial scale, displaying as it does sociological, institutional, and geopolitical qualities that are both distinctive and perhaps only realized in an emergent or superadditive fashion (as more than the sum of many parts, determinations, and relations). Here, there is a special role for those transversal methodologies that crosscut the tangled spatial and scalar relations of UCD. In the case of analyses that work closer to the ground, in more localized sites and settings, there is a broadly inverse obligation, to situate and to locate, to not only recognize but to problematize constitutive "outsides," moving articulations, network relations, and wider fields of causal conditioning and (co)determination. Here, there is a special role for those transversal methodologies that straddle more-than-local difference, that target borders, frontier zones, intersectional sites, liminal and interstitial spaces, and that probe conditions of existence and constitutive connections.

No matter, in other words, whether the methodological approach is microscopic or macroscopic, there is a shared concern with what might be framed as a dynamically "tectonic" ontology, with lurching and uneven terrains variously marked by underlying stresses and frictions, by a far-from-predictable skein of rifts and eruptions, and by checkerboard patterns of active crisis and comparative stability.[167] This suggests, in turn, an analytical optic that has an eye to the (unpredictably) moving terrain itself, and not on some normatively defined center, or on some equilibrium point imagined in the distance. Neither a frozen landscape nor a frictionless space, this is a sociologically cluttered and institutionally mediated terrain shaped by the interdependence of "successful" development and "underdevelopment," and by coexisting dynamics of abrupt change and glacial adaptation. This perspective, perhaps needless to say, is radically different from the planar and pacific conception of capitalism characteristic of the VoC literature, with its non-relational ontology and structured assumptions of horizontal regime competition, pretty much frozen in a late-twentieth-century form. Instead, variegated and recombinant capitalism is understood to be "fundamentally unruly, subject to perpetual reinvention and hence disruptive of institutional stability," as Chris Howell has put it, there being a "terraforming quality to capitalism that is likely to overwhelm the resilience of national institutions."[168] These terraforming dynamics are likely, from time to time, to overwhelm received categories of analysis too, calling for research methodologies that are both critical and reflexive.

Conclusion: Engaging Capitalism Conjuncturally

This chapter has revisited the problematic of capitalist variegation, and spatially uneven, recombinant development, first by historicizing the question of capitalist variety and then by pursuing several lines of critique and recomposition deriving from currents in the "post-VoC" literature. The VoC project, as Ugo Rossi has observed, ended up limiting itself to a "somewhat self-evident proposition: capitalism is varied because capitalist economies rely on spatiotemporally differentiated institutions."[169] This is certainly one reason why capitalism comes in different varieties, rather than in a standard form, but this chapter has suggested that the question of difference cuts deeper than this. Answers to questions about capitalism's spatiotemporality cannot be shoehorned into such a restrictive framework. Nevertheless, attempts to do so, which gained traction during the 1990s under the VoC rubric, have triggered what is proving to be a more diverse and ambitious research program. Taking its cues from this post-VoC literature, this chapter has worked with the problematics of variegation and UCD in order to engage a series of ontological and epistemological questions associated with theorizations of capitalism's spatiotemporality. Specifically, there has been an attempt to address the "disruptive" implications of variegation and UCD at the outset, rather than at the end of the analysis, to recall David Harvey's discussion of his treatment of uneven development in the *Limits to Capital*.[170] Constructing this alternative position has involved considerations, successively, of place and positionality, hybridity and holism, temporality and transformation, the conceptual principles and methodological implications of which are summarized in Table 9.1.

There is always a risk, of course, that the practically boundless challenges of theoretical elaboration and conceptual correctness end up crowding out, or indefinitely postponing, the no-less-demanding challenges associated with the construction of tractable and realizable methodological strategies. The latter is the charge of the chapter that follows, which seeks to explore

Table 9.1 Capitalist Variegation and Reflexive Methodologies

	Conceptual Resources ... and Axiomatic Principles	Methodological Cautions	Methodological Challenges	Conjunctural Maneuvers
Place and positionality	• Restructuring and locality • Relational analysis • Global sense of place ... prismatic optics, positionality	• Problematize pregiven categories and conceptual boundaries (case selection as a theoretical issue) • Question the use of ideal types and (artificially) isolated cases • Contra methodological internalism • More than local theory	• Positioning cases/places in relation to extra-local fields and networks • Attending to extra-local spaces and the global (also) as a place • Establishing (conceptually adequate) criteria for "provincialization" • Recognizing the global as a(nother) place	• Holding down the global • Targeting symptomatic cases • Problematizing positionality • Stress-testing theoretical propositions "out of place" • Making midlevel concepts, or abstractions-with-local-content • De/reconstructing received categories and cases
Hybridity and holism	• Spatial divisions of labor • Uneven and combined development ... interdependence, relationality	• Contra methodological centrism • Problematize standard or normative categories, together with their deployment as foils • Remember the "impurity principle" • Beware pregiven maps and empty wholes	• Encasing the macro • Addressing latent sources of (developmental) stagism and Eurocentricity • Determining points of analytical entry and exit • Establishing criteria for mapping difference	• Edge work, interstitial cases, and "off-center" research designs • Relationally located (and defined) cases • Reworking theory claims and midl-evel concepts across cases, places, and sites • Locating alternative (explanatory) fulcra and (potentially) pivotal sites • Interrogating institutional fixes

(*continued*)

Table 9.1 Continued

	Conceptual Resources ... and Axiomatic Principles	Methodological Cautions	Methodological Challenges	Conjunctural Maneuvers
Time and transformation	• Variegated capitalism • (Co)evolutionary and terraforming dynamics... articulation, recombination	• Contra sequentialism and stage theories • Beware extrapolating especially by way of "domestic analogies" • Beware path-dependency dependency	• Working past presentism through historicization, positioning cases in relation to arcs of transformation • Confronting complex combinations and "mixed" economies with variable geometries, rather than isolating one-sided abstractions • The "dirty work" of context-laden conjunctural analysis • Reification of spatial fixes	• Transversal methodologies • Incorporated comparisons • Following "entities-in-motion," searching for "vital signs" on moving terrains • Open social systems as emergent and more than/different to the sum of their parts • Interrogating moving patterns, "common differences," and divergent developments across cases and sites • Exploring (re)combinant configurations under stress • Working with/across open horizons

methodological strategies congruent with the arguments of this chapter regarding UCD and variegated capitalism. The methodological implications of these arguments, it must be said, are not singular. In principle, they can be addressed by way of an array of methodological strategies. The focus here, though, is on roads somewhat less traveled, at least in this particular context, but which are nevertheless potentially generative: relational comparison and conjunctural analysis. Unevenly codified, these complementary approaches will be examined in sequence, with the discussion of relational comparison serving as a prelude and entry point to the development of a more explicitly spatialized reading of the conjunctural method. In principle, the attention that is paid in conjunctural analysis to "analyzing situations," indeed problematizing situations, checks many of the boxes identified in the right-hand columns of Table 9.1. Conjunctural analyses are grounded in particular sites and situations, favoring substantive, concrete, and contextualized inquiries, although their tracing of causes and consequences is not ring-fenced. They offer the potential, in other words, to work with, and out from, the local—very much in the spirit of Massey's global sense of place—without being local*ist*. On the other hand, they also engage the global, and the relational "hinges" between the local and the global, as opposing to pushing these wider contexts of the local context into the explanatory background. As such, conjunctural analyses would appear to offer the potential of cutting a distinctive path between those more abstract treatments of UCD that speak largely of general tendencies and laws of motion, scarcely engaging with the particularities of local contexts and situations, and those on the other hand that become so absorbed with the particularities of local contexts and situations that extra-local dynamics, world-system conditions, and the wider contours of UCD itself tend to fade into the background. And they endeavor to do this, moreover, while remaining attentive to politics, institutions, and social agency in front-of-stage local situations, not in a voluntaristic manner but in ways that engage with wider conditions of existence and relations of interdependency.

This, it hardly needs to be said, is challenging terrain, and conjunctural analysis is no panacea. Ironically, conjunctural analysis retains a certain mystique in part *because* off-the-shelf routines and procedures are not readily available. In practice, the power of conjunctural analysis is typically demonstrated post hoc, in the consumption of the pudding, rather than by following some tried-and-tested recipe of methodological steps. Making the case for conjunctural analysis, the task of the next chapter, is consequently also a project of exploration and construction.

10

Situating Method

Exploring Conjunctural Capitalism(s)

With the discussion of capitalist variation and UCD in the previous chapter as its point of departure, this chapter is primarily concerned with questions of research design and methodology in geographical political economy, focusing in particular on the complementary approaches of relational comparison and conjunctural analysis. Relational comparison and conjunctural analysis each seek to explain, intervene, and theorize through the grounded but also structured contexts of place, positionality, and situation. Relational comparisons engage the stretched-out nature of social relations across space, while conjunctural analyses characteristically engage specific social formations (*qua* "combinations" of intersecting determinations), typically during moments of stress or crisis. They each tend to operate in the middle ranges of the explanatory register, being wary of unprincipled induction on the one hand and unmoored abstraction on the other, seeking instead to engage *through* situated analyses of articulation, intersection, and contestation. They do this in their somewhat different ways by "analyzing situations," to borrow Stuart Hall's Gramscian formulation, variously taking account of multiple (and more or less proximate) sources of causality, the mediating roles of politics and social struggle, the complex play of history, and the interdependencies of uneven spatial development.

Relational approaches to comparison emerged in critique of the conventional idea of side-by-side comparisons of supposedly like-for-like and discrete entities, such like cities or regions.[1] Their alternative is to invite more open-ended analyses of cases, situations, and subjects *in connection*. Taking cues, variously, from radical political economy, feminist theory, urban studies, postcolonial studies, global history, and comparative literature, relational approaches to comparison begin with the premise that subjects are formed "in relations," whether these be individuals, cities, or geopolitical entities—that they are, in other words, "relationed."[2] Watchwords here include interdependence, articulation, and mutual constitution; sites and subjects are encountered by virtue of their relationality, and with reference to their unique positionality within constitutive networks and power relations, not as discrete, bounded, or singular entities.[3] These methodological sensibilities find numerous echoes in conjunctural analysis, also a relational approach which for its part tends to be concerned with the contested political terrain of the historicized present, favoring searching, exploratory inquiries, and deeply contextualized modes of exposition.[4] The principles of conjunctural analysis have been largely recovered post hoc, to the extent that they can be closely specified in terms of an explicit methodological stance. If conjunctural analysis is Stuart Hall's "demanding gift" to the critical social sciences,[5] quite appropriately it is one that comes with "no guarantees" from a methodological perspective, being recognized more in exemplary execution than in explicit codification, and realized more through creative practice than through explicit rules or routines. Something similar might be said about the (no less demanding) method of relational comparison, which even as it has benefited from more explicit (critical) attention, is hardly reducible to a methodological formula or bundle of procedures.

This chapter delves into rationales for, and operationalizations of, relational comparison and conjunctural analysis, not with a view to boiling them down to some portable rubric, but in order to assess their methodological compatibility, first, with the principles of geographical political economy, and second, with variegated capitalism as an object of analysis. To this end, relational comparison and conjunctural analysis share antipathies to atomized reasoning, methodological individualism, and recourse to ideal types, recognizing instead the inescapably embedded nature of socioeconomic life; the constitution, in relations, of subjects and objects of analysis; and the resulting imperative to situate analyses not only historically but also geographically. In this sense, these methodological approaches are compatible with the ontologies of UCD, problematizing as they do the relative positionality of sites of inquiry in scalar terms and on moving terrains of transformation. As such, they engage and analyze concrete sites and situations (rather than isolated and circumscribed "cases," as such), in ways that resonate with conceptions of articulation and intersectionality, as well as with the classically Marxian understanding of the concrete as the synthesis of multiple determinations. It follows, moreover, that these are spaces of possibility and potential rather than predetermination.

As Tanya Li has remarked in the context of her own, quite distinctive approach to conjuncturally situated investigation, "[t]o analyze is to *tease apart*," in her case involving a combination of long-term ethnographic work and the dexterous theorizing of capitalist relations in frontier zones, "peeling back [of] layers of meaning and practice . . . tracking relations across different spans of space and time."⁶ The practice on conjunctural analysis, Li explains, is never a bounded or neatly circumscribed one, even as there is a persistent concern to loop back to subjects, sites, and situations of enduring concern. The conjunctures in question rarely present more than a contradictory unity, a provisional hanging together, revealed through the necessarily exploratory work of teasing out causal entanglements and heterogenous relations. These are very different moves, evidently, from those that attempt to "control for context," or work toward the refinement and stylization of ever more parsimonious, monocausal explanations. Conjunctural accounts are therefore characteristically busy: they are cluttered, thick with agency, rife with contradiction, and in Sewell's terms, "eventful."⁷ John Clarke, in conversation with Allan Cochrane, has equated "the *thinnest* version of conjunctural analysis," or what might be considered a minimalist definition, with an ability "to hold things up and say, 'Even if I don't know everything, I know that there is more than one thing going on.' "⁸ Conjunctural analyses, as Clarke's self-deprecating remark implies, are in practice almost never "thin," however. They are characteristically thick, being richly grounded in considerations of site, situation, and historical moment. Yet they nevertheless seek to transcend thick description, aspiring to what might be called *thick theorization*, as a contextually embedded mode of revelation, exposition, and analysis, grounded in multi-sided readings of causality and reserving a significant role for intermediate registers of abstraction, never detached from those situations of concern.

In relation to the notion, discussed in the previous chapter, of capitalism as a constructed or "configurational" phenomenon, these approaches have the potential to facilitate the exploration and mapping of different configurations or constellations of the moving parts that together constitute that variably constructed "system," or instituted order. Because these moving parts—inter alia, profit-driven accumulation, marketization and commodification, class relations, racialized dispossession and segmentation, regimes of social reproduction, private ownership and appropriation, and so on—do not present in essentially fixed, universal, and eternal states of constant conjunction, relational and conjunctural analyses have important roles to play in probing and teasing apart—for different times, places, and situations—how these variably constructed orders variously hang together; how they become provisionally normalized and stabilized, but also encounter moments of crisis and transformation; and what tolerances of adaption and *inconstant* conjunction they display across time and space. Again, this is a very different maneuver from the more orthodox practice of paring away the "merely" contingent or contextual in search of supposedly generalized or essential features, effectively "freezing" certain configurations in the form of normative assumptions and taxonomic categories, or decanting them into causally bounded ideal types. To encounter "capitalism" in relational and conjunctural terms is to problematize its differentiated and recombinant constitution across the moving terrain of uneven development, including as a more-than-the-sum-of-the-parts "meta-formation." Rather than conceptualizing a "unitary" and singular capitalism that only *becomes* differentiated through second-order encounters with a differentiated (external) world, this is to confront an *always unevenly constructed* capitalism, which can only exist in protean, variegated, and shape-shifting form. Variegated capitalism is therefore *simultaneously* grounded in a multiplicity of territorialized and networked forms; it is jointly configured through a plurality of conjunctural configurations, none of which should be confused with some pure-and-simple or classic form, or with free-standing "varieties." Since the meta-formation that is capitalism "in general" is not synonymous with, nor reducible to, any one of these conjunctural configurations (say, "American capitalism" or the "Bangalore model"), its complex reproduction occurs through and across this plurality of coexistent forms, not outside or "above" them.[9]

Explorations of variegated capitalism, in this sense, might be said to be necessarily and inescapably conjunctural, although that hardly settles the matter. One will search in vain, in fact, for a lineage of conjunctural thinking that is tidy, discrete, and closely documented.[10] However, certainly one of the best-known pathways runs through the work of Stuart Hall and his collaborators, and more classically to Gramsci and the late(r) Marx.[11] Two aspects of this legacy are particularly relevant in the present context. First, the embrace of conjunctural thinking invariably signals, quite unequivocally, a rejection of economic reductionism, in favor of more "integral" approaches that nevertheless take seriously, while refusing to isolate or essentialize, economic relations.[12] This can be read as a variation on Polanyi's embeddedness principle, inviting the substantivist analysis of actually existing socioeconomic worlds. Second, there is an explicit commitment to historicization and to modes of historically situated analysis that take account of the tangling and combination of different temporalities, extending if not necessarily to the *longue durée* then at least to the *durée moyenne*.[13] This is one reason to place conjunctural analysis in conversation with relational comparison, given that the latter is more explicitly concerned with the dimensions of spatiality and scale. In this vein, in their exploration of the opportunities and challenges for conducting *comparative* conjunctural analyses, Helga Leitner and Eric Sheppard have observed that:

> Spatialised conjunctural analysis [means going] one step further [stretching] explanatory frameworks not just backwards in time, but also outwards in space (identifying how local events are shaped by distant processes), and upwards and downwards in terms of geographical scale (whereby events at a particular scale may be shaped by both higher and lower scale processes). Importantly, spatiotemporality is conceptualised as much more than a Cartesian frame for conjunctural analysis: it is much more than stating when and where something happens. Drawing on the principles of socio-spatial theory, space and time themselves are active components in theorising the causal complexity of phenomena, processes and events—the socio-spatiotemporal dialectic . . . Spatialising conjunctural analysis also extends thinking about political intervention beyond place-based strategies attuned to local conditions, enabling it to take on board questions of political collaboration across space and of the politics of scale.[14]

The emergent project to spatialize conjunctural analysis has some affinities with work in global and historical anthropology, such as that associated with the journal *Focaal* and with Don Kalb and Herman Tak's parallel notion of "critical junctions." Kalb has described critical junctions as "multilevel relational mechanisms that link the global levels of structural power with the respective institutional fields of 'tactical power' on the scale of the nation-state and with the spaces of agential power of 'common people' in situated everyday circumstances."[15] Now, those working in the politics of scale tradition (invoked by Leitner and Sheppard and itself epistemologically adjacent to conjunctural analysis) would doubtless insist the various expressions of structural, institutional, and agential power referred to by Kalb and Tak are in fact more promiscuously distributed across scales, rather than being hierarchically sequestered in such a way, although there are certainly grounds for fruitful engagement here.[16]

Attending to the need to spatialize conjunctural methodologies, the chapter proceeds in two steps. The first moves from more conventional approaches to comparison to the relational approach developed most fully by Gillian Hart.[17] Comparative approaches of various kinds have self-evidently important roles to play in the analysis of socioeconomic diversity, not only as a family of methodological procedures but also in helping to realize the late-Polanyian project of comparative economy. Various forms of comparison are also vital, in principle, to the project of geographical political economy, although here they are not as commonplace as they might be.[18] Geographical political economy possesses a standard critique of the style of comparative analysis associated with the VoC approach, which not only corrals spatial difference in a restrictive and ultimately self-limiting way but is also for the most part non-relational. Yet while geographical political economy might be credited for its epistemological correctness, in practice the project is confronted by almost the inverse problem: a tendency to engage difference quite promiscuously, seeing it all over the place; recognizing spatial unevenness to be integral to the ongoing (re)production of capitalist and more-than-capitalist economies, and not some side effect, but doing so in ways that are methodologically diffuse and quite unruly—hence the strategy in this chapter to move somewhat more methodically, building more deliberatively in the direction of a methodological dialogue between relational comparison and conjunctural analysis.

From Regular to Relational Comparisons

Comparative thinking is integral to most forms of social-scientific research, whether or not they involve explicit recourse to comparative research designs or methods.[19] Charles Tilly's well-known schema of individualizing, variation-finding, universalizing, and encompassing approaches is usually taken to capture the basic repertoire of methodological options.[20] Individualizing comparisons work with the principle of contrast to identify a relatively small number of cases, which are then engaged in order to grasp and then explicate the particularities or "singularities" of each. Classically, this will take one case at a time, having little to say about common properties and patterns across cases. At the opposite end of the spectrum, universalizing comparisons endeavor to uncover generalized rules or laws that are deemed to govern empirical regularities. Here, the common thread is key, with phenomena traced across a multiplicity of cases. Variation-finding comparisons work in a systematic manner with revealed differences (including qualitative or in-kind differences, or quantitative differences of degree) in order to isolate pertinent principles of variation. Here, the concern is with the intensity or character of the phenomenon in question, as revealed across cases. Finally, encompassing comparisons probe differences across cases in order to understand the effects of cross-cutting and wider-scale processes.

Tilly saw encompassing comparisons as the most promising approach, since these characteristically "begin with a large structure or process . . . select[ing] locations within the structure or process," before seeking to explain "similarities or differences among those locations as consequences of their *relationships to the whole*."[21] Here, comparisons are drawn across sites or locations within a common, overarching system. While surely an advance on those approaches to comparison that posit the existence of independent and equivalent units of analysis, Tilly's treatment of encompassing comparison involves an explicit grounding in relation to historical processes, but it also *foregrounds* those processes, risking a form of functionalism in which the whole (pre)determines and effectively governs the parts.[22] In this respect, the parts (or "locations") tend also to be pregiven, and subordinated to that historical process, scant attention being paid to their own historical formation, situation, and interrelationships.

Explicitly relational approaches have been developed less as elaborations or varieties of the comparative method, and more as a critiques-cum-alternatives. Relational historians like Dale Tomich approach the capitalist world system not as a pregiven whole and omnipresent source of "external" causality, but as an emergent, reciprocal outcome of the interacting component parts, the latter moments or "locations" being analyzed not as self-contained entities but as "bundles of relations," which in their plurality represent "distinct yet mutually conditioning socioeconomic configurations."[23] The capitalist world system here is understood to be multi-configurational, one that can (only) be engaged from different sites of specificity.

Gillian Hart's rendering of a relationally comparative research method has proved to be especially influential, predicated as it was on a critique of orthodox approaches to comparative and multi-scalar inquiry. As Michael Ekers, Stefan Kipfer, and Alex Loftus have pointed out, Hart's method is "derived from a dialectical understanding of the relation between the concrete and the abstract," always grounded in the former while engaging the latter, in the service of an "extroverted historical materialist understanding of space and place."[24] Certainly, hers stands apart from those individualizing and variation-finding approaches that engage and analyze cases *as if* they are mutually independent isolates, proceeding on this basis to probe particularities and/or principles of variation, sometimes in ideal-typical terms. Hart distances her approach from traditions of universalizing and encompassing comparison as well, which tend to read cases in a manner subordinate to some overarching process or system-logic, effectively as variants or instantiations of a known, larger, or more "global" system. Her original rendering of the relational-comparative approach is offered as "a strategy that differs fundamentally from one that deploys ideal types, or that posits different 'cases' as local variants of a more general phenomenon."[25] Here, individualizing and variation-finding comparisons are critiqued for deferring to pregiven units and categories of analysis (rather than defining these in relation to the process or problem in question), effectively severing or sequestering the plethora of constitutive connections, interdependencies, and relations that exceed territorialized boundaries, while obscuring "external" sources of connectivity and conditions of existence. Hart also found these approaches to be agnostic, ambivalent, or effectively silent on the question of the nature of the world (or global system) within which bounded local cases are nominally located. Of course, it is the (presumed) nature of this world—its structuring forces, evolutionary tendencies, fault lines, and pressure points—that tends to play a leading, and sometimes overbearing, role in universalizing and encompassing comparisons, the "big story" to which these cases are yoked. For Hart, the problem with these approaches, especially in the wake of (critiques of) of orthodox globalization narratives, is that they are prone to slide into "top-down" modes of analysis, in which the drivers of change come, unilaterally and unidirectionally, from above (aptly characterized as "impact models"), in the wake of which there is only subjection, co-optation, and localized, against-the-odds resistance.

In this context, relational comparison arrives as a disruptive methodological intervention, motivated from the outset by critiques of structural determinism, essentialism, Eurocentrism, economism, and "globocentrism."[26] Correspondingly, it is positioned in varying degrees of tension with more conventional approaches to research design, case selection, and comparative analysis in fields like world-systems theory, sociology, global history, area studies, and (even) postcolonial studies. As a strategy, relational comparison has been formulated *"in opposition to"* both methodological localism and methodological globalism—the former having resort to bounded cases and Weberian ideal-types, and the latter tending to reduce cases to mere variants more general phenomena, or cogs in a larger machine.[27] Neither global nor local, in a one-sided fashion, but in a sense *both*, relational comparisons seek actively to problematize spatiotemporal positionality across a number of registers: First, they engage the more-than-local and the inter-local, situating and positioning sites of inquiry with reference to, but not "under," these wider (and often constitutive) relations, forces, processes, flows, and conditions of (local) existence. Second, they grapple with the ongoing production of sociospatial difference, both within and between research sites, difference being problematized in the form of intersections, articulations, translations, and frictions, the salience of which can be political as well as causal. Third, along with conjunctural analyses, they conceive the concrete as a realm of multiple determinations, recognizing inconstant causal conjunction to be an ontological condition; each conjunction is therefore geohistorically specific, and as a result is neither deterministically preordained nor voluntaristically free-willed.[28] And fourth, they position the "local" not just as a unique-yet-connected actually existing place in the world, but as a consequential starting or vantage point, as a domain of social experience, political engagement, and meaning-making, as a site of intersecting flows and articulating relations, and as a joint or hinge in more-than-local social processes and systems.

Hart explains that relational comparisons are fundamentally concerned with *how* key processes are "constituted in relation to one another," through a variety of power-laden social relations and practices, revealed within and across the "multiple, interconnected arenas of everyday life."[29] As such, they set out to explore

> connections and relations of mutual constitution—as well as slippages, openings, and contradictions—[in order to] generate new understandings of the possibilities for social change. . . . [B]ringing diverse but connected historical geographies into tension with one another helps to render taken-for-granted categories peculiar and open to question, as well as pointing to new connections, claims, and re-articulations. Relational comparison also focuses attention on the production of racial, ethnic, and gendered norms of difference as active constitutive forces propelling divergent trajectories of social-spatial change—and as crucial to any strategy of forging alliances.[30]

Hart's take on relational comparison has a number of affinities with parallel methodological currents and projects, even as its principles of pertinence are somewhat distinctive. The first of these is the inventively formulated but sparsely applied idea of incorporated comparison, introduced in the previous chapter: McMichael conceives of cases or study sites in terms of the dynamic (re)production of the world system, where the latter whole does not prefigure or govern the operation of the parts, but instead (co)exists in a state of contradictory, evolving, and unstable emergence. This approach "progressively *constructs* a whole as a methodological procedure by giving context to historical phenomena [and through the] comparative analysis of the 'parts' as moments in a self-forming whole."[31] With reference to Tilly's recommendation to begin with an—albeit *provisional*—"mental map of the whole system and a theory of its operation," following which the comparative examination of "units within [that] system" leads to incremental modifications of both "map and theory [as each] improve in use," McMichael advocates what amounts to a more grounded approach, being skeptical of the way in which, for Tilly, units of analysis tend to be pregiven and defined from outside or above.[32] Instead, McMichael is more concerned with the manner in which case-specific particulars successively "realize the general," where cases are domains of observation and loci of concern, rather than units of observation per se.

Hart broadly endorses McMichael's approach, but finds the treatment of space (and spatialized relations) somewhat truncated and inert. In contrast, her method of relational comparison evokes a more politicized and dynamic understanding of space-time, in the spirit of Henri Lefebvre and Doreen Massey. Second, Hart's approach resonates with the Berkeley variant of the extended case method, as practiced by Michael Burawoy and his collaborators, which seeks to extend ethnographic practice across space, time, and scale, "stress-testing" hunches, hypotheses, and proto-theories through multi-site investigations and "experiments."[33] (Burawoy, like Tilly, will begin with theory, along with its associated mental map, but will prioritize case selection based on observed *anomalies*, rather than functioning parts of the whole. The methodological strategy is therefore inherently disruptive, with the goal of reconstructing rather than affirming theory.) Endorsing Burawoy's style of critically engaged ethnography, Hart nevertheless finds its evocations of space and spatiality to be somewhat gestural, at least in earlier formulations. Against any lingering tendency to preserve the local as the ethnographic "hearth," Hart is insistent in her concern with manifestly pan-local or inter-local connections, with extra-local conditions for "local" possibility, and with the mutually constitutive interdependencies between places, events, entities, and identities. Third, Hart locates her approach in the tradition of critical realism, as practiced by Andrew Sayer and (rather more obliquely) by Doreen Massey, with its expressly relational understanding of generality (*generality²* in Sayer's terms), wherein parts and wholes are dialectically (or internally) related in ways that are necessary to their existence and causal liabilities, in contrast to positivist treatments of recurrent events and so-called representative cases (*generality¹*) in the context of an atomized ontology.[34] This said, relational comparisons typically have more to say about (and attach greater explanatory weight to) spatiotemporal contextualization than tends to be the case in textbook treatments of critical realism, where spatiality and spatial relations are less often ascribed explicit causal status.[35]

A further line of methodological complementarity can be found with a strand of work in comparative literature that, quite independently for a while, invoked the same terminology of relational comparison in the service of a broadly parallel purpose. Shu-mei Shih, who had earlier advocated a model of conjuncturally situated comparison under the banner of "Sinophone as method," has been making the case for a version of relational comparison founded on the ontological premise that "the world has always been an interconnected place and a site of infinite relations."[36] Shih's (separate) path to relational comparison comes via engagements with postcolonial studies, transnational history, chaos theory, and studies of creolization, later extending to radical geography.[37] She makes a case for tracing broad historical "arcs," literary arcs specifically, across multiple sites and situations, such as plantations, programs of decolonization, and Cold War friction zones. Mobilized in this way, relational comparison represents an explicitly *active* methodological procedure, one that makes rather than merely follows connections and (inter) relations, guided by ethical and political as well as scientific purpose. Bringing entities and subjects *into* relation is a deliberate methodological act. As Shih puts it, this is an act of "relationing," designed to set

> into motion relationalities between entities brought together for comparison ... bringing into relation terms that have been traditionally pushed apart from each other due to certain interests, especially interests of power. I consider the excavation of these relationalities to be the ethical practice of comparison, where minor sites or texts (social or cultural) from so-called peripheries or semi-peripheries ... can be brought to relation just as can major sites and texts. The work of the comparatist thereby partially equalises the uneven terrain of discursive power across the world. Relational comparison thus in turn breaks up the centre-periphery model of the world systems theory, as sites and texts from anywhere form a network of relations. ... Given that mapping the totality of infinite interconnections is a practical impossibility, relational comparison, as praxis, must also delimit its scope and scale depending on the problematiques being posed and issues being explored. The problematiques and issues will lead the cartography and geography of entities brought into relational comparison, and not the other way around.[38]

Echoing Jennifer Robinson's technique of "theorizing from elsewhere" in critical urban studies, this methodological maneuver involves "upsetting Eurocentrism and other power grids," including core-periphery models, thereby "altering our conception of the world," not with a view to replacing one (Euro)centric reading with a reversed-out or subaltern one, but instead to expose power-laden relations by pushing together (or "relationing") objects, texts, peoples, situations, and places that might otherwise be more conventionally separated—and in the process "scatter[ing] all centers."[39] This move seeks to transcend, as a conscious and reflexive methodological procedure, notions of insularity, "siloing," and disconnection implicit in the conventions of area-studies and the formal logics of comparison. Once again, there is a studied skepticism concerning pregiven containers and preformulated categories, coupled with a refusal simply to follow the well-trodden pathways. Consequently, research designs are shaped in proactive dialogue with questions of politics, ethics, theory, and method. And again, theory-building is equated more with map *making* than with the elaboration of preexisting mental maps. In a similar spirit comes Subrahmanyam's injunction to "redraw maps that emerge from the problematics we study rather than invent problematics to fit our pre-existent cartographies."[40]

The received map that Shih has sought to redraw, more specifically, is the one that has confined Taiwan within the power grid of Cold War geopolitics and the traditional rubrics of area studies. Here, the search is for a "new method for studying Taiwan," not just as a "node in a network, but [as a] *place* from which one theorises about the world, as ... a crucial place that is a co-producer or even initiator of global processes."[41] In a similar spirit, if quite coincidentally, Gillian Hart had earlier engaged Taiwan, as a dynamic and structuring presence on the "inside" of her long-term investigations in South Africa, once the town of Newcastle "became a node in a worldwide Taiwanese diaspora" following successive waves of investment in the local textiles sector: "On the face of it, at least, the Taiwanese knitwear complex in Newcastle bears a close resemblance to forms of network production that have functioned in Taiwan," she reported, yet the story of ongoing struggles around wages, working conditions, and productivity revealed no mechanical, one-to-one correspondence between industrial systems and social politics, "the production of knitwear and the production of difference [having] reinforced one another."[42] This "comparative move" was not just a matter of comparing one case (site or location) with another, but tracing what were deeply entangled experiences of sociospatial transformation, each locally refracted through particular articulations of class formation, managerial strategy, and racial, ethnic, and gendered difference. The superficial resemblances between "Taiwanese" patterns of industrial development in the different locations provided, in this case, a series of entry points into an unevenly developed terrain of mutual constitution and variable articulation. Eschewing teleology and structural determination on the one hand and voluntarism and radical contingency on the other, Hart invokes the idea of "multiple trajectories of socio-spatial change" as midlevel concepts mobilized in order to explore the "structured contingencies" of localized outcomes and situated politics.[43] In doing so, she is knowingly steering a course between what is stylized as a David Harvey position, emphasizing systemic tendencies for uneven capitalist development, and a Doreen Massey position, attending to a more granular and open reading of spatiality.[44]

In describing, quite candidly and reflexively, her somewhat improvised method of relational comparison, Hart provides the most extended explication and application of this approach. While her multi-year investigations have been anchored, politically and practically, in South Africa, the project nevertheless extended to discussions of Taiwanese investment practices, onshore and offshore, along with different experiences of agrarian transformation and labor reproduction across East Asia. "Relationality," in this sense, is not reducible to material connections between South Africa and East Asia, although it certainly includes this. (Hart examines material flows of Taiwanese capital and organizational practices, also making periodic reference to Asian "models from elsewhere" that were being promoted at the same as templates for post-apartheid development.) In this context, relationality extends to a dialogical analysis of different geohistorical configurations of accumulation dynamics, employment regimes, production and reproduction politics, social struggles, and so forth, notably those surrounding "Taiwanese" textile-manufacturing complexes in South Africa, China, and Taiwan itself. Patterns of industrial development exhibited in Taiwan and China are shown to be predicated on, and comingled with, particular histories of redistributive land reform, but when translated into the South African context, this has the effect of naturalizing a distinctive and especially acute form of racialized exploitation and dispossession. It is *out of* this particular confluence of circumstances, social struggles, and power relations that the local state is judged to have acquired a strategically significant role in the reconstitution of the neoliberalizing post-apartheid order.[45]

As a genre of representation and exposition, this demanding method of parallel, overlapping, and cross-referential analysis, involving not just one but several sites and situations, cannot be anything but densely documented, closely engaged, and intricately argued—in this respect bearing the burdens (and responsibilities) of multisite complexity in a way that again is more reminiscent of Doreen Massey than David Harvey. Stylization and complexity reduction are not really available options when it comes to this kind of relational comparison, which tends to *multiply* the demands of not only documentation and description but also analysis and explanation. What are brought into question, and into relation, are not mere instantiations or localizations of the same (otherwise known) array of "global processes," nor can their analysis defer "simply [to] methods for the detailed production of local knowledge" in the shape of theoretically neutral narratives.[46] Hart's task, instead, is to construct "concrete concepts that are adequate to [and indexed against] the historical and geographical complexity with which they are seeking to grapple."[47]

To recall Andrew Sayer's distinction between different "metaphysics" of methodological representation, which he characterizes as a series of coexisting and alternative (rather than mutually substituting) "ways of conceptually structuring the world in terms of objects and relations," Hart's method of relational comparison amounts to a particular take on the problem of handling, *pari passu*, the particular but at the same time interdependent.[48] Table 10.1 offers a heuristic representation of four, admittedly simplified, methodological positions, based on the two dimensions identified by Sayer, those of particularity/generality and independence/interdependence. There is no need to dwell, in the present context, on the non-relational modes of analysis described in quadrants *a* and *b* of this stylized methodological space, which

Table 10.1 Contrasting Methodological Orientations

Particular and independent	General and independent
Idiographic studies & empirical description	*Positivist regional science & spatial analysis*
Implicit presumption of a structureless social world, comprised of atomized facts, objects, events, places	Search for enduring regularities, realized as empirical patterns
Assumption of "external" and contingently related objects and places, standing alone, with independent conditions of existence	Generalizations codified as covering "laws"
	Phenomena classified according to taxonomic criteria (relating to formal characteristics), "externally" related objects and places
Limited theoretical ambition or penetration	Unreflexive theoretical posture
a	*b*
Particular and interdependent	**General and interdependent**
Uneven geographical development & extended case analysis	*Territorial development modeling & evolutionary political economy*
Problematizing situations and social formations as the complex synthesis of multiple determinations; theoretical recognition of a deeply structured and interconnected social world, configured by "internal," interlocking, and necessary relations	Generation of synthesized accounts and midlevel abstractions affirmed (but not reducible) to regularized patterns; theoretical recognition of a structured and interconnected social world
Uniqueness as articulation and inconstant conjunction; configurations positioned in space-time and on uneven terrains	Search for generalized logics of territorial development, agglomeration, and center-periphery relations
Explanatory value attached to "local" configurations and structured forms of coherence; skeptical of generalizations and essentialism	Deployment of causal rather than taxonomic groups; willingness to draw out generalizations linked to recurrent patterns, configurations, and abstract tendencies
Conjunctural analysis: problematizing part-whole relations, read through the prism of particular parts, through situations, crises, and social formations	System analysis: part-whole relations understood from the perspective of the whole (systematic and structured spatiality)
c	*d*

Source: Authors' formulation, derived from Sayer (1991, 2010)

skew toward empiricist and positivist modes of generalization (*generality1* in Sayer's schema), "typical" or ostensibly representative case studies, and ideal-typical modes of reasoning. These approaches tend to be weakly relational at best, in the sense that they presume a universe of atomized, independent, and self-acting objects/subjects, between which there exist only "external" relations, while the social world itself is *not* seen to be systematically structured, by asymmetrical power relations or by entrenched forms of social difference.

More pertinent for present purposes are quadrants c and d of Table 10.1, which are associated with non-positivist epistemologies and relational ontologies. Here, the social world is understood to be characteristically lumpy and uneven, while also being structured in enduring ways, which may or may not be revealed in the form of empirical regularities. Since relationality implies states of interdependency in the social world, objects, entities, events, and sites will often exhibit mutual conditions of existence, nominally exterior connections and relations shaping their "internal" capacities and liabilities. The (variable and alterable) manner in which local social worlds are assembled and articulated with one another is therefore held to make a significant difference. It follows that these approaches "involve a much greater concern with conceptualisation than [those summarized at quadrants a and b]; for, if all relations are conceived of as external, then the relata seem stable, simple and straightforward to conceptualise, whereas if many relations are internal, and hence effect the nature of the relata [as in quadrants c and d], one needs to make the conceptualisation of the objects sensitive to this fact."[49]

Hart's rendering of the relational-comparative method belongs in the bottom half of Table 10.1, being more adjacent to quadrant c than d. For his part, Sayer places Massey's spatial division of labor approach, the original spirit of the British localities program, and ethnographic studies sensitized to wider systems of meaning in this same category.[50] Broadly speaking, the approaches of Gillian Hart and Michael Burawoy belong somewhere in this vicinity too.[51] It is largely the domain of situated case-study investigations and small-n comparisons, in Steinmetz's terms,[52] whereas the modes of relational analysis located in quadrant d would more often take their cues from recurrent patterns or what Lawson calls "demi-regularities," working across a larger number of cases, situations, and sites, rather than homing in on the kinds of particularities and specificities that necessarily attach to relational *comparisons*.[53] If Hart's research program is an example of the latter, it should be noted that hers was a methodological path constructed through practice, beginning with a focused, but effectively unbounded, South African inquiry and spiraling out from that starting (and reference) point to a series of transnational explorations, rather than by way of a comparative research design conceptualized explicitly in advance. Once again, this highlights how the relational-comparative approach emerged less as a calculated methodological adaptation of the comparative research design, more as a critically guided alternative.

Drawing together the discussion in this part of the chapter, Table 10.2 outlines some methodological rules of thumb associated with relational comparison. Founded on a relational ontology, these approaches operate on the premise of an intricately interconnected, heterogeneous, and spatially uneven social world, such that no site or place can be meaningfully considered in isolation. Research sites (as entry points and loci of concern) are uniquely situated, demanding explicit attention to their relative positionalities; there is no place for "centric" or prototypical theorizing, or stage models premised on universal templates and developmental paths. Points of departure (and analytical focus) may be selected for strategic, political, or pragmatic reasons, or on the basis of theoretically informed research designs, although analysis will proceed in a relatively unbounded way, starting points being no more than that. Methodologically speaking, the feet must remain on the ground, but the gaze should extend over the horizon. These open-ended inquiries engage social worlds and social relations marked by ongoing transformation, contestation, and emergence; exploratory in character, they characteristically spiral outward, extending as appropriate to extra-local and boundary-exceeding domains of mutual constitution, networked capacities, framing relations, structuring contexts, and off-site conditions of existence. (In contrast to

Table 10.2 Some Rules of Thumb for Relational Comparison

Relational ontology: the world as an uneven and interdependent place; mutually related research sites are uniquely positioned in multipolar social worlds, understandings of which are duly constructed not given

Open horizons: not closed-system theorizing, but open-ended and relatively unbounded investigations, spiraling across sites and cases

Situated cases: a premium is placed on understanding the positionality research sites and subjects in wider networks, hierarchies, and (power) relations, which are not defined a priori but in their always-emergent form; cases are connected, but with no presumption of commensurability

Mutual entanglement: "relationed" research sites are not discrete and free-standing but mutually interconnected, and interdependent; each has a presence "inside" the other(s)

Fluid spatiality: socially produced rather than pregiven categories, boundaries, interrelations, and delimitations; investigations positioned on dynamic, uneven landscapes

Moving articulations: multisited inquiries of differently constituted and hybridized relations with attention to their localized (and contextualized) forms

closed-system theorizing, there is no a priori expectation of self-containment, endogenous logics, or internal coherence.)

Since research sites and subjects are located on moving terrains, cross-cut by transformative dynamics and power relations, their "outsides" are mutually constitutive, not inert or empty hinterlands. There is consequently an obligation actively to *situate cases* in relation to their constitutive others, and to more-than-local networks and domains, hierarchical relations, and power geometries. After McMichael and others, however, this is not just a matter of deriving units of analysis from a pregiven theory-map; rather, grounded inquiries become engines for the (re)generation of theoretical worldviews: "it is insufficient simply to place phenomena within empirically given chronological and geographical coordinates," Tomich explains, "Instead, the sociohistorical construction of temporal and spatial processes and relations must itself become an object of inquiry."[54] Likewise for Hart, uneven geographical development is not some inherited landscape on which relational comparisons are then executed; instead, the form and logic of uneven geographical development are engaged through these grounded inquiries. Furthermore, "comparative" research sites are relationed and interconnected; they are not presumed to be independent of one another, separately located as commensurable, like-to-like entities occupying parallel and autonomous positions on a lateral plane. It follows that research sites are mutually entangled, each having presences "inside" the other. Rather than free-standing, discrete, and independent "case-study areas," invoked in assessments of dis/similarity or contrast, research sites (co)exist in states of interconnection, entanglement, and interdependence, the content and character of which is properly subject to prior conceptualization, at least provisionally. (The social relations in question, those that connect research sites, might be those of competition, cooperation or collaboration, those connecting experimenters and emulators, positions on corporate supply-chains or intergovernmental networks, and so forth.) So while relational inquiries are relatively open-ended, they are not freely inductive, and neither should they be theoretically unprincipled "fishing expeditions." At the stage of research design and (starting) case selection, theoretically derived principles of pertinence, puzzles, anomalies, and paradoxes, together with opportunities for the stress-testing of concepts, categories, and propositions, all have active roles to play, since these are likely to inform the pathways and horizons of subsequent inquiries—more so, it ought to be expected, than flat-out surprises or empirical bolts from the blue.

Since space and scale are themselves understood in relational terms, the spaces and sites of research do not adhere or defer to pregiven or fixed categories, boundaries, and coordinates. Consistent with this relational sense of socially produced and fluid spatialities, research sites are not conceived as delimited spaces characterized by internal coherence or integrity, but as entry points and as domains of articulated relations. In this context, relational comparisons engage two or more sites of inquiry, or connectivities and mediations between these, with a view to documenting, problematizing, and ultimately theorizing "locally" variable configurations of social relations and causal potentialities, differently articulated power geometries, and distinctive forms of (re)combination, synthesis, and hybridity. This sense of differently constructed relations, from place to place, of *moving articulations*, represents the underlying rationale for dynamic and multisited investigations, since there is no expectation of predictable or fixed configurations, determinate (inter)relationships, or constant conjunctions.

From Conjunctural Analysis to Conjunctural Method

For all its allure, which if anything seems to be growing in recent years, conjunctural analysis remains somewhat elusive from a methodological perspective, witnessed principally in execution and seemingly resistant even to post hoc codification, including at the hands of its most accomplished practitioners.[55] What Stuart Hall once referred to as "the discipline of the conjuncture" involves a commitment (and indeed responsibility) "to theorise and analyse the concrete complexity of a social formation," married with an injunction to "keep on" theorizing through the circumstances of the contested (and historically produced) present.[56] (The "discipline" to which Hall refers has little to do with the pursuit of a formally specified methodological program; it is more a matter of the political exigencies of a given situation, linked to an exploration of its many determinations and implications.) According to Jeremy Gilbert, the pursuit of conjunctural analysis entails a "strategic political choice," to work intensively at intermediate (and intermediat*ing*) levels of abstraction, an explanatory space located, temporally, "between the specificity of the moment and the long *durée* of the epoch,"[57] and analytically, positioned between an abstract "theoreticism [as if] for its own sake [and] an excessive particularism [devoid of] any effort to situate or explain its objects of study with reference to any wider set of social relations or historical tendencies."[58] Situated historically, but not reducible either to a slice of time, nor to an artifact of periodization, conjunctural analysis demands attention to the tangling of temporalities and spatialities, the old and the new, the near and the far, as these are knotted together at particular sites, moments, and "problem spaces."[59] The injunction to "analyze situations" involves an exacting focus on specific articulations of cultural, ideological, political-economic, and socionatural relations, teasing apart the puzzles of multiple determination in and from those particular situations.[60] In practice, this means analyzing social formations (or sometimes "settlements") that have exhibited some measure of durability or institutionalization, albeit typically under conditions of stress, transformation, or crisis.

As with relational comparison, there are affinities here with Burawoy's model of reflexive science, and its favored methodological strategy, the extended case study. Conjunctural approaches seek to situate social action, social practices, and social processes within what are invariably complex, leaky, and "open" social systems.[61] They are skeptical of strictly inductive inquiries, operating within delimited and/or circumscribed explanatory boundaries, in which events are assumed to have endogenous, internal, or otherwise proximate causes, as if operating immediately behind the backs (or in the backyards) of social actors. But they are equally wary of those highly generalized, deductive, and abstracted accounts that run the opposite risk, hovering above the realm of contextual specificity and grounded conditions. If positivist approaches to science seek to *control for* the effects of situation and context, attempting to parse these away in search of generalized laws, conjunctural analyses make a countermove, "tak[ing] context as a point of departure but not [as a] point of conclusion."[62] As such, they invoke and engage horizons of analysis and action that exceed the immediate and everyday play of events, exploring the (mutually) constitutive effects of structuring processes and framing conditions—what have been characterized as the wider contexts of those more proximate contexts.[63]

Conjunctural analyses refuse to disengage from "the moment," and the worlds of everyday events and ongoing social struggles, while at the same time insisting that this immediate horizon of analysis is rarely sufficient. Fundamentally, they are addressed to "the complex formation of an historical moment."[64] Decisive moments such as the Brexit referendum, or watershed elections like those of Modi or Thatcher or Trump, clearly each have their own, relatively "proximate" characteristics, impulses, contradictions, and casts of social actors (or "causal groups"), to which must be attached analytical significance. But to circumscribe this too narrowly, or to focus exclusively on the realm of the immediate, the present, and the proximate, is to fail to situate and articulate such so-called particularities in relation to their constitutive relations and conditions of existence, and to the multiple histories, spatialities, and social projects that contributed to their making. In Gramscian terms, conjunctural analyses definitively engage the "immediate and transitory," but problematize their complex fusion with "the organic."[65]

Following Raymond Williams, John Clarke emphasizes how conjunctural modes of analysis seek to shed light on the "dynamic interactions" between the dominant, the residual, and the emergent, understood as multiple and overlapping temporalities, which will combine, coalesce, and conflict with one another in the context of specific social formations and geopolitical moments. Conjunctural analyses are disinclined to impose unidimensional master narratives or singular, overbearing frames of analysis, and as such have no place for mechanical or monological readings of history. Instead, they involve the careful sifting, parsing, and teasing apart—through the prism of a specific situation or moment—of different framings, temporalities, and spatialities. According to Clarke, as a "mode of thinking," conjunctural approaches seek to leverage three principal sources of explanatory value, all in the service of teasing out the ephemeral from the consequential, as "deeper" dynamics and determinations are sought amid the to-and-fro of everyday events and struggles:

- A configuration of time-space: not just the conventional here and now, but spatial relations and entangled temporalities;
- Attention to heterogeneous social forces and their political alignments;
- The principle of articulation, rather than the analysis of singularities.[66]

Exemplary projects of conjunctural analysis, since the landmark text *Policing the Crisis*,[67] have tended, in practice, to foreground historicizations of the cultural and the political. What might be considered a spatialized methodological imaginary is usually little more than implicit. Uneven spatial development may be presumed, but rarely is it actively problematized. (In contrast to relational comparisons, conjunctural inquiries typically focus on *a* configuration of time-space, anchored to a single, historicized site, or unfolding crisis, rather than multiple configurations.) Nevertheless, in the lexicon of cultural studies, where conjunctural approaches are effectively the methods of choice, suggestive and (at a minimum) metaphorical invocations of space and spatiality—mappings, terrains, problem spaces, and so forth—are widespread: "the aim of a conjunctural analysis," as Gilbert puts it, for example, "is always to map a social territory."[68]

Yet there is clearly more in play here than some mere geographical stage—hence the fact that Doreen Massey's relational conception of place and some of her characteristic methodological practices have occasionally been touchstones in these discussions. In her methodological practice, Massey "elaborated conjunctural analysis geographically," Pickles and Smith write, by way of a distinctive conception of "place and space as the temporary crystallization and materialization of flows and relations occurring at multiples scales."[69] Similarly, as John Clarke has observed, Massey's concern was to address the "*entangling* of different dynamics... in complex articulations as they groom, condition, interrupt and unsettle one another," not just temporally, but as "multiple spatial relations, such that politics come to play out on a terrain that combines and condenses multiple sites [and scales] whilst recognising that all of these are folded into one another."[70] Like Hart's approach, this lends itself to granular and situated modes of exposition and theorization, rather than parsimony, stylization, or brusque abstraction, coupled with close attention to the specificities of locally articulated relationships.[71]

Stuart Hall's self-styled "radical conjuncturalism" entails what Grossberg terms "radical contextuality." The premise here is that "everything is relationally constituted," to the point that there is nothing that "can be grasped apart from its context," where context denotes a tangle or knot of intersecting relations, the particular configurations of which may never rise to the level of the determinate or the necessary (in the critical-realist sense), but nevertheless exert "real effects."[72] Context, in this radical sense, is much more than a byword for background conditions. It signals the fact that so-called context cannot be held in abeyance, but barges in as an active, unstable, and politically mediated omnipresence. Context is alive. Grossberg explains that

> [a] context cannot be described as a fixed, seamless totality where everything is neatly slotted into place as a result of some ultimately simple principle of determination... At the same time, [we] cannot give in to the radical deconstructive impulse to abandon any claim to unity, totality or fixity. Relations are "fixed," but always and only temporarily, always open to change. Contexts are constructed as unities, but they are always unstable and their boundaries porous to varying degrees.... Additionally, radical contextuality suggests that both theory and politics can only be understood and judged in relation to a context.[73]

This notion of provisional unities is germane to the definition of conjuncture themselves, which are understood as the complex outcome of "an accumulation of multiple contexts, lines of force, determination, resistances, and contradictions, each with different temporalities and spatialities, always fractured and conflictual, along multiple axes and scales."[74] If conjunctures are spatiotemporally defined social formations, there is a measure medium-term stability here but not fixity, contradiction but not chaos, and movement but not patternless fluidity. And the political horizon is never foreclosed, even if the terrain can sometimes seem to be restricting or ossified. But if conjuncturalism requires contextualism, the two are not simply interchangeable. For where contextualism signifies an ontological condition of relationality, conjuncturalism must go a step further, to "define a set of critical analytical practices," more often than not brought to bear under conditions of political intensification or crisis, where the balance of forces is being called into question and contested.[75] The Kilburn Manifesto, a collaboration launched by the journal *Soundings* and led by Stuart Hall, Doreen Massey, and Michael Rustin, was in this sense conceived and executed as a "project of conjunctural analysis,"[76] addressed as it was to the unfolding, real-time moment, the particular "condensation," that was the crisis in the British social formation in the aftermath of the (global) financial crisis.[77] Echoing Gramsci, this is a reading of conjuncture defined as a confluence conditioning and (co)determining circumstances "in movement," understood as a contradictory "ensemble that gives rise to... ever new combinations."[78]

Hall developed an approach to conjunctural analysis through his explorations of the meaning and implications of "articulation." Agreeing with Foster-Carter that the notion of articulation rested on "an anatomical metaphor to indicate relations of linkage and effectively between different levels of all sorts of things," Hall added that this signaled a structured and yet heterogeneous combination (or "contradictory unity"), linking phenomena that "though connected... are not the same," going on to add:

> The unity formed by this combination or articulation, is always, necessarily, a "complex structure": a structure in which things are related, as much through their differences as through their similarities. This requires that *the mechanisms which connect dissimilar features must be shown*—since no "necessary correspondence" or expressive homology can be assumed as given. It also means—since the combination is a structure (an articulated combination) and not a random association—that there will be structured relations between its parts.[79]

This reading of conjuncture as a structured combination of causally diverse elements—which are not reducible to one another, which do not have the same conditions of existence, and which can only be synthesized or institutionalized in a provisional, still-contradictory manner—represents, in effect, a sine qua non of the concept of UCD, where conjuncture signals situation and relational positionality, while UCD indexes the structured and heterogeneous terrain on which plurality of conjunctural situations is located. And "combination" is their shared condition. The unbounded nature of conjunctural inquiries means that they are not confined to some discrete and separate set of "interior" relations, against which are positioned the "external" relations of UCD; these are but different sides of the same dialectical process, with conjunctural analyses focusing in particular on the instituted mechanisms that *connect* the diverse elements of each structured combination, focusing on how they are able to hang together.

None of this should give the impression, however, that conjunctures are somehow "mechanical" constructions. For Grossberg, conjunctures are analogous to "problem spaces." They are the sites and settings marked by struggles over understandings and interventions. As Massey said of the Kilburn Manifesto, this was an attempt to produce "serious political analysis [founded on a] searching movement between the precise shape of the here and now and fundamental questions of conceptualisation and epistemology."[80] It was addressed to a tangled knot of conjunctural circumstances and political mediations, a problem space or situated problematic. For Grossberg, this is analogous to a

> conceptual knot [the strands of which weave their] way through economic, political, cultural and social relations in unpredictable and nonlinear ways. These vectors do not follow straight lines that neatly transect the space of the conjuncture; rather they appear as plot lines meandering all over the space-time of the conjuncture, like an ever-changing spider web.[81]

Addressing "problem spaces" in this fashion, a conjunctural analysis can be thought of as a "map of the problematics," Grossberg concludes, confessing that every such effort is liable to be something of a failure—partial, incomplete, provisional, and contestable—the geographical metaphor pointing to a pragmatic imperative "to start somewhere," even if the explanatory destination cannot be known in advance; the best that can be hoped for being pointers in the direction of "temporary conclusions."[82] In this sense, Gillian Hart's research program, which took South Africa as its starting point and ultimate focus, but never its limit, was all along a conjunctural one.[83] The kinds of methodological maps that are developed through such exploratory inquiries can only be made through practice, analysis, and engagement; they are not reducible to preexisting methodological designs, nor are they readily portable from site to site, case to case, or context to context. As frustrating as this may be to acknowledge, "there is simply no prescriptive formula" for determining either the conceptual space of a conjuncture itself or the ultimate scope of a conjunctural analysis,[84] there being "no theory that would tell one in advance how to specify a conjuncture."[85] Unpredictable, unbounded, and unwieldy as it invariably is, "conjunctural analysis is [also] probably only sustainable as a collaborative practice."[86]

No stranger to collaborative practice herself, Doreen Massey was "convinced about the importance of thinking conjuncturally as a method," not least as a method for "getting to grips with the present and its troubles,"[87] the collective effort that was the Kilburn Manifesto having recognized the decisive "importance of thinking of things as complex moments, where different parts of the overall social formation may themselves, independently, be in crisis in various ways."[88] While a methodological take on conjunctural analysis at the subnational (urban and regional) scale might in principle be recovered from Massey's practice, surely a worthwhile project in its own right, this was not something that she addressed at length. The question of how Massey might have explicated this tacit methodological practice is an intriguing one, since the archive of self-identifying conjunctural inquiries scarcely deals with these more granular issues of "localized" spatiality, or indeed the questions of scale and scalar relations, beyond a recurring interest in exploring the increasingly "stressed hyphen" that both separates and unites the *nation-state*.[89] Characteristically, this extant body of self-identifying conjunctural analysis is generally wary of "global" formulations, its more grounded inquiries problematizing the national scale without necessarily transcending that scale in methodological terms.[90] Skeptical of universalist claims, it tends to approach the general through the prism (and medium) of the particular, and the global through the prism (and medium) of the national.

In principle, there is a sound rationale for exploring approaches to conjunctural analysis that extend the scalar reach "below" that of the national scale, acknowledging the fact that their particular value (added) tends to derive from the untangling of relatively complex and heterogeneous social formations, the contestation of hegemonic orders, and assessments of the shifting balance of social forces, which may preclude some highly localized applications. There are surely opportunities, however, for the development of conjunctural approaches at the metropolitan and regional scales.[91] Conjunctural analyses oriented to these scales might constructively take as a point of departure Ananya Roy's provocation, "What does it mean to think about contemporary urbanism via articulation rather than agglomeration?"[92] What this would mean, among other things, is avoiding the sequestration and separation of the urban and regional scales but instead operationalizing a fully relational and reflexive approach to scale, inter-scalar dynamics, and their complex reproduction. Conjunctural approaches in geographical political economy consequently cannot be confined to the scales of the subnational, even as inquiries that engage these scales (among others) certainly play to the field's comparative methodological advantage (in grounded, local studies, with an eye to the global). One of the challenges here will be to find ways *actively* to problematize UCD. Multisited, comparative analyses that trace contrasting but simultaneous transformations at the urban and regional scale are extremely valuable, albeit perhaps the most demanding option, in light of Michael Dear's sobering assessment of their (im)practicality.[93] Relational comparisons, especially those that follow particular threads or domains of connection, *sans* expectations concerning the more-or-less symmetrical size or "weight" of the cases/sites in question, clearly have great potential here. Yet the methodological challenges of truly *engaging*, rather than merely indexing or gesturing toward ambient conditions of UCD, undoubtedly remain. The "space" between case studies or fieldwork sites must itself be an object of exploration and theorization (being neither "empty," nor comprising only determinant forces). The imperative is to engage and problematize UCD, *to draw it in* as an active domain of concrete inquiry and reflexive theorization, in a manner jointly constitutive of the "internal" conditions, politics, and lives encountered in localized research sites. The gridlines of geographical diversity and difference may not be comprehensively mappable in advance of such situated inquiries, but neither is it appropriate to bracket off these nominally exterior worlds as if *terra incognita*. Studies of localized conjunctures carry the responsibility to expose and engage these wider domains, networks, and landscapes of transformation, from a variety of starting and vantage points.

Instead of deferring to single-site ideal types or paradigmatic cases, conjunctural analysis at the urban and regional scale invite multipolar investigations that "draw in" the moving terrain of UCD. This calls for non-reductionist and context-rich modes of explanation, attentive to local specificities and aspiring to political relevance as well as theoretical salience. This is a license to push the limits and tolerances of extant explanations, rather than to seek their affirmative reiteration, and an invitation to theoretical reconstruction allied to a logic of methodological selectivity favoring potentially confounding cases, boundary objects, and sites of contradiction, crisis, and conflict, as opposed to would-be "models." In the spirit of "stress-testing" preferred theories, the impetus for conjunctural inquiries of this kind, Leitner and Sheppard point out, might be "what *seems atypical and unexpected* given received theory," often expressed in moments of crisis or disjuncture.[94] At the same time, there is also a remit here for the kind of inquiries that are able to shed (new) light on the normalized, the routine, and the taken for granted, as Tanya Li puts it, to "look critically at conjunctures that *aren't* shaped by dramatic events."[95]

This kind advice ought to inform a "locational politics" of research design, (field) site selection, starting points, horizons of analysis, and spaces of engagement—none of which can be left implicit or unexamined in conjunctural studies. While they may also address the ostensibly "settled" conditions of normalization, conjunctural inquiries tend to favor disruptive and contrarian methodological maneuvers, and those that work with friction or tension from the outset (hence the concern with moments and sites of crisis, disjuncture, and dislocation). The politics of such sites and moments are invariably complex and frequently urgent.[96] In explanatory terms, too, there is surely truth in Tony Lawson's observation that "generative mechanisms become that much more accessible at . . . geohistorical turning point[s]."[97] Crises, dislocations, and transformative moments often expose the seams or "welds" in social systems, focusing as they do on situations in which combinatorial formations are coming under stress or breaking apart, and where new configurations are taking shape. These are times and places where futures not just uncertain but subject to active contestation, and where the question of the "place in the world" of cities and regions is likewise an unsettled and often politicized one. The injunction to maintain open explanatory horizons is in this sense both deliberate and necessary. Conjunctural analyses seek to work through the connections between politically situated case-study investigations, reflexively defined midlevel concepts and explanatory frames, and always revisable theoretical interpretations. They stage opportunities for the extension and reconstruction of social theory, in Burawoy's terms. And there, there is particular utility in theories that engage questions of variegation and UCD frontally, rather than late in the game; and it cautions against "tight-fit" theories, tailored to this or that (sometimes presumptively normative) situation, in favor of those that are more flexible and capacious, reserving an important role for their (re)design, interrogation, and development across sites and contexts. In practice, this means working back and forth between the investigation of concrete (local) situations, the identification of emergent patterns within and between local sites, and the continuous development and revision of emergent abstractions, probing provisional categories of analysis and seeking to hone and interrogate midlevel concepts along the way.

In this respect, conjunctural approaches in geographical political economy present invitations to *think through, and then across* particular sociospatial formations, taking full account of but not being limited to the scales of the subnational. Characteristically, the preferred explanatory pathway can be thought of as an intermediate or liminal one, navigated between the high altitudes of abstract theory (with its propensity to "read off," and then *down*, from theoretical propositions to prefigured local outcomes) and the alternative pole of contingency-freighted varieties of thick description (with their tendency to alight upon adjacent sources of causality, visible across shorter lines of sight that are unlikely to capture the patterning of configurations and relations *across* multiple sites and scales). Instead, by navigating an intermediate path, if not collapsing the distinction altogether, conjunctural explanations are sought—and ultimately constructed—on the terrain of the contextual, where their theory claims are typically situated, conditional, and embedded, rather than universal and unmediated. From this perspective, conjunctural investigations that begin at the regional or subnational scales position these as sites through which to explore the localized mediation and articulation of social formations, processes, and relations, in their often-contradictory condensations and configurations. Here, cities and regions are not seen as mere case studies or host environments for the illustration of generalized theory claims. Instead, they are spaces of combination, intersection, and particular "bundles" of social relations. One way to think of them is as junction points, or hinges, in more-than-regional networks, orders, and systems, analogous to the "joints of [a] social problem," as Ollman puts it.[98] For Pickles and Smith, the conjunctural analysis of regionalized economic formations is "always territorialized in some way," albeit not in a bounded or circumscribed fashion.[99]

Conjunctural investigations (at whatever scale) are placed in the service of the purposeful *reconstruction* of understandings, explanations, working concepts, hunches, and emergent theories, not as mere illustrations (or confirmations) of what is already supposedly known, but as reflexive interrogations and stress tests of received or emergent explanations and theory claims.[100] In Stuart Hall's terms, this involves "working the contradictory, stony ground of the present conjuncture," at the same time as "thinking large[r] concepts in terms of their application to concrete and specific situations."[101] These inquiries are neither ambivalent about extant theory nor single-mindedly committed to its defense, their purpose being to engage in critical dialogue with theories and concepts—with a view, ultimately, to their elaboration, reinterpretation, reconstruction, or, if necessary, rejection. The shaping of concepts and the development of theories, in this respect, are both continuous practices: research design, site section, and "fieldwork" are not pre-theoretical exercises, since the very premises of any such "starting" theories or orienting concepts must be problematized, and themselves subject to interrogation. Whether researchers locate themselves near to normative centers (e.g., "global city") or at the supposed margins (e.g., "peripheral region"), the obligation to theorize and problematize the relationship between "cases" and their "worlds" remains.

Theories, in other words, are always in the mix, and always in iterative dialogue with the various stages of empirical inquiry, (re)conceptualization, and explanation, one of the hallmarks of conjunctural analysis being the refusal to separate (or otherwise "insulate") the process of theorization. What is involved, though, is more the work of theorizing rather than applications of theory. As Stuart Hall once reflected:

> I would do without theory if I could! The problem is, I cannot. You cannot. Because the world presents itself in the chaos of appearances, and the only way in which one can understand, break down, analyze, grasp, in order to do something about the present conjuncture that confronts one, is to break into that series of congealed and opaque appearances with the only tools you have: concepts, ideas, and thoughts. To break into it and to come back to the surface of a situation or conjuncture one is trying to explain, having made "the detour through theory."[102]

The promise of (more) spatialized approaches to conjunctural analysis is to make the most of such detours *with* theory, in the spirit of the revisable map imagined by Tilly, but where questions of research design and execution have less to do with fixed and self-contained locations and more to do with directions of travel and relatively open explanatory horizons. And since there is no such thing as a theoretically neutral location, or for that matter a politically neutral one, the starting points of these journeys are mixed up with theory and politics, whether this is acknowledged or not. To explore "problem spaces" is to work at the limits of extant theory, or in sites that facilitate its express challenge. This does not mean that research sites have to occupy known locations in (fixed) theoretical frameworks, but it cannot mean dispensing with theoretical frameworks altogether. Rather, working at the limits of theoretical frameworks frequently involves the identification of puzzles or anomalies *in relation to* those frameworks. And as Jeffrey Paige has pointed out, "There would of course be no anomalies without theoretical frameworks."[103]

The goal here is to capitalize, reflexively, on the theory-laden nature of social-scientific inquiry, including the selection and justification of research sites and methodological tools. In principle, there are neither prescriptions nor restrictions on the choice of methodological tools, but self-identifying conjunctural inquiries have tended in practice to favor generally qualitative and often discourse-analytical or ethnographic approaches. Geographical political economists, accustomed to using a mixed toolbox of methodological techniques, tend to favor various kinds of closely focused engagement with research sites, many of them local. Conjunctural inquiries will often (productively) begin here, although the next moves often involve "spiraling" methodological maneuvers, exceeding these localized sites, and problematizing "complexity, contingency, and change . . . 'all the way down,'" as well as all the way out to other sites.[104] Conjunctural specificity, complexity, and contextualization, from this perspective, do not demarcate the limits of productive theorization; they are its means and its media. This is therefore not a recipe for complexity reduction or spartan styles of monocausal explanation, but rather for the progressive (re)construction of theoretically suggestive accounts of conjunctural situations and moments, explicitly positioned in historical and geographical terms.

In geographical terms, this means situating research sites in relation to the variously intimate and extended families that comprise closely related and sharply contrasting cases, near and far, so as to present opportunities for recognizing and interrogating recurrent configurations; for probing the translation and patterning of processes, practices, and events across multiple sites, situations, and cases; and for tracing constitutive relations and network connections between them. In historical terms, it means positioning research sites in relation to multiple temporalities and transformations, implying a span (or reach) of historical analysis sufficient to grasp different fields of "organic" constitution and arcs of change, from antecedent and emergent conditions through moments of frontal advance and crisis. And in scalar terms, the fact that cities and regions can never be reduced to pregiven, stable, autonomous, or definitively bounded entities means that conjunctural analyses must be multi-scalar, taking into account the relational constitution of the local with a host of other-scaled and extra-locally networked phenomena, including the (inter)state system and the web of transnational connections, symbolic as well as material. Working with, through, and out of urban and regional sites and scales, this strand of conjunctural analysis should seek explicitly to suture the local to extra-local horizons of analysis, positioning specific cases in relation to structuring contexts, and probing their mutual interactions. In this respect, conjunctural methods tend to favor cross-cutting and transversal modes of analysis, in dialogue with the production and refinement of content-bearing, midlevel abstractions.

Summarizing the discussion so far, Table 10.3 identifies some rules of thumb for conjunctural analysis. Also premised on relational thinking, these approaches recognize the multipolar ontology of the social world, each and every position in and perspective on which is situated, partial, and particular. Radically contextualizing approaches are embraced, those that encounter the world through situated and historicized social formations, or transformative political moments, the complexity and contingency of which are not readily reducible. Conjunctures are understood as provisionally normalized configurations of social relations, the spatiotemporalities of which get tangled up in particular ways. These social formations are usually situated,

Table 10.3 Some Rules of Thumb for Conjunctural Analysis

Multipolar ontology: premise of uneven and combinatorial development, a "lumpy" ontology of more than one (center, global form, or direction); critical of universalism, reductionism, and economism

Knotted formations: analysis encompasses relatively enduring or "instituted" historical formations, as the provisional synthesis of multiple determinations; subject to ongoing transformation, contestation, and crisis tendencies

Spatiotemporal positionality: exploring the fusion of "organic" movements of history and the terrain of the contested present; express concern to problematize positionality, reading and theorizing the general and the macro through "situations," and the prism of the particular

Thick theorization: contextualization and "conditioning" of theory claims, which are subject to ongoing reconstruction; working the middle ranges, with an emphasis on the interrogation and development of midlevel concepts; skeptical of both "floating" abstractions and unprincipled induction

Problematizing scale: cross-scalar analysis of "regionalized" formations, finding difference and division on the "inside," as well as interregionally—contextualizing "all the way out"

Crisis moments: rooted in multiple determinations and moving contradictions; dialectical analysis of hegemonic strategies, social settlements, and institutional regularization under conditions of stress and reconstruction; mapping contestations and counter-projects

---

in the first instance, in relation to arcs of historical development, being subject to ongoing transformation, contestation, and recurrent crisis tendencies, but will also be periodically stabilized under the sway of hegemonic projects or institutionalized social settlements. Furthermore, conjunctural analyses are predicated on the recognition (and problematization) of spatiotemporal positionality. They seek to "analyze situations," seeking to read and diagnose "the general," "the organic," and "the macro," not in purely abstract terms but through the prism of the grounded, the concrete, and the particular.

In their aspiration to deeply contextualized modes of inquiry, conjunctural approaches inhabit in the space between thick description and abstract theorizing—what is styled here as thick theorization. Middle-range inquiries are privileged, forging pathways between the micro and the macro, the systematic and the experiential, the organic and the immediate, the patterned and the particular, and higher- and lower-flying modes of inquiry, without completely detaching from any of these, as means to identify and explore articulations, mediations, localizations, condensates, and configurations. Characteristically, conjunctural analyses seek to work on the hinges, welds, articulations, and intersections between the flow of everyday events and struggles on the one hand, and "tectonic" shifts in historically embedded social formations on the other, while privileging neither in any permanent way. Unconvinced of the value of either abstract theoreticism (thin theorization) or unprincipled empirical induction (thick description), they must effectively begin with a provisional conceptual "map," if only to inform points of departure and initial directions of inquiry. Redrawing and reanimating these maps duly become methodological objectives in their own right.

Working transversally, the goal is to construct middle-range explanatory pathways with recourse neither to the kind of vulgar "verticalism" that privileges top-down, hierarchical relations in a unilateral manner, nor to the sort of free-form "horizontalism" that is vulnerable to localist and voluntarist modes of interpretation. Instead, conjunctural analyses problematize the tangled, cross-cutting, and "knotted" intersections of more-than-local processes and practices. They will often make spiraling maneuvers, methodologically speaking, from a chosen starting point or loci of concern, remaining anchored to these particular situations, but setting out to resist and overcome the stubborn, binary associations between the concrete/local and the abstract/global. They seek to contextualize "all the way out" while diagnosing general movements and tendencies through engagements on the "stony ground" of the present and the particular. Conjunctural analyses are well suited to the middle ranges in scalar terms, problematizing scale by conducting multi-scalar and cross-scalar inquiries of "regionalized" formations at expansive but less-than-global scales, and thereby internalizing significant degrees of heterogeneity, difference, and unevenness in social, political, and institutional conditions. Sometimes "sampling" on extended moments of crisis, conjunctural analyses seek to trace moving contradictions, as arenas of struggle, as motors of transformation, and as spaces of experimentation, mutation, and chance discovery.

Conclusion: Disruptive Methodologies

Relational comparison and conjunctural analysis each come with invitations to creative and disruptive modes of theorizing that, without doubt, are methodologically demanding—from provisional conceptualization and research design, through adaptive and relatively unbounded empirical inquiries, to the fashioning of alternative explanations, understandings, and interventions. These are methodological paths made by walking, often via way stations, "detours," and provisional destinations that cannot be fully anticipated in advance. Relational comparison and conjunctural analysis can both be considered to be emergent methodological approaches in the fields of geographical political economy, in the sense that the library of canonical texts remains rather sparse, coupled with only sporadic progress, to date, in the direction of serious methodological reflection and codification. The objective of this closing chapter has been to open up the discussion of the latter, seeking to identify complementarities and through-lines between the two approaches, in anticipation of an (at least) preliminary form of methodological consolidation. Since this too has been a journey, the concern has been to identify promising directions rather than fixed destinations.

Providing as they do an alternative repertoire of methodological optics, critically and orthogonally positioned in relation to more conventional methods, relational-conjunctural approaches offer the promise of transcending the tired binary of the general and the particular. Relational comparison purposefully problematizes the interdependent variegation of subnational-scale processes and practices across cities, regions, and more expansive territorial spaces, challenging more conventional norms of comparative case-study analysis, which misleadingly tend to treat territorialized study areas as if they were hermetic units of analysis possessed of some "interior" logic, integrity, or rationality. Methodologically speaking, relational approaches bring the elsewhere in; they open up lateral lines of connectivity, mutuality, and interdependence across the constantly moving landscapes of uneven development. Conjunctural analyses, on the other hand, engage the general *through* the historicized particular; they do not privilege the particular and the immediate over the general and organic, in a one-sided fashion, but neither do they encounter present situations as mere instantiations of generalized, macro-historical conditions. Instead, the particular is bound up in and dialectically constitutive of the general, the emergent and contradictory outcome a plurality of (interacting, mutually constitutive) particulars. The epistemological objects brought into focus through relational-conjunctural analysis are therefore neither self-contained sites, nor are they simply "cases of" more general phenomena; they are *cases in context*.

Relational-conjunctural approaches establish guardrails against methodological localism, methodological nationalism, and methodological globalism, while also cautioning against ideal-typical reasoning, decontextualized theory claims, and the ring-fencing of field sites and causal inquiries. They engage constitutive outsides—across spatial, networked, or scalar dimensions—not as a means of diminishing the local, the grounded and proximate, the up-close, and the experiential, which retain indispensable roles as methodological anchors, explanatory domains, and reference points, but in the form of an injunction always to contextualize, situate, and position research sites and case-study locations. They seek to overcome false separations between the "interiors" of case-study sites and the worlds ostensibly beyond, between endogenous capacities and exogenous forces, and between content-laden empirics and contentless abstraction. Relational-conjunctural approaches are disinclined to take the global or planetary as their point of departure or indeed ultimate scale of reference, although they are rarely timid in grappling with the terrains of the more-than-local. They engage with the more-than-local, however, from the perspective(s) of sociospatial positionality, as situated and situating methodologies. Metaphorically speaking, their (shared) ontology of the global bears little resemblance to a unified and preformed whole, as if some hard shell or inflexible container; rather, it presents as something more like an unsolvable Rubik's cube, each (entry) point within which is jointly constituted with (and connected to) others, the movements among which are nonlinear and cumulative, but nevertheless prone repeatedly to reveal new juxtapositions and combinations. The reflexive epistemologies of relational comparison and conjunctural analysis have been shaped accordingly, as strategies for engaging with and intervening in this moving sociopolitical puzzle.

A series of quite distinctive methodological values can be identified at the nexus of relational-comparative and conjunctural approaches. They problematize the situational and the positional, "locating" case studies and research sites in historical and geographical terms, rather than dissociating or abstracting them from their constitutive, structuring contexts, frames, and relations. They recognize mutual relations and interdependencies, including constitutive connections that spiral out from and variously connect research sites, in contrast to approaches that posit the existence of free-standing cases or decontextualized ideal types. They initiate theoretically informed but relatively open-ended explorations of spatial and scalar difference, without imposing, a priori, constraining expectations of normativity, centrality, or hierarchy, thereby circumventing some of the pitfalls of ethnocentric, paradigmatic, "top down" or excessively deductive theorizing. And not least, they transcend the arbitrary division of the general and the particular by way of a dialectical reformulation, engaging and grounding "the general" through particularized and situated sites, moments, and vantage points.

Finally, it bears emphasizing that these are not merely matters of epistemological correctness; they impinge directly on where, why, and with whom research is conducted, to what purpose and with what stakes. Relational-conjunctural approaches provide checks against political foreclosure, inevitablism, and monological thinking; they issue a remit for the active engagement of "situations," while calling attention to power geometries, alternative configurations, and open horizons. They provide a warrant for locally grounded, connected, and experience-near investigations in ways that engage but also exceed these more immediate spaces of agency and social action. It may be a fact of life that kind of work is resource-intensive, time-consuming, and effectively incompletable, often necessitating extended commitments and collaborations. Furthermore, it calls for degrees of attention to research design and to rigorous reflexivity that differ (and perhaps exceed) some of the established methodological norms in geographical political economy, where improvisation and creativity have often been valued over more exacting forms of codification, reflexivity, and transparency. It is one measure, in other words, of the work that there still is to do.

Notes

Chapter 1

1. See Peck (2012b).
2. Scott (2000, 484).
3. See Wilkinson (1981) and Gordon et al (1982).
4. See Peck (1989).
5. See Massey (1984), Sayer (1984, 1985), and Lovering (1989). For subsequent reflections, see Peck et al (2018) and Peck (2013b, 2018, 2022).
6. See Cooke P (1989) *Localities: the changing face of urban Britain*. London, UK: Routledge; Warde A (1989) Recipes for a pudding: a comment on locality. *Antipode* 21(3): 274–281.
7. This synthesis was perhaps most notoriously embodied by Patrick Minford, a monetarist economist and vocal advocate for the Thatcherite program, who was down the road at Liverpool University at the time. See Minford P (1985) *Unemployment: cause and cure*. Oxford, UK: Wiley-Blackwell.
8. See Robertson D B (1986) Mrs. Thatcher's employment prescription: an active neo-liberal labor market policy. *Journal of Public Policy* 6(3): 275–296; Dawes and Peck (2020).
9. See Polanyi (1944), Aglietta (1979), Offe (1985), and the discussion in Peck (1994, 2000).
10. See Peck (2020a, 2022a).
11. Harvey (2004, 545) has observed that "the introduction of space and matters geographical . . . into any theoretical framework usually exercises a disruptive effect on how the theory works. . . . My strategy has been to bring the Marxian theory to bear on spatial/geographical questions towards the end of the analysis. This was difficult. . . . But a decent theoretical understanding of uneven geographical development still remains to be written. . . . To do this requires, in my judgement, that the issues of spatio-temporality [are] integrated into the argument at the very start rather than at the end of the analysis." Harvey D (2004) Retrospect on *The Limits to Capital*. *Antipode* 36(3): 544–549.
12. See the further discussion in Chapter 4. See also Peck J (1998) Geographies of governance: TECs and the neo-liberalisation of "local interests." *Space and Polity* 2(1): 5–31; Brenner et al (2010); and Dawes and Peck (2020).
13. See Peck (2012b, 2018) and the discussion in Chapters 2 and 5.
14. Scott (2000, 495).
15. On "layering," rounds of investment, and definitions of the economic, see Massey D (1995) New directions in space. In G Gregory and J Urry (eds) *Social relations and spatial structures*. Basingstoke, UK: Macmillan, 9–19; Massey D (1997) Economic/non-economic. In R Lee and J Wills (eds) *Geographies of economies*, London, UK: Arnold, 27–36.
16. See the further discussion in Peck (2013b, 2022b).
17. The article that marks this moment perhaps better than any other is Linda McDowell's (1991) Life without father and Ford: the new gender order of post-Fordism. *Transactions of the Institute of British Geographers* 16(4): 400–419. See also Peck J and Omstedt M (2019)

Linda McDowell. In P A Atkinson, S Delamont and M Williams (eds) *The Sage encyclopedia of research methods*. London, UK: Sage, 1–8.
18. Barnes and Christophers (2018, 12).
19. On the donut-like form of the field, see Peck J and Olds K (2007) The Summer Institute in Economic Geography. *Economic Geography* 83(3): 309–318. See also Rosenman E, Loomis J and Kay K (2020) Diversity, representation, and the limits of engaged pluralism in (economic) geography. *Progress in Human Geography* 44(3): 510–533.
20. See Peck J (1990) Circuits of capital and industrial restructuring: adjustment in the Australian clothing industry. *Australian Geographer* 21(1): 33–52; Peck J (1990) Outwork and restructuring in the Australian clothing industry. *Labour and Industry* 3(2/3): 302–329; and Peck J (1992) "Invisible threads": homeworking, labour-market relations, and industrial restructuring in the Australian clothing trade. *Environment and Planning D: society and space* 10(6): 671–690.
21. See the discussion in Barnes et al (2007).
22. An "institutional" marker of this shift in emphasis and nomenclature is that, in 1992, the members of what had been known as the Industrial Activity and Area Development Study Group of the Institute of British Geographers (myself among them) voted to change the group's name, belatedly one might say, to the Economic Geography Study Group (and now Research Group).
23. The discussion around (dis)engaged pluralism in economic geography was initiated by Trevor Barnes and Eric Sheppard's (2010) article, "Nothing includes everything." See also Peck (2012b); Wray F, Dufty-Jones R, Gibson C, Larner W, Beer A, Le Heron R and O'Neill P (2013) Neither here nor there or always here and there? Antipodean reflections on economic geography. *Dialogues in Human Geography* 3(2): 179–199; Varró K (2015) Making (more) sense of political-economic geographies of continuity and change: dialoguing across ontological divides. *Progress in Human Geography* 39(1): 26–46; Rosenman E, Loomis J and Kay K (2020) Diversity, representation, and the limits of engaged pluralism in (economic) geography. *Progress in Human Geography* 44(3): 510–533.
24. See Yeung H W and Lin G (2003) Theorizing economic geographies of Asia. *Economic Geography* 79(2): 107–128; Pollard et al (2011); Werner M (2012) Contesting power/knowledge in economic geography: learning from Latin America and the Caribbean. In T J Barnes, J Peck and E Sheppard (eds) *The Wiley-Blackwell companion to economic geography*. Oxford, UK: Wiley-Blackwell, 132–145; Hassink R, Gong H and Marques P (2019) Moving beyond Anglo-American economic geography. *International Journal of Urban Sciences* 23(2): 149–169.
25. See, especially, the discussion in Barnes and Christophers (2018), chapter 2.
26. See, in addition to the discussion in Chapters 2, 5, and 10, Sayer A (1985) The difference that space makes. In D Gregory and J Urry (eds) *Social relations and spatial structures*. London, UK: Macmillan, 49–66; Jessop B (2000) The crisis of the national spatio-temporal fix and the tendential ecological dominance of globalizing capitalism. *International Journal of Urban and Regional Research* 24(2): 323–360; Block F (2003) Karl Polanyi and the writing of *The great transformation*. *Theory and Society* 32(3): 1–32; and Peck et al (2018).
27. Michael Storper's (1997) *Regional world* is arguably the definitive contribution in this vein.
28. See Coe and Yeung (2015).
29. Doreen Massey's influence has perhaps been the most decisive here, nowhere better illustrated than in her concepts of power geometries and the "global sense of place." See Massey D (1991) A global sense of place. *Marxism Today* 35(6): 24–29; Massey D (1993)

Power-geometry and a progressive sense of place. In J Bird, B Curtis, T Putnam and L Tickner (eds) *Mapping the futures: local cultures, global change*. London, UK: Routledge, 59–69.
30. Alongside David Harvey's extensive contributions, the foundational work is Neil Smith's (1984) *Uneven development*.
31. Sayer A (1985) The difference that space makes. In D Gregory and J Urry (eds) *Social relations and spatial structures*. London, UK: Macmillan, 49–66.

Chapter 2

1. Darwin to Hooker, August 1, 1857; Darwin Correspondence Database, http://www.darwinproject.ac.uk/entry-2130.
2. See Hodgson (2015, 31–34).
3. Hodgson (2015, 32, emphasis added).
4. See the further discussion in Chapters 9 and 10.
5. After Mufti (2005, 475), a theory culture can be understood as "the *habitus* that regulates 'theory' as a discrete set of practices." Mufti A R (2005) Global comparativism. *Critical Inquiry* 31(2): 472–489.
6. See the discussion in Sheppard E (2016) Heterodoxy as orthodoxy: prolegomenon for a geographical political economy. In G L Clark, M P Feldman, M S Gertler and D Wójcik (eds) *The new Oxford handbook of economic geography*. Oxford, UK: Oxford University Press, 159–178.
7. Barnes and Christophers (2018, 11–15, 26–28) may have provided the most compelling "extended" definition of economic geography, one that culminates in, even if it cannot be entirely reduced to, the following: "an analytical attentiveness to, and explanatory emphasis upon, the substantive implication of place, space, scale, landscape, and environment in (what are deemed to be) 'economic' processes."
8. Barnes and Sheppard (2010, 199).
9. Sheppard et al. (2012, 18).
10. Anon (1894) Defence not defiance. *Cornhill Magazine* (March): 286–296, 295.
11. Tarrow S (2002) From lumping to splitting: specifying globalization and resistance. In J Smith and H Johnston (eds) *Globalization and resistance: transnational dimensions of social movements*. Oxford, UK: Rowman and Littlefield, 229–249, 234.
12. Kindleberger C P (2000) Lumpers and splitters in economics, a note. *American Economist* 44(1): 88–92, 88.
13. Dow (2000, 157, emphasis added).
14. Lawson (2015, 26).
15. See Fourcade et al. (2015).
16. Lawson (2015, 32).
17. Lawson (2015, 3); Colander D, Holt R P, and Rosser J B (2004) The changing face of mainstream economics. *Review of Political Economy* 16(4): 485–500, 492.
18. Dow (2000, 168).
19. Strassmann D L (1994) Feminist thought and economics; or, what do the Visigoths know? *American Economic Review, Papers and Proceedings* 84(2): 153–158, 153–154.
20. Paul Romer, quoted in Sussman A L (2015) Paul Romer on "mathiness" and the state of economics. *Wall Street Journal*, August 15. http://blogs.wsj.com/economics/2015/08/17/qa-paul-romer-on-mathiness-and-the-state-of-economics/ (accessed March 22, 2021); see

also Romer P M (2015) Mathiness in the theory of economic growth. *American Economic Review, Papers & Proceedings* 105(5): 89–93. For more on Paul Romer and his turn toward more "applied" economics, see Ebner N and Peck J (2022) Fantasy island: Paul Romer and the multiplication of Hong Kong. *International Journal of Urban and Regional Research* 46(1): 26–49.
21. Fourcade et al. (2015, 96).
22. Fourcade et al. (2015, 96).
23. Benton R (1982) Economics as a cultural system. *Journal of Economic Issues* 16(2): 461–469. See also Galbraith J K (1971) *Economics, peace, and laughter*. Boston, MA: Houghton Mifflin; Geertz C (1973) *Interpretation of cultures*. New York, NY: Basic Books.
24. Fourcade M et al. (2015, 107).
25. Brown W (2015) *Undoing the demos: neoliberalism's stealth revolution*. New York, NY: Zone, 31, 36.
26. Dow (2000, 163).
27. Lawson (2015, 26, emphasis added).
28. See Vidal and Peck (2012); Fourcade M (2009) *Economists and societies*. Princeton, NJ: Princeton University Press.
29. On the orthodox treatment of the market, and the condition of marketcentricity, see Peck (2020b).
30. Lawson (2015, 45, original emphasis).
31. The phrase is from Barnes and Sheppard (2010, 195).
32. See Foster J, Muellerleile C, Peck J, and K Olds (2007) Circulating economic geographies: citation patterns and citation behaviour in economic geography, 1982–2006. *Transactions of the Institute of British Geographers* 32(3): 295–312.
33. Clark G L (1998) Stylized facts and close dialogue: methodology in economic geography. *Annals of the Association of American Geographers* 88(1): 73–87, 75, 74.
34. This is further discussed in Chapter 3; see also Grabher G (2006) Trading routes, bypasses, and risky intersections: mapping the travels of networks between economic sociology and economic geography. *Progress in Human Geography* 30(2): 163–189.
35. See Barnes and Sheppard (2010).
36. Scott A J (2000) Economic geography: the great half-century. *Cambridge Journal of Economics* 24(4): 483–504, 493.
37. This term was coined by Eric Sheppard (2011). See also Pike A, Birch K, Cumbers A, MacKinnon D and McMaster R (2009) A geographical political economy of evolution in economic geography. *Economic Geography* 85(2): 175–182; Jones A (2016) Political economic geographies: a pluralist direction? *Progress in Human Geography* 40(5): 697–706.
38. See Peck (2012b, 2012c).
39. Sheppard (2011); Swyngedouw E (2009) Political economy. In D Gregory, R Johnston, and G Pratt (eds) *Dictionary of human geography*. Malden: Wiley-Blackwell, 547–549, 548.
40. Sheppard (2011, 320–321).
41. Gibson-Graham (1996, 3).
42. Gibson-Graham (1996, 3).
43. See Gibson-Graham J-K, Cameron J and Healy S (2013) *Take back the economy*. Minneapolis: University of Minnesota Press; Cameron J and Gibson K (2020) Action research for diverse economies. In J-K Gibson-Graham and K Dombroski (eds) *The handbook of diverse economies*. Cheltenham, UK: Edward Elgar, 511–519.
44. Gibson-Graham (2008, 619).

45. Gibson-Graham (1996, 9).
46. Gibson-Graham (2008, 618).
47. Gibson-Graham (2008, 619–620). On pattern recognition, see Gibson-Graham J-K, Cameron J and Healy S (2013) *Take back the economy*. Minneapolis: University of Minnesota Press, 7–8.
48. Barnes and Sheppard (2010, 194).
49. Polanyi (1977, xl). In the *Grundrisse*, Marx (1973, 105) was similarly critical of "those economists who smudge over all historical differences and see bourgeois relations in all forms of society." Polanyi's relationship with Marxism is a complex matter. He can be read as a creative post-Marxist or as a muted anti-Marxist, among other positions. See Burawoy (2003); Dale (2010); Block and Somers (2014); and also Peck et al. (2020).
50. Adaman F and Madra Y M (2002) Theorizing the "third sphere": a critique of the persistence of the "economistic fallacy." *Journal of Economic Issues* 36(4): 1045–1078, 1046, emphasis added.
51. This qualified concession to market rationality would later attract criticism on the grounds that the applicability of neoclassical theory ought to be questioned in nominally market economies too, although there were perhaps circumstantial reasons, relating to the McCarthyite climate, for Polanyi's acceptance of a provisional division of labor between his insurgent heterodoxy and orthodox economics (see Peck, 2013a). As if to underline the point that contemporary borrowings from Polanyi require some careful *re*interpretation, he once remarked (problematically) that the "last two centuries produced in Western Europe and North America an organization of man's [*sic*] livelihood to which the rules of choice happened to be singularly appropriate [consisting of] a system of price-making markets" (Polanyi, 1957, 244), having previously declared (polemically) the market mentality to be practically "obsolete," the legacy of a failed historical experiment in liberal capitalism (Polanyi, 1947, 109).
52. See Fusfeld D B (1957) Economic theory misplaced: livelihood in primitive society. In K Polanyi, C M Arensberg, and H W Pearson (eds) *Trade and market in the early empires: economies in history and theory*. Chicago, IL: Henry Regnery, 342–356; LeClair E E (1962) Economic theory and economic anthropology. *American Anthropologist* 64(6): 1179–1203.
53. Polanyi (1947, 113).
54. See the discussion in Hodgson (2015) and Peck (2020b).
55. See Halperin (1994); Gudeman (2001); Dalton G (1969) Theoretical issues in economic anthropology. *Current Anthropology* 10(1): 63–102.
56. Polanyi (1947, 112); see also Sahlins (1972) and Rosser J B and Rosser M V (1995) A comparison of comparative economic anthropologies. *History of Economics Review* 23: 96–107.
57. Polanyi (1959, 166, emphasis added).
58. Fusfeld D B (1957) Economic theory misplaced: Livelihood in primitive society. In K Polanyi, C M Arensberg and H W Pearson (eds) *Trade and market in the early empires: economies in history and theory*. Chicago, IL: Henry Regnery, 342–356, 354; Dalton G (1968) Introduction. In G Dalton (ed) *Primitive, archaic, and modern economies: essays of Karl Polanyi*. Garden City, NY: Doubleday-Anchor, ix–liv, xi.
59. An institutional manifestation of the comparative economists' positive program was the establishment in the early 1960s of the Association of Comparative Economics (later the Association of Comparative Economic Studies), which would launch the journals *Comparative Economic Studies* and the *Journal of Comparative Economics*. Polanyi apostle George Dalton was president of this group in the late 1960s, working to capitalize on the

"theoretical affinity between economic anthropology and [the study of] comparative economic systems." Stanfield J R (1980) The institutional economics of Karl Polanyi. *Journal of Economic Issues* 14(3): 593–614, 594. See also Dalton G (1968) Introduction. In G Dalton (ed) *Primitive, archaic, and modern economies: essays of Karl Polanyi*. Garden City, NY: Doubleday-Anchor, ix–liv.

60. Rotstein A (1957) Introductory note. In K Polanyi, C M Arensberg and H W Pearson (eds) *Trade and market in the early empires: economies in history and theory*. Chicago, IL: Henry Regnery, xvii–xviii, xviii.
61. The Polanyi group may have been more secure than they should have been in their understanding of the "facts" of economic diversity, although such declarations of empirical certainty were usually advanced in the service of theoretical reflexivity: "One of the peculiarities of economic anthropology," Dalton (1968, xxxviii) wrote, is that "neither the facts nor the folk views of primitive [sic] economic life are in doubt. The ethnographic record is large and detailed. What is in doubt is the most useful theoretical approach to organize the many descriptive accounts." Polanyi (1947, 112) was inclined to report the "facts" in a similarly bald manner. Matters of presentation aside, this raises the question of what one might venture to say, well over half a century later, about the received condition of the accumulated geographical "record," and its theoretical "organization." How far from exhaustive, really, have been the discipline's manifestly incomplete efforts at mapping expressed-geographical diversity? How do prevailing theoretical frameworks encounter, organize, and explain those nodes and coordinates of diversity that have been documented?
62. Dalton G (1968) Introduction, ix–liv, x.
63. Polanyi (1957, 244).
64. Stanfield J R (1980) The institutional economics of Karl Polanyi. *Journal of Economic Issues* 14(3): 593–614, 595.
65. These issues are further discussed in Chapters 9 and 10. See also Adaman F and Madra Y M (2002) Theorizing the "third sphere": a critique of the persistence of the "economistic fallacy." *Journal of Economic Issues* 36(4): 1045–1078.
66. For suggestive examples, see Saxenian (1996), Gertler (2004), and McDowell (2011). See also the discussion in Barnes et al. (2007).
67. See Polanyi (1959, 168).
68. These themes are taken up again in Chapter 10.
69. For some early contributions, see Hanson and Pratt (1995) and Bagguley P, Mark-Lawson J, Shapiro D, Urry J, Walby S and Warde A (1990) *Restructuring: place, class, and gender*. London, UK: Sage. For a complementary research agenda, see Pollard et al. (2011). For reflections on some of the policy implications of local economic diversity, see Lovering J (1988) The local economy and local economic strategies. *Policy and Politics* 16(3): 145–158.

Chapter 3

1. In longer form, parts of this chapter were originally published as Peck J (2005) Economic sociologies in space. *Economic Geography* 81(2): 129–176. I am grateful to Taylor & Francis Ltd. for permission to reproduce material from this article in revised form (License number 5358290005502).
2. Saxenian A (1994) *Regional advantage: culture and competition in Silicon Valley and Route 128*. Cambridge, MA: Harvard University Press; Saxenian A (2001) Inside-out: regional

networks and industrial adaptation in Silicon Valley and Route 128. In M Granovetter and R Swedberg (eds) *The sociology of economic life*. New York, NY: Westview Press, 357–375.
3. See Hirsh et al. (1987).
4. Stark D (2000) *For a sociology of worth*. Working paper. New York, NY: Center on Organizational Innovation, Columbia University, https://www.researchgate.net/publication/251651120_For_a_Sociology_of_Worth, 2.
5. Parsons T (1935) Sociological elements in economic thought I. Historical. *Quarterly Journal of Economics* 49(3): 414–453 and (1935) Sociological elements in economic thought II. The analytical factor view. *Quarterly Journal of Economics* 49(4): 646–667.
6. See Granovetter (1990); Velthuis O (1999) The changing relationship between economic sociology and institutional economics: from Talcott Parsons to Mark Granovetter. *American Journal of Economics and Sociology* 58(4): 629–649.
7. Swedberg R and Granovetter M (1992) Introduction. In M Granovetter and R Swedberg (eds) *The sociology of economic life*. Boulder, CO: Westview Press, 1–18, 7.
8. Granovetter (1985, 504). Compare Krippner et al. (2004).
9. Granovetter M (1990, 98, emphasis added).
10. See Swedberg R (1997) New economic sociology: what has been accomplished, what is ahead? *Acta Sociologica* 40(2): 161–182.
11. See Swedberg and Granovetter (2001).
12. Smelser and Swedberg (1994, 3).
13. Williamson O E (1994) Transaction cost economics and organization theory. In N J Smelser and R Swedberg (eds) *The handbook of economic sociology*. Princeton, NJ: Princeton University Press, 77–107; see also Zafirovski M (1999) Economic sociology in retrospect and prospect: in search of its identity within economics and sociology. *American Journal of Economics and Sociology* 58(4): 583–627.
14. Guillén M F, Collins R, England P and Meyer M (2002) The revival of economic sociology. In M F Guillén, R Collins, P England and M Meyer (eds) *The new economic sociology*. New York, NY: Russell Sage Foundation, 1–32.
15. Williamson (1975, 20).
16. See Block F (1991) Contradictions of self-regulating markets. In M Mendell and D Salée (eds) *The legacy of Karl Polanyi: market, state and society at the end of the twentieth century*. New York, NY: St. Martin's Press, 86–106; and Fligstein (2001).
17. Guillén et al. (2002, 7).
18. Frank R (1996) The political economy of preference falsification: Kuran's private truths, public lies. *Journal of Economic Literature* 34(1): 115–123, 117.
19. See Granovetter (2002).
20. Baron J N and Hannan M T (1994) The impact of economics on contemporary sociology. *Journal of Economic Literature* 32(3): 1111–1146, 1114.
21. Smelser and Swedberg (1994, 4).
22. Smelser and Swedberg (1994, 18).
23. Granovetter (1990, 94).
24. Swedberg R (2004) On the present state of economic sociology (1990s). *Economic Sociology—European Economic Newsletter* 5(2): 2–17, 4.
25. Bourdieu P (2000) Making the economic habitus: Algerian workers revisited. *Ethnography* 1(1): 17–41, 39.

26. Powell W W and Smith-Doerr L (1994) Networks and economic life. In N J Smelser and R Swedberg (eds) *The handbook of economic sociology*. Princeton, NJ: Princeton University Press, 368–402, 369.
27. Becker G (1976) *The economic approach to human behavior*. Chicago, IL: University of Chicago Press, 14, 5.
28. Granovetter (1990, 95).
29. Granovetter (1990, 98, 106).
30. Smelser and Swedberg (1994, 20).
31. See Baron J N and Hannan M T (1994) The impact of economics on contemporary sociology. *Journal of Economic Literature* 32(3): 1111–1146; Davern M E and Eitzen D S (1995) Economic sociology: an examination of intellectual exchange. *American Journal of Economics and Sociology* 54(1): 79–88.
32. Keen S (2003) Economists have no ears. In E Fullbrook (ed) *The crisis in economics*. London, UK: Routledge, 74–76.
33. Hirshleifer J (1985) The expanding domain of economics. *American Economic Review* 85(6): 53–68, 53. The more *cultural* expressions of this phenomenon, which continue to proliferate decades later, include the rise of pop economics in the shape of the freakonomics franchise and the ascendancy of a new generation of guru economists, recognized more for their marketing and communication skills than for their scientific accomplishments. See Peck J (2016) Economic rationality meets celebrity urbanology: exploring Edward Glaeser's city. *International Journal of Urban and Regional Research* 40(1): 1–30.
34. Granovetter (2002, 37).
35. Granovetter (2002, 38).
36. Collins R (1995) Review of "The handbook of economic sociology." *Contemporary Sociology* 24(3): 300–304, 302; Bowles S (1995) Review of "The handbook of economic sociology." *Contemporary Sociology* 24(3): 304–307, 306.
37. Zelizer V A (2002) Enter culture. In M F Guillén, R Collins, P England and M Meyer (eds) *The new economic sociology*. New York, NY: Russell Sage Foundation, 101–125, 109.
38. See Alexander J C (1992) Some remarks on "agency" in recent sociological theory. *Perspectives* 15(1): 1–4; Emirbayer M and Goodwin J (1994) Network analysis, culture, and the problem of agency. *American Journal of Sociology* 103(6): 271–307.
39. Granovetter (1985, 506–507).
40. Granovetter (1985, 507, emphasis added); Granovetter (2002, 38).
41. Zelizer V A (2002) Enter culture. In M F Guillén, R Collins, P England and M Meyer (eds) *The new economic sociology*. New York, NY: Russell Sage Foundation, 101–125, 107.
42. Granovetter (1990, 107).
43. Barber (1995, 406–407).
44. Bowles S (1995, 304–307, 306–307).
45. Arrighi G (2001) Braudel, capitalism, and the new economic sociology. *Review* 24(1): 107–123, 108.
46. See Krippner et al. (2004).
47. See Polanyi (1944); Block F (1994) The roles of the state in the economy. In N J Smelser and R Swedberg (eds) *The handbook of economic sociology*. Princeton, NJ: Princeton University Press, 691–710; Jessop (2002) The social embeddedness of the economy and its implications for economic governance. In F Adaman and P Devine (eds) *Economy and society: money, capitalism and transition*. Montreal: Black Rose Books, 192–222.
48. Polanyi (1977), quoted in Krippner (2001, 780).

49. Krippner et al. (2004, 112).
50. Granovetter (2002, 54).
51. Williamson O E (1994) Transaction cost economics and organization theory. In N J Smelser and R Swedberg (eds) *The handbook of economic sociology*. Princeton, NJ: Princeton University Press, 77–107, 98.
52. Krippner (2001, 799–800).
53. Quoted in Swedberg R (1997) New economic sociology: what has been accomplished, what is ahead? *Acta Sociologica* 40(2): 161–182, 171.
54. Granovetter, for his part, stated, "It would be to go too far to replace the market with network analysis . . . one should rather try to combine them." Quoted in Swedberg R (1990) *Economics and sociology*. Princeton, NJ: Princeton University Press, 104.
55. Zelizer V A (2002) Enter culture. In M F Guillén, R Collins, P England and M Meyer (eds) *The new economic sociology*. New York, NY: Russell Sage Foundation, 101–125, 117.
56. See Block (2003).
57. See Podolny J M and Page K L (1998) Network forms of organization. *Annual Review of Sociology* 24: 57–76; Krippner (2001); Granovetter (2002).
58. Block (2002, 224).
59. Block (2002, 224, emphasis added).
60. Blim M (2000) Capitalisms in late modernity. *Annual Reviews of Anthropology* 29: 25–38, 33.
61. Fligstein N (2002) Markets as politics: a political-cultural approach to market institutions. In N W Biggart (ed) *Readings in economic sociology*. Oxford, UK: Blackwell, 197–218, 200.
62. Hodgson (1984).
63. Polanyi (1957, 250).
64. See Block F and Somers M R (1984) Beyond the economistic fallacy: the holistic science of Karl Polanyi. In T Skocpol (ed) *Vision and method in historical sociology*. Cambridge, UK: Cambridge University Press, 47–84; Lie (1991); Swedberg and Granovetter (2001); and Block (2003).
65. Barber (1995, 400).
66. See Peck (2021).
67. See Clark G L (1998) Stylized facts and close dialogue: methodology in economic geography. *Annals of the Association of American Geographers* 88(1): 73–87.
68. See the further discussion in Peck (2019b).
69. Stark D and Bruszt L (2001) One way or multiple paths: for a comparative sociology of East European capitalism. *American Journal of Sociology* 106(4): 1129–1137, 1131.
70. Burawoy M (2001) Neoclassical sociology: from the end of communism to the end of classes. *American Journal of Sociology* 106(4): 1099–1120, 1114, 1116.
71. Stark D and Bruszt L (2001) One way or multiple paths: for a comparative sociology of East European capitalism. *American Journal of Sociology* 106(4): 1129–1137, 1131.
72. See Peck (2004).
73. Burawoy M (2001) Neoclassical sociology: from the end of communism to the end of classes. *American Journal of Sociology* 106(4): 1099–1120, 1118.
74. See Block F (1994) The roles of the state in the economy. In N J Smelser and R Swedberg (eds) *The handbook of economic sociology*. Princeton, NJ: Princeton University Press, 691–710; O'Neill M (1997) Bringing the qualitative state into economic geography. In R Lee and J Wills (eds) *Geographies of economies*. London, UK: Arnold, 290–301; Fligstein (2001).

75. See Gerber T and Hout M (1998) More shock than therapy: market transition, employment, and income in Russia, 1991-1995. *American Journal of Sociology* 104(1): 1-50; Grabher G and Stark D (1997) Organizing diversity: evolutionary theory, network analysis and postsocialism. *Regional Studies* 31(5): 533-544; Fligstein N and Sweet A S (2002) Constructing politics and markets: an institutionalist account of European integration. *American Journal of Sociology* 107(5): 1206-1243.
76. See the discussion in Chapter 4.
77. Polanyi (1944, 140-141).
78. Barber (1995, 394-395).
79. See Larner W (2000) Theorising neo-liberalism: policy, ideology, governmentality. *Studies in Political Economy* 63(1): 5-26; Dezalay Y and Garth B G (2002) *The internationalization of palace wars*. Chicago, IL: University of Chicago Press; Tickell and Peck (2003); Peck (2010).
80. See Naim M (2000) Fads and fashion in economic reforms: Washington consensus or Washington confusion? *Third World Quarterly* 21(3): 505-528; Peck and Tickell (2002); Peck and Theodore (2019).
81. See Smith C (1989) *Auctions: the social construction of value*. Berkeley, CA: University of California Press; Evans P (1995) *Embedded autonomy: states and industrial transformation*. Princeton, NJ: Princeton University Press; Abolafia M (1996) *Making markets: opportunism and restraint on Wall Street*. Cambridge, MA: Harvard University Press; Block (2000); Fligstein (2001).

Chapter 4

1. See Peck (2009, 2010a), Peck and Theodore (2012b), and Dawes and Peck (2020). The body of this chapter was originally published as Peck J (2013) Explaining (with) neoliberalism. *Territory, Politics, Governance* 1(2): 132-157. I am grateful to Taylor & Francis for permission to reproduce material from this article in revised form (License number 5358281477412).
2. The genre of repudiations might warrant a study in its own right. In lieu of this, some examples include: Barnett C (2005) The consolations of neoliberalism. *Geoforum* 36(1): 7-12; Venugopal R (2015) Neoliberalism as concept. *Economy and Society* 44(2): 165-187; Dunn B (2017) Against neoliberalism as a concept. *Capital and Class* 41(3): 435-454. For further reflections, rather more reflexively voicing skepticism or ambivalence, or raising concerns about polysemy and conceptual foreclosure, see Ferguson J (2010) The uses of neoliberalism. *Antipode* 41(1): 166-184; Dean M (2014) Rethinking neoliberalism. *Journal of Sociology* 50(2): 150-163; Ganti T (2014) Neoliberalism. *Annual Review of Anthropology* 43: 89-104.
3. See Brenner et al. (2010), Peck et al. (2010, 2013), and Peck (2017a).
4. The first paper that I can recall that set up the issues in these terms, in a manner that was both proximate and relevant to my own research questions, was Robertson D B (1986) Mrs. Thatcher's employment prescription: an active neo-liberal labor market policy. *Journal of Public Policy* 6(3): 275-296. See also Dawes and Peck (2020).
5. See Peck and Miyamachi (1994).
6. See Peck (2000), Peck and Tickell (2002), and Tickell and Peck (2003).
7. See Peck and Tickell (2002) and Brenner and Theodore (2002).

8. See Brenner et al. (2010).
9. See Collier (2012), Dean (2012), and Latour (2007).
10. See Peck (2009, 2010b).
11. For a recent discussion, see Davies W and Gane N (2021) Post-neoliberalism? An introduction. *Theory, Culture and Society* 38(6): 3–28
12. Centeno M A and Cohen J N (2012) The arc of neoliberalism. *Annual Review of Sociology* 38(1): 317–340, 312.
13. See, notably, Mirowski P and Plehwe D (eds) (2009) *The road from Mont Pèlerin*. Cambridge, MA: Harvard University Press; Jones D S (2012) *Masters of the universe: Hayek, Friedman, and the birth of neoliberal politics*. Princeton, NJ: Princeton University Press.
14. Dean (2012, 69, 86).
15. Hall (2011, 706).
16. See Crouch (2011); Slobodian Q and Plehwe D (2020) Introduction. In D Plehwe, Q Slobodian, and P Mirowski (eds) *Nine lives of neoliberalism*. London, UK: Verso, 1–17.
17. See Peck et al. (2010), Blyth (2013), and Peck J (2016) We are all Keynesians again ... *and always? Dialogues in Human Geography* 6(2): 135–145.
18. Elliot L (2011) Three years on, it's as if the crisis never happened. *Guardian*, May 30, 22.
19. See Independent Evaluation Office of the International Monetary Fund (2011) *IMF performance in the run-up to the financial and economic crisis*. Washington, DC: IEO-IMF.
20. Capturing these continuities suggested a "still neoliberalism" position, although this would have to be verified, not simply assumed. Versions of these "still" questions apply across all of neoliberalism's gyrations and adaptations, of course, accepting that the project-cum-program itself is never "still" (see Peck and Theodore, 2019).
21. See C Calhoun and G Derluguian (eds) (2011) *Business as usual the roots of the global financial meltdown*. New York, NY: New York University Press.
22. Kalb (2012, 318). See also Davis M (2011) Spring confronts winter. *New Left Review* 72: 5–15.
23. See Bond (2009) Realistic postneoliberalism: a view from South Africa. *Development Dialogue* 51(1): 193–211; Peck et al. (2010).
24. Crouch (2011, 179).
25. Compare Jessop B, Bonnett K, Bromley S, and Ling T (1988) *Thatcherism*. Cambridge, UK: Polity; Hall S and Jacques M (eds) (1989) *New times*. London, UK: Lawrence & Wishart; and Skidelsky R (ed) *Thatcherism*. Oxford, UK: Blackwell.
26. See Hall (2003b) and Jessop B (2004) New Labour's doppelte Kehrtwende: Anmerkungen zu Stuart Hall und eine alternative Perspektiv zu New Labour. *Das Argument* 256: 494–504.
27. Ferguson J (2010) The uses of neoliberalism. *Antipode* 41(1): 166–184, 171; Tickell and Peck (2003, 179).
28. Piven F F (1995) Is it global economics or neo-laissez-faire? *New Left Review* 213: 107–115.
29. See Nononi D M (2008) Is China becoming neoliberal? *Critique of Anthropology* 28(2): 145–176; Chu Y and So A Y (2010) State neoliberalism: the Chinese road to capitalism. In Y Chu (ed) *Chinese capitalisms: historical emergence and political implications*. Basingstoke, UK: Palgrave Macmillan, 73–99. Weber I M (2018) China and neoliberalism: moving beyond the China is/is not neoliberal dichotomy. In D Cahill, M Cooper, M Konings and D Primrose (eds) *The Sage handbook of neoliberalism*. London, UK: Sage, 219–233. And see the further discussion in chapter 6.
30. See Hall (2011) and Gamble A (1988) *The free economy and the strong state: the politics of Thatcherism*. London, UK: Macmillan.

31. See Brenner et al. (2010), and for a perspective from the neoliberal "truth spot" that was colonial Hong Kong, see Peck J (2021) Milton's paradise: situating Hong Kong in neoliberal lore. *Journal of Law and Political Economy* 2(1): 189–211.
32. Hall (2011, 727–728).
33. Hall (2003b, 22).
34. See the discussion of these terms in Chapter 2.
35. Gledhill J (2004) Neoliberalism. In D Nugent and J Vincent (eds) *A companion to the anthropology of politics*. Oxford, UK: Blackwell, 332–348, 336. See also Brenner and Theodore (2002); Saad-Filho A and Johnston D (eds) (2005) *Neoliberalism: a critical reader*. London, UK: Pluto Press; Peck et al. (2018).
36. Tretjak K and Abrell E (2011) Fracturing neoliberalism: ethnographic interventions. *New Proposals* 4(2): 29–32, 29. See also Ong (2006) and Kingfisher and Maskovsky (2008).
37. Kingfisher and Maskovsky (2008, 118, emphasis added); Ferguson J (2010) The uses of neoliberalism. *Antipode* 41(1): 166–184, 171.
38. Kingfisher and Maskovsky (2008, 119); Gledhill J (2004) Neoliberalism. In D Nugent and J Vincent (eds) *A companion to the anthropology of politics*. Oxford, UK: Blackwell, 332–348.
39. The phrase is from Ong (2006, 14). See also Ong (2007).
40. See Collier S J (2011) *Post-Soviet social: neoliberalism, social modernity, biopolitics*. Princeton, NJ: Princeton University Press; Fairbanks R (2012) On theory and method: critical ethnographic approaches to urban regulatory restructuring. *Urban Geography* 33(4): 545–565.
41. Collier (2012, 189); cf. Brenner et al. (2010); Peck et al. (2018).
42. Latour (2007).
43. The approach apparently advised by Latour (2007, 190).
44. For further discussion, see Brenner et al (2010), Peck et al. (2018), and Peck and Theodore (2019).
45. For a discussion of the quasi-viral form of neoliberalization, see Sparke M and Williams O D (2022) Neoliberal disease: COVID-19, co-pathogenesis and global health insecurities. *EPA: Economy and Space* 54(1): 15–32.
46. Jessop (2000).
47. See Bourdieu (1998), Brenner and Theodore (2002), and Peck et al. (2018).
48. Compare Wacquant L (2012) Three steps to a historical anthropology of actually existing neoliberalism. *Social Anthropology/Anthropologie Sociale* 20(1): 66–79.
49. Cahill (2012, 177).
50. Cahill (2012, 115).
51. Hilgers M (2012) The historicity of the neoliberal state. *Social Anthropology/Anthropologie Sociale* 20(1): 80–94. See also Hilgers M (2011) The three anthropological approaches to neoliberalism. *International Social Science Journal* 61(202): 351–364.
52. Collier (2012, 194).
53. Collier (2012, 194); cf. Peck (2010a).
54. Dean (2012, 75).
55. See Peck and Tickell (1994b, 1995, 2012); Albo G (2007) Neoliberalism and the discontented. In L Panitch and C Leys (eds) *Global flashpoints*. London, UK: Merlin Press, 354–362.
56. See Clarke J (2008) Living with/in and without neo-liberalism. *Focaal* 51(1): 135–147.
57. Collier (2012, 186).
58. Collier (2012, 191). See Brenner et al. (2010) and Peck and Theodore (2012b).
59. Collier (2012, 191).

60. See Burawoy (2011), Peck and Theodore (2012a), and the further discussion in Chapter 10.
61. Collier S J (2011) *Post-Soviet social: neoliberalism, social modernity, biopolitics*. Princeton, NJ: Princeton University Press, 12.
62. See the discussion in Chapters 2 and 7.
63. See Leitner H, Peck J and Sheppard E S (2007) Squaring up to neoliberalism. In H Leitner, J Peck and E S Sheppard (eds) *Contesting neoliberalism: urban frontiers*. New York, NY: Guilford, 311–327.

Chapter 5

1. The DEMOLOGOS research program (2004–2007) was coordinated by Frank Moulaert and involved Bob Jessop, Ngai-Ling Sum, Andreas Novy, Flavia Martinelli, Erik Swyngedouw, and Alvin So, among others. See Moulaert F and Jessop B (2013) Theoretical foundations for the analysis of socio-economic development in space. In F Martinelli, F Moulaert and A Novy (eds) *Urban and regional development trajectories in contemporary capitalism*. London, UK: Routledge, 18–44; Novy A, Mehmood A and Moulaert F (2013) The DEMOLOGOS methodology for analysing urban and regional trajectories. In F Martinelli, F Moulaert, and A Novy (eds) *Urban and regional development trajectories in contemporary capitalism*. London, UK: Routledge, 45–62; Peck J and Theodore N (2013) Chicago beyond Fordism: between regulatory crisis and sustainable growth. In F Martinelli, F Moulaert, and A Novy (eds) *Urban and regional development trajectories in contemporary capitalism*. London, UK: Routledge, 173–194.
2. Brenner N, Peck J and Theodore N (2005) Neoliberal urbanism: cities and the rule of markets. *WP1 Discussion Papers*, DEMOLOGOS. Newcastle: Global Urban Research Unit; Peck J and Theodore N (2005) Comparing capitalisms: theorizing the persistence of institutional variation. *WP1 Discussion Papers*, DEMOLOGOS. Newcastle: Global Urban Research Unit. See also Peck et al. (2009).
3. The body of this chapter was originally published as Peck J and Theodore N (2007) Variegated capitalism. *Progress in Human Geography* 31(6): 731–772. I am grateful to Sage Publishing for permission to reproduce material from this article in revised form.
4. Boyer (2005, 1).
5. Some exceptions to this general rule, where geographers engage VoC problematics, or where varieties scholarship signals explicitly spatial questions, beyond its default methodological nationalism, include the following: Christopherson S (2002) Why do national labor market practices continue to diverge in the global economy? The "missing link" of investment rules. *Economic Geography* 78(1): 1–20; Coates D (2005) Paradigms of explanation. In D Coates (ed) *Varieties of capitalism, varieties of approaches*. Basingstoke, UK: Palgrave, 1–25; Bathelt H and Gertler M S (2005) The German variety of capitalism: forces and dynamics of evolutionary change. *Economic Geography* 81(1): 1–9; Dunford M (2005) Old Europe, new Europe and the USA: comparative economic performance, inequality and market-led models of development. *European Urban and Regional Studies* 12(2): 149–176; Clark G L and Wojcik D (2007) *The geography of finance: corporate governance in a global marketplace*. Oxford, UK: Oxford University Press; and Crouch (2005).
6. Soskice D (1990) Wage determination: the changing role of institutions in advanced industrial economies. *Oxford Review of Economic Policy* 6(4): 36–61; Soskice D (1991) The institutional infrastructure for international competitiveness: a comparative analysis of

the UK and Germany. In A B Atkinson and R Bruneta (eds) *The new Europe*. London, UK: Macmillan, 45–66.
7. Soskice (1999, 110–111).
8. Albert (1993, 15).
9. See Olson M (1965) *The logic of collective action: public goods and the theory of groups*. Cambridge, MA: Harvard University Press; Goldthorpe J H (ed) (1984) *Order and conflict in contemporary capitalism*. Oxford, UK: Clarendon Press; Esping-Anderson G (199) *The three worlds of welfare capitalism*. Cambridge, UK: Polity.
10. See Best M (1990) *The new competition: institutions of industrial restructuring*. Cambridge, MA: Harvard University Press; Streeck W (1997) German capitalism: does it exist? Can it survive? In C Crouch and W Streeck (eds) *Political economy of modern capitalism*. London, UK: Sage, 33–54; Herrigel G (1993) Large firms, small firms, and the governance of flexible specialization: the case of Baden Wurttemberg and socialized risk. In B Kogut (ed) *Country competitiveness*. Oxford, UK: Oxford University Press, 15–35; Dicken P, Forsgren M, and Malmberg A (1994) The local embeddedness of transnational corporations. In A Amin and N Thrift (eds) *Globalization, institutions, and regional development in Europe*. Oxford, UK: Oxford University Press, 23–45; Boyer R (2003) The embedded innovation systems of Germany and Japan: distinctive features and futures. In K Yamamura and W Streeck (eds) *The end of diversity? Prospects for German and Japanese capitalism*. Ithaca, NY: Cornell University Press, 147–182; Grabher G (ed) (1993) *The embedded firm: on the socioeconomics of industrial networks*. London, UK: Routledge.
11. Hollingsworth and Boyer (1997, 2).
12. Hollingsworth and Boyer (1997, 2, emphasis added).
13. Hollingsworth and Boyer (1997, 2).
14. Hollingsworth and Boyer (1997, 36); see also Coates (2000) and (2005b).
15. Hollingsworth and Boyer (1997, 5); see also Crouch (2005).
16. Boyer and Hollingsworth (1997, 435).
17. Boyer and Hollingsworth (1997, 437); see also Schmidt (2002).
18. Boyer and Hollingsworth (1997, 458, 461).
19. Boyer and Hollingsworth (1997, 434, 442).
20. Hall and Soskice (2001, 3, 5).
21. Hall and Soskice (2001, 5, 4).
22. See Milgrom P and Roberts J (1992) *Economics, organization and management*. Englewood Cliffs, NJ: Prentice Hall.
23. Hall and Soskice (2001, 13, 9).
24. Hall and Soskice (2001, 8).
25. Hall and Soskice (2001, 8).
26. Hall and Soskice (2001, 21); see also Pontusson J (2005) *Inequality and prosperity: social Europe vs. liberal America*. Ithaca, NY: Cornell University Press.
27. Hall and Soskice (2001, 57).
28. See Hall and Gingerich (2009).
29. Goodin R E (2003) Choose your capitalism. *Comparative European Politics* 1(2): 203–213, 206.
30. See Amable (2003) and Boyer (2005).

31. See Kenworthy L (2006) Institutional coherence and macroeconomic performance. *Socio-Economic Review* 4(1): 69–91; Watson M (2003) Ricardian political economy and the "varieties of capitalism" approach: specialization, trade and comparative institutional advantage. *Comparative European Politics* 1(2), 227–240.
32. See Allen M (2004) The varieties of capitalism paradigm: not enough variety? *Socio-Economic Review* 2(1): 87–108; Brewster C, Wood G, and Brookes M (2006) Varieties of capitalism, varieties of firm. In G Wood and P James (eds) *Institutions, production, and working life*. Oxford, UK: Oxford University Press, 217–234.
33. Hall and Soskice (2001, 63).
34. Hall and Soskice (2001, 64).
35. See Amable (2003), Boyer (2005b) and Coriat B, Petit P and Schméder G (eds) (2006) *The hardship of nations: exploring the paths of modern capitalism*. Cheltenham, UK: Edward Elgar.
36. Boyer (2005, 529).
37. See Duménil G and Lévy D (2004) *Capital resurgent*. Cambridge, MA: Harvard University Press.
38. Sorge (2005).
39. Campbell J L (2007) Complexity and simplicity in "The global and the local." *Socio-Economic Review* 5(1), 181–186, 183.
40. Streeck and Thelen (2005); Hall and Thelen (2009).
41. Streeck and Thelen (2005, 1).
42. See Friedman (2005).
43. Hall and Soskice (2001, 8).
44. Hall and Soskice (2001, 27).
45. Hall and Gingerich (2009, 452–453).
46. Hall and Soskice (2001, 9).
47. Hall and Gingerich (2009, 453).
48. On market essentialism, see Barber (1977, 1995) and Lie J (1997) The sociology of markets. *Annual Review of Sociology* 23: 341–360.
49. Thelen K (2001) Varieties of labour politics in the developed democracies. In P A Hall and D Soskice (eds) *Varieties of capitalism: the institutional foundations of comparative advantage*. Oxford, UK: Oxford University Press, 71–103; Allen M (2004) The varieties of capitalism paradigm: not enough variety? *Socio-Economic Review* 2(1): 87–108; Blyth M (2003) Same as it never was: temporality and typology in the varieties of capitalism. *Comparative European Politics* 1(2): 215–225, 219.
50. See Watson (2003).
51. Hodgson (2015); Jessop and Sum (2006).
52. See Vitols S (2001) Varieties of corporate governance: comparing Germany and the UK. In P A Hall and D Soskice (eds) *Varieties of capitalism: the institutional foundations of comparative advantage*. Oxford, UK: Oxford University Press, 337–360; Thelen K (2001) Varieties of labour politics in the developed democracies. In P A Hall and D Soskice (eds) *Varieties of capitalism: the institutional foundations of comparative advantage*. Oxford, UK: Oxford University Press, 71–103.
53. Hall and Soskice (2001, 63–64).
54. Hall and Soskice (2001, 63).

55. See Schmidt (2002); Jackson and Deeg (2006).
56. Streeck and Thelen (2005, 7, 4).
57. See Pierson P (1994) *Dismantling the welfare state? Reagan, Thatcher, and the politics of retrenchment*. Cambridge, UK: Cambridge University Press; Pierson P (2004) *Politics in time: history, institutions, and social analysis*. Princeton, NJ: Princeton University Press.
58. Deeg and Jackson (2007, 9).
59. Deeg and Jackson (2007, 9).
60. See Hall and Thelen (2009).
61. Goodin R E (2003) Choose your capitalism. *Comparative European Politics* 1(2): 203–213, 211–212.
62. Hall P A and Soskice D (2003) Varieties of capitalism and institutional change: a response to three critics. *Comparative European Politics* 1(2): 241–250, 243, 245.
63. See Streeck W and Yamamura K (eds) (2001) *The origins of nonliberal capitalism: Germany and Japan in comparison*. Ithaca, NY: Cornell University Press; Yamamura K and Streeck W (eds) (2003) *The end of diversity? Prospects for German and Japanese capitalism*. Ithaca, NY: Cornell University Press.
64. Hall and Thelen (2009, 22).
65. Hall and Thelen (2009, 23).
66. Hirst P and Thompson G (1996) *Globalization in question*. Cambridge, UK: Polity.
67. See Dicken et al. (1997).
68. Boyer (2000, 274, 302).
69. See Howell (2003); Deeg and Jackson (2007).
70. Howell (2003, 112); Jackson and Deeg (2006).
71. See, especially, Brenner (2004).
72. See Strange S (1997) The future of global capitalism: or will divergence persist forever? In C Crouch and W Streeck (eds) *Political economy of modern capitalism*. London, UK: Sage, 182–191.
73. See Jessop (2000).
74. See Dicken et al. (1997); Amin A (2002) Spatialities of globalisation. *Environment and Planning A* 34(3): 385–399; Amin A (2004) Regulating economic globalization. *Transactions of the Institute of British Geographers* 29(2): 217–233.
75. See Chapter 9; see also Hart (2002) and Harvey (2006).
76. Howell (2003, 122).
77. Stark D and Bruszt L (2001) One way or multiple paths: for a comparative sociology East European capitalism. *American Journal of Sociology* 106(4): 1129–1137, 1131; see also Crouch (2005).
78. See Crouch (2005) and Jackson and Deeg (2006).
79. Burawoy M (2001) Neoclassical sociology: from the end of communism to the end of classes. *American Journal of Sociology* 106(4): 1099–1120, 1103.
80. Pontusson (2005, 164).
81. See the discussion in Chapters 2 and 3.
82. See Chapter 2 and Peck (2012b, 2016).
83. Watson (2003, 228).
84. First published in French in 1991, see Albert (1993).

Chapter 6

1. The body of this chapter was originally published as Peck J and Peck J and Zhang J (2013) A variety of capitalism . . . with Chinese characteristics? *Journal of Economic Geography* 13(3): 357–396. I am grateful to Oxford University Press for permission to reproduce material from this article in revised form (License number 5357260841130).
2. On Chinese capitalism, or otherwise, see Arrighi (2007) and Meyer (2011). From a heterodox VoC perspective, Amable identifies five types of capitalism, according to their institutional forms and complementarities—the market-based, the social-democratic, the continental European, the Mediterranean, and the Asian models. Given that the social-democratic model is essentially Scandinavian, this means that: "Except for the market-based model . . . all other types of capitalism have a geography-based denomination. This is for the sake of simplicity and should not be taken too literally. It does not mean that geographical or 'cultural' factors are the most important factors or explain the coherence of different types of capitalism" (Amable, 2003, 14).
3. Compare Hart-Landsberg M and Burkett P (2004) *China and socialism: market reforms and class struggle*. New York, NY: Monthly Review Press; Silver B and Arrighi G (2000) Workers north and south. In L Panitch and C Leys (eds) *Working classes, global realities*. New York, NY: Monthly Review Press, 53–76.
4. See Arrighi (2007, 79, 81).
5. Economist (2012) State capitalism. *Economist* January 28: 3–18, 4.
6. Witt (2010, 3).
7. Fligstein and Zhang (2011).
8. Haley G T, Tan C T, and Haley U C V (1998) *New Asian emperors*. Oxford, UK: Butterworth-Heinemann.
9. See McNally (2006); Zhang and Peck (2013).
10. See Arrighi (2007), cf. Harvey (2005); Chang H-J (2010) *23 things they don't tell you about capitalism*. New York, NY: Bloomsbury Press.
11. See Carney M, Gedajlovic E and Yang X (2009) Varieties of Asian capitalism: toward an institutional theory of Asian enterprise. *Asia Pacific Journal of Management* 26(3): 361–380; Hancké B, Rhodes M and Thatcher M. (eds) (2008) *Beyond varieties of capitalism: conflict, contradictions, and complementarities in the European economy*. Oxford, UK: Oxford University Press; Lane (2007).
12. Popov (2007); McGregor R (2010) *The party*. New York, NY: HarperCollins.
13. McNally (2006, 10, 16); McNally (2007, 179).
14. Hamilton G G (1985) Why no capitalism in China? Negative questions in historical, comparative research. *Journal of Developing Societies* 1: 187–211.
15. Arrighi (2007, 24).
16. Baum R and Shevchenko A (1999) The "state of the state." In M Goldman and R MacFarquhar (eds) *The paradox of China's post-Mao reform*. Cambridge, MA: Harvard University Press, 333–362.
17. See McNally (2008a).
18. Unnamed Chinese commentator, quoted in McNally (2008a, 235).
19. Fewsmith (2008, 38).
20. Saich (2010, 78–79).
21. Saich (2010, 87–88).

22. Deng X (1994) *Selected works of Deng Xiaoping*, volume 2. Beijing: Renmin Chubanshe, 232–233.
23. Quoted in Yu G (2005) Accomplishments and problems: a review of China's reform in the past twenty-three years. In T Y Cao (ed.) *The Chinese model of modern development*. London, UK: RoutledgeCurzon, 23–53, 37.
24. See Kornai (2009).
25. See Stark (1996); Eyal G, Szelény I and Tonsley E (1997) *Making capitalism without capitalists*. London, UK: Verso.
26. See Zhang and Peck (2013).
27. McNally (2006, 20–21).
28. Szelény (2010).
29. See Popov (2007).
30. See McNally (2008c); Szelény (2010); Huang (2008).
31. Nee V and Opper S (2007) On politicized capitalism. In V Nee and R Swedberg (eds) *On capitalism*. Stanford, CA: Stanford University Press, 93–127, 94.
32. Naughton (2007).
33. Deng Y, Morck R, Wu J and Yeung B (2011) Monetary and fiscal stimuli, ownership structure, and China's housing market. *NBER Working Paper*, No. 16871, NBER, Cambridge, MA.
34. McGregor R (2010) *The party*. New York, NY: HarperCollins.
35. Szelény (2010, 207); Liew (2005).
36. Deng Y, Morck R, Wu J, and Yeung B (2011) Monetary and fiscal stimuli, ownership structure, and China's housing market. *NBER Working Paper*, No. 16871, NBER, Cambridge, MA.
37. Amin S (2010) *Eurocentrism*. New York, NY: Monthly Review Press; Blaut J (1993) *The colonizer's model of the world: geographical diffusionism and Eurocentric history*. New York, NY: Guilford Press; Hamilton G G (1985) Why no capitalism in China? Negative questions in historical, comparative research. *Journal of Developing Societies* 1: 187–211.
38. See Yeung (2004); McNally (2007).
39. McNally (2006, 2008c); Heilbroner R (1985) *The nature and logic of capitalism*. New York, NY: W W Norton; Heilbroner R (1993) *21st Century capitalism*. New York, NY: W W Norton.
40. See Ong A (2004) The Chinese axis: zoning technologies and variegated sovereignty. *Journal of East Asian Studies* 4(1): 69–96; Zhang (2012).
41. Gallagher M E (2005) *Contagious capitalism: globalization and the politics of labor in China*. Princeton, NJ: Princeton University Press, 14.
42. See OECD [Organisation for Economic Co-operation and Development] (2003) *China in the world economy*. Paris: OECD; Wang X (2004) The contribution of the non-state sector to China's economic growth. In R Garnaut and L Song (eds) *China's third economic transformation*. New York, NY: Routledge, 15–28; McNally (2008c); Kornai (2009); Huang (2008).
43. See Meyer (2011); Deans (2004).
44. See Wederman A H (2003) *From Mao to market: rent seeking, local protectionism, and marketization in China*. New York, NY: Cambridge University Press.
45. Cai F, Park A, and Zhao Y (2008) The Chinese labor market in the reform era. In L Brandt and T Rawski (eds) *China's great economic transformation*. Cambridge, UK: Cambridge University Press, 167–214.
46. Zhang (2012).
47. Rofel L (2007) *Desiring China: experiments in neoliberalism, sexuality, and public culture*. Durham, NC: Duke University Press; Ku C (2010) The "spirit" of capitalism in

China: contemporary meanings of Weber's thought. In Y Chu (ed) *Chinese capitalisms: historical emergence and political implications*. Basingstoke, UK: Palgrave Macmillan, 19–45.
48. McNally (2008c, 31).
49. Liew (2005); Tsai K S (2007) *Capitalism without democracy: the private sector in contemporary China*. Ithaca, NY: Cornell University Press.
50. Dickson (2003) and (2008).
51. Dickson (2003, 164).
52. See Benjamin D, Brandt L, Giles J, and Wang S (2008) Income inequality during China's economic transition. In L Brandt and T Rawski (eds) *China's great economic transformation*. Cambridge, UK: Cambridge University Press, 729–775; Gustafsson B, Li S, and Sicular T (eds) (2008) *Inequality and public policy in China*. New York, NY: Cambridge University Press.
53. Deng X (1993) *Selected works of Deng Xiaoping 1982–1992*, vol. 3. Beijing: Renmin Chubanshe, 172.
54. See Wade (1990); Evans (1995); Whitley (1999).
55. See Breslin S (2006) Serving the market or serving the party: neo-liberalism in China. In R Robison (ed) *The neo-liberal revolution: forging the market state*. New York, NY: Palgrave Macmillan, 114–134.
56. White G and Wade R (1988) Developmental states and markets in East Asia: an introduction. In G White (ed) *Developmental states in East Asia*. Basingstoke, UK: Macmillan Press, 1–29, 19, original emphasis.
57. See Lane (2007); Popov (2007).
58. Szelény (2010, 201–202).
59. See Evans (1995); Deans (2004); Weiss L (2000) Developmental states in transition: adapting, dismantling, innovating, not "normalizing." *Pacific Review* 13(1): 21–55.
60. Deans (2004).
61. Deans (2004, 134).
62. Suttmeier R P and Yao X (2004) China's post-WTO technology policy: standards, software, and the changing nature of techno-nationalism. *Special Report* 7, National Bureau of Asian Research, Seattle, WA.
63. Montinola G, Qian Y and Weingast B (1995) Federalism, Chinese style: the political basis for economic success in China. *World Politics* 48(1): 50–81; Weingast B (1995) The economic role of political institutions: market-preserving federalism and economic development. *Journal of Law, Economics, and Organization* 11(1): 1–31; Jin H, Qian Y and Weingast B (2005) Regional decentralization and fiscal incentives: federalism, Chinese style. *Journal of Public Economics*, 89(9–10): 1719–1742.
64. Li H and Zhou L-A (2005) Political turnover and economic performance: the incentive role of personnel control in China. *Journal of Public Economics* 89(9–10): 1743–1762.
65. Xu (2011).
66. Gallagher M E (2005) *Contagious capitalism: globalization and the politics of labor in China*. Princeton, NJ: Princeton University Press.
67. Naughton (2007).
68. Xu (2011).
69. Oi (1995); Oi J C (1999) *Rural China takes off: institutional foundations of economic reform*. Berkeley: University of California Press.
70. See Oi (1995); Naughton (2007); Huang (2008).
71. Arrighi (2007, 363).

72. Naughton B (1995) *Growing out of the plan: Chinese economic reform, 1978–1993*. New York, NY: Cambridge University Press.
73. Naughton (2007, 281).
74. Xu (2001); Bai C, Du Y and Tao Z (2004) Local protectionism and regional specialization: evidence from China's industries. *Journal of International Economics* 63(2): 297–317.
75. Naughton (2007).
76. Tsui K Y and Wang Y (2004) Between separate stoves and a single menu: fiscal decentralization in China. *China Quarterly* 177: 71–90.
77. Yang D and Wang H (2008) Dilemmas of local governance under the development zone fever in China: a case study of the Suzhou region. *Urban Studies* 45(5–6): 1037–1054; Tao R, Su F, Liu M and Cao G (2010) Land leasing and local public finance in China's regional development: evidence from prefecture-level cities. *Urban Studies* 47(10): 2217–2236.
78. Hsing (2010, 5–6).
79. Tsui K Y (2011) China's infrastructure investment boom and local debt crisis. *Eurasian Geography and Economics* 52(5): 686–711.
80. Naughton B (2009) Loans, firms, and steel: is the state advancing at the expense of the private sector? *China Leadership Monitor* 30. Stanford, CA: China Leadership Monitor.
81. Hsing (2010).
82. See Segal A and Thun E (2001) Thinking globally, acting locally: local governments, industrial sectors, and development in China. *Politics and Society* 29(4): 557–588; Remick E J (2002) The significance of variation in local states: the case of twentieth century China. *Comparative Politics* 34(4): 399–418; Oi (1995).
83. See Zhang and Peck (2013).
84. Tao R and Yang D (2008) *The revenue imperative and the role of local government in China's transition and growth*. Paper presented at 2008 Chicago Conference on China's Economic Transformation, University of Chicago, July 16.
85. Saich T (2002) The blind man and the elephant: analysing the local state in China. In L Tomba (ed) *On the roots of growth and crisis: capitalism, state and society in East Asia*. Milan: Annale Feltrinelli, 75–99.
86. See Xu (2011); Pei (2006); Dickson (2008).
87. Howell J (2006) Reflections on the Chinese state. *Development and Change* 37(2): 273–297, 291.
88. Chu and So (2010).
89. Harvey (2005, 150).
90. So A Y (2007) Globalization and the transition from neoliberal capitalism to state developmentalism in China. *International Review of Modern Sociology* 33(special issue): 61–76; see also Liew (2005).
91. Qin H (2009) China's low human rights advantage. *China Rights Forum* 1: 85–89.
92. So A Y (2009) Rethinking the Chinese developmental miracle. In H Hung (ed) *China and the transformation of global capitalism*. Baltimore, MD: Johns Hopkins University Press, 50–64, 53.
93. So A Y (2009) Rethinking the Chinese developmental miracle. In H Hung (ed) *China and the transformation of global capitalism*. Baltimore, MD: Johns Hopkins University Press, 50–64, 57, 61, emphasis added.
94. For a range of positions, see Chu and So (2010); Kipnis A (2007) Neoliberalism reified: *suzhi* discourse and tropes of neoliberalism in the People's Republic of China. *Journal of the Royal Anthropological Institute* 13(2): 383–400; Nonini D M (2008) Is China

becoming neoliberal? *Critique of Anthropology* 28(2): 145–176; Ji M (2006) Neoliberal developmentalism: state-led economic liberalization in China. Unpublished doctoral dissertation, Department of Political Science, Cornell University. See also the discussion in Chapter 4.
95. Huang (2008).
96. See Zhang and Peck (2013).
97. Zhang K H (2005) Why does so much FDI from Hong Kong and Taiwan go to mainland China? *China Economic Review* 16(3): 293–307; Weidenbaum M and Hughes S (1996) *The bamboo network*. New York, NY: Free Press; Lever-Tracy C, Ip D and Tracy N (eds) (1996) *The Chinese diaspora and mainland China: an emerging economic synergy*. London, UK: Macmillan; Hsing (1998).
98. Hsing (1998, 8).
99. Arrighi (2007, 351).
100. See Carney M, Gedajlovic E and Yang X (2009) Varieties of Asian capitalism: toward an institutional theory of Asian enterprise. *Asia Pacific Journal of Management* 26(3): 361–380.
101. Smart J and Smart A (1991) Personal relations and divergent economies: a case study of Hong Kong investment in South China. *International Journal of Regional and Urban Research* 15(2): 216–233.
102. Redding S G (1993) *The spirit of Chinese capitalism*. Berlin: Walter de Gruyter; Boisot M and Child J (1996) From fiefs to clans and network capitalism: explaining China's emerging economic order. *Administrative Science Quarterly* 41(4): 600–629; Jacques M (2009) *When China rules the world*. Harmondsworth, UK: Penguin.
103. Whyte M K (1995) The social roots of China's economic development. *China Quarterly* 144: 999–1019; Whyte M K (1996) The Chinese family and economic development: obstacle or engine? *Economic Development and Cultural Change* 45(1): 1–30.
104. See Whyte (2009).
105. Yeung (2004); McNally (2008b).
106. Amable (2003); cf. Yeung (2004).
107. McNally (2006).
108. Xin K and Pearce J L (1996) Guanxi: connections as substitutes for formal institutional support. *Academy of Management Journal* 39(6): 1641–1658; Peng Y (2004) Kinship networks and entrepreneurs in China's transitional economy. *American Journal of Sociology* 109(5): 1045–1074.
109. Wank D L (1999) *Commodifying communism: business, trust and politics in a Chinese city*. Cambridge, UK: Cambridge University Press; Dickson (2008).
110. Saich (2010).
111. Dickson (2003) and (2008).
112. So A Y (2003) The making of the cadre-capitalist class in China. In J Cheng (ed) *China's challenges in the twenty-first century*. Hong Kong: City University of Hong Kong Press, 475–501; Sun Y (2004) *Corruption and market in contemporary China*. Ithaca, NY: Cornell University Press.
113. Andreas J (2009) *Rise of the red engineers: the cultural revolution and the origins of China's new class*. Stanford, CA: Stanford University Press.
114. Sun Y (2004) *Corruption and market in contemporary China*. Ithaca, NY: Cornell University Press.
115. Naughton B (2010) The turning point in housing. *China Leadership Monitor* 33. Stanford, CA: China Leadership Monitor.

116. Wang X (2010) The current situation, problems and countermeasures of the national income distribution. *Journal of China National School Administration* 3: 23–27.
117. Pei (2006, 88–90); Fewsmith (2008, 274).
118. Dickson (2008).
119. Wright T (2010) *Accepting authoritarianism: state-society relations in China's reform era*. Stanford, CA: Stanford University Press.
120. Buckley C (2011) China internal security spending jumps past army budget. *Reuters* March 4. https://www.reuters.com/article/us-china-unrest-idUSTRE7222RA20110305; Fewsmith J (2012) "Social management" as a way of coping with heightened social tensions. *China Leadership Monitor* 36. Stanford, CA: China Leadership Monitor.
121. Dickson (2008).
122. Wright T (2010) *Accepting authoritarianism: state-society relations in China's reform era*. Stanford, CA: Stanford University Press, 179.
123. Hamilton G G and Biggart N W (1988) Market, culture, and authority: a comparative analysis of management and organization in the Far East. *American Journal of Sociology* 94(Supplement): S52–S94; Redding S G (1993) *The spirit of Chinese capitalism*. Berlin: Walter de Gruyter; Whitley (1999).
124. Whitley (1999).
125. Saich (2010, 390–391); Pei (2006, 18).
126. See Peck and Miyamachi (1994).
127. See Zhang and Peck (2013).
128. See the discussion in Chapter 7. For the original formulation, see Polanyi (1957).
129. See Peck (2012b, 2012c), and the further discussion in Chapters 7 and 10.
130. See Burawoy (2009), and the discussion in Chapter 10.
131. Arrighi (2007); Whyte (2009).
132. See Qin H (2009) China's low human rights advantage. *China Rights Forum* 1: 85–89.
133. Wu F (2008) China's great transformation: neoliberalization as establishing a market society. *Geoforum* 39: 1093–1096.
134. See Zhang and Peck (2013).
135. Kornai (2009); Szelény (2010).
136. Burawoy (2003, 52).
137. See, respectively, Hann C (2009) Land, labor, and money in eastern Xinjiang. In C Hann and K Hart (eds) *Market and society: the great transformation today*. Cambridge, UK: Cambridge University Press, 256–271; Deyo F C and Agartan K (2007) Reforming East Asian labor systems: China, Korea, and Thailand. In A Bugra and K Agartan (eds) *Reading Karl Polanyi for the twenty-first century: market economy as a political project*. Basingstoke, UK: Palgrave Macmillan, 191–218.
138. See Chapter 7.
139. See Jessop (2012).
140. See Peck (2021); Serra N and Stiglitz J E (eds) (2008) *The Washington consensus reconsidered: towards a new global governance*. New York, NY: Oxford University Press; Ramo J C (2004) *The Beijing consensus: notes on the new physics of Chinese power*. London, UK: Foreign Policy Centre.
141. Whyte (2009, 388).

Chapter 7

1. In geography, little changed on this front until the publication, a decade later, of Hanson and Pratt's (1995) *Gender, work and space*, which opened up new questions for a project that would later become known as labor geography. Galvanized by Andrew Herod (1998, 2001), *qua* project this would take as its primary focus the reorganization of unionized and newly mobilized workers. While this influential line of research would become synonymous with proper-noun Labor Geography, the pluralized domain of "small-l" labor geographies also included significant flanks that explored, from the early 1980s, workplace and labor-process issues from a restructuring perspective, and which would subsequently engage a wider array of questions concerning the gendering and racialization of work, regulation and policy, and social reproduction. See McDowell (1997), Wright (2006), Werner (2015), and the commentaries in Peck (2013b, 2018).
2. Offe (1985).
3. Polanyi (1944).
4. See the discussion in Chapter 3, and in Peck J (2016) Polanyian pathways. *Economic Geography* 92(2): 226–233; Peck (2020a).
5. Harvey D (1973) *Social justice in the city*. Baltimore, MD: Johns Hopkins University Press; Harvey (2005).
6. See Amin A and Thrift N (1994) Living in the global. In A Amin and N Thrift (eds) *Globalization, institutions and regional development in Europe*. Oxford, UK: Oxford University Press, 1–22; Hess M (2004) "Spatial" relationships? Towards a reconceptualization of embeddedness. *Progress in Human Geography* 28(2): 165–186; Grabher G (2006) Trading routes, bypasses, and risky intersections: mapping the travels of networks between economic sociology and economic geography. *Progress in Human Geography* 30(2): 163–189; Rossi (2013).
7. See Peck and Tickell (1994a); Tickell and Peck (1995).
8. This was illustrated in a day of sessions on Polanyian economic geographies that I organized with Sally Randles and Martin Hess at the 2012 meetings of the Association of American Geographers. The sessions attracted a large and diverse audience principally comprising the Polanyi-curious, with just a scattering (if that) of self-identifying Polanyians. A succession of excellent papers was presented, mostly by early-career researchers, while the more senior scholars who served as discussants and panelists tended to portray their own relationship with the Polanyian project as selective, orthogonal, or somewhat ambivalent. A selection of papers and commentaries were subsequently published in *Environment and Planning A* 45(7) in July 2013. Commentators and discussants at the AAG sessions included: Amy Glasmeier, Gillian Hart, John Pickles, Scott Prudham, Katharine Rankin, Erica Schoenberger, Adrian Smith, and Richard Walker.
9. Block and Somers (2014, 7).
10. See also Peck (2020a).
11. Hann and Hart (2011, 147).
12. The body of this chapter was originally published as Peck J (2013) For Polanyian economic geographies. *Environment and Planning A* 45(7): 1545–1568. I am grateful to Sage for permission to reproduce material from this article in revised form.
13. Hann and Hart (2011, 55).
14. Polanyi-Levitt (1990, 1).

15. Humphreys (1969, 169).
16. Cangiani M (1994) Prelude to *The Great Transformation*: Karl Polanyi's articles for *Der Oesterreichische Volkswirt*. In K McRobbie (ed) *Humanity, society and commitment: on Karl Polanyi*. Montréal: Black Rose Books, 7–24, 16.
17. Humphreys (1969, 173).
18. Humphreys (1969, 175).
19. A lifelong socialist, Polanyi himself was nevertheless always wary of formal party affiliations. See Dale (2016).
20. See Polanyi et al. (1957); Polanyi (1977).
21. Polanyi (1959, 162); (1960, 329).
22. Kaplan D (1968) The formal-substantive controversy in economic anthropology: reflections on its wider implications. *Southwestern Journal of Anthropology* 24(3): 228–251; Löfving (2005).
23. Those watching closely—indeed stalking the corridors at Columbia, where Polanyi taught—were nevertheless aware of the threat posed by Polanyian socioeconomics, as the Hungarian temporarily became a target of the arch-neoliberal Volker Fund in the early 1960s (revealingly, this neo-Austrian hatchet job was entitled "Down with primitivism"). See Rothbard M N (2004 [1961]) Down with primitivism. *Mises Institute* September 17. https://mises.org/library/down-primitivism-thorough-critique-polanyi (accessed December 19, 2021).
24. Halperin (1984, 257).
25. Halperin (1994, 43).
26. Coser (1984, 171–172).
27. See also Burawoy (2003); Cangiani (2011); Dale (2010).
28. See Isaac (2005).
29. See Dalton G (1990) Writings that clarify theoretical disputes over Karl Polanyi's work. *Journal of Economic Issues* 24(1): 249–261; Jenkins A (1977) "Substantivism" as a theory of economic forms. In B Hindess (ed) *Sociological theories of the economy*. London, UK: Macmillan, 66–91.
30. Isaac (2005, 20).
31. Dale G (2010) Social democracy, embeddedness and decommodification: on the conceptual innovations and intellectual affiliations of Karl Polanyi. *New Political Economy* 15(2): 369–393.
32. Block (2003).
33. See Burawoy (2003); Cangiani (2011); Dale (2010).
34. Burawoy (2003, 214). See also Cohen D (2018) Between perfection and damnation: the emerging geography of markets. *Progress in Human Geography* 42(6): 898–915.
35. Saul M (2005) Africa south of the Sahara. In J G Carrier (ed) *A handbook of economic anthropology*. Cheltenham, UK: Edward Elgar, 500–514, 503.
36. Polanyi's (1959, 174) historical perspective was that "a recession of markets from their nineteenth century peak [had] set in." Apparently confirming that he did not see the substantivist project as a solely extra-capitalist endeavor, Polanyi went on to comment that, "[e]ven in regard to the market-system itself [i.e. advanced capitalism], the market as the sole frame of reference is out of date" (1959, 184). Slipping into depression in the 1960s, Hayek may have come to share Polanyi's view that the historical trend was *away from* market society, not toward some imminent (neo)liberal restoration (see Peck, 2010a). On this score at least, both were proved to be wrong.

37. Dalton (1965, 17). Ironically, Goldwater's ill-fated presidential run of 1964—the year of Polanyi's death—is now recognized as the first stirring of a distinctively *neoliberal* ascendancy in the United States. Milton Friedman served as one of Goldwater's economic advisors, one of the few politicians who did not go on to disappoint the economist (see Peck, 2010a).
38. McRobbie K (1994) From class struggle to the "clean spring." In K McRobbie (ed) *Humanity, society and commitment: on Karl Polanyi*. Montréal: Black Rose Books, 45–80; Peck (2010a).
39. Dale (2010, 248).
40. Polanyi-Levitt K and Mendell M (1987) Karl Polanyi: his life and times. *Studies in Political Economy* 22(1): 7–39, 22; Block (2012).
41. Polanyi-Levitt (1990, 1).
42. McRobbie K (1994) Introduction. In K McRobbie (ed) *Humanity, society and commitment: on Karl Polanyi*. Montréal: Black Rose Books, vii–x, ix.
43. Coser (1984, 173).
44. See the discussion in Chapter 3.
45. It might be fairer to say, for example with reference to alternate interpretations of the "hard" (or radical) Polanyi and his "softer" (or reformist) alter ego, that *both* readings are historiographically credible, and legislating decisively or finally in favor of one over the other is impossible. See Dale (2010).
46. Gudeman (2001, 84).
47. Block and Somers (1984, 71).
48. On retroduction in heterodox economics, see Downward P and Mearman A (2007) Retroduction as mixed-methods triangulation in economic research: reorienting economics into social science. *Cambridge Journal of Economics* 31(1): 77–99; Fleetwood S (2001) Causal laws, functional relations and tendencies. *Review of Political Economy* 13(2): 201–220; Jones A and Murphy J T (2011) Theorizing practice in economic geography: foundations, challenges, and possibilities. *Progress in Human Geography* 35(3): 366–392. On the tensions between methodological holism and heterogeneity, see Peck (2012b, 2012c) and Brenner et al. (2011).
49. See Gemici (2008); Despain H G (2011) Karl Polanyi's metacritique of the liberal creed: reading Polanyi's social theory in terms of dialectical critical realism. *Journal of Critical Realism* 10(3): 277–302.
50. See Block (2000); Gudeman (2001).
51. See Halperin (1994); Silver B J and Arrighi G (2003) Polanyi's "double movement": the belle epoques of British and US hegemony compared. *Politics and Society* 31(2): 325–355.
52. Humphreys (1969, 180). See also the discussion in Peck (2012b, 2012c).
53. See Dowling J H (1979) The goodfellows vs. the Dalton gang: the assumptions of economic anthropology. *Journal of Anthropological Research* 35(3): 292–308.
54. Polanyi (1957, 247).
55. See Halperin (1984, 1994).
56. "Descriptions shall provide details of social situations and processes, spelling out who does what, to whom, under what circumstances, how frequently, and to what affect," Polanyi wrote, "Quantitative determination of phenomena is sought wherever possible. Locational patterns, processes, mechanisms, operations and their functioning may be illustrated to advantage through the use of models" (unpublished notes from 1956, quoted in Halperin, 1994, 44).

57. Polanyi (1959, 170).
58. Block and Somers (1984, 69); Polanyi, quoted in Dale G (2011) Lineages of embeddedness: on the antecedents and successors of a Polanyian concept. *American Journal of Economics and Sociology* 70(2): 306–339, 317.
59. See Vidal and Peck (2012).
60. Polanyi (1977, xl); Hann and Hart (2011, 70).
61. Polanyi (1959, 174, emphasis added).
62. Kaplan D (1968) The formal-substantive controversy in economic anthropology: reflections on its wider implications. *Southwestern Journal of Anthropology* 24(3): 228–251, 236–237.
63. Halperin (1994, 209).
64. Polanyi (1959, 162–163).
65. Polanyi (1959, 166, 168).
66. Polanyi advocated these quasi-realist positions as early as the mid-1920s, partly in conversation with Karl Popper, as Humphreys (1969) notes. "Terms and definitions constructed without reference to factual data are hollow, while a mere collecting of facts without a readjustment of our [theoretical] perspective is barren," Polanyi wrote, "To break this vicious circle, conceptual and empirical research must be carried forward *pari passu* [side by side]. Our efforts shall be sustained by the awareness that there are no shortcuts on this trail of inquiry" (1977, liv–lv). On critical realism and the extended case approach, see Burawoy (2009); Sayer (1984); Despain H G (2011) Karl Polanyi's metacritique of the liberal creed: reading Polanyi's social theory in terms of dialectical critical realism. *Journal of Critical Realism* 10(3): 277–302; and the further discussion in Chapter 10.
67. Hann and Hart (2011, 57).
68. Polanyi (1960, 330).
69. Block and Somers (1984, 63).
70. See the discussion in Chapter 3, and also Vidal and Peck (2012).
71. Polanyi (1957, 244).
72. Polanyi (1977, 31); Polanyi, quoted in Halperin (1994, 47).
73. See Halperin (1994).
74. See also see Sheppard (2011).
75. See Peck (2020a); Peck et al. (2020); Rantisi N M, Berndt C and Peck J (2020) Conclusion: "market research." In C Berndt, J Peck, and NM Rantisi (eds) *Market/place: exploring spaces of exchange*. Newcastle upon Tyne, UK: Agenda, 269–283.
76. Fusfeld D J (1994) Karl Polanyi's lectures on General Economic History: a student remembers. In K McRobbie (ed) *Humanity, society and commitment: on Karl Polanyi*. Montréal: Black Rose Books, 1–6, 4, emphasis added.
77. Polanyi (1957, 256).
78. What Polanyi took from the ethnographic evidence on "primitive" peoples, Dale observes, was that the absence of utilitarian or instrumentalist motives "was evidently a function of the structure of their societies [which duly] opened a window onto new ways of construing 'the economy' that were radically different to the contemporary capitalist norm." Dale G (2011) Lineages of embeddedness: on the antecedents and successors of a Polanyian concept. *American Journal of Economics and Sociology* 70(2): 306–339, 318.
79. Cook S (1966) The obsolete "anti-market" mentality: a critique of the substantive approach to economic anthropology. *American Antrhropologist* 68(2): 323–345, 337, original emphasis.

80. See Godelier M and Parce B (1972) *Rationality and irrationality in economics*. New York, NY: Monthly Review Press; Meillassoux C (1972) From reproduction to production. *Economy and Society* 1(1): 93–105; Halperin (1994).
81. See Jenkins A (1977) "Substantivism" as a theory of economic forms. In B Hindess (ed) *Sociological theories of the economy*. London, UK: Macmillan, 66–91.
82. Löfving (2005, 11). See also Hann and Hart (2011) and Isaac (2005).
83. See Pålsson Syll L (2005) The pitfalls of postmodern economics: remarks on a provocative project. In S Löfving (ed) *Peopled economies: conversations with Stephen Gudeman*. Uppsala, Sweden: Interface, 83–114.
84. Halperin (1994, 9, original emphasis).
85. The formulation is from Halperin (1994, 10).
86. See Berndt C and Boeckler M (2009) Geographies of circulation and exchange: constructions of markets. *Progress in Human Geography* 33(4): 535–551; Peck (2012b); Berndt C, Peck J and Rantisi N M (eds) *Market/place: exploring spaces of exchange*. Newcastle upon Tyne, UK: Agenda.
87. The absence of color may have been intentional of course, after Halperin's interpretation (1994, 50).
88. Polanyi (1944, 141).
89. Burawoy (2003, 198, 206).
90. Land, labor, and money are pseudo-commodities in Polanyi's terms, since they are socially, ecologically, and politically (re)produced, not made for (sale in) the market, and only partly (mal)regulated by price mechanisms.
91. See Block (2012); Harvey (2005); Fraser N (2011) Marketization, social protection, emancipation: toward a neo-Polanyian conception of capitalist crisis. In C Calhoun and G Derluguian (eds) *Business as usual: the roots of the global financial meltdown*. New York, NY: New York University Press, 137–158; Watts M (2007) What might resistance to neoliberalism consist of? In N Heynen, J McCarthy, S Prudham and P Robbins (eds) *Neoliberal environments*. New York, NY: Routledge, 273–278.
92. Burawoy (2003, 231–232).
93. There are affinities here with Gramscian and regulationist understandings of "chance discovery," and with Jessop's understanding of strategic selectivity and crisis-mediated governance. See Lipietz (1987); Jessop B and Knio K (eds) (2019) *The pedagogy of economic, political and social crises: dynamics, construals and lessons*. London, UK: Routledge.
94. See the further discussion in Peck (2021).
95. See the discussion in Chapter 3, and Krippner (2001).
96. Compare Block (2003) and Burawoy (2003). See also Gemici (2008); Krippner (2001); Krippner et al. (2004); Vidal and Peck (2012).
97. Dalton (1965, 2).
98. Polanyi (1959, 168).
99. See Gudeman (2001); Halperin (1984).
100. Berthoud G (1990) Toward a comparative approach: the contribution of Karl Polanyi. In K Polanyi-Levitt (ed) *The life and work of Karl Polanyi*. Montréal: Black Rose Books, 171–182, 171.
101. Polanyi (1977, 14).
102. Wright (2010).
103. See Peck (2012b).
104. After Gudeman (2001).

105. See Crouch (2011); Peck (2020b).
106. See Block (2012).
107. Polanyi (1959, 182, 184). See also Paton J and Cahill D (2020) Thinking socially and spatially about markets. In C Berndt, J Peck and N M Rantisi (eds) *Market/place: exploring spaces of exchange*. Newcastle upon Tyne, UK: Agenda, 29–48; Peck (2020a).
108. See Hart (2002, 2018), and the further discussion in Chapter 10.
109. See Bugra A and Agartan K (eds) (2007) *Reading Karl Polanyi for the twenty-first century: market economy as a political project*. New York, NY: Palgrave Macmillan; Hann C and Hart K (eds) (2009) *Market and society: the great transformation today*. Cambridge, UK: Cambridge University Press; Harvey M, Ramlogan R and Randles S (eds) (2007) *Karl Polanyi: new perspectives on the place of the economy in society*. Manchester, UK: Manchester University Press; Rodrigues W and Santos N S (2020) Karl Polanyi and substantivism in economic development. *Brazilian Journal of Political Economy* 40: 86–99; Almond P and Connolly H (2020) A manifesto for "slow" comparative research on work and employment. *European Journal of Industrial Relations* 26(1): 59–74; Hann C (2021) One hundred years of substantivist economic anthropology. *Working Paper* #205, Max Planck Institute for Social Anthropology, Halle/Saale, Germany.
110. Polanyi (1960, 332).

Chapter 8

1. In addition to Matthew Tonts and Paul Plummer, the group comprised Neil Argent, Julia Horsley, Misty Lawrie, Danny MacKinnon, and Eric Sheppard. See the account in Plummer P and Tonts M (2013) Geographical political economy, dirt research and the Pilbara. *Australian Geographer* 44(3) 223–226.
2. The phrase is from Henry Lawson's *The roaring days* (1889), quoted in Ellem (2017).
3. Ellem (2017).
4. See, for example, Pearson (2009); Altman and Hinkson (2010); Altman (2010); and Langton and Mazel (2012).
5. Howitt (1989, 155, emphasis added).
6. Cleary (2011, 127).
7. The remainder of this chapter reproduces and combines material originally published as Peck J (2013) Polanyi in the Pilbara. *Australian Geographer* 44(3): 243–264 and Peck J (2013) Excavating the Pilbara: a Polanyian exploration. *Geographical Research* 51(3): 227–242. I am grateful to Taylor & Francis for permission to reproduce material from the article in *Australian Geographer* in revised form (License Number 5358281394397) and to John Wiley and Sons for permission to reproduce material from the article in *Geographical Research* in revised form (License Number 5357270592245).
8. Pearson (2009, 373).
9. Block F (2001) Introduction. In K Polanyi, *The great transformation*. Boston, MA: Beacon Press, xviii–xxxviii. See also Halperin (1994); Dale G (2011) Lineages of embeddedness: on the antecedents and successors of a Polanyian concept. *American Journal of Economics and Sociology* 70(2): 306–339.
10. Barber (1995, 407).

11. Pearson H W (1957) Parsons and Smelser on the economy. In K Polanyi, C M Arensberg and H W Pearson (eds) *Trade and market in the early empires*. New York, NY: Free Press, 307–319; Dalton (1965); Halperin (1994).
12. Polanyi (1977, xl).
13. Block and Somers (1984, 63).
14. Polanyi-Levitt K (2007) Preface: the English experience in the life and work of Karl Polanyi. In M Harvey, R Ramlogan, and S Randles (eds) *Karl Polanyi: new perspectives on the place of the economy in society*. Manchester, UK: Manchester University Press, xi–xvi, xiv.
15. Cangiani M (2011) Karl Polanyi's institutional theory: market society and its "disembedded" economy. *Journal of Economic Issues* 45(1): 177–198, 180.
16. Cleary (2011, 127); Howitt (1989, 167).
17. ABC (2011) The world economy needs hard work: Albanese. Australian Broadcasting Corporation Transcripts, August 7, 2011.
18. See Stockbridge M E (1976) *Dominance of giants*. Department of Social Work, University of Western Australia, Perth, WA.
19. Cleary (2011); Regional Development Australia (2010) *Preliminary Pilbara regional plan*. Karratha, WA: RDA.
20. Ellem B L (2004) *Hard ground*. Port Hedland, WA: Pilbara Mineworkers Union, 13–14.
21. Cleary (2011).
22. Miller J W (2011) The $200,000-a-year mine worker. *Wall Street Journal* November 16, B1.
23. Cousins D and Nieuwenhuysen J P (1984) *Aboriginals and the mining industry*. Sydney, NSW: Allen and Unwin; Thompson H (1987) The Pilbara iron ore industry: mining cycles and capital-labour relations. *Journal of Australian Political Economy* 21: 66–82; Cleary (2011); Langton and Mazel (2012).
24. Howitt (1989, 157).
25. Taylor J and Scambary B (2005) *Indigenous people and the Pilbara mining boom*. Canberra, ACT: ANU E Press.
26. See Altman (2012).
27. See Langton and Mazel (2012).
28. Harvey B and Gawler J (2003) Aboriginal employment diversity in Rio Tinto. *International Journal of Diversity in Organizations, Communities and Nations* 3: 195–209, 208.
29. See Trigger D (2005) Mining projects in remote Aboriginal Australia: sites of the articulation and contesting of economic and cultural futures. In D Austin-Broos and G Macdonald (eds) *Culture, economy and governance in Aboriginal Australia*. Sydney, NSW: Sydney University Press, 41–62; Holcombe (2006); Altman (2010).
30. Cleary (2011, 127).
31. See Altman (2007); Sercombe (2008).
32. See Peterson N (2005) What can the pre-colonial and frontier economics tell us about engagement with the real economy? Indigenous life projects and the conditions for development. In D Austin-Broos and G Macdonald (eds) *Culture, economy and governance in Aboriginal Australia*. Sydney, NSW: Sydney University Press, 7–18.
33. Newman P, Armstrong R and McGrath N (2005) *Pilbara regional sustainability strategy*. Institute for Sustainability and Technology Policy, Murdoch University, Perth, WA; McHugh L (2011) *Pilbara prospects 2020*. West Perth, WA: Future Directions International.
34. See Pini B, McDonald P and Mayes R (2012) Class contestations and Australia's resource boom: the emergence of the "cashed-up bogan." *Sociology* 46(1): 142–158.
35. Knight Frank (2010) *Pilbara region overview*. Perth, WA: Knight Frank.

36. Ellem (2004, 23).
37. Leaver R (2010) An Australian international political economy? The high road and the low road. *Australian Journal of International Affairs* 64(1): 123–129.
38. Lawrie M, Tonts M and Plummer P (2011) Boomtowns, resource dependence and socio-economic well-being. *Australian Geographer* 42(2): 139–164.
39. See Tonts M, Plummer P and Lawrie M (2012) Socio-economic wellbeing in Australian mining towns: a comparative analysis. *Journal of Rural Studies* 28(3): 288–301; Newman P, Armstrong R and McGrath N (2005) *Pilbara regional sustainability strategy*. Institute for Sustainability and Technology Policy, Murdoch University, Perth, WA.
40. Taylor J and Scambary B (2005) *Indigenous people and the Pilbara mining boom*. Canberra, ACT: ANU E Press.
41. Botsman P (2010) After emancipation: the Pilbara, Australian Aboriginal economic development and the mining tax. https://www.workingpapers.com.au/papers/after-emancipation-pilbara-australian-aboriginal-economic-development-and-mining-tax.
42. Ngarda Ngarli Yarndu Foundation (2009) *Outcomes from the Indigenous Pilbara dialogue*. South Hedland, WA: NNYF, 5.
43. Ashby I (2012) Industry builds indigenous opportunity. *Australian Financial Review*, February 1, 55.
44. Indigenous Business Australia (2009) Mining opportunities in the Pilbara. *Inspire* 3: 13–15, 14–15.
45. See Business Council of Australia (2009) *Many connections, one goal: closing the gap*. Melbourne, VIC: BCA; Cleary (2011, 135). See also Holcombe (2010).
46. See Jordan K and Mavec D (2010) Corporate initiatives in indigenous employment: the Australian Employment Covenant two years on. *CAEPR Working Paper 74/2010*, Centre for Aboriginal Economic Policy Research, Australian National University, Canberra, ACT; Freed J (2011) Forrest stands by landholder deal. *Australian Financial Review*, July 19, 9; *YMAC News* (2011) Historic agreement between Pilbara traditional owners and Rio Tinto Iron Ore. *YMAC News* 14, 3–5; Cleary (2011).
47. Altman and Hinkson (2010, 188).
48. Hughes H and Hughes M (2010) Indigenous employment, unemployment and labour force participation: facts for evidence based policies. *CIS Policy Monograph 107*, Centre for Independent Studies, St Leonards, NSW, 16.
49. Sahlins (1972).
50. Buckley and Wheelwright (1988).
51. Dufty N F (1984) *Industrial relations in the Pilbara iron ore industry*. Perth, WA: Western Australian Institute of Technology, 5.
52. Fisk E K (1981) Foreword. In E Young (ed) *Tribal communities in rural areas*. Development Studies Centre. Canberra, ACT: ANU, vii–vix, vii.
53. McLeod (1984, 33). A mostly self-educated, white bush worker, McLeod served as a mediator on behalf of Aboriginal workers. He was also a conduit to the Australian Communist Party and other progressive interests in Perth. According to Hess (1994, 70), McLeod enjoyed "the trust of the Pilbara Aboriginal people [which he combined with] some knowledge of Marxism," the latter mostly gleaned from AM radio broadcasts.
54. Maddock K (1974) *The Australian Aborigines*. Sydney, NSW: Penguin Books, 27.
55. McLeod (1984, 17).
56. Buckley and Wheelwright (1988, 18).
57. See Young E (1981) *Tribal communities in rural areas*. Canberra, ACT: ANU Press.

58. Altman and Hinkson (2010); Holcombe (2010).
59. Rowley (1972, 67).
60. Polanyi (1944, 146); Marx (1976, 875).
61. Buckley and Wheelwright (1988, 20).
62. Buckley and Wheelwright (1988).
63. Marx (1976, 933).
64. Rowley (1972, 68).
65. Rose D B (1991) *Hidden histories*. Canberra, ACT: Aboriginal Studies Press, 151.
66. See Olive (2007).
67. Rowley (1972, 192).
68. Wilson (1980, 155).
69. Rowley (1972, 198).
70. Buckley and Wheelwright (1988, 25).
71. See Wilson (1980).
72. Wilson (1980, 157).
73. See Young E (1981) *Tribal communities in rural areas*. Canberra, ACT: ANU Press.
74. On the ascription of contingent status in wage labor markets, see Peck (1996); Peck J and Theodore N (2012) Politicizing contingent labor: countering neoliberal labor-market regulation ... from the bottom up? *South Atlantic Quarterly* 111(4): 741–761.
75. See Wilson (1980); Holcombe (2006).
76. Stuart D (1959) *Yandy*. Melbourne, VIC: Georgian House.
77. Hess (1994, 68).
78. Federal negotiations resulted in Aboriginal pay rates being set at 15% of the basic rate, plus food and accommodation, after employers objected to a proposed 50% rate. See Stevens F S (1981) *Black Australia*. Sydney, NSW: Alternative Publishing Co-operative.
79. Wilson (1980, 162).
80. McLeod (1984, 40).
81. Hess (1994, 68).
82. See Hess (1994).
83. Broome R (2010) *Aboriginal Australians*. Crows Nest, NSW: Allen and Unwin, 144.
84. See Wilson (1980).
85. Holcombe (2006, 7, emphasis added); Howitt (1989, 158).
86. Roberts J (1978) *From massacres to mining*. London, UK: War on Want, 89.
87. McLeod (1984, 119).
88. Duffield R (1979) *Rogue bull*. Sydney, NSW: Collins.
89. Quoted in Coyne M and Edwards L (1980) *The Oz factor*. East Malvern, VIC: Royal Blind Society, 68.
90. Altman (2012).
91. Rowley C D (1971) *The remote Aborigines*. Canberra, ACT: ANU Press, 259.
92. Roberts J (1978) *From massacres to mining*. London, UK: War on Want; Howitt (1989).
93. Olive (2007, 176).
94. Howitt (1989, 160).
95. Tonkinson R (1974) *The Jigalong mob*. Menlo Park, NSW: Cummings, 150.
96. Cleary (2011).
97. Edmunds M (1989) *They get heaps*. Canberra, ACT: Aboriginal Studies Press, 49.
98. Neil et al. (1982, 11).
99. Hamersley Holdings Ltd (1972) *Annual report*. Melbourne, VIC: Hamersley Holdings, 18.

100. Neil et al. (1982, 13).
101. Brealey (1980, 149).
102. A study by psychiatrists Burvill and Kidd found that "the men drink large quantities of alcohol when not working [and] the women tend to be bored." High rates of neurosis and anxiety disorder were diagnosed among women in the towns, spiking in the temporary caravan parks. Burvill W and Kidd C B (1975) The two town study: a comparison of psychiatric illness in two contrasting Western Australian mining towns. *Australasian Psychiatry* 9: 85–92, 86. See also Stockbridge M E (1976) *Dominance of giants*. Department of Social Work, University of Western Australia, Perth, WA; Brealey (1980).
103. Lawrence Howroyd, quoted in Neil et al. (1982, 9).
104. Quoted in Brealey (1980, 149).
105. Commonwealth of Australia (1974) *The Pilbara study*. Canberra, ACT: AGPS, 8.2, 8.
106. Commonwealth of Australia (1974) *The Pilbara study*, 8.2, 11–12.
107. Howroyd L H (1974) Shay Gap. *Architecture Australia* 63 (June), 53–56, 53.
108. Commonwealth of Australia (1974) *The Pilbara study*, 8.2, 12.
109. Howitt (1989, 167).
110. Commonwealth of Australia (1974) *The Pilbara study*, 8.2, 13–14.
111. The term is from Ellem B L (2003) Re-placing the Pilbara's mining unions. *Australian Geographer* 34(3): 281–296; see also Ellem (2017).
112. Brealey (1980, 151).
113. Brealey (1980); Neil et al. (1982).
114. Thompson H (1981) "Normalization": industrial relations and community control in the Pilbara. *Australian Quarterly* 53(3): 301–324, 307.
115. Smith and Thompson (1987).
116. See Ellem (2017).
117. See Smith and Thompson (1987).
118. Smith and Thompson (1987, 304); see also Ellem (2017).
119. See Ellem (2017).
120. Storey K (2001) Fly-in/fly-out and fly-over: mining and regional development in Western Australia. *Australian Geographer* 32(2): 133–148, 135; Cleary (2011).
121. Chamber of Minerals and Energy Western Australia (2005) *Fly in/fly out*. Perth, WA: CMEWA.
122. Ellem B L (2003) Re-placing the Pilbara's mining unions. *Australian Geographer* 34(3): 281–296, 286.
123. Watts J (2004) *Best of both worlds*. Karratha, WA: Pilbara Regional Council, 9.
124. Haslam McKenzie F (2010) Fly-in fly-out: the challenges of transient populations in rural landscapes. In G W Luck, D Race, and R Black (eds) *Demographic change in Australia's rural landscapes*. Collingwood, VIC: CSIRO, 353–374, 363.
125. Pilbara Area Consultative Committee (2008) *The Pilbara plan*. Karratha, WA: PACC; Newman P, Bilsborough D, Reed P, and Mouritz M (2010) *Pilbara cities*. West Perth, WA: Future Directions International.
126. See Pilbara Development Commission (2010) *Strategic plan 2010–2013*. Karratha, WA: PDC.
127. Western Area Regional Development Council (2010) *Extractive industry sustainable and regional development*. West Perth, WA: Syme Marmion, i.
128. Western Area Regional Development Council (2010) *Extractive industry sustainable and regional development*, 42–48, 26

129. Norman J (2010) On the ground in Karratha. *ABC North West WA*, February 1.
130. Turner R (2011) Depression the dark side of mining boom. *Australian*, March 12, 6.
131. Premier Colin Barnett, quoted in Weber D (2010) Workers at Woodside's Pluto project defy Federal Court order. *Australian Broadcasting Corporation Transcripts*, January 28.
132. Julie Pope, Karratha Chamber of Commerce, quoted in Burrell A (2010) Town has no pity for fly-in "whingers." *Australian*, February 6, 1, 8.
133. Ellem B L (2003) New unionism in the old economy: community and collectivism in the Pilbara's mining towns. *Journal of Industrial Relations* 45(3): 423–431.
134. See Johnson P (2009) *Fly-in fly-out and regional impact assessments*. Perth, WA: Regional Development Council.
135. Pick D, Dayaram K, and Butler B (2008) Neo-liberalism, risk and regional development in Western Australia: the case of the Pilbara. *International Journal of Sociology and Social Policy* 28(11–12): 516–527, 519; Haslam McKenzie F (2010) Fly-in fly-out: the challenges of transient populations in rural landscapes, 364.
136. Knight Frank (2010) *Pilbara region overview*. Perth, WA: Knight Frank.
137. Williams R (2011) How the resources boom split the golden state. *Sydney Morning Herald*, December 3, 6.
138. See Olive (2007); Holcombe (2010).
139. Brown J (1981) Infrastructure policies in the Pilbara. In E J Harman and B W Head (ed) *State, capital and resources in the north and west of Australia*. Perth, WA: University of Western Australia Press, 237–256; Dufty N F (1984) *Industrial relations in the Pilbara iron ore industry*. Perth, WA: Western Australian Institute of Technology.
140. McLeod (1984, 36).
141. Altman and Hinkson (2010, 198).
142. Hughes H and Hughes M (2010) Indigenous employment, unemployment and labour force participation: facts for evidence based policies. *CIS Policy Monograph 107*, Centre for Independent Studies, St Leonards, NSW, 14, 17.
143. See Pearson (2009); Altman and Hinkson (2010).
144. See Johns G (2008) The Northern Territory intervention in Aboriginal affairs: wicked problem or wicked policy? *Agenda* 15(2): 65–84; Langton M (2008) Trapped in the Aboriginal reality show. *Griffith Review* 19: 145–162; Altman (2010).
145. See Department of Families Housing Community Services and Indigenous Affairs (2009) *Closing the gap on Indigenous disadvantage*. Canberra, ACT: Commonwealth of Australia.
146. See Kowal E (2008) The politics of the gap: Indigenous Australians, liberal multiculturalism, and the end of the self-determination era. *American Anthropologist* 110(3): 338–348; Altman (2009).
147. Altman and Hinkson (2010, 193).
148. Pearson (2009, 143).
149. Ah Mat (2003, 3).
150. Ah Mat (2003, 3, 9).
151. See Ngarda Ngarli Yarndu Foundation (2009) *Outcomes from the Indigenous Pilbara dialogue*. South Hedland, WA: NNYF.
152. Sercombe (2008, 20).
153. See Peterson N (1993) Demand sharing: reciprocity and the pressure for generosity among foragers. *American Anthropologist* 95(4): 860–874; Holcombe (2010); Sercombe (2008).
154. Altman (2009, 11).

155. Altman (2010, 271).
156. Ah Mat (2003, 3, 6).
157. Pearson (2009, 370).
158. Quoted in Williams R (2011) How the resources boom split the golden state. *Sydney Morning Herald* December 3, 6.
159. Langton M (2010) The shock of the new: a postcolonial dilemma for Australianist anthropology. In J Altman and M Hinkson (eds) *Culture crisis*. Sydney, NSW: UNSW Press, 91–115, 92.
160. Polanyi (1977, p. xl).

Chapter 9

1. See Sheppard (2011); Peck (2016, 2017b); Brenner (2019).
2. See Rosenberg (2005); Makki (2015); Anievas and Nisancioglu (2015); Rioux S (2015) Mind the (theoretical) gap: on the poverty of international relations theorising of uneven and combined development. *Global Society* 29(4): 481–509; Matin K and Anievas A (eds) (2016) *Historical sociology and world history: uneven and combined development over the longue durée*. London, UK: Rowman & Littlefield International; Rosenberg J (2013) The "philosophical premises" of uneven and combined development. *Review of International Studies* 39(3): 569–597.
3. Coates (2015, 13); see also Hancké (2009).
4. See Clark B (2016) *The evolution of economic systems: varieties of capitalism in the global economy*. Oxford, UK: Oxford University Press; Dicken P (2015) *Global shift*, 7th edition. London, UK: Sage; Menz G (2017) *Comparative political economy*. Oxford, UK: Oxford University Press; Vermeiren M (2021) *Crisis and inequality*. Cambridge, UK: Polity.
5. See Hancké et al. (2009), Streeck (2011a), and the further discussion in Chapter 5.
6. On the "frontal" formulation that is advanced capitalism, and its recent travails, see Peck (2021).
7. See Streeck (2011b); Heyes J, Lewis P and Clark I (2012) Varieties of capitalism, neoliberalism and the economic crisis of 2008–? *Industrial Relations Journal* 43(3): 222–241; Coates (2015); Šitera D (2015) On new travels in space-time: theoretical rediscoveries after the crisis in (comparative) capitalism(s). *New Perspectives* 23(2): 77–91.
8. Bohle and Greskovits (2009, 382).
9. See Wallerstein et al. (2013); Streeck (2016).
10. See Coates (2015); Bruff et al. (2015); Šitera D (2015) Varieties in comparative capitalisms research: a critical juncture. *New Perspectives* 23(2): 141–156; Menz G (2017) *Comparative political economy*. Oxford, UK: Oxford University Press; Vermeiren M (2021) *Crisis and inequality*. Cambridge, UK: Polity.
11. Ebenau M, Bruff I, and May C (2015) Introduction: comparative capitalisms research and the emergence of critical, global perspectives. In M Ebenau, I Bruff and C May (eds) *New directions in comparative capitalisms research*. London, UK: Palgrave Macmillan, 1–8, 2–3.
12. Bruff et al. (2015, 34); see also Hancké et al. (2009).
13. For recent discussions of UCD, see Hudson R (2016) Rising powers and the drivers of uneven global development. *Area Development and Policy* 1(3): 279–294; Peck (2016); Sheppard (2016); Dunford M and Liu W (2017) Uneven and combined development.

Regional Studies 51(1): 69–85; Hadjimichalis C (2018) *Crisis spaces: structures, struggles and solidarity in South Europe*. London, UK: Routledge; Phelps N A, Atienza M and Arias M (2018) An invitation to the dark side of economic geography. *Environment and Planning A* 50(1) 236–244; Werner M (2019) Geographies of production I: global production and uneven development. *Progress in Human Geography* 43(5): 948–958; Rolf S (2021) *China's uneven and combined development*. Cham: Springer Nature; Alami I and Dixon A (2023) Uneven and combined state capitalism. *EPA: Economy and Space* 55(1): 72–99.

14. Harvey D (2004) Retrospect on *The Limits to Capital*. *Antipode* 36(3): 544–549, 545.
15. Stuart Hall, quoted in McCabe (2007, 38).
16. Jessop B (2014) Capitalist diversity and variety: variegation, the world market, compossibility and ecological dominance. *Capital and Class* 38(1): 45–58, 46.
17. Hall (1991b, 42).
18. On the terraforming dynamics of capitalism and its dynamic, fractal ontology, see Jessop (2012, 2015, 2018) and Chris Howell in Howell C, Culpepper P D and Rueda D (2015) On Kathleen Thelen, varieties of liberalization and the new politics of social solidarity. *Socio-Economic Review* 13(2): 399–409.
19. See Brenner (2019, chapter 8).
20. Economist (1992) A world history, chapter 13: the disastrous 21st Century. *Economist*, December 26: 17–19, 17.
21. Friedman T L (1999) *The lexus and the olive tree: understanding globalization*. New York, NY: Farrar, Straus and Giroux, 102.
22. Wooldridge A (2012) The visible hand. *Economist*, January 21: 3–5, 3.
23. See Jacques, M. (2009) *When China rules the world*. New York, NY: Penguin; Wang H (2009) *The end of the revolution: China and the limits of modernity*. London, UK: Verso; cf. Peck (2021); Karl R E (2020) *China's revolutions in the modern world*. London, UK: Verso.
24. See Rosenberg J and Boyle C (2019) Understanding 2016: China, Brexit and Trump in the history of uneven and combined development. *Journal of Historical Sociology* 32(1): e32–58.
25. Mezzadra and Neilson (2019, 21–22).
26. Mezzadra and Neilson (2019, 22, emphasis added).
27. "The country that is more developed industrially only shows, to the less developed," Marx famously wrote, "the *image of its own future*" (Marx, 1976, 91, emphasis added). But see the discussion in Shanin (1983).
28. See Hall (2003a), Streeck (2011a); Jessop (2018); Westra R (2015) Travels to socialism interrupted: origins of the varieties of capitalism debate. *New Perspectives* 23(2): 124–131.
29. See Selwyn B (2011) Trotsky, Gerschenkron and the political economy of late capitalist development. *Economy and Society* 40(3): 421–450; Ashman S and Fine B (2013) Neoliberalism, varieties of capitalism, and the shifting contours of South Africa's financial system. *Transformation: Critical Perspectives on Southern Africa* 81(1): 144–178; Henderson J, Appelbaum R P and Ho S Y (2013) Globalization with Chinese characteristics: externalization, dynamics and transformations. *Development and Change* 44(6): 1221–1253; Anievas and Nisancioglu (2015).
30. Wallerstein et al. (2013).
31. Streeck (2011a).
32. See Piore and Sabel (1984); Dore (1986); Lipietz (1987).

33. Rosenberg (2005, 6) contends that it was the *combination* of the breakdown of the Soviet system and neoliberalism's "deregulating thrust" that generated an "enormous sense of temporal acceleration and spatial compression" out of which emerged a new generation of overdrawn and ideologically freighted theories of globalization. See also Dicken et al. (1997); Tickell and Peck (2003).
34. See Greider W (1997) *One world, ready or not: the manic logic of global capitalism*. New York, NY: Simon and Schuster.
35. See the discussion in Chapter 5 for more details. Nominally "close" to the neoclassical textbook version of a free-market economy, LMEs are held to be governed by arm's length and openly competitive relations, and by formal contracts and price signals, their more fluid capital and labor markets enabling both rapid adjustment and radical innovation. Meanwhile, as the others of this free-market model, CMEs are characterized by "more social" forms of coordination, cooperation, and corporatist governance, by patient capital markets and longer-term employment relationships.
36. Hall and Soskice (2001, 8, 21). See also the discussion in Chapter 5.
37. Hancké (2009); Coates (2015); Martin C J (2014) Getting down to business: varieties of capitalism and employment relations. In A Wilkinson, G Wood and R Deeg (eds) *The Oxford handbook of employment relations: comparative employment systems*. Oxford, UK: Oxford University Press, 65–85.
38. Streeck (2011a, 426); see also Albert (1993); Blyth (2003).
39. Coates (2015, 19).
40. Hodgson (2015, 11).
41. See Howell C (2003) Varieties of capitalism: and then there was one? *Comparative Politics* 36(1): 103–124; Bruff I (2011) What about the elephant in the room? Varieties of capitalism, varieties in capitalism. *New Political Economy* 16(4): 481–500; Streeck (2011b); Piore (2016).
42. It had been for "expositional purposes," Hall and Soskice (2003, 243–244) later explained, that LMEs and CMEs were presented as "ideal types . . . focused on the American and German cases that exemplify them, but the point of the analysis was not simply to describe two types of economies but to develop new formulations about the principal dimensions distinguishing one political economy from another in more general terms, with an emphasis on dimensions of difference consequential for national policy and performance."
43. Bohle and Greskovitz (2009, 375, emphasis added).
44. See Massey (1991b, 1999); Anievas and Nisancioglu (2015).
45. Hall (1991a, 39, 23). For Stuart Hall, the global was not some unpatterned, extraterrestrial space or a zone of pure mystification: during the 1990s, globalization was being reimagined, and unevenly enacted, according to a hegemonically American template, in the sense of "the global [as] the self-representation of the dominant particular" (Hall, 1991b, 67; 1991a, 27). This representational regime may have beckoned the end of history in the name of a unified free-market capitalism, but the nation-state, rather than "backing off," seemed instead to be heading "into an even deeper trough of defensive exclusivism," including the renewal of ugly nationalisms, racisms, and social antagonisms (Hall, 1991a, 25).
46. Hall (1991b, 62, 67).
47. Hancké et al. (2009, 298); Blyth (2003).
48. Bohle and Greskovits (2009, 355, 359, 355).
49. Crouch (2009, 83, 78).
50. Sayer (1992, 138).

51. See Blyth (2003); Crouch (2009).
52. Michael Piore (2016, 238) has also criticized what he regards as the VoC paradigm's ahistorical and ad hoc institutionalism: "My major problem with the VoC literature is the way in which it characterizes the United States as a 'liberal market economy' [which] clashes sharply with the way in which the United States economy was organized in the immediate postwar decades." While he does not entirely embrace this conceptual terminology, postwar Fordism and more recent waves of financialization seem more relevant to explaining the "transition" in the United States, Piore observes, than could a static comparison drawn (only) with Germany and preoccupied with "the internal coherence of these two systems," in the absence both of historical analysis and an explicit theory of capitalism (2016, 239).
53. Coates (2015, 23).
54. Ebenau M (2015) Directions and debates in the globalization of comparative capitalisms research. In M Ebenau, I Bruff and C May (eds) *New directions in comparative capitalisms research*. London, UK: Palgrave Macmillan, 45–61, 53, 58.
55. Streeck (2011a, 439, 441, original emphasis).
56. Coates (2015, 22).
57. See, for example, Milanović B (2019). *Capitalism, alone*. Cambridge, MA: Belknap Press. For a critique of this new variant of binary theorizing, see Peck (2021).
58. Jackson G (2018) Socioeconomics in 2018: more global, more ethnographic and less comfortable, please. *Socio-Economic Review* 16(1): 1–3, 1–2.
59. See Bohle D and Greskovits B (2012) *Capitalist diversity on Europe's periphery*. Ithaca, NY: Cornell University Press; Glassner V (2013) Central and Eastern European industrial relations in the crisis: national divergence and path-dependent change. *Transfer* 19(2): 155–169.
60. See Bizberg I (2014) Types of capitalism in Latin America. *Revue Interventions Économiques* 49: 1–31; Fernández V R, Ebenau M and Bazza A (2018) Rethinking varieties of capitalism from the Latin American periphery. *Review of Radical Political Economics* 50(2): 392–408.
61. See McNally (2007, 2008c), and the discussion in Chapter 6.
62. See Hausmann R, Hidalgo C A, Bustos S, Coscia M, Simoes A and Yildirim M A (2013) *The atlas of economic complexity*. Cambridge, MA: MIT Press; Witt M A, Kabbach de Castro L R, Amaeshi K, Mahroum S, Bohle D and Saez L (2018) Mapping the business systems of 61 major economies: a taxonomy and implications for varieties of capitalism and business systems research. *Socio-Economic Review* 16(1): 5–38.
63. Hancké et al. (2009, 276–277).
64. See Hall (1991b); Streeck (2011a); Clarke J (2014) Imagined, real and moral economies. *Culture Unbound* 6: 95–112.
65. Crouch (2009, 89).
66. Hall (1991a, 29, 32).
67. Jessop (2018, 215–216, original emphasis).
68. See Harvey (1982); Smith N (2008 [1984]) *Uneven development: nature, capital, and the production of space*, 3rd edition. Athens, GA: University of Georgia Press.
69. See Massey (1984); Allen J, Massey D, and Cochrane A (1998) *Rethinking the region*. London, UK: Routledge; Morgan K and Sayer A (1988) *Microcircuits of capital*. Cambridge, UK: Polity.
70. Anievas and Nisancioglu (2015, 9, original emphasis).
71. Anievas and Nisancioglu (2015); Jessop (2018, 210).

72. Massey (1995, 296). See also Clarke (2018), Peck et al. (2018), and for a parallel approach to content-rich abstraction, Mezzadra and Neilson (2019).
73. See Chapters 2 and 3. See also Barnes and Christophers (2018).
74. Moore J W (2017) Value in the web of life, or, why world history matters to geography. *Dialogues in Human Geography* 7(3): 326–330, 327.
75. Anievas and Nisancioglu (2015, 6). See also Lee (2017); Glassman J (2018) Geopolitical economies of development and democratization in East Asia: themes, concepts, and geographies. *EPA: Economy and Space* 50(2): 407–415.
76. Jessop (2018, 215).
77. See Streeck (2011a).
78. Massey (1991a).
79. Massey (1994, 155, 154).
80. See Massey (1995); Li (2014).
81. Massey (1995, 318).
82. See Sheppard (2002).
83. Massey (1995, 303).
84. See Chernilo D (2010) Methodological nationalism and the domestic analogy: classical resources for their critique. *Cambridge Review of International Affairs* 23(1): 87–106.
85. Sheppard E (2019) Globalizing capitalism's raggedy raggedly fringes: thinking through Jakarta. *Area Development and Policy* 4(1): 1–27, 14, original emphasis. See also Leitner and Sheppard (2020).
86. Go J and Lawson G (2017) Introduction: for a global historical sociology. In J Go and G Lawson (eds) *Global historical sociology*. Cambridge, UK: Cambridge University Press, 1–34, 30.
87. See Brenner (2019). Doreen Massey famously underlined the political as well as explanatory stakes here with her rhetorical question, "In what sense a regional problem?" Massey D (1979) In what sense a regional problem? *Regional Studies* 13(2): 233–243.
88. Anievas and Nisancioglu (2015, 5).
89. Hobson J M (2017) Worlding the rise of capitalism: the multicivilizational roots of modernity. In J Go and G Lawson (eds) *Global historical sociology*. Cambridge, UK: Cambridge University Press, 221–240, 224.
90. Sayer (1992, 237).
91. Lowe L (2005) Insufficient difference. *Ethnicities* 5(3): 409–414.
92. See Boyer (2005); Crouch (2009).
93. See Hancké (2009).
94. Anievas and Nisancioglu (2015, 9).
95. Quoted at People's Forum, "Marx and Capital: the Book, the Concept, the History," https://peoplesforum.org/events/marx-and-capital-the-book-the-concept-the-history/2018-08-06/.
96. Fraser and Jaeggi (2018); Hodgson (2015).
97. Anievas and Nisancioglu (2015, 8–9).
98. Massey (1995, 302).
99. Massey (1995, 325, 304).
100. Massey (1995, 327, 314–315, emphasis added). See also Peck et al. (2018).
101. See Clarke (2018); Grayson D and Little B (2017) Conjunctural analysis and the crisis of ideas. *Soundings* 65: 59–75.
102. McMichael (2000, 671).

103. See McMichael (1990).
104. Massey (1995, 313); Henriques J, Morley D and Goblot V (2017) The politics of conjuncture. In J Henriques and D Morley with V Goblot (eds) *Stuart Hall: conversations, projects and legacies*. London, UK: Goldsmiths Press, 69–77, 73.
105. See, for example, Jessop's (2018, 216) approach to the "insertion of economic spaces into the hierarchically structured world system." Incorporated comparisons, rather than eschewing these systemic formulations, ought instead to engage them.
106. Massey (1995, 315).
107. Massey D (2004) Geographies of responsibility. *Geografiska Annaler: Series B, Human Geography* 86(1): 5–18, 8.
108. Rosenberg (2006, 323). For Rosenberg, the "domestic" and the "national" (along with the local) possess no constitutive essence prior to various forms of intersocietal interaction; this absence of pre-interactive essences sets up a chicken and egg problem (the constitution of local societies does not precede the moment of interaction, but the space of global interaction does not exist independently of its constituent elements), for which the solution must be to treat the national and the international as coeval, even as they are not the same, in part due to the absence of a "higher" form of political authority and means of effective regulation at the international scale.
109. See the discussion in Brenner (2019), especially chapter 8.
110. Makki (2015, 491).
111. For Massey, "place is relational, and can be seen as neither a bounded enclosure, or a privileged site of meaning-making, but rather as a subset of the interactions which constitute [social] space, a local articulation within a wider whole" (Massey, 1994, 4).
112. Quoted in Rubel and Manale (1975, 252).
113. Marx, letter to Sorge, September 27, 1877 (quoted in Rubel and Manale, 1975, 306).
114. Shanin (1983, 17, emphasis added).
115. Marx (1971, xxiii–xxiv). In the preface to the German edition, Marx speaks both of the mundane and the more portentous reasons behind his decision to work from this "classic ground," complaining about the wretched state of "social statistics" on the continent in comparison to England, but also remarking that the "physicist either observes physical phenomena where they occur in their most typical form and most free from disturbing influence, or, wherever possible, he makes experiments under conditions that assure the occurrence of the phenomenon in its normality" (Marx, 1971, xxiii).
116. Marcello Musto (2020, 3, 4) has documented just how central these questions of Russian (under)development, and the sociospatial preconditions for revolution, were for the "late" Marx, observing that "he was highly wary of transferring interpretative categories across completely different historical or geographical fields . . . Marx thought the study of new political conflicts, new themes, and geographical areas to be fundamental for this ongoing critique of the capitalist system." Musto M (2020) *The last years of Karl Marx*. Stanford, CA: Stanford University Press.
117. Sayer and Corrigan (1983); Jessop (2018).
118. Shanin (1983, 19, 15, 29, emphasis added). Marx wrote that, "*If* Russia wants to become a capitalist nation after the example of the West European countries . . . *then, once drawn into* the whirlpool of the capitalist economy, she will have to endure its inexorable laws like other profane nations" (Letter to Sorge, September 27, 1877, quoted in Sayer and Corrigan, 1983, 79, original emphasis).
119. Shanin (1983, 22).

120. Marx (1981, 792).
121. Rosenberg (2006, 318, emphasis added).
122. Crouch C, Schröder M and Voelzkow H (2009) Regional and sectoral varieties of capitalism. *Economy and Society* 38(4): 654–678, 656–657.
123. See Peck (2022b).
124. Massey (1994, 155).
125. Hodgson (2015, 388).
126. Hodgson G M (1996) Varieties of capitalism and varieties of economic theory. *Review of International Political Economy* 3(3): 380–433, 412, 414.
127. Gidwani V and Wainwright J (2014) On capital, not-capital, and development: after Kalyan Sanyal. *Economic and Political Weekly* 49(34): 40–46, 41. See also Sanyal K (2013) *Rethinking capitalist development: primitive accumulation, governmentality and postcolonial capitalism*. New Delhi: Routledge India; Anievas and Nisancioglu (2015).
128. Clarke (2017, 82; 2018, 201–202).
129. Polanyi (1959, 168).
130. See the discussion in Chapter 7.
131. Selwyn B (2011) Trotsky, Gerschenkron and the political economy of late capitalist development. *Economy and Society* 40(3): 421–450, 422.
132. Recognizing, and working with, specificity is not the same as simple disaggregation. See Massey (1995, 318). Although, for his part, Charles Tilly made the case for resisting a retreat into the study of ever-increasing number of cases along with "finer and finer comparisons," because "with the multiplication of cases and the standardization of categories for comparison the theoretical return declines more rapidly than the empirical return rises" (Tilly, 1984, 144).
133. Barber (1995, 407).
134. Lee (2017).
135. See Kasmir and Gill's intervention and the commentaries collected in Kasmir S and Gill L (2018) No smooth surfaces: the anthropology of unevenness and combination. *Current Anthropology* 59(4): 355–377.
136. See Rosenberg (2006).
137. See the further discussion in Peck (2019a).
138. Trotsky (2008 [1932], 890). Contra Sayer and Corrigan (1983), this suggests that (serious) methodological and interpretative consequences follow from the decision to begin with, and theorize from, the "classical ground" of English capitalism. Even if this was, at the time, merely a preemptive clarification for German readers of the original text, the implications ran deeper than that, as the later, "more conjunctural" Marx would surely have conceded.
139. Clarke (2018, 205). See Massey D (2017) The Soundings conjunctural projects: the challenge right now. In J Henriques and D Morley with V Goblot (eds) *Stuart Hall: conversations, projects and legacies*. London, UK: Goldsmiths Press, 86–93.
140. Sayer and Corrigan (1983, 79) defended Marx's use of such arch-models on the grounds that these were critical heuristics, "summary devices to present conclusions rather than essential tools or premises of analysis," arguments they use to refute assertions of teleology and crude evolutionism in *Capital 1*.
141. Jessop (2018, 215).
142. Wolf (2010 [1982], 73, 385).

143. Hobsbawm E (1983) The movement of capitalism. *Times Literary Supplement*, October 28: 1181–1182, 1181; Eriksen T H (2010) Foreword to the 2010 edition. In E R Wolf, *Europe and the people without history*, ix–xvii. Berkeley, CA: University of California Press, xi, ix. See also Don Kalb's commentary on the potentially disruptive notion of UCD, in response to Kasmir and Gill's "no smooth surfaces." Kalb D (2018) Trotsky versus Boas. *Current Anthropology* 59(4): 367–369.
144. Wolf (2010 [1982], 3).
145. Hecht S (2018) Europe and the people without history, by Eric Wolf. *Journal of Peasant Studies* 45(1): 220–225, 220.
146. Hobsbawm E (1983) The movement of capitalism. *Times Literary Supplement* October 28: 1181–1182, 1182.
147. Wolf (2010 [1982], 25, 391).
148. Rosenberg (2006, 322–323).
149. Callinicos, in Callinicos A and Rosenberg J (2008) Uneven and combined development: the social-relational substratum of "the international?" An exchange of letters. *Cambridge Review of International Affairs* 22(1): 77–112, 88.
150. Smith N (2006) The geography of uneven development. In B Dunn and H Radice (eds) *100 years of permanent revolution: results and prospects*. London, UK: Pluto, 180–195.
151. Trotsky (2008 [1932], 4–5). For a discussion of the "missing C" in uneven development, see Peck (2019a).
152. Allinson and Anievas (2009, 490, emphasis added).
153. Rosenberg (2006); Makki (2015).
154. Trotsky L (1969 [1928]) *The permanent revolution & results and prospects*. New York, NY: Pathfinder, 146; Makki (2015).
155. Rosenberg (2006); Allinson and Anievas (2009, 52, 54); Makki (2015).
156. Rosenberg (2006, 327).
157. For a discussion of the scaling of austerity politics, see Peck (2014).
158. See Collier S J (2012) Neoliberalism as big Leviathan, Or . . . ? A response to Wacquant and Hilgers. *Social Anthropology* 20(2): 186–195; Peck and Theodore (2012b).
159. Shanin (1983, 31).
160. Chakrabatty D (2007 [2000]) *Provincializing Europe: postcolonial thought and historical difference*. Princeton, NJ: Princeton University Press, 48.
161. See Hodgson (2015); Peck (2019b).
162. Massey (1999); Rosenberg (2006).
163. See Burawoy (2009); Crouch (2009).
164. See Fraser and Jaeggi (2018); Peck (2021).
165. Massey (1995, 310); Anievas and Nisancioglu (2015).
166. Pickles and Smith et al. (2016, 46). They clarify that this deeply contextualist conception of socioeconomic differentiation, which finds difference on the constitutive "inside" of capitalist formations, "is not an argument to see regional economies as non-capitalist, or to call for some kind of culturalist, nativist or alternative exceptionalist explanation of social and economic difference."
167. Admittedly, there are echoes here of the geological metaphor for the spatial division of labor, one that Doreen Massey always resisted on the grounds that the metaphor did not appear to allow for the agentic fluency, relational interdependencies, and combinatorial complexity she had in mind (Massey, 1995, 321). Without wishing to overburden the metaphor, however, it should be recognized that tectonics are anything but static or inert,

neither do they imply any consistent patterning, or directionality, in the movements of the "surface" layer, where the dynamics of transformative change are uneven in both spatial and temporal terms.
168. Howell C, Culpepper P D and Rueda D. (2015) On Kathleen Thelen, varieties of liberalization and the new politics of social solidarity. *Socio-Economic Review* 13(2): 399–409, 401.
169. Rossi (2012, 352).
170. Harvey D (2004) Retrospect on *The Limits to Capital*. *Antipode* 36(3): 544–549.

Chapter 10

1. See Ward K (2010) Towards a relational comparative approach to the study of cities. *Progress in Human Geography* 34(4): 471–487; Peck (2015).
2. See, especially, Shih et al. (2018) and Hart (2018b).
3. Localities were situated this way, for example, in Doreen Massey's spatial division of labor approach, which problematized how the social relations of corporate and employment regimes were being restructured, (re)divided, and reconstituted through space, and their intricate, iterative articulations with gender relations, state policies, and local politics. See Massey (1995); Hart (2018a).
4. Stuart Hall's extended project on Thatcherism and its extended aftermath, which began at a time when Britain's social settlement appeared to be "coming apart at the seams" (quoted in MacCabe, 2007: 24), represents perhaps the paradigmatic example of a conjunctural analysis, within which "crisis" was more of a protracted and multilayered condition than it was an "event." Conjunctural analyses tend to be associated with such historical moments of crisis, although there are also applications in "normal times" (see Li, 2014; Leitner and Sheppard, 2020).
5. Clarke (2019, 132).
6. Li (2014, 16–17, emphasis added).
7. Sewell W H (2008) The temporalities of capitalism. *Socio-Economic Review* 6(3): 517–537.
8. Clarke J and Cochrane A (2019) Allan Cochrane. In J Clarke, *Critical dialogues: thinking together in turbulent times*. Bristol, UK: Policy Press, 119–134, 131, emphasis added. For an especially revealing illustration of Clarke's approach, see his work on the politics of Brexit: Clarke J (2019) A sense of loss? Unsettled attachments in the current conjuncture. *New Formations* 96/97: 132–146.
9. See Peck (2019a, 2019b, 2021).
10. A useful source, while also illustrating the complex genealogy, is Koivisto and Lahtinen (2012).
11. See Clarke (2017); Grossberg (2019); Decoteau C L (2018) Conjunctures and assemblages: approaches to multicausal explanation in the human sciences. In T Rutzou and G Steinmetz (eds) *Critical realism, history, and philosophy in the social sciences*. Bingley, UK: Emerald, 89–118; Spielman D (2018) Marxism, cultural studies, and the "principle of historical specification": on the form of historical time in conjunctural analysis. *Lateral* 7.1, https://csalateral.org/issue/7-1/marxism-cultural-studies-historical-specification-conjunctural-analysis-spielman/; Jefferson T (2021) *Stuart Hall, conjunctural analysis and cultural criminology: a missed moment*. Cham: Palgrave Macmillan; Carley R F (2021) *Cultural studies methodology and political strategy: metaconjuncture*. Cham: Palgrave Macmillan.

12. For discussion and exemplification of integral modes of analysis, see Jessop and Sum (2006); Sum and Jessop (2013).
13. Stuart Hall, for his part, tended to think of conjunctures in terms of medium-term historical shifts in the social terrain, and in something resembling regulationist timescales (although he never subscribed to this school of thought per se), such as the arc of the postwar settlement in Britain, its extended decomposition, and neoliberal reconstruction. Echoing Braudel, Sewell equates conjunctural conditions with horizons of analysis that are relatively long term, running to decades, positioned between the extended rhythms of glacial or structural history on the one hand and the fleeting movement of contingent events on the other. See Hall (2007). On space, time, and Gramsci, see Jessop B (2005) Gramsci as a spatial theorist. *Critical Review of International Social and Political Philosophy* 8(4): 421–437; Kipfer S (2013) City, country, hegemony: Antonio Gramsci's spatial historicism. In M Ekers, G Hart, S Kipfer and A Loftus (eds) *Gramsci: space, nature, politics*. Oxford, UK: Wiley-Blackwell, 83–103; Sewell W (2005) *Logics of history*. Chicago, IL: University of Chicago Press.
14. Leitner and Sheppard (2020, 495).
15. Kalb D (2011) Headlines of nation, subtexts of class: working class populism and the return of the repressed in neoliberal Europe. In D Kalb and G Halmai (eds) *Headlines of nation, subtexts of class*. New York, NY: Berghahn Books, 1–36, 11–12. See also Kalb D and Tak H (2006) (eds) *Critical junctions: anthropology and history beyond the cultural turn*. New York, NY: Berghahn Books.
16. On the politics of scale, see Swyngedouw E (2000) Authoritarian governance, power, and the politics of rescaling. *Environment and Planning D: Society and Space* 18(1): 63–76; Brenner N (1999) Beyond state-centrism? Space, territoriality, and geographical scale in globalization studies. *Theory and Society* 28(1): 39–78; Leitner H and Miller B (2007) Scale and the limitations of ontological debate: a commentary on Marston, Jones and Woodward. *Transactions of the Institute of British Geographers* 32(1): 116–125. See also Peck (2002).
17. See Hart (2002, 2004, 2018b).
18. See Peck (2012b); Barnes and Christophers (2018). See also the discussion in Chapters 2, 3, and 7.
19. See Swanson G E (1971) Frameworks for comparative research: structural anthropology and the theory of action. In I Vallier (ed) *Comparative methods in sociology*. Berkeley, CA: University of California Press, 141–202; Steinmetz G (2004) Odious comparisons: incommensurability, the case study, and "small N's" in sociology. *Sociological Theory* 22(3): 371–400; Ragin C (1987) *The comparative method*. Berkeley, CA: University of California Press; Abu-Lughod J (1975) The legitimacy of comparisons in comparative urban studies: a theoretical position and an application to North African cities. *Urban Affairs Review* 11(1): 13–35; Ward K (2008) Toward a comparative (re)turn in urban studies? Some reflections. *Urban Geography* 29(5): 405–410; McFarlane C (2010) The comparative city: knowledge, learning, urbanism, *International Journal of Urban and Regional Research* 34(4): 725–742; Jacobs J M (2012) Comparing comparative urbanisms. *Urban Geography* 33(6): 904–914; Robinson J (2016) Comparative urbanism: new geographies and cultures of theorizing the urban. *International Journal of Urban and Regional Research* 40(1): 187–199; Peck (2015); Lawson (1997).
20. Tilly (1984, 82–83).
21. Tilly (1984, 125, emphasis added).
22. See Wolf (1982); McMichael (1990).

23. Tomich D (1994) Small islands and huge comparisons: Caribbean plantations, historical unevenness, and capitalist modernity. *Social Science History* 18(3): 339–358, 340; Tomich D W (2004) *Through the prism of slavery: labor, capital, and world economy*. Lanham, MD: Rowman & Littlefield.
24. Ekers M, Kipfer S and Loftus A (2020) On articulation, translation, and populism: Gillian Hart's postcolonial Marxism. *Annals of the American Association of Geographers* 110(5): 1577–1593, 1583.
25. Hart (2006, 996).
26. See Coronil F (2000) Towards a critique of globalcentrism: speculations on capitalism's nature. *Public Culture* 12(2): 351–374; Mignolo W D (2012) *Local histories/global designs: coloniality, subaltern knowledges, and border thinking*. Princeton, NJ: Princeton University Press; Hart (2018b).
27. Hart (2018b, 374, emphasis added).
28. For Gramsci, this involved constructing a path between economic essentialism ("economism") and what he called "ideologism," defined as an exaggerated sense of voluntaristic agency. See Koivisto and Lahtinen (2012).
29. Hart (2006, 996).
30. Hart (2018b, 374–375).
31. McMichael (1990, 336, original emphasis). See also McFarlane C and Robinson J (2012) Introduction—experiments in comparative urbanism. *Urban Geography* 33(6): 765–773; Peck (2015).
32. Tilly (1984, 125); McMichael (1990, 388–389).
33. Burawoy et al. (2000); Burawoy (2009).
34. See Sayer (1991, 2010); Massey (1995).
35. See Sayer (1985); Lawson (1997).
36. Shih et al. (2018, 220, 210). See also Shih S (2013) Comparison as relation. In R Felski and S S Friedman (eds) *Comparison: theories, approaches, uses*. Baltimore, MD: Johns Hopkins University Press, 79–98.
37. See Shih S (2016) Theory in a relational world. *Comparative Literature Studies* 53(4): 722–746.
38. Shih et al. (2018, 212).
39. Shih S (2015) World studies and relational comparison. *PMLA* 130(2): 430–438, 437, 435; Robinson J (2016) Comparative urbanism: new geographies and cultures of theorizing the urban. *International Journal of Urban and Regional Research* 40(1): 187–199.
40. Subrahmanyam S (2005) *Explorations in connected history*. New Delhi: Oxford University Press, 3.
41. Shih et al. (2018, 209, 211, emphasis added).
42. Hart (2002, 167, 168, 170).
43. Hart (2002, 295–298).
44. See Chapter 9 on the differences between Harvey's and Massey's approaches to UCD.
45. Hart (2002, 311; 2018b, 375–376).
46. Hart (2006, 982).
47. Hart (2004, 97).
48. Sayer (1991, 302).
49. Sayer (1991, 302).
50. See Massey (1995); Peck et al. (2018).

51. See Burawoy (2009); Hart (2018a); Sayer A (2018) Ontology and the politics of space. In M Werner, J Peck, R Lave and B Christophers (eds) *Doreen Massey: critical dialogues*. Newcastle upon Tyne, UK: Agenda, 103–112.
52. Steinmetz G (2004) Odious comparisons: incommensurability, the case study, and "small N's" in sociology. *Sociological Theory* 22(3): 371–400.
53. Lawson (1997, 204) states, "A demi-regularity, or *demi-reg* for short, is precisely a partial event regularity which *prima facie* indicates the occasional, but less than universal, actualization of a mechanism or tendency, over a definite region of time-space." See also Jessop B (2005) Critical realism and the strategic relational approach. *New Formations* 56: 40–53.
54. Tomich D (1994) Small islands and huge comparisons: Caribbean plantations, historical unevenness, and capitalist modernity. *Social Science History* 18(3): 339–358, 343.
55. See Hall (1988a); Grossberg (2019). Larry Grossberg (2019: 40) has reflected, "I realised that I did not have, and I could not find anywhere . . . a well-theorised understanding of how conjunctural analysis is to be done, and how a conjuncture is defined or constituted."
56. Hall (1988a, 162).
57. Grossberg (2019, 42).
58. Gilbert (2019, 5).
59. Clarke (2018); Grossberg (2019).
60. Hall (1986).
61. Burawoy (2009).
62. Burawoy M (1998) The extended case method. *Sociological Theory* 16(1): 4–33, 13.
63. See Brenner et al. (2010), and the further discussion in Chapter 4.
64. Koivisto and Lahtinen (2012, 276).
65. "A common error in historico-politico analysis," Gramsci wrote, is "presenting causes as immediately operative which in fact only operate indirectly, or . . . asserting that the immediate causes are the only effective ones" (quoted in Koivisto and Lahtinen, 2012, 270).
66. Clarke (2019, 132).
67. Hall S, Critcher C, Jefferson T, Clarke J, and Roberts B (1978) *Policing the crisis*. London, UK: Macmillan.
68. Gilbert (2019, 15).
69. Pickles and Smith et al. (2016, 43).
70. Clarke (2018, 203, original emphasis).
71. See Peck et al. (2018).
72. Hall, quoted in MacCabe (2007, 41–42); Grossberg (2019, 46). See also Davis A (2019) Failure is always an option: the necessity, promise and peril of radical contextualism. *Cultural Studies* 33(1): 46–56.
73. Grossberg (2019, 47–48).
74. Grossberg (2019, 51).
75. See the discussion in Grossberg (2007, 107–111).
76. Massey D (2014) The Kilburn manifesto: after neoliberalism? *Environment and Planning A* 46(9): 2034–2041, 2034.
77. As Hall explained, the Kilburn manifesto represented a strategic intervention, predicated on an analysis of the political-economic situation of the United Kingdom, in the context of post-financial crisis patterns of restructuring in capitalism and the late-neoliberal malaise in British politics: "We must set about disrupting the current common sense. . . . This is a moment for challenging, not adapting to, neoliberalism's new reality, and for making a leap." Hall S (2013) The neoliberal victory must be challenged. *Guardian*, April 24, 30.

See also Hall S, Massey D and Rustin M (2015) *After neoliberalism? The Kilburn manifesto*. London, UK: Lawrence and Wishart.
78. According to Gramsci, "A conjuncture may be defined as the set of circumstances which determine the market at a given phase of these circumstances if these circumstances, however, are conceived of as in movement" (quoted in Koivisto and Lahtinen, 2012, 269).
79. Foster-Carter A (1978) The modes of production controversy. *New Left Review* 107: 47–77, 54; Hall S (2021 [1980]) Race, articulation and societies structured in dominance. In P Gilroy and R W Gilmore (eds) *Stuart Hall: selected writings on race and difference*. Durham, NC: Duke University Press, 195–245, 220, emphasis added.
80. Massey D (2014) The Kilburn manifesto: after neoliberalism? *Environment and Planning A* 46(9): 2034–2041, 2035.
81. Grossberg (2019, 52). See also Pickles and Smith et al. (2016, 43).
82. Grossberg (2019, 52, 42).
83. For her part, Hart (2004, 14, emphasis added) explains that, "I *start from* the question of how [sites, places, events, cases] are formed in relation to one another and to a larger whole."
84. Gilbert (2019, 8).
85. Grossberg (2019, 56).
86. Clarke (2019, 146). See also Clarke (2017); Grossberg (2019, 38); and Leitner and Sheppard (2020, 499). Leitner and Sheppard write that "conjunctural analysis is extremely ambitious and conjunctural comparison even more so. The latter requires deep familiarity and engagement with multiple places and their geohistorical, cultural and biophysical contexts, in addition to familiarity with larger-scale processes, connectivities and path dependence. This typically exceeds the expertise and scope of any single scholar. Conjunctural comparison thus necessitates convening teams of scholars who collectively bring the necessary range of knowledge and expertise to the project, while negotiating the politics of difference that inevitably emerge within such teams."
87. Clarke (2018, 201).
88. Hall and Massey (2010, 59).
89. See Clarke (2018); Grossberg (2019).
90. Grossberg (2007, 109) declares that "conjunctures are largely constituted as national formations [while being] deeply and increasingly articulated into and by international, transnational and global practices, relations, processes and institutions."
91. Doreen Massey's (2007) *World City* might be considered a model of sorts, although again the text is not as methodologically reflexive as it might have been. For a discussion of conjunctural approaches in urban and regional studies, see Peck (2017a) and Leitner and Sheppard (2020).
92. Roy A (2016) Who's afraid of postcolonial urban theory? *International Journal of Urban and Regional Research* 40(1): 200–209, 206.
93. See Dear M (2005) Comparative urbanism. *Urban Geography* 26(3): 247–251; compare the discussion of collaborative approaches in Leitner and Sheppard (2020).
94. Leitner and Sheppard (2020, 496, emphasis added).
95. Li (2014, 9, emphasis added). See also the discussion in Sheppard et al. (2020).
96. See Hall and Massey (2010); Grossberg (2019).
97. Lawson (1997, 209).
98. Ollman B (2003) *Dance of the dialectic*. Urbana: University of Illinois Press, 19.
99. Pickles and Smith et al. (2016, 48).

100. See Burawoy (2009).
101. Hall (1986, 6); Hall, quoted in Koivisto and Lahtinen (2012, 274).
102. Hall (2018 [2007], 310).
103. Paige J M (1999) Conjuncture, comparison, and conditional theory in macrosocial inquiry. *American Journal of Sociology* 105(3): 781–800, 798.
104. Grossberg L (2015) Learning from Stuart Hall, following the path with heart. *Cultural Studies* 29(1): 3–11, 8, 7. See also Roman L G (2015) Conjunctural thinking—"pessimism of the intellect, optimism of the will": Lawrence Grossberg remembers Stuart Hall. *Discourse* 36(2): 185–199, 192; Peck (2017a).

Bibliography

Adaman F and Madra Y M (2002) Theorizing the "third sphere": a critique of the persistence of the "economistic fallacy." *Journal of Economic Issues* 36(4): 1045–1078.
Aglietta M (1979) *A theory of capitalist regulation: the US Experience*. London, UK: Verso.
Ah Mat R (2003) The moral case for Indigenous capitalism. Paper presented at the Native Title conference, Australian Institute of Aboriginal and Torres Strait Islander Studies and Central Land Council, Alice Springs, NT, June 3–5.
Albert M (1993) *Capitalism vs. capitalism*. London, UK: Whurr.
Allinson J C and Anievas A (2009) The uses and misuses of uneven and combined development: an anatomy of a concept. *Cambridge Review of International Affairs* 22(1): 47–67.
Altman J (2007) The Indigenous hybrid economy: a realistic sustainable option for remote communities? *CAEPR Topical Issue* No. 2, Centre for Aboriginal Economic Policy Research, Australian National University, Canberra.
Altman J (2009) *Beyond closing the gap*. Centre for Aboriginal Economic Policy Research, Australian National University, Canberra, ACT.
Altman J (2010) What future for Indigenous Australia? Economic hybridity and the neoliberal turn. In J Altman and M Hinkson (eds) *Culture crisis*. Sydney, NSW: UNSW Press, 259–280.
Altman J (2012) Indigenous rights, mining corporations, and the Australian state. In S Sawyer and E T Gomez (eds) *The politics of resource extraction*. Basingstoke, UK: Palgrave Macmillan, 46–74.
Altman J and Hinkson M (2010) Very risky business: the quest to normalise remote Aboriginal Australia. In G Marston, J Moss, and J Quiggin (eds) *Risk, responsibility and the welfare state*. Melbourne, VIC: Melbourne University Press, 185–211.
Amable B (2003) *The diversity of modern capitalism*. Oxford, UK: Oxford University Press.
Anievas A and Nisancioglu K (2015) *How the West came to rule: the geopolitical origins of capitalism*. London, UK: Pluto Press.
Arrighi G (2007) *Adam Smith in Beijing*. London, UK: Verso.
Barber B (1977) Absolutization of the market: some notes on how we got from there to here. In D Dworkin, G Bermaut and P Brown (eds) *Markets and morals*. Washington, DC: Hemisphere, 15–31.
Barber B (1995) All economies are "embedded": the career of a concept, and beyond. *Social Research* 62(2): 387–413.
Barnes T J (1996) *Logics of dislocation: models, metaphors and meanings of economic space*. New York, NY: Guilford Press.
Barnes T J and Christophers B (2018) *Economic geography: a critical introduction*. Oxford, UK: Wiley-Blackwell.
Barnes T J, Peck J, Sheppard E, and Tickell A (2007) Methods matter: transformations in economic geography. In Tickell A, Sheppard E, Peck J and Barnes T J (eds) *Politics and practice in economic geography*. London, UK: Sage, 1–24.
Barnes T J and Sheppard E (2010) "Nothing includes everything": towards engaged pluralism in Anglophone economic geography. *Progress in Human Geography* 34(2): 193–214.
Block F (1990) *Postindustrial possibilities: a critique of economic discourse*. Berkeley, CA: University of California Press.
Block F (2000) Deconstructing capitalism as a system. *Rethinking Marxism* 12(3): 83–98.

Block F (2002) Rethinking capitalism. In N W Biggart (ed) *Readings in economic sociology*. Oxford, UK: Blackwell, 219–230.
Block F (2003) Karl Polanyi and the writing of "The great transformation." *Theory and Society* 32(3): 1–32.
Block F (2012) Varieties of what? Should we still be using the concept of capitalism? In J Go (ed) *Political power and social theory* 23. Bingley, UK: Emerald, 269–291.
Block F, Somers M R (1984) Beyond the economistic fallacy: the holistic social science of Karl Polanyi. In T Skocpol (ed) *Vision and method in historical sociology*. Cambridge, UK: Cambridge University Press, 47–84.
Block F and Somers M R (2014) *The power of market fundamentalism: Karl Polanyi's critique*. Cambridge, MA: Harvard University Press.
Blyth M (2003) Same as it never was: temporality and typology in the varieties of capitalism. *Comparative European Politics* 1(2): 215–225.
Blyth M (2013) *Austerity: the history of a dangerous idea*. New York, NY: Oxford University Press.
Bohle D and Greskovits B (2009) Varieties of capitalism and capitalism "tout court." *European Journal of Sociology/Archives Européennes de Sociologie* 50(3): 355–386.
Bourdieu P (1998) *Acts of resistance*. Cambridge, UK: Polity.
Boyer R (1990) *The regulation school: a critical introduction*. New York, NY: Columbia University Press.
Boyer R (2000) The political in the era of globalization and finance: focus on some *régulation* school research. *International Journal of Urban and Regional Research* 24(2): 274–322.
Boyer R (2005) How and why capitalisms differ. *Economy and Society* 34(4): 509–557.
Boyer R and Hollingsworth J R (1997) From national embeddedness to spatial and institutional nestedness. In J R Hollingsworth and R Boyer (eds) *Contemporary capitalism: the embeddedness of institutions*. Cambridge, UK: Cambridge University Press, 433–484.
Brealey T B (1980) Popular myths and folklore concerning planning in new mining towns in Australia. *Man-Environment Systems* 10(3–4): 146–152.
Brenner N (2004) *New state spaces: urban governance and the rescaling of statehood*. Oxford, UK: Oxford University Press.
Brenner N (2019) *New urban spaces: urban theory and the scale question*. Oxford, UK: Oxford University Press.
Brenner N, Peck J and Theodore N (2010) Variegated neoliberalization: Geographies, modalities, pathways. *Global Networks* 10(2): 182–222.
Brenner N and Theodore N (2002) Cities and the geographies of "actually existing neoliberalism." In N Brenner and N Theodore (eds) *Spaces of neoliberalism: urban restructuring in North America and Western Europe*. Oxford, UK: Blackwell, 2–32.
Bruff I, Ebenau M, and May C (2015) Fault or fracture? The impact of new directions in comparative capitalisms research on the wider field. In M Ebenau, I Bruff, and C May (eds) *New directions in comparative capitalisms research*. London, UK: Palgrave Macmillan, 28–44.
Buckley K and Wheelwright T (1988) *No paradise for workers*. Melbourne, VIC: Oxford University Press.
Burawoy M (1985) *The politics of production: factory regimes under capitalism and socialism*. London, UK: Verso.
Burawoy M (2003) For a sociological Marxism: the complementary convergence of Antonio Gramsci and Karl Polanyi. *Politics and Society* 31(2): 193–261.
Burawoy M (2009) *The extended case method*. Berkeley, CA: University of California Press.
Burawoy M, Blum J A, George S, Gille Z, Gowan T, Haney L, Klawitter M, Lopez S, Riain S O and Thayer M (2000) *Global ethnography*. Berkeley, CA: University of California Press.
Cahill D (2012) The embedded neoliberal economy In D Cahill, L Edwards and F Stilwell (eds) *Neoliberalism: beyond the free market*. Cheltenham, UK: Edward Elgar, 110–127.

Cangiani M (2011) Karl Polanyi's institutional theory: market society and its "disembedded" economy. *Journal of Economic Issues* 45(1): 177–198.

Chu Y and So A Y (2010) State neoliberalism: the Chinese road to capitalism. In Y Chu (ed) *Chinese capitalisms: historical emergence and political implications*. Basingstoke, UK: Palgrave Macmillan, 73–99.

Clarke J (2017) Doing the dirty work: the challenges of conjunctural analysis. In J Henriques and D Morley with V Goblot (eds) *Stuart Hall: conversations, projects and legacies*. London, UK: Goldsmiths Press, 79–85.

Clarke J (2018) Finding place in the conjuncture: a dialogue with Doreen. In M Werner, J Peck, R Lave, and B Christophers (eds) *Doreen Massey: critical dialogues*. Newcastle upon Tyne, UK: Agenda, 201–213.

Clarke J (2019) A sense of loss? Unsettled attachments in the current conjuncture. *New Formations* 96/97: 132–146.

Cleary P (2011) *Too much luck*. Melbourne, VIC: Black.

Coates D (2000) *Models of capitalism: growth and stagnation in the modern era*. Cambridge, UK: Polity Press.

Coates D (2005a) Paradigms of explanation. In D Coates (ed) *Varieties of capitalism, varieties of approaches*. Basingstoke, UK: Palgrave, 1–25.

Coates D (ed) (2005b) *Varieties of capitalism, varieties of approaches*. Basingstoke, UK: Palgrave.

Coates D (2015) Varieties of capitalism and "the great moderation." In M Ebenau, I Bruff and C May (eds) *New directions in comparative capitalisms research*. London, UK: Palgrave Macmillan, 11–27

Coe N M and Yeung H (2015) *Global production networks*. Oxford, UK: Oxford University Press.

Collier S J (2012) Neoliberalism as big Leviathan, or . . . ? A response to Wacquant and Hilgers. *Social Anthropology/Anthropologie Sociale* 20(2): 186–195.

Coser L A (1984) *Refugee scholars in America*. New Haven, CT: Yale University Press.

Crouch C (2005) *Capitalist diversity and change: recombinant governance and institutional entrepreneurs*. Oxford, UK: Oxford University Press.

Crouch C (2009) Typologies of capitalism. In B Hancké (ed) *Debating varieties of capitalism*. Oxford, UK: Oxford University Press, 75–94.

Crouch C (2011) *The strange non-death of neoliberalism*. Cambridge, UK: Polity.

Dale G (2010) *Karl Polanyi: the limits of the market*. Cambridge, UK: Polity.

Dale G (2016) *Karl Polanyi: a life on the left*. New York, NY: Columbia University Press.

Dalton G (1965) Primitive, archaic, and modern economies: Karl Polanyi's contribution to economic anthropology and comparative economy. In J Helm, P Bohannan and M Sahlins (eds) *Essays in economic anthropology*. Seattle, WA: University of Washington and American Ethnological Society, 1–24.

Dawes S and Peck J (2020) Contextualizing neoliberalism: an interview with Jamie Peck. In S Dawes and M Lenormand (eds) *Neoliberalism in context: governance, subjectivity and knowledge*. Cham: Palgrave Macmillan, 289–309.

Dean M (2012) Free economy, strong state. In D Cahill, L Edwards and F Stilwell (eds) *Neoliberalism: beyond the free market*. Cheltenham, UK: Edward Elgar, 69–89.

Deans P (2004) The People's Republic of China: the post-socialist developmental state. In L Low (ed) *Developmental states: relevancy, redundancy or reconfiguration?* New York, NY: Nova, 133–146.

Deeg R and Jackson G (2007) Towards a more dynamic theory of capitalist variety. *Socio-Economic Review* 5(1): 149–179.

Dicken P, Peck J and Tickell A (1997) Unpacking the global. In R Lee and J Wills (eds) *Geographies of economies*. London, UK: Arnold, 158–166.

Dickson B J (2003) *Red capitalists in China*. New York, NY: Cambridge University Press.

Dickson B J (2008) *Wealth into power: the Communist Party's embrace of China's private sector.* New York, NY: Cambridge University Press.
Dore R (1986) *Flexible rigidities: industrial policy and structural adjustment in the Japanese economy, 1970–1980.* London, UK: Athlone Press.
Dow S C (2000) Prospects for the progress of heterodox economics. *Journal of the History of Economic Thought* 22(2): 157–170.
Ellem B (2017) *The Pilbara: from the deserts profits come.* Crawley, WA: UWAP Scholarly.
Evans P (1995) *Embedded autonomy: states and industrial transformation.* Princeton, NJ: Princeton University Press.
Fewsmith J (2008) *China since Tiananmen: from Deng Xiaoping to Hu Jintao.* Cambridge, UK: Cambridge University Press.
Fligstein N (2001) *The architecture of markets: economic sociology of twenty-first century societies.* Princeton, NJ: Princeton University Press.
Fligstein N and Zhang J (2011) A new agenda for research on the trajectory of Chinese capitalism. *Management and Organization Review* 7(1): 39–62.
Foucault M (2008) *The birth of biopolitics.* Basingstoke, UK: Palgrave.
Fourcade M, Ollion E and Algan Y (2015) The superiority of economists. *Journal of Economic Perspectives* 29(1): 89–114.
Fraser N and Jaeggi R (2018) *Capitalism: a conversation in critical theory.* Cambridge, UK: Polity.
Friedman T L (2005) *The world is flat: a brief history of the twenty-first century.* New York, NY: Farrar, Straus, and Giroux.
Gemici K (2008) Karl Polanyi and the antinomies of embeddedness. *Socio-Economic Review* 6(1): 5–33.
Gertler M S (2004) *Manufacturing culture: the institutional geography of industrial practice.* Oxford, UK: Oxford University Press.
Gibson-Graham J-K (1996) *The end of capitalism (as we knew it): a feminist critique of political economy.* Oxford, UK: Blackwell.
Gibson-Graham J-K (2006) *A postcapitalist politics.* Minneapolis: University of Minnesota Press.
Gibson-Graham J-K (2008) Diverse economies: performative practices for "other worlds." *Progress in Human Geography* 32(5): 613–632.
Gilbert J (2019) This conjuncture: for Stuart Hall. *New Formations* 96: 5–37.
Gordon D M, Edwards R and Reich M (1982) *Segmented work, divided workers: the historical transformation of labor in the United States.* New York, NY: Cambridge University Press.
Granovetter M (1985) Economic action and social structure: the problem of embeddedness. *American Journal of Sociology* 91(3): 481–510.
Granovetter M (1990) The old and the new economic sociology: a history and an agenda. In R Friedland and A F Robertson (eds) *Beyond the marketplace: rethinking economy and society.* New York, NY: Aldine de Gruyter, 89–112.
Granovetter M (2002) A theoretical agenda for economic sociology. In M F Guillén, R Collins, P England and M Meyer (eds) *The new economic sociology: developments in an emerging field.* New York, NY: Russell Sage Foundation, 35–60.
Gregory D and Urry J (eds) (1985) *Social relations and spatial structures.* Basingstoke, UK: Macmillan.
Grossberg L (2007) Stuart Hall on race and racism: cultural studies and the practice of contextualism. In B Meeks (ed) *Culture, politics, race and diaspora: the thought of Stuart Hall.* Kinston, Jamaica: Ian Randle, 98–119.
Grossberg L (2019) Cultural Studies in search of a method, or looking for conjunctural analysis. *New Formations* 96/97: 38–68.
Gudeman S (2001) *The anthropology of economy.* Oxford, UK: Wiley-Blackwell.

Hall P A and Gingerich D W (2009) Varieties of capitalism and institutional complementarities in the political economy: an empirical analysis. *British Journal of Political Science* 39(3): 449–482.
Hall P A and Soskice D (2001) An introduction to varieties of capitalism. In P A Hall and D Soskice (eds) *Varieties of capitalism: the institutional foundations of comparative advantage.* Oxford, UK: Oxford University Press, 1–68.
Hall P A and Soskice D (2003) Varieties of capitalism and institutional change: a response to three critics. *Comparative European Politics* 1(2): 241–250.
Hall P A and Thelen K (2009) Institutional change in varieties of capitalism. *Socio-Economic Review* 7(1): 7–34.
Hall S (1986) Gramsci's relevance for the study of race and ethnicity. *Journal of Communication Inquiry* 10(2): 5–27.
Hall S (1988a) *The hard road to renewal: Thatcherism and the crisis of the Left.* London, UK: Verso.
Hall S (1988b) The toad in the garden: Thatcherism among the theorists. In C Nelson and L Grossberg (eds) *Marxism and the interpretation of culture.* Urbana: University of Illinois Press, 35–57.
Hall S (1991a) Old and new identities, old and new ethnicities. In A D King (ed) *Culture, globalization and the world-system.* Basingstoke, UK: Macmillan, 41–68.
Hall S (1991b) The local and the global: globalization and ethnicity. In A D King (ed) *Culture, globalization and the world-system.* Basingstoke, UK: Macmillan, 19–39.
Hall S (2003a) Marx's notes on method: a "reading" of the "1857 Introduction." *Cultural Studies* 17(2): 113–149.
Hall S (2003b) New Labour's double shuffle. *Soundings* 24: 10–24.
Hall S (2011) The neo-liberal revolution. *Cultural Studies* 25(6): 705–728.
Hall S (2018 [2007]) Through the prism of an intellectual life. In D Morley (ed) *Stuart Hall: essential essays*, Volume 2. Durham, NC: Duke University Press, 301–324.
Hall S and Massey D (2010) Interpreting the crisis. *Soundings* 44: 57–71.
Halperin R H (1984) Polanyi, Marx, and the institutional paradigm in economic anthropology. In B L Isaac (ed) *Research in economic anthropology*, Volume 6. Greenwich, CT: JAI Press, 245–272.
Halperin R H (1994) *Cultural economies past and present.* Austin: University of Texas Press.
Hancké B (2009) Beyond varieties of capitalism. In B Hancké (ed) *Debating varieties of capitalism.* Oxford, UK: Oxford University Press, 1–17.
Hancké B, Rhodes M and Thatcher M (2009) Beyond varieties of capitalism. In B Hancké (ed) *Debating varieties of capitalism.* Oxford, UK: Oxford University Press, 273–300.
Hann C and Hart K (2011) *Economic anthropology: history, ethnography, culture.* Cambridge, UK: Cambridge University Press.
Hanson S and Pratt G (1995) *Gender, work, and space.* New York, NY: Routledge
Hart G (2002) *Disabling globalization.* Berkeley, CA: University of California Press.
Hart G (2004) Geography and development: critical ethnographies. *Progress in Human Geography* 28(1): 91–100.
Hart G (2006) Denaturalizing dispossession: critical ethnography in the age of resurgent imperialism. *Antipode* 38(5): 977–1004.
Hart G (2018a) Becoming a geographer: Massey moments in a spatial education. In M Werner, J Peck, R Lave and B Christophers (eds) *Doreen Massey: critical dialogues.* Newcastle upon Tyne, UK: Agenda, 75–88.
Hart G (2018b) Relational comparison revisited: Marxist postcolonial geographies in practice. *Progress in Human Geography* 42(3): 371–394.
Harvey D (1982) *The limits to capital.* Oxford, UK: Basil Blackwell.
Harvey D (2005) *A brief history of neoliberalism.* Oxford, UK: Oxford University Press.

Harvey D (2006) *Spaces of global capitalism: a theory of uneven geographical development*. London, UK: Verso.
Herod A (ed) (1998) *Organizing the landscape: geographical perspectives on labor unionism*. Minneapolis, MN: University of Minnesota Press.
Herod A (2001) *Labor geographies: workers and the landscapes of capitalism*. New York, NY: Guilford Press.
Hess M (1994) Black and red: the Pilbara pastoral workers' strike 1946. *Aboriginal History* 18(1): 65–83.
Hirsch P, Michaels S, and Friedman R (1987) "Dirty hands" versus "clean models": is sociology in danger of being seduced by economics? *Theory and Society* 16(3): 317–336.
Hodgson G M (1984) *The democratic economy: a new look at planning, markets and power*. Harmondsworth, UK: Penguin.
Hodgson G M (2015) *Conceptualizing capitalism: institutions, evolution, future*. Chicago, IL: University of Chicago Press.
Holcombe S (2006) Early indigenous engagement with mining in the Pilbara: lessons from a historical perspective. *CAEPR Working Paper 24/2004*, Centre for Aboriginal Economic Policy Research, Australian National University, Canberra, ACT.
Holcombe S (2010) Sustainable Aboriginal livelihoods and the Pilbara mining boom. In I Keen (ed) *Indigenous participation in Australian economies*. Canberra, ACT: ANU E Press, 141–164.
Hollingsworth J R and Boyer R (1997) Coordination of economic actors and social systems of production. In J R Hollingsworth and R Boyer (eds) *Contemporary capitalism: the embeddedness of institutions*. Cambridge, UK: Cambridge University Press, 1–48.
Howell C (2003) Varieties of capitalism: and then there was one? *Comparative Politics* 36(1): 103–124.
Howell J (2006) Reflections on the Chinese state. *Development and Change* 37(2): 273–297.
Howitt R (1989) Resource development and Aborigines: the case of Roebourne 1960–1980. *Australian Geographical Studies* 27(2): 155–169.
Hsing Y (1998) *Making capitalism in China*. New York, NY: Oxford University Press.
Hsing Y (2010) *The great urban transformation: politics of land and property in China*. Oxford, UK: Oxford University Press.
Huang Y (2008) *Capitalism with Chinese characteristics: entrepreneurship and the state*. New York, NY: Cambridge University Press.
Humphreys S C (1969) History, economics, and anthropology: the work of Karl Polanyi. *History and Theory* 8(2): 165–212.
Isaac B L (2005) Karl Polanyi. In J G Carrier (ed) *A handbook of economic anthropology*. Cheltenham, UK: Edward Elgar, 1–25.
Jackson G and Deeg R (2006) How many varieties of capitalism? Comparing the comparative institutional analyses of capitalist diversity. *MPIfG Discussion Paper* 06/2, Max Planck Institute for the Study of Societies, Cologne, Germany.
Jessop B (1990) Regulation theories in retrospect and prospect. *Economy and Society* 19(2): 153–216.
Jessop B (2000) The crisis of the national spatio-temporal fix and the tendential ecological dominance of globalizing capitalism. *International Journal of Urban and Regional Research* 24(2): 323–360.
Jessop B (2012) Rethinking the diversity and variability of capitalism: on variegated capitalism in the world market. In G Wood and C Lane (eds) *Capitalist diversity and diversity within capitalism*. London, UK: Routledge, 209–237.
Jessop B (2015) Comparative capitalisms and/or variegated capitalism. In M Ebenau, I Bruff, and C May (eds) *New directions in comparative capitalisms research*. London, UK: Palgrave Macmillan, 65–82.

Jessop B (2018) The world market, "North-South" relations, and neoliberalism. *Alternative Routes* 29: 207–228.
Jessop B and Sum N L (2006) *Beyond the regulation approach: putting capitalist economies in their place*. Cheltenham, UK: Edward Elgar.
Kalb D (2012) Thinking about neoliberalism as if the crisis was actually happening. *Social Anthropology/Anthropologie Sociale* 20(3): 318–330.
Kingfisher K and Maskovsky J (2008) Introduction: the limits of neoliberalism. *Critique of Anthropology* 28(2): 115–126.
Koivisto J and Lahtinen M (2012) Conjuncture, politico-historical. *Historical Materialism* 20(1): 267–277.
Kornai J (2009) Socialism and the market: conceptual clarification. In J Kornai and Y Qian (eds) *Market and socialism*. Basingstoke, UK: Palgrave Macmillan, 11–24.
Krippner G R (2001) The elusive market: embeddedness and the paradigm of economic sociology. *Theory and Society* 30(6): 775–810.
Krippner G, Granovetter M, Block F, Biggart N, Beamish T, Hsing Y, Arrighi G, Mendell M, Hall J, Burawoy M, Vogel S and O'Riain S (2004) Polanyi symposium: a conversation on embeddedness. *Socio-Economic Review* 2(1): 109–135.
Lane D (2007) Post-state socialism: a diversity of capitalisms. In D Lane and M Myant (eds) *Varieties of capitalism in post-communist countries*. Basingstoke, UK: Palgrave Macmillan, 13–39.
Langton M and Mazel O (2012) The "resource curse" compared: Australian Aboriginal participation in the resource extraction industry and distribution of impacts. In M Langton and J Longbottom (eds) *Community futures, legal architecture*. New York, NY: Routledge, 23–44.
Latour B (2007) *Reassembling the social*. New York, NY: Oxford University Press.
Lawson T (1997) *Economics and reality*. London, UK: Routledge.
Lawson T (2015) *The nature and state of modern economics*. London, UK: Routledge.
Lee C K (2017) *The specter of global China*. Chicago: University of Chicago Press.
Leitner H and Sheppard E (2020) Towards an epistemology for conjunctural inter-urban comparison. *Cambridge Journal of Regions, Economy and Society* 13(3): 491–508.
Li T M (2014) *Land's end: capitalist relations on an indigenous frontier*. Durham, NC: Duke University Press.
Lie J (1991) Embedding Polanyi's market society. *Sociological Perspectives* 34(2): 219–235.
Liew L H (2005) China's engagement with neo-liberalism: path dependency, geography and party self-reinvention. *Journal of Development Studies* 41(2): 331–352.
Lipietz A (1987) *Mirages and miracles: the crises of Global Fordism*. London, UK: New Left Books.
Löfving S (2005) Introduction: peopled economies. In S Löfving (ed) *Peopled economies: conversations with Stephen Gudeman*. Uppsala, Sweden: Interface, 1–28.
Lovering J (1989) The restructuring debate. In R Peet and N J Thrift (eds) *New models in geography*, Volume 1. London, UK: Unwin Hyman, 198–223.
MacCabe C (2007) An interview with Stuart Hall, December 2007. *Critical Quarterly* 50(1–2): 12–42.
Makki F (2015) Reframing development theory: the significance of the idea of uneven and combined development. *Theory and Society* 44(5): 471–497.
Marx K (1971) Preface to the first German edition. In K Marx *Capital*, Volume 1. German edition. London, UK: Lawrence and Wishart, 5–7.
Marx K (1973) *Grundrisse*. New York, NY: Vintage.
Marx K (1976) *Capital*, Volume 1. Harmondsworth, UK: Penguin.
Marx K (1981) *Capital*, Volume 3. Harmondsworth, UK: Penguin.
Massey D (1984) *Spatial divisions of labour: social structures and the geography of production*. London, UK: Methuen.

Massey D (1991a) A global sense of place. *Marxism Today* June: 24–29.
Massey D (1991b) The political place of locality studies. *Environment and Planning A* 23(2): 267–281.
Massey D (1994) *Space, place and gender*. Cambridge, UK: Polity.
Massey D (1995) *Spatial divisions of labour: social structures and the geography of production*, 2nd edition. Basingstoke, UK: Macmillan.
Massey D (1999) *Power-geometries and the politics of space-time*. Heidelberg: University of Heidelberg, Germany.
Massey D (2007) *World city*. Oxford, UK: Wiley.
Massey D and Allen J (eds) (1988) *Uneven re-development*. London, UK: Hodder and Stoughton.
McDowell L (1997) *Capital culture: gender at work in the City*. Oxford, UK: Wiley.
McDowell L (2011) *Redundant masculinities: employment change and white working class youth*. Oxford, UK: John Wiley & Sons.
McLeod D (1984) *How the west was lost*. Port Hedland, WA: D W McLeod.
McMichael P (1990) Incorporating comparison within a world-historical perspective: an alternative comparative method. *American Sociological Review* 55(3): 385–397.
McMichael P (2000) World-systems analysis, globalization, and incorporated comparison. *Journal of World-Systems Research* 6(3): 668–689.
McNally C A (2006) Insinuations on China's emergent capitalism. *East-West Center Working Paper: Politics, Governance, and Security Series* 15, East-West Center, Honolulu, HI.
McNally C A (2007) China's capitalist transition: the making of a new variety of capitalism. *Comparative Social Research* 24: 177–203.
McNally C A (2008a) Conclusion: capitalism in the dragon's lair. In C A McNally (ed) *China's emergent political economy: capitalism in the dragon's lair*. London, UK: Routledge, 228–244.
McNally C A (2008b) The institutional contours of China's emergent capitalism. In C A McNally (ed) *China's emergent political economy: capitalism in the dragon's lair*. London, UK: Routledge, 105–125.
McNally C A (2008c) Reflections on capitalism and China's emergent political economy. In C A McNally (ed) *China's emergent political economy: capitalism in the dragon's lair*. London, UK: Routledge, 17–35.
Meyer M W (2011) Is it capitalism? *Management and Organization Review* 7(1): 5–18.
Mezzadra S and Neilson B (2019) *The politics of operations*. Durham, NC: Duke University Press.
Naughton B (2007) *The Chinese economy: transitions and growth*. Cambridge, MA: MIT Press.
Neil C C, Brealey T T, and Jones J A (1982) The development of single enterprise resource towns. *CHS Occasional Paper* No 25, Centre for Human Settlements, University of British Columbia, Vancouver, BC.
Offe C (1985) *Disorganized capitalism: contemporary transformation of work and politics*. Cambridge, UK: Polity.
Oi J C (1995) The role of the local state in China's transitional economy. *China Quarterly* 144: 1132–1149.
Olive N (2007) *Enough is enough*. North Freemantle, WA: Freemantle Arts Centre Press.
Ong A (2007) Neoliberalism as a mobile technology. *Transactions of the Institute of British Geographers* 32(1): 3–8.
Pearson N (2009) *Up from the mission*. Melbourne, VIC: Black.
Peck J (1989) Reconceptualizing the local labour market: space, segmentation and the state. *Progress in Human Geography* 13(1): 42–61.
Peck J (1992a) Labor and agglomeration: labor control and flexibility in local labor markets. *Economic Geography* 68(4): 325–347.
Peck J (1992b) TECs and the local politics of training. *Political Geography* 11: 335–354.

Peck J (1994) Regulating labour: the social regulation and reproduction of local labour-markets. In A Amin and N Thrift (eds) *Globalization, institutions and regional development in Europe.* Oxford, UK: Oxford University Press, 147–176.
Peck J (1996) *Work-place: the social regulation of labor markets.* New York, NY: Guilford.
Peck J (2000) Doing regulation. In G L Clark, M P Feldman and M S Gertler (eds) *The Oxford handbook of economic geography.* Oxford, UK: Oxford University Press, 61–80.
Peck J (2002) Political economies of scale: fast policy, interscalar relations, and neoliberal workfare. *Economic Geography* 78(3): 331–360.
Peck J (2004) Constructions of neoliberalism. *Progress in Human Geography* 28(3): 392–405.
Peck J (2009) Zombie-Neoliberalismus und der beidhändige Staat. *Das Argument* 282: 644–650.
Peck J (2010a) *Constructions of neoliberal reason.* Oxford, UK: Oxford University Press.
Peck J (2010b) Zombie neoliberalism and the ambidextrous state. *Theoretical Criminology* 14(1): 104–110.
Peck J (2012a) Austerity urbanism: American cities under extreme economy. *City* 16(6): 626–655.
Peck J (2012b) Economic geography: island life. *Dialogues in Human Geography* 2(2): 113–133.
Peck J (2012c) On the waterfront. *Dialogues in Human Geography* 2(2) 165–170.
Peck J (2013a) Disembedding Polanyi: exploring Polanyian economic geographies. *Environment and Planning A* 45(7): 1536–1544.
Peck J (2013b) Making space for labour. In D Featherstone and J Painter (eds) *Spatial politics: essays for Doreen Massey.* Oxford, UK: Wiley-Blackwell, 99–114.
Peck J (2014) Pushing austerity: state failure, municipal bankruptcy, and the crises of fiscal federalism in the USA. *Cambridge Journal of Regions, Economy & Society* 7(1): 17–44.
Peck J (2015) Cities beyond compare? *Regional Studies* 49(1): 160–182.
Peck J (2016) Macroeconomic geographies. *Area Development and Policy* 1(3): 305–322.
Peck J (2017a) Transatlantic city, part 1: conjunctural urbanism. *Urban Studies* 54(1): 4–30.
Peck J (2017b) Uneven regional development. In D Richardson, N Castree, M F Goodchild, A Kobayashi, W Liu and R A Marston (eds) *The Wiley-AAG international encyclopedia of geography.* Oxford, UK: Wiley-Blackwell, 7270–7282.
Peck J (2018) Pluralizing labour geography. In G L Clark, M P Feldman, M S Gertler and D Wójcik (eds) *The new Oxford handbook of economic geography.* Oxford, UK: Oxford University Press, 465–484.
Peck J (2019a) Combination. In T Jazeel, A Kent, K McKittrick, N Theodore, S Chari, P Chatterton, V Gidwani, N Heynen, W Larner, J Peck, J Pickerill, M Werner and M W Wright (eds) *Keywords in radical geography: Antipode at 50.* Oxford, UK: Wiley, 50–55.
Peck J (2019b) Problematizing capitalism(s): big difference? *EPA: Economy and Space* 51(5): 1190–1196.
Peck J (2020a) Polanyi in space. In R Desai and K Polanyi Levitt (eds) *Karl Polanyi and twenty-first-century capitalism.* Manchester, UK: Manchester University Press, 250–268.
Peck J (2020b) Where are markets? In C Berndt, J Peck and N M Rantisi (eds) *Market/place: exploring spaces of exchange.* Newcastle upon Tyne, UK: Agenda, 49–68.
Peck J (2021) On capitalism's cusp. *Area Development and Policy* 6(1): 1–30.
Peck J (2022a) Confessions of a recovering regulation theorist. In Hillier B, Phillips R and Peck J (eds) *Regulation theory, space, and uneven development: conversations and challenges.* Vancouver, BC: 1984 Press, 169–188.
Peck J (2022b) Hard work: restructuring, realism, and regions. In G Calder and B Sanghera (eds) *Ethics, economy and social science: dialogues with Andrew Sayer.* London, UK: Routledge, 139–152.
Peck J, Berndt C and Rantisi N M (2020) Introduction: exploring markets. In C Berndt, J Peck, and N M Rantisi (eds) *Market/place: exploring spaces of exchange.* Newcastle upon Tyne, UK: Agenda, 1–26.

Peck J and Miyamachi Y (1994) Regulating Japan? Regulation theory versus the Japanese experience. *Environment and Planning D: Society and Space* 12(6): 639–674.

Peck J and Theodore N (2012a) Follow the policy: a distended case approach. *Environment and Planning A* 44(1): 21–30.

Peck J and Theodore N (2012b) Reanimating neoliberalism: process-geographies of neoliberalization. *Social Anthropology* 20(2): 177–185.

Peck J and Theodore N (2015) *Fast policy: experimental statecraft at the thresholds of neoliberalism*. Minneapolis: University of Minnesota Press.

Peck J and Theodore N (2019) Still neoliberalism? *South Atlantic Quarterly* 118(2): 245–265.

Peck J, Theodore N, and Brenner N (2009) Neoliberal urbanism: models, moments, and mutations. *SAIS Review of International Affairs* 29(1): 49–66.

Peck J, Theodore N, and Brenner N (2010) Postneoliberalism and its malcontents. *Antipode* 41(S1): 94–116.

Peck J, Theodore N, and Brenner N (2013) Neoliberal urbanism redux? *International Journal of Urban and Regional Research* 37(3): 1091–1099.

Peck J, Theodore N, and Brenner N (2018) Actually existing neoliberalism. In D Cahill, M Cooper, M Konings and D Primrose (eds) *The Sage handbook of neoliberalism*. London, UK: Sage, 3–15.

Peck J and Tickell A (1994a) Jungle law breaks out: neoliberalism and global-local disorder. *Area* 26(4): 317–326.

Peck J and Tickell A (1994b) Searching for a new institutional fix: the after-Fordist crisis and the global-local disorder. In A Amin (ed) *Post-Fordism: a reader*. Oxford, UK: Blackwell, 280–316.

Peck J and Tickell A (1995) The social regulation of uneven development: regulatory deficit, England's South East, and the collapse of Thatcherism. *Environment and Planning A* 27(1): 15–40.

Peck J and Tickell A (2012) Apparitions of neoliberalism: revisiting "Jungle law breaks out." *Area* 44(2): 245–257.

Peck J, Werner M, Lave R and Christophers B (2018) Out of place: Doreen Massey, radical geographer. In M Werner, J Peck, R Lave and B Christophers (eds) *Doreen Massey: critical dialogues*. Newcastle upon Tyne, UK: Agenda, 1–38.

Pei M (2006) *China's trapped transition: the limits of developmental autocracy*. Cambridge, MA: Harvard University Press.

Pickles J and Smith A, with Begg R, Buček M, Roukova P and Pástor R (2016) *Articulations of capital: global production networks and regional transformations*. Oxford, UK: Wiley Blackwell.

Piore M J (2016) Varieties of capitalism theory: its considerable limits. *Politics and Society* 44(2): 237–241.

Piore M J and Sabel C F (1986) *The second industrial divide*. New York, NY: Basic Books.

Polanyi K (1944) *The great transformation*. Boston, MA: Beacon Press.

Polanyi K (1947) Our obsolete market mentality: civilization must find a new thought pattern. *Commentary* 3(2): 109–117.

Polanyi K (1957) The economy as instituted process. In K Polanyi, C M Arensberg and H W Pearson (eds) *Trade and market in the early empires: economies in history and theory*. Chicago, IL: Henry Regnery, 243–269.

Polanyi K (1959) Anthropology and economic theory. In M F Fried (ed) *Readings in anthropology*, Volume 2. New York, NY: Crowell, 161–184.

Polanyi K (1960) On the comparative treatment of economic institutions in antiquity, with illustrations from Athens, Mycenae, and Alalakh. In C H Kraeling and R M Adams (eds) *City invincible*. Chicago, IL: University of Chicago Press, 329–350.

Polanyi K (1969) Theoretical issues in economic anthropology. *Current Anthropology* 10(1): 63–102.
Polanyi K (1977) *The livelihood of man*. New York, NY: Academic Press.
Polanyi K, Arensberg C M and Pearson H W (eds) (1957) *Trade and market in the early empires: economies in history and theory*. New York, NY: Free Press.
Polanyi-Levitt K (1990) The origins and significance of *The Great Transformation*. In K Polanyi-Levitt (ed) *The life and work of Karl Polanyi*. Montréal, QC: Black Rose Books, 111–124.
Pollard J, McEwan C and Hughes A (eds) (2011) *Postcolonial economies*. London, UK: Zed.
Pontusson J (2005) Varieties and commonalities of capitalism. In D Coates (ed) *Varieties of capitalism, varieties of approaches*. Basingstoke, UK: Palgrave, 163–188.
Popov V (2007) Shock therapy versus gradualism reconsidered: lessons from transition economies after 15 years of reforms. *Comparative Economic Studies* 49(1): 1–31.
Rosenberg J (2005) Globalization theory: a post mortem. *International Politics* 42(1): 2–74.
Rosenberg J (2006) Why is there no international historical sociology? *European Journal of International Relations* 12(3): 307–340.
Rosenberg J (2007) International relations—the "higher bullshit": a reply to the globalization theory debate. *International Politics* 44(4): 450–482.
Rossi U (2013) On the varying ontologies of capitalism: embeddedness, dispossession, subsumption. *Progress in Human Geography* 37(3): 348–365.
Rowley C D (1972) *The destruction of Aboriginal society*. Ringwood, VIC: Penguin.
Rubel M and Manale M (1975) *Marx without myth*. Oxford, UK: Basil Blackwell.
Sahlins M D (1972) *Stone age economics*. Chicago, IL: Aldine.
Saich T (2010) *Governance and politics of China*. Basingstoke, UK: Palgrave Macmillan.
Saxenian A (1996) *Regional advantage: culture and competition in Silicon Valley and Route 128*. Cambridge, MA: Harvard University Press.
Sayer A (1984) *Method in social science: a realist approach*. London, UK: Hutchinson.
Sayer A (1985) Industry and space: a sympathetic critique of radical research. *Environment and Planning D: Society and Space* 3(1): 3–29.
Sayer A (1991) Behind the locality debate: deconstructing geography's dualisms. *Environment and Planning A* 23(2): 283–308.
Sayer A (2010) *Method in social science: a realist approach*, 2nd edition. London, UK: Routledge.
Sayer D and Corrigan P (1983) Late Marx: continuity, contradiction and learning. In T Shanin, *Late Marx and the Russian road: Marx and "the peripheries of capitalism."* New York, NY: Monthly Review Press, 77–94.
Schmidt V A (2002) *The European futures of capitalism*. Oxford, UK: Oxford University Press.
Scott A J (1988) *Metropolis: from the division of labor to urban form*. Berkeley, CA: University of California Press.
Scott A J (2000) Economic geography: the great half-century. *Cambridge Journal of Economics* 24(4): 483–504.
Sercombe H (2008) Living in two camps: the strategies goldfields Aboriginal people use to manage in the customary economy and the mainstream economy at the same time. *Australian Aboriginal Studies* 2008(2): 16–31.
Shanin T (1983) *Late Marx and the Russian road: Marx and "the peripheries of capitalism."* New York, NY: Monthly Review Press.
Sheppard E (2011) Geographical political economy. *Journal of Economic Geography* 11(2): 319–331.
Sheppard E (2016) *Limits to globalization: the disruptive geographies of capitalist development*. Oxford, UK: Oxford University Press.
Sheppard E, Barnes T J and Peck J (2012) The long decade: economic geography, unbound. In T J Barnes, J Peck and E Sheppard E (eds) *The Wiley-Blackwell companion to economic geography*. Oxford, UK: Wiley-Blackwell, 1–24.

Sheppard E, Leitner H, and Peck J (2020) Doing urban studies: navigating the methodological terrain. In H Leitner, J Peck, and E Sheppard (eds) *Urban studies inside/out: theory, method, practice*. London, UK: Sage, 21–44.

Shih S, Harrison M, Chiu K, and Berry M (2018) Linking Taiwan studies with the world. *International Journal of Taiwan Studies* 1: 209–227.

Smelser N J and Swedberg R (1994) The sociological perspective on the economy. In N J Smelser and R Swedberg (eds) *The handbook of economic sociology*. Princeton, NJ: Princeton University Press, 3–26.

Smith H and Thompson H (1987) Industrial relations and the law: a case study of Robe River. *Australian Quarterly* 59(3–4): 297–304.

Smith N (1984) *Uneven development: nature, capital, and the production of space*. Oxford, UK: Basil Blackwell.

Sorge A (2005) *The global and the local: understanding the dialectics of business systems*. Oxford, UK: Oxford University Press.

Soskice D (1999) Divergent production regimes: coordinated and uncoordinated market economies in the 1980s and 1990s. In H Kitschelt, P Lange, G Marks and J D Stephens (eds) *Continuity and change in contemporary capitalism*. Cambridge, UK: Cambridge University Press, 101–164.

Stark D (1996) Recombinant property and East European capitalism. *American Journal of Sociology* 101(4): 993–1027.

Storper M (1997) *The regional world*. New York, NY: Guilford Press.

Storper M and Scott A J (eds) (1992) *Pathways to industrialization and regional development*. London, UK: Routledge.

Storper M and Walker R (1989) *The capitalist imperative*. Oxford, UK: Basil Blackwell.

Streeck W (2011a) E pluribus unum? Varieties and commonalities of capitalism. In M Granovetter and R Swedberg (eds) *The sociology of economic life*, 3rd edition. Philadelphia, PA: Westview Press, 419–455.

Streeck W (2011b) Taking capitalism seriously: towards an institutionalist approach to contemporary political economy. *Socio-Economic Review* 9(1): 137–167.

Streeck W (2016) *How will capitalism end? Essays on a failing system*. London, UK: Verso.

Streeck W and Thelen K (2005) Introduction: institutional change in advanced capitalist economies. In W Streeck and K Thelen (eds) *Beyond continuity: institutional change in advanced capitalist economies*. Oxford, UK: Oxford University Press, 1–39.

Sum N L and Jessop B (2013) *Towards a cultural political economy: putting culture in its place in political economy*. Cheltenham, UK: Edward Elgar.

Swedberg R and Granovetter M (1992) Introduction. In M Granovetter and R Swedberg (eds) *The sociology of economic life*. Boulder, CO: Westview Press, 1–18.

Swedberg R and Granovetter M (2001) Introduction to the second edition. In M Granovetter and R Swedberg (eds) *The sociology of economic life*. Boulder, CO: Westview Press, 1–28.

Szelény I (2010) Capitalism in China? Comparative perspectives. In Y Chu (ed) *Chinese Capitalisms: historical emergence and political implications*. Basingstoke, UK: Palgrave Macmillan, 199–223.

Tickell A and Peck J (1992) Accumulation, regulation and the geographies of post-Fordism: missing links in regulationist research. *Progress in Human Geography* 16(2): 190–218.

Tickell A and Peck J (1995) Social regulation *after* Fordism: regulation theory, neo-liberalism and the global-local nexus. *Economy and Society* 24(3): 357–386.

Tickell A and Peck J (2003) Making global rules: globalisation or neoliberalisation? In J Peck and H Yeung (eds) *Remaking the global economy: economic-geographical perspectives*. London, UK: Sage, 163–181.

Tilly C (1984) *Big structures, large processes, huge comparisons.* New York, NY: Russell Sage Foundation.
Trotsky L (2008) *History of the Russian revolution.* Chicago, IL: Haymarket Books.
Vidal M and Peck J (2012) Sociological institutionalism and the socially constructed economy. In T J Barnes, J Peck, and E Sheppard (eds) *The Wiley-Blackwell companion to economic geography.* Oxford, UK: Wiley-Blackwell, 594–611.
Wade R (1990) *Governing the market: economic theory and the role of government in East Asian industrialization.* Princeton, NJ: Princeton University Press.
Wallerstein I, Collins R, Mann M, Derluguian G and Calhoun C (2013) *Does capitalism have a future?* Oxford, UK: Oxford University Press.
Watson M (2003) Ricardian political economy and the "varieties of capitalism" approach: specialization, trade and comparative institutional advantage. *Comparative European Politics* 1(2): 227–240.
Werner M (2015) *Global displacements: the making of uneven development in the Caribbean.* Oxford, UK: Wiley.
Whitley R (1999) *Divergent capitalisms: the social structuring and change of business systems.* Oxford, UK: Oxford University Press.
Whyte M K (2009) Paradoxes of China's economic boom. *Annual Review of Sociology* 35: 371–392.
Whyte M K (2010) *One country, two societies: rural-urban inequality in contemporary China.* Cambridge, MA: Harvard University Press.
Wilkinson F (ed) (1981) *The dynamics of labour market segmentation.* London, UK: Academic Press.
Williamson O E (1975) *Markets and hierarchies.* New York, NY: Free Press.
Wilson J (1980) The Pilbara Aboriginal social movement: an outline of its background and significance. In R M Berndt and C H Berndt (eds) *Aborigines of the West.* Perth, WA: University of Western Australia Press, 151–168.
Witt M A (2010) China: what variety of capitalism? *INSEAD Faculty & Research Working Paper* 2010/88/EPS. INSEAD, Fontainebleau, France.
Wolf E R (2010 [1982]) *Europe and the people without history.* Berkeley, CA: University of California Press.
Wright E O (2010) *Envisioning real utopias.* New York, NY: Verso.
Wright M (2006) *Disposable women and other myths of global capitalism.* New York, NY: Routledge.
Xu C (2011) The fundamental institutions of China's reforms and development. *Journal of Economic Literature* 49(4): 1076–1151.
Yeung H (2004) *Chinese capitalism in a global era: towards a hybrid capitalism.* London, UK: Routledge.
Yeung H and Lin G (2003) Theorizing economic geographies of Asia. *Economic Geography* 79(2): 107–128.
Zhang J (2012) From Hong Kong's capitalist fundamentals to Singapore's authoritarian governance: the policy mobility of neo-liberalising Shenzhen, China. *Urban Studies* 49(13): 2853–2871.
Zhang J and Peck J (2013) Variegated capitalism, Chinese-style: regional models, multi-scalar constructions. *Regional Studies* 50(1): 52–78.

Index

For the benefit of digital users, indexed terms that span two pages (e.g., 52–53) may, on occasion, appear on only one of those pages.

Aboriginal economies, 194–96, 199–206, 215–19, 220–21. *See also* economics, Aboriginal; economy, customary; Indigenous communities; Indigenous socioeconomies
abstraction, 47, 80–81, 115, 171, 238–39, 249, 298. *See also* midlevel theorizing; theorizing
accumulation, capital, 142–43, 237–40, 264
actually existing economies, 9–10, 19–20, 30–31, 35–36, 132, 173, 186. *See also* economy
actually existing markets, 41–42, 176–77, 180, 184–86, 221
actually existing neoliberalism. *See* neoliberalism: actually existing
advanced capitalism. *See* capitalism: advanced
Altman, Jon, 188, 216, 218–19
American model (of capitalism), 2, 19, 65–66, 113–14, 116, 227–29, 232–33
Anglo-centrism, 12–13
Anievas, Alexander, 240, 245–48
anomalies, 16–17, 21, 279, 286, 297
anticapitalism, 35–36, 168
anti-essentialism, 31–32, 38–39. *See also* essentialism; poststructuralism
Antipode (journal), 72
Arrighi, Giovanni, 61, 133, 138, 147, 152, 158
articulation, 177–78, 238, 248–51, 270–71, 283f, 285t, 286–87, 293–94
    Block, Fred, 64
    Hall, Stuart, 249–50, 289
    Hart, Gillian, 278, 281
    Marx, Karl, 227
    Massey, Doreen, 244, 248–51, 289–90
    Polanyi, Karl, 220

austerity, 73, 76–77, 79–80, 262
Australian Employment Covenant (AEC), 198–99

Barber, Bernard, 60–61, 65–66, 68, 71, 191–92
Barnes, Trevor, ix, 10–11, 21–22, 40–41, 48, 307n.7
Baron, James, 56
BHP Billiton, 197–99, 207, 219
Bibby, Peter, ix, 6–7
binaries, 65–66, 71, 78–79, 177–78, 300–1
Block, Fred, 63–65, 69, 71, 161–62, 167, 169, 182, 191
bogan culture. *See* culture, bogan
Boyer, Robert, 103, 105–7, 111–12, 122
Braudel, Fernand, 61, 347n.13
Braverman, Harry, 56–57
Brenner, Neil, ix, 102–3, 225–26
BRICS (Brazil, Russia, India, China, South Africa), 226–27
Brief History of Neoliberalism, A (Harvey), 161
Brown, Wendy, 27–28
Bruszt, Laszlo, 66–67, 125
Buckley, Ken, 200–1, 203
Burawoy, Michael, 16–17, 66–68, 125–26, 167, 179–82, 288

Cahill, Damien, 92
camps, 191, 194, 196–99, 211, 213, 220–21
capital accumulation. *See* accumulation, capital
Capital (Marx), 227, 236–37, 252–54, 258
capital-labor relations, 3–4, 35–36, 108, 188, 191, 197, 248. *See also* industrial relations; regulation: labor

capitalism, 17, 34–38, 66–68, 103, 124–28, 165–66, 180–81, 219, 225, 226–37, 247–48, 263–64. *See also* anticapitalism; liberal capitalism; more-than-capitalism; variegated capitalism; varieties of capitalism
  advanced, 35–36, 67–68, 113–14, 164–65, 173–74, 180–81, 193, 222–23, 239–40
  American, 2, 19, 65–66, 113–14, 116, 227–29, 232–33
  Chinese, 133–37, 138–57
  configurative conceptions of, 240, 247–48, 256–58, 263–64, 272–73, 276
  diversity of, 17, 35–36, 64, 87, 105, 125, 222–26, 230, 235–36
  financialized, 32–33, 37–38, 81–82, 84–85, 111–12, 122, 180
  free-market, 68, 112–13, 166, 167–68, 226, 228, 232–33, 234, 236–37
  German, 109–10, 112, 116–17, 232–33
  global(izing), 81–82, 112–13, 140–41, 144–45, 146, 167, 183, 222, 230–34, 237
  guanxi, 65, 135*t*, 152–56
  pastoral, 195, 203–6, 220–21
  platform, 222–23
  polymorphous, 125, 237–38, 247, 263–64
  power-elite, 152–56
  socially embedded, 29, 71, 92, 103–6, 167, 232–33
  state, 133, 142, 144–51, 156–57, 201, 226
  terraforming, 225–26, 237, 265–66, 267*t*, 339n.18
Capitalisme contre capitalisme (Albert), 104–5, 129–30, 229
capitalocentrism, 35–38, 46–47
case studies. *See* extended case methodology
CCP. *See* Chinese Communist Party
Chicago School of Economics, 68–69
Chinese Communist Party, 134–36, 138–40, 142, 144, 146–47, 152, 157–58
Chinese model (of capitalism), 133–37, 138–57
Christophers, Brett, 11, 307n.7
Clark, Gordon, 30–31
Clarke, John, 256, 258, 271–72, 289
class
  analysis, 59–61, 66–67
  relations, 8–9, 10–11, 35–36, 55–56, 124–25, 144, 150, 154, 210
closed system theorizing, 25–26, 29, 250, 285–86

Coates, David, 229–30, 233–34
coexistence, 28–29, 116, 159, 167, 272–73
Cold War, 68–69, 132, 163–64, 166–67, 227, 279–81
Collier, Stephen, 88, 92–93, 95–97, 99
Collins, Jane, 50–51
Collins, Randall, 59
Columbia University, 164–65
combination, 17, 44, 125–26, 174–75, 177–78, 252, 254, 257–58, 261–62, 291–92. *See also* recombination
commodities, fictive. *See* fictive commodities
Community Development Employment Program (CDEP), 215–16, 218–19
community economies collective, 37–38. *See also* Gibson-Graham, J. K.
company towns, 191, 196–97, 207–15
comparative economy, 20, 24, 42–46, 157, 159, 162–64, 182–85, 187–88, 207–15, 256, 274–75. *See also* comparative political economy
comparison, 45–46, 103, 110, 169–70, 182–85, 189, 193, 275–87
  relational, 17, 184, 266–69, 275–87, 293–94 (*see also* relational analysis; relational perspective; relationality)
complexity. *See* theorizing: complexity
conjunction, inconstant, 272–73, 283*f*
conjunctural analysis, 1–2, 17, 47, 76–77, 98, 243–45, 256, 258, 262, 267*t*, 270–75, 283*f*, 287–300. *See also* explanation; comparison: relational; extended case methodology; more-than-local relations; problem spaces (methodological); relational analysis; theorizing: conjunctural; theorizing: contextual
consumer culture. *See* culture, consumer
context, 16–17, 51–52, 55–56, 59–60, 70, 164, 191–92, 235–36, 288, 290–91, 299–300, 299*t*
  of context, 88, 288
  "radical" contextuality, 290, 298–99
  theorization of (*see* theorizing: contextual)
coordinated market economies. *See* varieties of capitalism: coordinated market economies
coordination, mode of, 107–10, 114, 118–19, 159
corporate culture. *See* culture: corporate

corporate social responsibility, 198, 217, 220–21
crisis, 72, 74–75, 82, 94–95, 122, 180–81, 201, 226–27, 233–34, 290–91, 294. *See also* global financial crisis
crisis management, 68–69, 74–75, 84–85
critical realism, 3–4, 172–73, 279, 330n.66
Crouch, Colin, 83, 232–33, 235–36
culture
   bogan, 194, 197, 208, 211–12
   consumer, 209–10
   corporate, 194–95, 210–11
   "culturalist" explanation, 196, 221, 259–60, 345n.166 (*see also* explanation)
   dependency, 199, 217–18
   industrial, 195, 199, 208
   market, 43, 62, 143–44, 192, 196 (*see also* neoliberalism)
   neoliberal, 97–98, 216 (*see also* neoliberalism)
   union, 210 (*see also* labor movement; regulation, labor; unions)
   welfare, 15–16, 199, 215–19
culturalism. *See* culture: "culturalist" explanation
customary economy. *See* economy, customary

Dalton, George, 166–67, 170–71, 177–78
Darwin, Charles, 18–20, 23–24, 49
Darwinism, social, 202, 203
Dean, Mitchell, 79–80, 93
decentralization, 146–48, 155
deduction, 25–26, 30–31, 54, 172, 186, 192, 235, 288. *See also* explanation; induction; retroduction
Deeg, Richard, 118–19
deindustrialization, 10–11, 83–84, 228
demand sharing, 200–1, 218. *See also* economy, customary; Indigenous socioeconomies
DEMOLOGOS, 102–3, 317n.1
Deng, Xiaoping, 138–40, 142–44, 152, 226
dependency culture. *See* culture: dependency
deregulation, 8–9, 68–69, 96–97, 102, 111, 121, 180, 228
determinism, economic, 89–90, 167, 182–83, 277–78. *See also* economism
determinism, institutional, 235
development, uneven. *See* uneven and combined development; uneven spatial development

developmental state, 35, 93–94, 145–46, 150–51, 159, 228. *See also* state
dialectics, 89–90, 98, 169–70, 179–82
Dicken, Peter, ix, 6–7
difference, 13–14, 18–20, 162–63, 183, 235–37, 274–75, 277–78
   economic, 2–3, 21, 32, 36, 44–49, 101, 186, 221
   finding, 88, 108, 183, 247, 263–64, 275, 299*t*
   social, 248, 278, 282–84
discourse, 73–74, 91, 129, 139, 213
   globalization, 14, 112–13, 228, 230 (*see also* globalization)
   neoliberal, 72, 73–74, 112–13, 115, 129 (*see also* neoliberalism)
disembedding, 62, 65–66, 71, 176–77, 181. *See also* embeddedness
disequilibrium, 8–9, 21, 118, 127*t*, 141, 192–93, 236–37. *See also* equilibrium
Disorganized Capitalism (Offe), 160
diversity, 19, 46–48, 224, 235–36, 255–56
   capitalist, 35–38, 64, 66–67, 105, 125–26, 222–26, 230, 235–36
   economic, 31–32, 44–45, 193
   neoliberal, 87
division of labor, spatial. *See* spatial division of labor
double movement, 91, 150–51, 159, 164, 179–82, 192–93. *See also* Polanyi, Karl
Dow, Sheila, 24–25
Durkheim, Émile, 56–57

Economic Approach to Human Behavior (Becker), 57
economic geography, 1–7, 10–11, 24, 103, 123–28, 129–30, 161–63. See also geographical political economy; industrial geography; perspective, in economic geography; place, in economic geography; positionality, in economic geography
   project, 4–5, 11–12, 19–20, 222
   theory-culture of, 6, 10–12, 20–23, 30–41, 48–49, 103–4, 173–74, 240–41
Economic Geography (journal), 50
economic imaginaries. *See* imaginaries, economic
economic sociology, 1–2, 30, 50–51, 60, 64, 173–74

economics
- Aboriginal, 187–88, 200–1, 218–19
- Chicago School (*see* Chicago School of Economics)
- heterodox, 5, 12–15, 20–21, 24–25, 28–31, 38–39, 40–41, 70, 102–3, 131, 168, 172, 178
- institutional, 1–2, 19, 52, 103, 113
- neoclassical, 24–26, 34, 41, 56–58, 69–70, 109–10, 115, 165, 170–74, 230, 236–37
- orthodox, 8–9, 20–21, 24–29, 34, 54, 58, 115

economism, 3–4, 145, 220, 277–78, 299t, *See also* determinism, economic

economistic fallacy (Polanyi), 41, 220

economy
- camp (*see* camps)
- customary, 189, 194–96, 200, 217–21 (*see also* Indigenous socioeconomies)
- embedded (*see* embedded economy)
- instituted, 13–14, 19–20, 157, 172, 174–75, 182–83, 189–90, 220–21, 256–57
- mixed (*see* mixed economy)
- planned (*see* planned economy)
- resource, 188–89, 190–91, 195, 197, 198, 199–200, 206–7, 213–14
- socially constructed, 52–55, 65, 244, 247, 272–73
- subsistence, 177, 201, 203–4

Ellem, Bradon, 188, 194, 210–11

Elliot, Larry, 82

embeddedness, 13–14, 15, 52, 55–57, 61–66, 71, 92, 115–16, 176–77, 181–82, 190–91, 232–33, 256. *See also* disembedding
- always, 13–14, 63–64, 69–70, 103–4
- everywhere, 13–14, 69–70, 190–91, 246, 271

engaged pluralism. *See* pluralism: engaged

Engels, Friedrich, 252, 254

equilibrium, 19, 25, 32, 54–55, 57, 111, 117–19, 141. *See also* disequilibrium

essentialism, 38, 42–43, 237, 277–78, 283f, *See also* anti-essentialism; reductionism
- market, 63–64, 116, 173–74 (*see also* economism; market: "shape of things")

ethnocentrism, 42–43, 45–46, 166, 178, 182–83, 302

ethnography, 77–78, 87, 92–93, 234, 256–57, 271–72, 284–85, 297–98
- global, 172–73, 279. *See also* Burawoy, Michael; extended case methodology

Eurocentrism, 9, 74–75, 131–32, 142–43, 227, 239–40, 259, 267t, 277–78, 280–81

Europe and the People without History (Wolf), 259–60

European social model, 107–8, 127t, 232–33

European Union, 68, 102–3, 262

eventful analysis, 271–72

exchange, 44–47, 54–55, 62–63, 138, 163, 171, 175, 176t, 201. *See also* integration, mode of; market
- relations, 41–43, 155–56, 218
- unequal, 3, 31–32

experimentation, 68–69, 118, 142–43, 146–47, 152, 157–58

explanation, 30–31, 48–49, 50–59, 95, 99–100, 131, 189–91, 219–20, 256–57, 295–96, 297–98. *See also* conjunctural analysis; deduction; induction; theorizing; midlevel theorizing; relational analysis

exploration. *See* mapping

extended case methodology, 98, 279, 283f, 288. *See also* Burawoy, Michael; ethnography: global

federalism, 146, 149–50

feminism, 12, 24–25, 33, 35–36, 173t, 270–71

feminist geography, 10–11, 40–41

fictive commodities, 179–80

FIFO. *See* fly in, fly out (workers)

financialized capitalism. *See* capitalism: financialized

fix, spatial, 196–97, 211

flexible specialization, 235–36. *See also* post-Fordism

fly in, fly out (workers), 190–91, 194, 196–98, 211–14

Fordism, 35, 74–75, 107, 156–57, 206, 341n.52, *See also* post-Fordism; Keynesian welfare state; regulation theory

formalism, 25–26, 29–30, 41–43, 66, 165, 169–74, 177, 192

Foucauldian analysis, 93, 96–97, 99

Fourcade, Marion, 27

free-market capitalism. *See* capitalism: free-market; market: free

Friedman, Milton, 93–94, 166–67, 329n.37

functionalism, 102, 106, 113, 275–76

Geertz, Clifford, 27

Index

gender, 8–9, 10–11, 59, 208–9, 256, 278, 281
geographical political economy, 24, 34–35, 37–39, 99, 162, 169–70, 173t, 187, 222, 224–25, 236–39, 240–41, 270–71, 274–75, 295–96. *See also* economic geography; political economy
geography, economic. *See* economic geography
geography, industrial. *See* industrial geography
German model (of capitalism), 109–10, 112, 116, 117, 232–33
Gibson-Graham, J. K., 35–40
Gledhill, John, 87–88
global capitalism. *See* capitalism: global(izing)
global cities, 35, 294–95, 298
Global Conference on Economic Geography, 18
global ethnography. *See* ethnography: global
global financial crisis, 2, 72, 73, 79, 83, 212–13, 222, 226, 233–35, 290–91. *See also* capitalism: financialized; crisis; Great Recession
global production networks, 14, 31–32
"global sense of place" (Massey), 243–44, 250–51, 266–69, 306–7n.29
globalization, 3, 10–11, 13–14, 71, 85, 226–31, 251. *See also* capitalism: global(izing); impact models
  critique of, 85, 121–22, 251, 276–77
  debates, 124, 129–30, 231
  decade, 2, 168–69, 226–28
Goodin, Robert, 111, 120
governance, 7–9, 238–39. *See also* regulation
  corporate, 108, 117, 135t, 148–49
  economic, 123–24, 125, 152, 192–93
  regimes, 70, 91
Gramsci, Antonio, 167, 180, 273, 290–91, 348n.28, 349n.65
Gramscian analysis, 144, 158, 255–56, 270, 288, 331n.93
Granovetter, Mark, 52–54, 57–59
Great Recession, 79–80, 83
Great Transformation, The (Polanyi), 160–61, 164–69, 179. *See also* Polanyi, Karl
Grossberg, Larry, 290, 292
Grundrisse (Marx), 227, 309n.49
guanxi. *See* capitalism: *guanxi*

Hall, Peter, 108–12, 114–15, 117–18, 124–25, 229, 231–33, 235

Hall, Stuart, 224–25, 231, 236–37, 297
  articulation, 249–50, 289–91
  conjunctural analysis, 249–50, 270–71, 273, 287–88, 290–91, 296
  neoliberalism, 80–81, 86
Halperin, Rhoda, 165–66, 170–72, 178–79
Hancké, Bob, 234–35
Handbook of Economic Sociology (Smelser and Swedberg), 54, 59
Hannan, Michael, 56
Hart, Gillian, 274–75, 278, 281, 284–85, 286, 289–90, 292
  articulation, 278, 281
  relational comparison, 276–78
Harvey, David, 9–10, 150, 161, 222, 224–25, 238–40, 247, 266, 281–82
Hayek, Friedrich, 91–92, 93–94, 107–8, 167–68
hegemony, 35–36, 46–47, 75, 81–82, 85–88, 93–98, 100–1, 226–27, 293–94
Hess, Michael, 205
Hinkson, Melinda, 188, 216
historical materialism, 167, 191, 276–77
historicization, 189, 225–26, 267t, 273, 289, 298–99
Hodgson, Geoffrey, 19, 65, 116, 230, 247, 255–56, 264. *See also* "impurity principle"
holism, 162–63, 168–69, 183–84, 188–89, 220–21, 266, 267t. *See also* part-whole relations
Hollingsworth, J. Rogers, 105–6
Homo economicus, 42–43, 53, 55, 59–60, 171
Hong Kong, 152
householding, 44–47, 174–75, 176t. *See also* integration, mode of
Howell, Chris, 124–25, 150, 265–66
Howitt, Richie, 188, 193–94, 206
Huxley, Thomas, 18–19
hybridity, 157, 169–70, 254–56, 286–87
  capitalist, 66–68, 116, 125, 264
  economic, 16–17, 44–47, 65–66, 134, 152, 177–78, 218–20
  neoliberal, 78–79, 83–85, 88–90

ideal type
  cases, 109–10, 114, 134–36, 294
  reasoning, 90, 222, 232–33, 235, 246, 272–73, 276–77, 301–2
imaginaries, economic, 31–32, 36, 162–63, 181–84, 228, 234–35, 256, 264

impact models (of globalization), 98, 276–77
"impurity principle" (Hodgson), 65, 116, 255–56, 264
India, 35, 125, 226, 253, 258
Indigenous communities, 189, 195, 206, 215
Indigenous socioeconomies, 188–91, 196, 198–201, 216–21. *See also* Aboriginal economies; economics: Aboriginal; economy: customary
individualism, methodological. *See* methodological individualism
induction, 11–12, 54, 172–73, 186, 244, 270, 286, 288, 299–300. *See also* deduction; explanation; retroduction
industrial culture. *See* culture: industrial
industrial geography, 5–7, 12, 77–78. *See also* economic geography; restructuring, industrial
industrial relations, 105, 109, 135*t*, 149, 188, 210–11. *See also* capital-labor relations; regulation: labor
industrial restructuring. *See* restructuring: industrial
inequality, 64, 144, 150–51, 226–27
institutional economics. *See* economics: institutional
institutionalism, 11, 14–15, 34, 106, 110–11, 112–15, 117–21, 124–26, 171–72, 224, 229–30, 235–37. *See also* methodological institutionalism
integration, mode of, 44, 162–63, 174–78, 179–80, 192, 219–20. *See also* exchange; householding; reciprocity; redistribution
interdependencies, untraded. *See* untraded interdependencies
interdependency, 9–10, 19–20, 21, 66, 78–79, 125–26, 203, 217–18, 248–49, 252, 254, 284
interdisciplinarity, 14, 58, 71, 103, 113, 169–70, 256. *See also* economics: heterodox; pluralism; postdisciplinarity
internalism, methodological. *See* methodological internalism
international, the, 64, 110–11, 112, 231, 241–42, 250–51, 262
International Monetary Fund, 82
intersectionality, 7–8, 14, 47, 244, 265, 271, 300

Jackson, Gregory, 118–19

Japan, 110–11, 115, 119–20, 135*t*, 156–57, 199–200, 226, 228, 235–36
Jessop, Bob, 83–84, 90, 225, 237–38, 240, 243

Kaplan, David, 171–72
Keynes, John Maynard, 82
Keynesian welfare state, 74–75, 93–94, 107. *See also* New Deal; welfare
Keynesianism, 150–51, 180, 227
Kilburn manifesto, 290–93, 349–50n.77
Kindleberger, Charles, 23–24

labor
    contingent, 197, 202–3, 217–18
    demand, 7–8, 73–74
    regulation (*see* regulation: labor)
    relations (*see* capital-labor relations)
    supply, 7–8, 73–74, 149, 194, 196–97, 203, 207
labor market, 7–9, 73–74, 160, 202–3, 207
labor market segmentation theory, 1–2, 7–8, 12
labor movement, 15–16, 84–85, 210–11. *See also* labor unions
labor unions, 5–6, 9, 105, 134–36, 135*t*, 149, 209–11, 213–14
laissez-faire, 68, 133, 168, 179, 180–81. *See also* discourse: neoliberal; market: free; neoliberalism
land, 141–42, 143–44, 148–49, 154–55, 175, 179, 195, 198, 200–2, 206
Lawson, Tony, 24–26, 29, 284–85, 294–95
Lee, C. K., 256–57
Leitner, Helga, ix, 274, 294
Li, Tanya, 271–72, 294
liberal capitalism, 102, 113–15, 132–33, 163–65, 180
liberal market economies. *See* varieties of capitalism: liberal market economies
Limits to Capital, The (Harvey), 224–25, 266, 305n.11. *See also* Harvey, David
Lloyd, Peter, ix, 6–7
localism, 95, 245–46, 250–51, 266–69, 277–78, 300–2
longue-durée, 128, 189–90, 273
lumping, 18–24, 30–33, 37–41, 44–45, 47–48, 78, 86–87, 99

macroeconomic geography, 66, 95, 128–30, 242–43, 265, 299–300, 299*t*. *See also* economic geography; geographical political economy

Makki, Fouad, 251, 261–62
Manchester University, 6–7
mapping, 69–70, 98, 173t, 234–35, 236–37, 247, 249, 278–81, 293–94, 299–300
market, 27–29, 41–43, 52–53, 54–55, 62–64, 91, 107–8, 115–16, 138, 170–71, 176–77, 185. *See also* exchange; marketization; more-than-markets
   actually existing (*see* actually existing markets)
   centricity, 37, 41–42, 46–47, 53, 179, 236–37, 255–56, 308n.29
   contradictions of, 73–75, 176–77, 179–81, 192–93, 254–56
   culture, 43, 62, 143–44, 192, 196 (*see also* neoliberalism)
   essentialism (*see* essentialism: market)
   free, 65–66, 68, 93–94, 132, 226, 228–29, 232–33. *See also* discourse: neoliberal; laissez-faire; neoliberalism
   labor (*see* labor market)
   making, 71
   non-market, 41, 114, 116, 117, 178, 181, 183–84 (*see also* more-than-markets)
   rule, 9, 37–38, 40, 73–75, 79–83, 85–86, 96f, 100, 140, 159, 180 (*see also* neoliberalism)
   "shape of things" (Polanyi), 41, 166, 171, 183–84, 192, 220
   socialism, 84–85, 139–44, 149–50, 226 (*see also* socialist market economy)
   society, 41–42, 179, 217
   world, 237–38, 240, 243, 249–50
marketization, 8–9, 42–43, 68–69, 91, 96–97, 136–37, 179–80, 192–93. *See also* market; neoliberalization
Marx, Karl, 56–57, 201, 227, 236–37, 247, 252–54, 258, 263. *See also* Marxism; neoMarxist
Marxism, 11, 34, 56–57, 160–61, 165–67, 173t, 180–81. *See also* Marx, Karl; neoMarxism
Massey, Doreen, 3–4, 8–9, 50, 222, 238–41, 243–45, 248–51, 279, 281–82, 289–93. *See also* "global sense of place"
McCarthyism, 165–67, 309n.51
McLeod, Don, 200, 205, 215, 334n.53
McMichael, Philip, 249, 278–79, 286
McNally, Christopher, 137, 141, 142–44
Melbourne University, 12
Mercosur, 262
methodological globalism, 277–78

methodological individualism, 3–4, 55–56, 58–59, 169–72, 173, 183, 271
methodological institutionalism, 70, 158, 162–63, 171–72, 173t, *See also* institutionalism
methodological internalism, 95–96, 96f, 131, 245–46, 249, 262–63, 267t, 300
methodological localism, 95, 245–46, 277–78, 300, 301–2
methodological nationalism, 9, 14, 50–51, 102, 113, 123–24, 127t, 131, 222–23, 245–46, 254–55, 258, 301–2, 307n.6
methodological substantivism, 16–17, 169–85, 219–20. *See also* substantivism
methodology, 5, 17, 161–63, 169–85, 187, 189, 242–43, 249, 267t, 270, 297–98. *See also* conjunctural analysis; extended case methodology; research design
Mezzadra, Sandra, 226–27
midlevel theorizing, 20–21, 30–31, 44–46, 77–78, 124–25, 172, 176–77, 249–50, 281, 283f, 287–88, 294–95. *See also* explanation
mining, 189, 191, 194–200, 203–4, 206–15
mixed economy, 81–82, 136–37, 167–68, 176–78, 255–56. *See also* combination
mode of coordination. *See* coordination, mode of
mode of integration. *See* integration, mode of
mode of regulation. *See* regulation, mode of
modeling, 20–21, 25–28, 51–52, 118–19, 171, 283f, *See also* models
models, 56, 102, 111–12, 124–25, 178, 240–41, 259, 281–82. *See also* impact models; stage models
monetary relations, 45, 65, 200, 207
Moore, Jason, 242
more-than-capitalism, 35, 169–70, 175, 181, 222–23, 236–37, 255–56, 274–75. *See also* capitalism
more-than-local relations, 9–10, 78–79, 87–90, 99–100, 241–42, 255–58, 265, 277–78, 286, 300, 301–2. *See also* conjunctural analysis; macroeconomic geographies
more-than-markets, 179–80, 185. *See also* market; marketization
"more-than-one," ontology of (Rosenberg), 254–56, 262–63

nationalism, 146, 226–27

nationalism, methodological. *See* methodological nationalism
Neilson, Brett, 226–27
neoclassical economics. *See* economics: neoclassical
neoliberalism, 15–16, 72–101, 119–23, 150–51. *See also* neoliberalization; Washington consensus
   actually existing, 81–82, 87, 91, 92–93
   China, 73, 85, 132, 145, 150–51
   cultures of, 97–98, 216
   hegemonic, 74–75, 79, 86, 93–94, 96–98, 101
   ideational, 79–80, 87–88, 91–92, 101
   policies, 81–82
   roll-back, 76
   roll-out, 76
   thought collective, 79–80
   utopia (*see* utopia: market)
neoliberalization, 15–16, 73–75, 91–95, 99–100
   failing forward, 76–77
   processual, 75, 78–79, 89–90
   as transformative process, 75, 81–82, 86, 92, 93–94, 100–1, 118
   variegated, 76–78, 95–96
neoMarxism, 10–11, 35–36, 167, 224. *See also* Marxism
New Deal, 164. *See also* Keynesian welfare state; welfare
new economic sociology, 15, 50, 52–64, 160–61, 168–69. *See also* economic sociology
new international division of labor, 228
New York, 82, 94–95, 164–65, 166
Nisancioglu, Kerem, 240, 245–48
nomenklatura, 142, 144, 146, 148–49, 154–55
normalization, 53–54, 82, 85, 196–97, 210, 214–15, 264, 294–95
North West Industry Research Unit (Manchester University), 6–7

Offe, Claus, 73–74, 160
ontology, 3–4, 15–16, 29–30, 41, 174–75, 176–77, 200–1, 277–78. *See also* "more-than-one," ontology of
   neoliberal, 91, 95
   relational, 285–86, 285*t*, 290–91, 298–99, 299*t*
   uneven development, 30–31, 222, 254–56, 262–66, 279–80
open system theorizing, 29–31, 270–71, 288

orthodox economics. *See* economics: orthodox
Oxford University, 18

Parsons, Talcott, 52–53, 56–58, 60–61, 63–64, 191–92
part-whole relations, 98, 185, 188–89, 191–92, 275–76, 278, 283*f*, *See also* holism; more-than-local relations
pastoral capitalism. *See* capitalism: pastoral
paternalism, 203, 205, 207–11, 215–18
path dependency, 6, 15, 38, 76, 96*f*, 102, 112, 113–14
   and China, 140–41, 157–58
   path interdependency, 78–79 (*see also* interdependency)
patronage, 142, 146–47, 148
Pearson, Noel, 190–91, 217, 219
Peel, Thomas, 201
perspective, in economic geography, 3, 6, 12, 20–23, 33, 222, 243–44, 249–50
Perth (Western Australia), 187, 194, 202, 206, 211, 213
Pilbara, the (Western Australia), 187–89, 193–95
place, in economic geography, 3, 162, 241–45, 262, 267*t*
planned economy, 139–40, 145
platform capitalism. *See* capitalism: platform
pluralism, 2–3, 6, 22, 28–29, 56–57, 169–70. *See also* economics: heterodox; interdisciplinarity; postdisciplinarity
   disengaged, 48, 306n.23
   engaged, 12–14, 48–49
Polanyi, Karl, 160–61, 163–68, 183
   articulation, 219–20
   double movement, 159, 160, 164, 169–70, 192–93
   economistic fallacy, 41, 220 (*see also* economism)
   embeddedness, 15, 24, 65–66, 164–65, 181, 191, 273 (*see also* embeddedness)
   "market shape of things," 41, 166, 171, 183–84, 192, 220
   "primacy of politics," 168, 184
socioeconomics, 1–2, 5–6, 16–17, 160–62, 183, 188–89, 255–56 (*see also* comparative economy)
substantivist approach, 3–4, 9, 24, 41, 43, 163, 166–67, 170–74, 183, 192 (*see also* substantivism)

Policing the Crisis (Hall et al), 289
political economy, 1–2, 9–10, 14–15, 34, 77–78, 161, 167
    comparative, 47–48, 66–67, 102–3, 124–25, 129, 131–32, 233–34 (*see also* comparative economy)
    firm-centered, 104–6, 108–11, 115, 127t, 131, 136–37, 229–30, 231–32, 235
    geographical (*see* geographical political economy)
positionality, in economic geography, 3, 21–22, 220, 243–45, 249, 267t, 277–78, 285–86, 298–99
positivism, 25–26, 58, 172–73, 279, 282–84, 288. *See also* post-positivism
postcolonial studies, 222–23, 240, 255–56, 270–71, 279–80
postdisciplinarity, 1–2, 6, 14, 164–65, 168–69, 182–83. *See also* economics: heterodox; interdisciplinarity; pluralism
post-Fordism, 74–75. *See also* flexible specialization; Fordism
post-neoliberalism, 73, 79–80, 83, 100–1. *See also* neoliberalism
post-positivism, 127t, 284, 288. *See also* positivism; theorizing: reflexive
post-socialism, 66–67, 136–37, 141–42, 145–46, 152, 157. *See also* socialism
poststructuralism, 12, 33, 34–36, 38–41, 79, 87–88. *See also* anti-essentialism
problem spaces (methodological), 287–88, 289, 292, 297

race, 55–56, 203, 204, 207, 256, 272–73, 278, 281
rational choice, 41–43, 52–57, 108, 113, 120–21, 127t, 171–73, 229–30
rationalism, 183
rationality, 27–28, 29, 53, 63–64, 91, 182–83, 246
Reagan, Ronald, 68–69, 86–87, 168
Reaganomics, 73–74, 86–87
realism, critical. *See* critical realism
real utopias. *See* utopias: real
reciprocity, 44–45, 65–66, 152–56, 175, 176t, 192, 200–1, 217–18. *See also* integration, mode of
recombination, 66–67, 112, 125, 189–90, 261–62. *See also* combination
redistribution, 46–47, 65–66, 159, 164–65, 175, 176t, 192, 200, 213, 217–18, 220–21. *See also* integration, mode of

reductionism, 3–4, 28, 29, 38, 54–55, 56, 80–81. *See also* essentialism
regulation. *See also* deregulation
    dilemmas of, 8–9, 73–74, 106
    labor, 73–74, 105, 121, 135t, 143–44, 202–3
    mode of, 41–42, 161
regulation theory, 1–2, 5–6, 12, 74–75, 105–6, 111–12, 116, 122, 156–57, 160–61, 177–78
relations
    labor (*see* capital-labor relations; industrial relations)
    monetary (*see* monetary relations)
    more-than-local (*see* more-than-local relations)
relational analysis, 3–4, 95–96, 100–1, 167, 219–20, 248–51, 262–63, 289–91. *See also* relational comparison; relational perspective; relationality
relational comparison. *See* comparison; relational
relational perspective, 131–32, 181, 188–89, 240–43, 247–49, 300–3. *See also* relational analysis; relationality
relationality, 3–4, 85, 100–1, 103, 254, 262–63, 281–82, 284
representativeness, 254, 282–84
reproduction, social, 7–8, 194, 196–98, 210–11, 215, 219–20, 249, 255–56
rescaling, 71, 122–23. *See also* scale
research design, 16–17, 45–48, 179, 185–86, 242–43, 267t, 270, 277–78, 284–86, 296–97. *See also* methodology
resource economies. *See* economy: resource
restructuring
    approach, 1–2, 3–4, 77–78 (*see also* restructuring: industrial)
    capitalist, 35–38, 102, 128–30, 188, 236–37
    industrial, 7–8, 9–11, 77–78 (*see also* industrial geography)
    neoliberal, 90–92, 122–23 (*see also* neoliberalism; neoliberalization)
    present, 9–10, 35, 86, 240–41
    process, 3–4, 188
    regulatory, 75, 93–94
    research program, 8–9, 50, 77–78
    state, 73–74, 92
retroduction, 169, 329n.48, *See also* deduction; explanation; induction
Rhodes, Martin, 234–35
Rio Tinto, 193–95, 197, 206, 207, 214, 219

Romer, Paul, 27, 307–8n.20
Rosenberg, Justin, 250–51, 260–61. *See also* "more-than-one," ontology of
Rotstein, Abe, 43
Royalties for the Regions (R4R), 213–15
Russia, 35, 158, 164, 226, 252–53, 258

Sayer, Andrew, 3–4, 8–9, 14–15, 50, 232–33, 246, 279, 283*f*
scale, 71, 112, 122–25, 241–44, 273–74, 293–96, 299*t*, 300. *See also* rescaling
  politics of, 95, 107, 153, 274, 347n.16
Schumpeter, Joseph, 56–57
Scott, Allen, 7, 9–10, 33
segmentation theory. *See* labor market segmentation theory
Seidman, Gay, 50–51
Sercombe, Howard, 218
Shanin, Teodor, 252–54, 263
Sheppard, Eric, ix, 21–22, 34–35, 40–41, 48, 244–45, 274, 294
Shih, Shu-mei, 279–81
shock therapy, 68–69, 94–95, 141–42, 145–46, 152, 158. *See also* neoliberalism; Washington consensus
Smelser, Neil, 54, 56–57, 58, 59
socialism, 138, 139–44, 145, 148–49, 150–51. *See also* post-socialism
  Christian, 83–85
  market, 134, 140
  state, 15–16, 139–44
socialist market economy, 139–40, 157, 159. *See also* market; socialism
Social Justice and the City (Harvey), 161
social license, 195, 198, 217, 220–21
social reproduction. *See* reproduction, social
social system of production, 71, 105–6, 107–8
socioeconomics, 1–2, 5–6, 52, 69–70, 101, 162, 183, 186, 219, 255–56. *See also* economic sociology; economics
sociology, economic. *See* economic sociology
SOE. *See* state owned enterprises
Somers, Margaret (Peggy), 161–62, 169
Soskice, David, 104–5, 108–12, 114–15, 117–18, 124–25, 229, 231–33, 235
South Africa, 226, 281–82, 284–85, 292
spatial division of labor, 7–9, 31–32, 238–39, 248, 284–85
Spatial Divisions of Labour (Massey), 248. *See also* Massey, Doreen; restructuring: approach
spatial fix. *See* fix, spatial

spatiality, 1–2, 20–21, 125, 225–26, 238, 279
splitting, 18–24, 30–33, 38–41, 44–46, 48–49, 77–78, 86–87, 99
stadial development. *See* stage models
stage models, 167, 177, 227, 239–40, 248, 253–54, 261–62, 263, 285–86. *See also* models; teleology
Stark, David, 51–52, 66–67, 125
state, 73–74, 76–77, 90, 128, 142, 144–46, 150–52, 201
  capitalism (*see* capitalism: state; state owned enterprises)
  developmental (*see* developmental state)
  local, 148–50, 281–82
  small, 68, 78, 85–86, 92, 229 (*see also* neoliberalism)
  welfare (*see* welfare state)
state owned enterprises, 134–37, 141–44, 148–49, 154
Strassman, Diana, 26
Streeck, Wolfgang, 112, 118, 120–21, 228, 233–34, 243
stress testing (of theory claims), 16–17, 46–47, 157–58, 263–64, 267*t*, 279, 286, 294. *See also* theorizing
strikes, 204–6, 210–11, 213–14. *See also* labor unions
structural adjustment, 68–69, 86–87. *See also* Washington consensus
"structure of feeling" (Williams), 22
substantivism, 3–4, 41, 43, 169–74, 192, 221, 256. *See also* methodological substantivism
Summer Institute in Economic Geography, 11–12
Swedberg, Richard, 54, 56–57, 58, 59
synecdoche, 254
Szelényi, Iván, 141–42, 145–46

Taiwan, 152, 281–82
Tarrow, Sidney, 23–24
teleology, 42–43, 124, 167, 181, 192, 253, 281, 287–88
Thatcher, Margaret, 7–9, 68–69, 83–90, 97–98
Thatcher, Mark, 234–35
Thatcherism, 2, 68–69, 73–74, 86–87
Thelen, Kathleen, 112, 118, 121
Theodore, Nik, ix, 102–30
theorizing
  centric, 220, 239–40, 256–59

closed system (*see* closed system theorizing)
coherence, 91–93, 106, 113–14, 127*t*, 131–32, 140–41, 254–55
complexity, 56, 61, 235–36, 238–41, 243, 253, 274, 282, 287–88, 297–98
conjunctural, 73, 76–77, 161–62, 224–25, 265
contextual, 4–5, 15, 30–31, 70, 162, 266–69, 288, 299–300, 299*t* (*see also* conjunctural analysis; theorizing: conjunctural; theorizing: situated)
embedded, 273, 295–96, 299–300
ethnocentric, 45–46, 302
Foucauldian, 93, 96–97, 99
heterogeneity, 185
ideal-typical, 109–10, 114, 127*t*, 191–92, 222, 240, 246, 249–50, 276–77, 282–84, 301–2
midlevel (*see* midlevel theorizing)
open system (*see* open system theorizing)
political economic, 87, 95–96, 165 (*see also* political economy)
poststructuralist, 87, 95 (*see also* poststructuralism)
reflexive, 3–4, 178, 186
relational, 95–96, 220
situated, 49, 73, 250, 295–96
stress-testing (*see* stress testing [of theory claims])
"thick," 271–72
theory of regulation. *See* regulation theory
think tanks, 68–69, 104–5
third sector, 45, 47
Third Way, 228–30
Tickell, Adam, ix
Tilly, Charles, 275–76, 278–79, 297, 344n.132
Trade and Market in the Early Empires (Polanyi et al), 43. *See also* Polanyi, Karl
transaction costs, 59, 106
transduction, 44–45, 172–73
transversal analysis, 219–20, 250–51, 261–63, 265, 267*t*, 298
Trotsky, Leon, 252–53, 258, 261–62, 263–64. *See also* uneven and combined development
trust, 14, 54–55, 59, 107, 120, 155–56

unemployment, 6–8, 73–74, 134–36, 198–99, 215–16
uneven and combined development, 17, 124, 128, 222–23, 225–26, 238–40, 251–54, 258, 260–64, 291–92, 299*t*, 338–39n.13, *See also* combination; recombination; uneven development; uneven spatial development
uneven development, 9–10, 222, 224–25, 251–54, 272–73, 281
uneven spatial development, 3–4, 34–35, 76–79, 240, 242, 283*f*, 286
union culture. *See* culture: union
unions. *See* labor unions
United States–Mexico–Canada Agreement, 262
universalism, 13–14, 38, 184, 192, 299*t*
University of Manchester. *See* Manchester University
University of Melbourne. *See* Melbourne University
University of Oxford. *See* Oxford University
University of Wisconsin-Madison, 50–51
untraded interdependencies, 14
utopias, 100, 164
  market, 68, 85–86, 91
  neoliberal, 85–86, 92, 93–94
  real, 183–84

variegated capitalism, 103–4, 125, 126–30, 127*t*, 131–32, 237–38, 243, 247, 264, 267*t*
variegation, 15–17, 31–32, 40–41, 65–66, 103–4, 123–24, 174–79, 230–31, 237–38, 263–64, 266. *See also* variegated capitalism
varieties of capitalism, 16–17, 102, 105–11, 125–28, 127*t*, 222–23
  China, 134–36, 135*t*, 157–58, 222–23
  coordinated market economies, 102, 127*t*, 133–36, 229, 233
  liberal market economies, 102, 127*t*, 133–36, 229, 232–33
Varieties of Capitalism (Hall and Soskice), 108, 111, 120
Vienna, 163–64

Wade, Robert, 145
Washington Consensus, 87, 134, 150, 152, 159. *See also* neoliberalism
welfare, 149, 199, 215–19. *See also* culture: welfare; Keynesian welfare state; New Deal
welfare state, 9, 15–16, 84–85, 90, 105, 149, 215–16, 227, 229–30. *See also* Keynesian welfare state
Wheelwright, Ted, 200–1, 203
White, Gordon, 145

Wilberforce, Samuel, 18–19
Williams, Raymond, 22, 86, 289
Williamson, Oliver, 54–55, 59, 62
Wolf, Eric, 259–60
world market. *See* market: world
world system, 132, 185, 225, 233–34, 236–38, 242, 246, 258, 276, 278. *See also* world systems theory

world systems theory, 160–61, 277–78, 280. *See also* world system
Wright, Erik Olin, 50–51, 183–84

Yandy, 204

Zelizer, Viviana, 59–60, 63–64
Zhang, Jun, ix, 131–59